ALL EYES
ARE UPON US

ALL EYES ARE UPON US

Race and Politics
from
Boston to Brooklyn

JASON SOKOL

UNIVERSITY OF MASSACHUSETTS PRESS
Amherst and Boston

Copyright © 2014 by Jason Sokol
This edition published by arrangement with Basic Books,
an imprint of Perseus Books, LLC, a subsidiary of Hachette Book Group, Inc.,
New York, New York, USA. All rights reserved.

Paperback edition published by University of Massachusetts Press, 2017
Printed in the United States of America
All rights reserved

ISBN 978-1-62534-286-7 (paper)

Designed by Linda Mark
Set in Janson Text
Printed by Maple Press, Inc.

Cover design by Sally Nichols
Cover photo of Edward W. Brooke during his campaign to be elected Massachusetts
Attorney General, Nov. 3, 1962. Photo by Bob Dean (The Boston Globe via Getty Images)

Library of Congress Cataloging-in-Publication Data
A catalog record for this book is available from the Library of Congress.

British Library Cataloguing-in-Publication Data
A catalog record for this book is available from the British Library.

For Nina, with love

Contents

Introduction: The Northern Mystique   ix

PART I: NORTH OF JIM CROW

1. And to Think That It Happened in Springfield   3
   Pioneering Pluralism, Practicing Segregation
   (1939–1945)

2. Something in the Air   31
   Jackie Robinson's Brooklyn (1947–1957)

3. "If We Were Segregationists"   71
   The Struggle to Integrate Northeastern Schools
   (1957–1965)

PART II: FORERUNNERS

4. The Color-Blind Commonwealth?   103
   The Election of Edward Brooke (1966)

5. Shirley Chisholm's Place   137
   Winning New York's 12th Congressional
   District (1968)

PART III: **MIRRORS**

6. **"The North Is Guilty"**   171
   Abraham Ribicoff's Crusade (1970)

7. **"This Bedeviling Busing Business"**   193
   The Long 1970s, the Trials of Edward Brooke,
   and the Fall of the North (1968–1979)

PART IV: **THE DEATH AND LIFE OF THE NORTH**

8. **A Tale of Two Hartfords**   233
   Politics and Poverty in a Land of Plenty
   (1980–1987)

9. **The Ghost of Willie Turks**   259
   Racial Violence and Black Politics in
   New York City (1982–1993)

10. **The North Rises Again**   291
    Deval Patrick, Barack Obama, and
    the Twenty-First Century (2006–2012)

Acknowledgments   *315*

Notes   *319*

Bibliography   *361*

Index   *373*

Introduction

The Northern Mystique

For Edward Brooke, the North pulsed with promise. Brooke first set foot in New England during World War Two, when his army regiment trained in Massachusetts. He was a native of Washington, D.C., and Washington was a Jim Crow city. When the war ended, Brooke moved to Boston and enrolled in law school. He voted for the first time in his life. And he did much more. Brooke was elected the state's attorney general in 1962; four years later, he won election to the United States Senate. Brooke achieved all of this in a state that was 97 percent white. What constituted political reality in Massachusetts—an African American man winning one million white votes—was the stuff of hallucinations below the Mason-Dixon line.

At the same time, an open secret haunted America's northern states. As the nation gazed at southern whites' resistance to the civil rights movement—at the Klansmen and demagogues, attack dogs and cattle prods—many recoiled in horror. Northerners told themselves that such scenes emanated from a backward land, a dying region, a place apart. Yet rampant segregation in cities across the country rendered racial inequality a national trait more than a southern aberration. When black migrants streamed north during and after World War Two, James Baldwin reflected, "they do not escape Jim Crow: they merely encounter another, not-less-deadly variety." They moved not to New York, but to Harlem and Bedford-Stuyvesant; not to Chicago, but to the South Side; not to Boston, but to Lower Roxbury.[1]

Here were the two sides to race in the Northeast, embodied in Brooke's political success and in Baldwin's cautionary tale. The cities of the Northeast were simultaneously beacons of interracial democracy and strongholds of racial segregation.

Both stories—seemingly contradictory stories—unfolded side by side, at the same moments, in the same places. Black neighborhoods congealed in the years after World War Two as segregated schools proliferated across the urban Northeast. The numbers of black northerners in poverty and behind bars would continue to grow. And yet these cities and states also incubated movements for racial equality. African Americans scored advances at the polls, in the courtrooms, and in the region's cultural arenas as well.

The two stories are rarely told together. The North as a land of liberty holds power in the popular mind. When the idea of "northern history" enters into the public consciousness, it often comes attached to the American Revolution or the Civil War. This was the home of the minutemen, righteous abolitionists, and the noble Union army. Many schools still teach about slavery and segregation as distinctly southern sins. And the North continues to bask in its enlightened glow. To travel from Boston to New York is to take in Harvard and Broadway, high culture and high ideals. Northern states are blue states; they have powered American liberalism and provided the first black president with his largest margins of victory. To many Americans, the North remains a higher place.

To scholars, however, the North as a land of liberty has become a straw man. No reflective historian any longer believes it. Scholars have focused on the North's dark side. They have shown slavery's deep roots in New England and New York City. Histories of twentieth-century America reveal the North's bloody record of racial violence, and its stunningly segregated landscape of affluent white suburbs and destitute brown cities. In recent works of history, the North and the South emerge as rough racial equivalents: the South had Mississippi; the North had the Boston busing crisis. If the progressive side of the North enters into these stories, it is depicted as a rhetorical mask that hides the reality of racism.[2]

The truth is that both stories are real, and they have coexisted—albeit uneasily. This kind of truth can be difficult to assimilate. It does not fit with a portrait of American history as the story of freedom. Neither does it jibe with an understanding of America as the story of oppression. The larger tale weaves together these warring strands—it is a story befitting a nation that boasts an African American president as well as staggering racial and economic inequality.

The Northeast has been, and remains, the most American of regions. This is not because it is a glittering model of freedom and democracy. It is because the Northeast has long held genuine movements for racial democracy, and for racial segregation, within the same heart. The Northeast best illuminates the conflict that stands at the center of American race relations.

As late as 2011, the head of Boston's National Association for the Advancement of Colored People (NAACP) noted that his city still had an unsavory reputation among African Americans. "Boston is definitely a city that has two sides," reflected Michael Curry. "Maybe we should own that." He referred to Boston's abolitionist heritage on the one hand, and its history of white racism on the other. He was hinting that Boston's inhabitants should find a way to embrace that ambiguity. By contrast, most other American cities have one-sided racial histories. The side of racism, segregation, and oppression has always won out.[3]

This book does not downplay the brutality of racial violence or the persistence of segregation. Indeed, it documents this ugly history. But it takes seriously the advantages that African Americans have had in the North, and it makes much of the region's traditions of political and racial progressivism.

Among the advantages of northern life, none was more important than the fact that African Americans could vote. Blacks exercised this crucial right of American citizenship. As their numbers grew after World War Two, they influenced the political culture of northern cities and states, making these places more malleable and more democratic. African Americans elected some of their own. They placed their hands on the levers of urban political machines. They forced white officials to support civil rights legislation at the local and national levels. Their electoral clout also fueled interracial and multiracial coalitions, creating an atmosphere in which white voters would support black candidates.

All of this helps to present a history of recent America in which the election of a black president was imaginable—and possible. Barack

Obama's election is pictured here not as a shocking break from America's racial past, but as the triumph of one of its strands. The campaigns and careers of many black Northeastern politicians—Ed Brooke, Shirley Chisholm, and Deval Patrick, among others—show that Obama has forerunners in the realm of electoral politics. There were traditions of interracial politics upon which Obama could draw. The Northeast, more than any other region, supplied those historical antecedents.*

Many of the Northeast's African American leaders were descended from southern slaves. Their forebears had participated in the migrations to the North. Those transplants believed most deeply in the region's promise. But they also rubbed against its sharpest edges—shunted into its ghettoes, assigned to its crumbling schools, filtered through its menial jobs. African Americans remained suspended between the Northeast's reputation and its economic realities. Some of them made it to the top, leading states and cities, showcasing and confirming the region's mystique; many more lay at the bottom, still clawing and grinding, mute testaments to the bankruptcy of that promise. They explored the contours of a place that leaped far ahead of the rest of America. And yet it also reflected, illuminated, and reinforced the nation's worst demons.

That the Northeast possessed these two sides does not mean they forever fought to a standstill. They changed in shape and form and degree. At certain moments in the twentieth century, the white backlash won out. At other times, interracial progress stepped to the fore. The overall story contains forward marches and backward retreats, triumph and failure, and everything in between.

The North's mystique had a chronology, and a dynamic history, of its own. It soared to prodigious heights in the 1940s, inspired by the democratic ambitions of World War Two and nudged along by the rising black freedom struggle. Northeasterners saw themselves as leaders. Their cities were models for the nation and the world. With the "Springfield Plan" of the early 1940s, the city of Springfield, Massachusetts, declared war on racial, religious, and ethnic prejudice. In 1947, Jackie Robinson's breakthrough set the pace for experiments in interracial democracy. Though these wartime and postwar struggles did not establish equality in eco-

---

*The Northeast was not the only region that supplied such antecedents. For instance, Mayor Tom Bradley of Los Angeles was an important forerunner in the realm of interracial politics.

nomics or power, they laid cultural foundations for the coming years. Yet after the war, racial segregation became more entrenched in neighborhoods and schools. Northern blacks began to wage assaults on such conditions. The NAACP often led the charge. In 1964, for example, the NAACP took aim at the segregation that existed in Springfield's schools. A long legal battle ensued.

Just as northern school segregation was coming to light in the 1960s, interracial politics had its beginnings. Some white northerners embraced this promise, as seen through Ed Brooke's Senate election in Massachusetts and Shirley Chisholm's congressional triumph in Brooklyn. The difference is that while Brooke won more than one million white votes, Chisholm crafted a diverse coalition of African American, Puerto Rican, and white voters—including the Jews of Crown Heights as well as the Polish Catholics of Greenpoint. Still, racism flourished and inequalities continued to deepen in Brooke's Massachusetts as well as Chisholm's Brooklyn. Victories at the ballot box were significant but fragile.

The northern mystique was bruised and battered in the 1970s, and ultimately beaten by the school busing controversy. In 1970, at the instigation of Connecticut's Abraham Ribicoff, the Senate erupted in a heated debate over northern segregation. And in 1974, blood was spilled in the streets of Boston. The Northeast no longer seemed like a land of breakthroughs. It became a mirror for America's troubles—shaping and reflecting, rather than surmounting, the nation's racial and political divisions. The 1970s witnessed the fall of the North.

The old interracial ideals dissolved in a vapor of racial strife and economic hardship. Factories were shuttered in the 1970s and 1980s; white residents departed the region's once-proud cities, leaving behind impoverished urban cores that many racial minorities called home. First in Hartford, then in New York City and New Haven, African American mayors rose to power. As black poverty worsened, however, the electoral triumphs seemed emptier than ever.

In the early twenty-first century, the northern mystique began to rise from the ashes. Massachusetts, and then the nation, was reborn by a new black politics. Deval Patrick ran for governor in 2006, asking Bay State residents to "vote your aspirations." He encouraged the citizens of Massachusetts to position themselves on the frontier of interracial democracy—to see themselves as a model once again.[4]

At its broadest, this book tells the story of a region, and a people, first standing as the nation's beacon—then as its mirror, its outcast, and finally as a harbinger.

While the South was weighted down by its racial history, all blood and terror and tragedy, it made a certain sense that a humorist dared to unwrap the riddle of race in the North.

Margaret Halsey first gained notoriety for her 1938 satire of British life, *With Malice Toward Some*. She worked in an interracial canteen during World War Two, and her writing took a more serious turn. Halsey greeted the postwar world with a slim but devastating volume entitled *Colorblind: A White Woman Looks at the Negro*. Her upbringing on the outskirts of Yonkers, New York, had approximated that of many whites in the prewar Northeast. "There were no Negroes in the rather remote suburban neighborhood where I grew up, and none in the grammar school I attended. The only mammy I had was the white lady who had put herself to the inconvenience of bearing me, and as a child I never saw Negroes except in the streets and stores." To Halsey, the African Americans who populated northern cities were truly invisible men and women: "Nobody ever talked about them at all." Such an existence produced within her a combination of "innocence, ignorance, indifference, and inexperience," an amalgam she thought quite typical among white Americans of every region. Even so, Halsey believed that if America would ever solve its "race situation," those who resided above the Mason-Dixon line would lead the way. "The North has a greater responsibility than the South because it has the superior equipment for dealing with the problem. . . . It is a richer section of the country, with all that that implies in terms of general levels of health and education. And while many Northern citizens are prejudiced against Negroes, that prejudice is not usually trained into them so intensively." Here was the northern mystique, or at least one iteration of it. Halsey portrayed the North, in relative terms, as a place of cultural and racial enlightenment.[5]

There was nothing straightforward about white northerners' racial attitudes. Impulses toward democracy and discrimination warred within a single mind or body; beliefs in equality were just as dogged as crass stereotypes. As Halsey reflected, "there is not room for these two reactions—the democratic one and the popular-legend one—in the same person at the same time. Not, that is, if the person is to be at all comfortable." *Colorblind* demonstrated this excruciating discomfort—the unease resulting from whites' attempts to unify two opposites, to stride toward racial progress even as they nursed vicious stereotypes and policed the boundaries of racial segregation.[6]

At the time of *Colorblind*'s publication, James Baldwin was twenty-one years old and just beginning his writing career. While only ten miles separated Baldwin's childhood world from Halsey's, his native Harlem and her "remote suburban neighborhood" could scarcely have felt farther apart. Still, the two writers arrived at strikingly similar conclusions about race in the North. The white northerner "never sees Negroes," Baldwin wrote in 1961. "Northerners never think about them whereas Southerners are never really thinking of anything else. Negroes are, therefore, ignored in the North and are under surveillance in the South, and suffer hideously in both places." Though Baldwin bought into no great notions about northern progress, he knew the power of the mystique. "Northerners indulge in an extremely dangerous luxury. They seem to feel that because they fought on the right side during the Civil War . . . they can ignore what is happening in Northern cities because what is happening in Little Rock or Birmingham is worse." He questioned the premise that one region was more enlightened than the other. Baldwin related with approval his own brother's observation that "the spirit of the South is the spirit of America."[7]

Except for one critical distinction. It was the difference of history, of regional heritage—the spell that the past cast over the present. "The Southerner remembers, historically and in his own psyche, a kind of Eden in which he loved black people and they loved him," Baldwin wrote. "Historically, the flaming sword laid across this Eden is the Civil War. . . . Everything, thereafter, is permitted him except the love he remembers and has never ceased to need." The result was an "indescribable torment" that afflicted "every Southern mind." This hysteria was the white southerner's alone. "None of this is true for the Northerner." White northerners took their regional history in stride.[8]

In the North, the burden feels light: the burden of the past, the weight of history, the stories and sagas that form its fabric. To northerners, collective history does not bewitch. It looms as a source of aspiration and inspiration.

Those who came up in Dixie shouldered the "burden of southern history," in historian C. Vann Woodward's famous formulation. The past was an encumbrance to unload; history was something to overcome. Transplanted Mississippian Willie Morris, an author and the editor of *Harper's* magazine, carried within him the "agonies I had seen in my own past." Agony and anguish were the names for the southerner's ordeal. By contrast, the northern experience admitted of no such torment. In the Northeast, the past operated differently. It was something to affirm.[9]

There is in the North a mystique about the past that continues to influence the present. It is a set of ideas and ideals, a cultural complex that interacts with the stuff of electoral politics, public policy, urban and suburban landscapes, and structures of inequality. During and after World War Two, this regional mystique held its greatest strength in the corridor from Boston to Brooklyn. In this same time period, it would meet its stiffest challenge—a challenge posed by millions of black migrants from the South and by the burgeoning civil rights revolution.

As many northerners saw it, their region stood not as the embodiment of a painful duel between two American traditions. Instead, they fought nobly on one side of that battle. The Northeast's unique spirit grew out of a selective interpretation of its past: this story featured the Pilgrims, who sought freedom on the shores of the New World, and the Puritans. John Winthrop, the Puritan leader, famously declared: "We shall be as a city upon a hill, the eyes of all people are upon us." Connecticut's citizens bound themselves to key democratic principles in the first written constitution. And whereas New England's settlers led the way toward one vision of American liberty, New Yorkers pioneered a form of intercultural pluralism. In the words of historians Frederick Binder and David Reimers, New York City fashioned a "climate of interethnic harmony" from its founding.[10]

Boston and New York became de facto capitals of the nation. To Supreme Court Justice Oliver Wendell Holmes, Boston was the "hub of the universe." E. B. White, the author and essayist, observed that New York "is to the nation what the white church spire is to the village—the visible symbol of aspiration and faith, the white plume saying that the way is up." The Northeast, as the site of the Revolutionary War's beginnings, also became known as the birthplace of American freedom. It was not that chattel slavery bypassed the Northeast, but that it died there decades before the Civil War. When the war broke out, Northeasterners took up arms against the slave South. After the Civil War, newly freed slaves relied upon northerners in Congress—those Radical Republicans who pursued the "unfinished revolution" known as Reconstruction.[11]

This story of the Northeastern past reigned in the regional imagination. It accented the adventuresome spirit of the Puritans and played down the extent to which they excluded all who believed in different creeds. It scarcely acknowledged settlers' persecution of Native Americans, the centrality of African slavery in many northern cities, episodes of brutal racial violence like the New York City Draft Riots, or the fact that Jim Crow laws had their origins in Massachusetts. In the region's collective history, the narrative of freedom had no room in it for these less savory realities.

Northeasterners of various stripes found uses for the lofty version of regional history. Into the middle of the twentieth century, the mystique helped to frame how northerners would grapple with the stormy present. The mystique informed African Americans' expectations, raising their hopes for equality and deepening their frustrations when the hopes went unfulfilled. Even when the rhetoric about liberty rang hollow, northern blacks could embarrass white leaders for failing to actualize this version of history. African Americans thus exposed the gap between the unceasing language of freedom and the inequalities that defined northern life.

This was nothing particularly new in America—the white embrace of freedom with one hand and the tightening of the rope with the other. But it had a different urgency in the decades after World War Two. The civil rights movement exposed the enormity of the chasm that separated America's ideals from its practices. Martin Luther King Jr. referred to this as a distinctly American pathology, one rooted deeply in history. "Ever since the Declaration of Independence, America has manifested a schizophrenic personality on the question of race," King wrote. "She has been torn between selves—a self in which she has proudly professed democracy and a self in which she has sadly practiced the antithesis of democracy." This American schizophrenia has played out most powerfully in the Northeast. No region professed democracy more proudly than this one. And in the Northeast, the battle between racial democracy and its antithesis actually seemed like a fair fight—at least for a time.[12]

UTTER THE PHRASE "THE SOUTH," AND ABSORB THE IMAGES IT INVITES: plantations and porticoes, white necks burned red by the sun, black backs whipped raw. Southern history is filled with extraordinary images of racism. The cast of characters ranges from antebellum slaveholders to hooded Klansmen. "The South" carries an established meaning in the American mind.

In contrast, Americans' impressions of the North are far more diffuse. This makes the North both easier and harder to think about, to write about, and to argue about than the South. There is an opening to define "the North," and to give it a story, yet few previous definitions to set oneself up against.

Twenty-first-century political maps paint the regions in red and blue, signifying two worlds at war inside one national soul. To many northerners, the South still feels foreign—marked by its politics, culture, and race relations, even its weather and its food. In turn, many southerners hold fast to their regional identity, separating themselves from elitist liberals up north. Comparisons inevitably begin with prominent touchstones: Union against Confederacy, snow versus sun, New England foliage juxtaposed against Mississippi magnolias, Vermont maple syrup and Georgia pecan pie. Southerners, in twangs or drawls, still boast about life's easier rhythms and slower pace. Northerners, through hard Boston accents or the coarse cadences of Brooklyn, continue to think of their environs as the hub of the universe; the South stands as retrograde or inscrutable or both.

Through the centuries, the North has been defined as all that the South was not. Historian James Cobb asserts, "Not only was the North every*where* the South was not, but in its relative affluence and presumed racial enlightenment, it had long seemed to be every*thing* the impoverished and backward South was not as well." Perceptions began to change in the late-1960s. African Americans forced southern whites to bury their Jim Crow signs; buildings burned in northern cities; the ugly faces of resistance to integration appeared in Chicago and New York and Boston.[13]

Southern journalists raced to deliver Dixie's eulogy. They argued that the South's problems had become similar to others across America; inequities now lurked in the texture of society rather than the letter of the law. According to Harry Ashmore, the longtime editor of the *Arkansas Gazette*, "the race problem is no longer the exclusive or even the primary property of the South." The most important difference between North and South had vanished.[14]

Through the 1960s, scholars as well as civil rights leaders questioned the racial meaning of the Mason-Dixon line. In 1961, historian Leon Litwack opened *North of Slavery* with a trenchant observation: the Mason-Dixon line "is a convenient but often misleading geographical division." Malcolm X stood before a Harlem audience in 1964 and declared: "America is Mississippi. There's no such thing as a Mason-Dixon line—it's America. There's no such thing as the South—it's America. . . . And the mistake that you and I make is letting these *Northern* crackers shift the weight to the Southern crackers." Malcolm's rhetoric was more fiery, but his message was the same.[15]

In a 1964 book, historian Howard Zinn argued that the South had only distilled the national essence into its purest form. Dixie was America at its crudest. If the rest of the country had long attempted to conceal or dismiss the racial blights all over its face, then the South, leaping onto the front pages in the 1960s, acted as a mirror that showed America its imperfections. Zinn listed a number of stereotypically southern traits—racism, provincialism, conservatism, violence, and militarism—that were actually basic American ones. "The South . . . has simply taken the national genes and done the most with them. . . . Those very qualities long attributed to the South as special possessions are, in truth, *American* qualities, and the nation reacts emotionally to the South precisely because it subconsciously recognizes itself there." Zinn titled his book *The Southern Mystique*.[16]

In most definitions of the North, it was everywhere other than the South. Historian Thomas Sugrue's *Sweet Land of Liberty*, published in 2008, defined the North as every state outside of the Old Confederacy. Sugrue's "sweet land" encompassed Los Angeles, Seattle, and even Wichita, Kansas, as well as Philadelphia and New York. Civil War scholar Richard Current had gone further. In Current's 1982 lectures, he asserted that "defining the North" was a "less serious difficulty" than defining the South. The North was "simply the rest of the country." The region was tied together by a common lack—that it was not the South.[17]

Kirkpatrick Sale, a writer and scholar, identified two competing regions: the Northeast and the Southern Rim. In Sale's 1975 *Power Shift*, his "Northeast" started with Maine, stretched down to New Jersey and Pennsylvania, and extended as far west as Illinois and Wisconsin. To establish the "Southern Rim," Sale drew a line from San Francisco in the West to North Carolina in the East, subsuming everything beneath it. Sale defined the Northeast as the traditional manufacturing belt of America. It housed large foreign-born populations and had centers of finance and industry. "There are some who would like to divide this quadrant in half, creating some sort of 'Midwest' that begins around the Pennsylvania-Ohio border—but there is, alas, no evidence whatsoever that there are real distinctions between the two regions." Sale dismissed those who would split the Midwest from the Northeast.[18]

Perhaps he had Jean Gottmann in mind. Gottmann, a French geographer, published the 1961 opus *Megalopolis*. Gottmann's Megalopolis stood as the urbanized eastern seaboard, reaching from Boston's northern ring (in New Hampshire) to Washington's southern suburbs (in Virginia). It was an uninterrupted stream of big cities and suburbs. "Nowhere else have men ever built anything comparable," Gottmann wrote. Megalopolis was the "Main Street of the Nation" as well as America's "chief façade toward the rest of the world." In this swath of land "has been developed a kind of supremacy, in politics, in economics, and possibly even in cultural activities." It contained "*on the average*, the richest, best educated, best housed, and best serviced group of such size . . . in the world." Megalopolis boasted "greater opportunity for advancement" than any other region.[19]

All Eyes Are Upon Us focuses on a smaller slice of the Northeast: Massachusetts, Connecticut, and New York. This area distills the qualities often associated with the North: cultural enlightenment, political liberalism, and racial progress. Here was the core of the northern mystique. In this region's cities and towns, the sense of history seemed stronger and older than elsewhere. The outposts of higher education proved more plentiful, the wealth-mongerers more wealthy. In comparison with the mid-Atlantic, the physical and psychological distance from the Midwest and the South was even greater. And while white southerners flocked to the Midwest and the mid-Atlantic during the Second Great Migration, neither New York, Connecticut, nor Massachusetts experienced a significant in-migration of southern whites. The cities of the mid-Atlantic and the Midwest—Chicago and Philadelphia among them—often held larger numbers of African Americans. But Massachusetts, Connecticut, and New York fashioned a reputation as the nation's motor of political and racial progress. This was a sort of super-North.[20]

Over the last seventy-five years, this part of the Northeast has become a definable political region. These states eventually tethered themselves to New Deal–style liberalism—no foregone conclusion in the historic stronghold of the Republican Party, the land of the Brahmins and Wall Street. By the end of the twentieth century, this area contained no swing states. It was solid blue. In the twenty presidential elections from 1936 to 2012, the three states voted Republican for only Dwight Eisenhower and Ronald Reagan. In contrast, New Jersey voted Republican every year from 1968 to 1988. At the state level, most candidates for governor or senator considered themselves to be racial liberals. The Northeastern Republicans—Ed Brooke, Frank Sargent, Jacob Javits, Nelson Rockefeller, Thomas Meskill, and even Prescott Bush—were progressives on civil rights issues, from fair employment legislation in the 1940s to the civil rights laws of the 1960s. They supported significant government regulation. All of this helped to make the Northeast a political region of its own.[21]

The Kennedy brothers played no small part in forging this political identity. They kept the flame of liberalism burning from the end of World War Two up to 2009. John F. Kennedy and Edward Kennedy both represented Massachusetts in the House of Representatives and the Senate; Robert F. Kennedy was a senator from New York. Before John F. Kennedy moved into the White House, he gave a farewell speech in Boston. The "democratic institutions" of the Bay State "have served as beacon lights for other nations, as well as our sister states," Kennedy declared. He invoked Pericles's address to the Athenians, which "has long been true of this commonwealth: 'We do not imitate—for we are a model to others.'" The Kennedys, with their outsized influence, shaped understandings of the North and its mystique.[22]

There are good arguments for extending *All Eyes Are Upon Us* beyond Massachusetts, Connecticut, and New York. New Jersey has often resembled Connecticut and New York in its urban-suburban structure and its state policies; Philadelphia, and the surrounding towns on the Main Line, breathe with some of the pioneering sense of history that one finds around Boston; Providence, Rhode Island, resembles many of the small cities in Massachusetts and Connecticut, and Rhode Island's politics have often mirrored those of the Bay State. But the big cities in New Jersey and Pennsylvania—namely, Newark and Philadelphia—

rarely possessed even the patina of "good race relations" that suffused New York and New England. Rhode Island had Brown University and Newport, but little else to trick itself into thinking it was a façade to the rest of the world. None of these other places—the Philadelphia area, New Jersey, or Rhode Island—brimmed with a similar sense of self-importance. Just as crucial, few observers perceived them as such. Ask a resident of Itta Bena or Iowa City, Mill Valley or Mineola, what places most define the North in political and cultural terms. Some of them might include Chicago, the most touted terminus of the Great Migration. Others would mention Minnesota, the heart of snow country. But almost every list will begin with Boston or New York City, and will incorporate Harvard or Yale, Broadway or Beacon Hill.

This book tries to articulate something that may seem both familiar and novel. Everybody knows what the North is and what it means, yet nobody does.

IN THE SCHOLARSHIP ON THE CIVIL RIGHTS MOVEMENT, THE CLASSICAL portrait held that the regions were marked by their difference. The South had Jim Crow and the North supposedly did not. Clearly, this perspective needed revision. But some of the most recent scholarship threatens to replace this old facile argument with a new one. Scholars now highlight the most blatant examples of northern racism. Yet these extreme cases tell us less about the whole. In addition, such studies underplay the fact that the South had an all-white politics, a racial etiquette of its own, and a unique history of slave societies, secession, and lynching.[23]

In the South of the 1960s, "a gesture could blow up a town." So wrote James Baldwin. A southern black man could no more look a white woman in the eye than he could drink from the "whites only" water fountain; he could no sooner omit "ma'am" from the end of a sentence than he could represent his state in the U.S. Senate. As Baldwin noted, the most important regional difference was not found in basic racial attitudes. The difference was that "it has never been the North's necessity to construct an entire way of life on the legend of the Negro's inferiority."[24]

When faced with the stifling atmosphere in the South, just a little room to exhale could mean the world. Lewis Steel was an attorney for the NAACP. A native New Yorker, he worked on school segregation lawsuits in the North. He had no illusions about the racism that festered in northern cities. Steel also traveled to the Deep South more than once. He was in Baton Rouge, Louisiana, in 1964, when James Chaney, Michael Schwerner, and Andrew Goodman went missing in Mississippi. He realized that to work for the NAACP in the Deep South was to put one's life on the line. The North acted as a safety valve. "The instant I got on the plane" back to New York, "I could breathe," Steel said. "They could never breathe." In the North, "I was safer. There is no doubt about it. I could sleep in a hotel. I wasn't worried about somebody breaking into my room and killing me." This was a distinct advantage that Steel held over his southern brethren.[25]

In this context, the North's very existence was important. Jackie Robinson, Ed Brooke, Shirley Chisholm, and the NAACP's Robert Carter— they were all crucial reminders that a Jim Crow nation still contained some sense of promise.

African Americans who migrated from the South threw these regional differences into sharp relief. They did not totally escape Jim Crow, but many still felt they had traded up. Robert Williams, who left Georgia for New York, was among the uprooted millions. Of paramount importance, he reflected, was "feeling like a man. You can't do that in the South, they just won't let you." Northern cities answered some of their prayers. As another migrant told a reporter in 1956, "I'd rather be a lamppost in New York than the mayor of a city in Alabama." A writer for *The New Yorker* would later put it this way: Black migrants exchanged the "unnameable horrors" of southern life for the "mundane humiliations" of their new land.[26]

For novelist Ralph Ellison, the journey to the North exacted a price. "In relation to their Southern background, the cultural history of Negroes in the North reads like the legend of some tragic people out of mythology, a people which aspired to escape from its own unhappy homeland to the apparent peace of a distant mountain." The escapees "made some fatal error in judgment and fell into a great chasm of maze-like passages that promise ever to lead to the mountain but end ever against a wall." They swapped the South's racial hell for the Sisyphean futility of the North. But Ellison's point was "not that a Negro is worse off in the North than in the South." Because that wasn't so. The point was that they had become refugees in the North. For Ellison, the South remained exceptional because of the black cultural treasures that it possessed. The South always beckoned as a homeland for African Americans, one by turns endearing and excruciating.[27]

African Americans' ability to achieve equality all too often depended upon white northerners. Whites frequently helped to forge racial breakthroughs in what might be termed "symbolic" realms—on baseball diamonds, in human-relations programs, in state laws and in electoral politics. But economic inequalities and spatial segregation deepened by the day. Still, "symbolic" advances had real value. They helped to form the very fabric of northern society. And on the question of what was possible in the North, they constructed a high ceiling.

White northerners were a heterogeneous bunch—divided by class, religion, ethnicity, and nationality. In Massachusetts, the rivalry between poor Irish Catholics and well-off Yankee Protestants was as important as the line separating white from black. New York had far more Jews than anywhere else in America, helping to distinguish that city's culture and politics. In Brooklyn and Boston, one was Irish, Italian, or Jewish as much as "white."

Yet important generalizations emerged. There was a surprising amount of agreement among whites when it came to race. Liberal leaders and purveyors of the white backlash alike believed that their region was a bastion of racial tolerance. Louise Day Hicks led the white resistance against school integration in Boston. At the same time, she championed her city's enlightenment. "The important thing is that I know *I'm* not bigoted," Hicks said. "To me that word means all the dreadful Southern segregationist Jim Crow business that's always shocked and revolted me." By the same token, many liberals blanched at the prospects of open housing and school integration. Racial conservatives and progressives shared a vast middle ground. They could agree that they were more advanced than southerners, that African Americans could rise high in the North, and that African Americans ought neither move next door nor enroll their children in majority-white schools.[28]

Gunnar Myrdal explored this apparent contradiction in his 1944 treatise, *An American Dilemma*. Myrdal was a Swedish scholar who conducted one of the great studies of American race relations. Among white northerners, he observed, "almost everybody is against discrimination in general, but, at the same time, almost everybody practices discrimination in his own personal affairs." When racial equality remained a matter of principle, whites were all for it. But they exhibited prejudice when integration threatened to affect their everyday lives. "The ordinary American follows higher ideals and is more of a responsible democrat when he votes as a citizen . . . than when he just lives his own life as an anonymous individual." Myrdal was surprised that northerners did not try to strip blacks of the franchise. In the realm of politics and elections, white northerners actually lived up to the "American Creed."[29]

Over the decades, a glue has held the conflicting sentiments together. Most white northerners agreed that their society ought to be color-blind. This allowed them to cast votes for black leaders. At the same time, even as city officials presided over segregated school systems, these officials claimed they were not segregating—because they fancied themselves as color-blind.

While such claims to color blindness often proved empty, they presented an opening that African Americans could seize. This was what made white northerners' racism so different: there were enormous holes in between their professed ideals and their practices, and African Americans could blow those holes wide open. The gap between a white liberal yearning and a segregated reality left room—small but meaningful room—for racial progress.

In February 1970, Abraham Ribicoff delivered a devastating speech on the Senate floor. The Connecticut senator raised his voice in support of an amendment offered by John Stennis, the longtime Mississippi segregationist. Stennis's proposal would standardize federal action on school integration across the country. If legislators wished to intensify desegregation efforts in Mississippi schools, Stennis proposed, they would have to do the same in New York and Connecticut. Most observers dismissed the Stennis proposal as but another white southern ploy—a way to blast the North, slow down the integration process, and get Dixie off the hook. But Ribicoff took the bait. He declared that if segregation was wrong in the South, it was wrong everywhere. He stood before the Senate and pronounced the North "guilty of monumental hypocrisy."[30]

Suddenly senators and journalists were debating the contours of northern racism and segregation. Robert Sherrill, a liberal southerner writing in *The Nation*, hammered Abraham Ribicoff. Sherrill acknowledged, "Everyone knows that the North has been no saintly station of xxvi = ALL EYES ARE UPON US

racial benevolence. . . . The North's callousness toward Negroes . . . is long-standing." But Sherrill zeroed in on the distinctions between North and South. Dixie remained unsurpassed in its racial cruelty. "The hundreds of lynchings . . . and the intentional deprivation of even rudimentary education to millions of people—such actions are not found in the record of any region outside the South." Sherrill granted that white northerners "shoot Panthers, stuff blacks into slums," and "flee integrated neighborhoods." He also noted that white northerners "feel about the blacks" as southerners did. But those factors did not comprise the totality of the region's racial practices. The North possessed other traditions. It pioneered civil rights laws and elected black leaders. There was always more dissent in the North. The northern states contained a wider range of "legitimate" views about race and democracy. Juxtaposed against the South, "other sentiments do prevail in other regions and it is *only* these other sentiments in other regions—which the South calls hypocrisy—that have ever given the black man a chance in this country." Call it a democratic tradition, or mere rhetoric, or the frail stuff of aspiration. But if the nation was ever to realize its better angels, it had to draw from this shallow but potable well of racial democracy.[31]

Whites in the Northeast were not eager to establish racial equality. But their region's history contained within it the sparks of possibility.

PART I

NORTH OF JIM CROW

ONE

And to Think That
It Happened in Springfield

Pioneering Pluralism, Practicing Segregation
(1939–1945)

WHEN THE NAZIS OCCUPIED PRAGUE IN MARCH 1939, New York City was preparing to host the World's Fair. From their Northeastern perch, America's political leaders and media barons eyed Hitler's advance across the Atlantic as well as the persistence of lynching and segregation in the Jim Crow South. In a world threatened by totalitarianism, they saw their region as the last best hope for democracy.

The World's Fair had its grand opening on April 30 in Flushing Meadows, Queens. The fair supplied tastes of the technological future with exhibits on RCA's new television and the vehicles conjured by General Motors' Futurama. At another exhibit, luminescent beams entranced attendees with a rosy version of tomorrow's cities. It was called "Democracity." A "weird violet light," as Meyer Berger described it in the *New York Times*, "gives Democracity that mystic quality." This was all too much for E. B. White. The commercial exhibits sat in a "murky bath of canned reverence," White harrumphed in the pages of *The New Yorker*. Yet certain parts of the fair still enthralled. The scale of the whole enterprise could awe and inspire, giving the visitor "that temporary and exalted feeling of being in the presence of something pretty special, something full of aspiration." It was a time of lofty dreams and of real import—a time when the world order hung in the balance.[1]

On September 29, the governor of New York delivered a speech at the fair. Herbert Lehman was the first Jew to be elected governor in any American state. His own victory had proved that Americans could overcome biases. "It is not too hopeful to believe that the day will come when we will build a world . . . of . . . justice, equality, and tolerance." In a world threatened by Nazism, "equality" depended upon a pluralist cast of mind and an accepting way of life. It had less to do with systemic injustice. Amid a dragging economic depression, Lehman took a swipe at the "undemocratic arrayal of class against class." Lehman framed the problem in terms of Americans' ability to stamp out racism and nativism. The primary task was to remove bigotry from Americans' behavior. "Fanaticism and intolerance are not yet dead even here. . . . We who love our country must labor to develop that goodwill and understanding among all."[2]

These were the platitudes of a politician. But they also captured an ethos that would become central to wartime America. This rhetoric rose to its highest point in the Northeast, where citizens forged the most serious attempts to foster tolerance, practice pluralism, and strengthen democracy. Such was the charge of the Springfield Plan.

AT THE END OF THE 1930S, THE CITY OF SPRINGFIELD, MASSACHUSETTS, claimed no particular distinction. The Bay State's third-largest city had appeared briefly on the national stage, but that seemed long ago. Daniel Shays and his band of farmers had waged a rebellion in Springfield during the young republic's first years; John Brown made a temporary home there well before the violent abolitionist drenched himself in martyr's blood. Springfield housed the first United States National Armory along with the Smith & Wesson gun factory, but this was as far as its boasts could extend. The game of basketball, invented at the Springfield YMCA, was still in its infancy. Theodor Seuss Geisel's first children's book, *And to Think That I Saw It on Mulberry Street*, had hit bookstores only in 1937—when Dr. Seuss himself was far away from the Mulberry Street of his native Springfield.

Springfield was described by many an observer as a "typical American city." It held a population of 150,000, about 40 percent (60,000) of whom were Yankee Protestants. Irish Americans numbered 25,000, French-Canadian Americans counted for 20,000 of the population, and Italian Americans 15,000. The city was also home to more than 8,000 Jews and 3,200 African Americans. Springfield's thirty-nine public schools, according to the *New York Times* education editor Benjamin Fine, were "as typical and normal as can be found anywhere." Fine both created and reinforced the perception that the Northeast was normative; it was representative of, and constitutive of, America as a whole. Indeed, there *was* something archetypal about Springfield. It had a real smattering of ethnicities and religions; residents fancied themselves as forward-looking, though many in this old manufacturing center nursed conservative streaks; and as a small city, it stood somewhere between a metropolis and a town. Even its name—Springfield—shouted normalcy. Almost every state had a town called Springfield. The Massachusetts version was the largest.[3]

In 1939, Springfield's public schools returned the city to prominence. It started as more of a plan than a Plan. John Granrud was its driving force. An Iowa native, Granrud earned a degree from Columbia University's Teachers College—where faculty members were developing and promoting theories of intercultural education. Granrud arrived in Springfield in 1927 at the age of thirty-two, eager to put those ideas into practice. He began as assistant superintendent of schools and in 1933 ascended to the position of superintendent. At that point, the Springfield public school system employed but one black teacher: Olive Rainey. She retired in 1936. Granrud started to recruit more black teachers and administrators, and he reformed the hiring process. The Springfield School Committee would evaluate all applications for teaching jobs "without regard to race, creed, or nationality." The School Committee had previously maintained a quota limiting Catholics to 10 percent of the teaching force. So Granrud initiated a policy in which the three major faiths—Protestant, Catholic, and Jewish—would all have representatives on the Evaluating Committee. His committees spawned additional committees, none more storied than the one that assembled in the fall of 1939.[4]

The World War Two era was a popular time for committees and councils—no problem seemed too small to prevent another gathering of the curious, the credentialed, and the concerned. Granrud appointed the Committee on Education for Democracy in October 1939. In devising this experiment he had assistance from Clyde Miller, a professor at Columbia's Teachers College, and from the National Conference of Christians and Jews. Granrud's committee was comprised of six teachers and principals from Springfield. It studied ways to teach democracy in the schools and to curb racial and religious prejudice. The committee concluded that children's prejudices were most often the product of "forces and factors outside the school, such as the home, the street, the club, and sometimes even the church." Thus any educational program could not be confined to the schools; it had to reach into the adult world and the city at large. The committee also found that previous attempts to foster democratic ways of thinking were "too idealized." Students had been fed the line that "we in this country had already achieved a perfect democracy." Yet students' daily experiences clashed with such idealizations—especially for African American children—and led to disillusionment. So the committee recommended emphasizing America's imperfections and the obstacles to democracy. Furthermore, the schools ought to teach the histories of different racial and religious groups. Here were the outlines for a program in multicultural education, a way to foster democratic thinking and living.[5]

The world seemed up for grabs in 1940. Dangers lurked everywhere from Nazi Germany and Joseph Stalin's Soviet Union to Senator Theodore Bilbo's Mississippi. Protofascist appeals also gathered steam above the Mason-Dixon line: the weekly radio broadcasts of Father Coughlin, a controversial Roman Catholic priest, were wildly popular in parts of the North, and Gerald L. K. Smith's far-right movement collected supporters. For those who continued to believe in religious freedom and interracial democracy, it was a time to ponder what had gone wrong—and how to make it right.

In the parlance of that era's social science, teaching students democracy would be like inoculating them against illness. Professor Clyde Miller recounted a meeting led by Smith, an anti-Semite who would soon found the America First Party. Smith was "spreading a disease just as terrible as typhoid or tuberculosis." Programs like the Springfield Plan might provide an antidote. Miller saw in them "an attempt to build such strong emotional health in the community as to immunize thousands of children, their parents and other adults, against the contagious phobias which are spread by demagogues like Smith, like Coughlin, like Hitler." Racial and religious prejudices were "diseases" that children could catch; experts had only to find the remedy and distribute it. Schools could cure illness rather than transmit it. This might not have been so straightforward in the American South, where the entire social system and cultural fabric were defined by racial discrimination. But northern schools had no such encumbrance. They could become the crucibles of a new religious pluralism and a new racial order, injecting children with the sweet syrup of democracy.[6]

AMERICA WAS AWASH IN ETHNIC AND RACIAL VIOLENCE. IN THE LATE-1930S and early-1940s, anti-Semitic violence erupted in Boston, in Bridgeport, Connecticut, and in Manhattan's Washington Heights neighborhood. In 1943, deadly race riots broke out in Detroit and Harlem. Amid this wreckage, Americans increased their efforts to promote programs for racial and religious tolerance. Yet the inherent limits of that term—tolerance—were apparent from the outset. Tolerance meant that people had only to learn how to stand one another. It implied no effort to embrace racial diversity or social equality, or even to understand other cultures—just to permit their presence.[7]

The crafters of the Springfield Plan realized this. Springfield teachers Clarence Chatto and Alice Halligan wrote, "Tolerance implies that we endure something, we put up with it, we allow it to exist, while we go on our superior way." They concluded that "tolerance is not enough." As Nancy Flagg would report in *Vogue*, "the Springfield School Department has a horror of those large loose words. 'Tolerance' especially gives them a fit of bad nerves: they think it implies condescension, and what they're working for is equality." This was easy enough for the proponents of the Springfield Plan to declare. But what did it actually look like when a city attempted to pioneer this sort of pluralism?[8]

Granrud continued his reforms in hiring. From the school administration to the classrooms and on down to the maintenance workers, he hoped students would encounter a crazy quilt of races, religions, and ethnicities. The point was to build an entire educational infrastructure that might make small children participants in an interracial democracy.

The Springfield Plan stressed the experiential dimensions of education. Teachers were to become living embodiments of their lessons. In an age when most textbooks presented the Civil War as an unfortunate battle over states' rights, and Reconstruction as a "tragic era," Springfield teachers would take their classes on excursions to John Brown's former home. Fifth graders at the Lincoln Elementary School would devote a unit to "the Negro people of Springfield." And teachers would connect the study of Reconstruction to the persistence of employment discrimination in Springfield.[9]

Courses in ninth-grade social studies centered on "The Contributions of Nationalities to Springfield." They encouraged students "to understand that all groups have the right, in a democratic city, to equal opportunities: civic, economic, educational, and social." In 1940, the idea of cultivating anything that smacked of "social equality" among the races was more than forward-looking. It seemed positively futuristic. One class took trips to the offices of the *Springfield Union*, and trolled the newspaper's archives for the biographies and achievements of local African Americans and immigrants. By 1944, Benjamin Fine of the *New York Times* could report that black children "have shaken off their inferiority and now are proud of their origins." The stigma of second-class citizenship had seemingly lifted from their shoulders.[10]

Each of Springfield's junior high schools created tangible testaments to intercultural education. In order to "develop a sympathetic attitude toward all racial and nationality groups," explained Chatto and Halligan, students conducted fieldwork. They interviewed city residents of various backgrounds and collected heirlooms from different cultures. The ninth graders at Forest Park Junior High School produced a seventy-five-page book titled *Pioneer Spirits*, containing the biographies of sixty foreign-born Springfield residents. On one level, this was standard junior high school fare. Many students simply wrote essays about their parents or grandparents. But the Springfield Plan brought to it a crucial dimension: the conscious realization and celebration of difference. Still, most of the biographical sketches embraced boosterish portraits of American life. Immigrants boasted of the paradise they found on these shores. The title, *Pioneer Spirits*, was "chosen to emphasize the fact that the pioneers who made America came on the 'Aquitania' as well as on the 'Mayflower.'" That so many of those who made America also came on slave ships was not a fact recognized in *Pioneer Spirits*.[11]

In the city's three high schools, the Springfield Plan combated prejudice with more sophistication. Tenth graders devoted a unit to "The Beginnings of Mankind." As Chatto and Halligan reported, it was based on the revolutionary concept that "so far as physical structure, intellect, and ability are concerned, all races of men are in sober truth created equal." Eleventh graders studied the difference between the "American Dream" and "American Reality." In classrooms, students "examined their own prejudices . . . and discussed them freely." High school seniors studied how racism and propaganda operated. Before implementation of the Springfield Plan, the students had taken tests that measured their own levels of prejudice. By 1943, many high schoolers believed they had made progress toward overcoming those prejudices. It was not as though the Springfield Plan ushered in a whole new world. But it did construct a novel educational environment. Students considered their own stereotypes, white children learned about black spirituals, and they were taught that social equality among the races was a goal of American society rather than a bugaboo.[12]

To many reporters, the most shocking spectacle of all was the Festival of Lights at Springfield's Washington School. This elementary school in the Forest Park neighborhood contained a larger Jewish population than any other school. In 1940, Washington School principal Rosa Bowker decided that the annual Christmas pageant conflicted directly with the spirit of the Springfield Plan. It excluded one-third of the students. So Bowker appointed a committee of parents who represented a range of religions. The committee recommended a "two-way Festival of Lights," as described in *Woman's Home Companion*, featuring a Christmas pageant followed by a Hanukkah ceremony. Jewish candles would share the stage with a Christian cross. A rabbi, a rector, and a priest all gave their blessings.[13]

The event was a hit among the school's students and parents. It inspired interreligious festivals across the city and interfaith gatherings at many Springfield churches. One junior high school class drew a "tree of religions." This raised the hackles of some Catholics. Edward Bernard, a recent graduate of Cathedral High School, charged that the tree of religions "reduced all faiths to the same level." Bernard alleged that the attendance of Catholic children at non-Catholic services violated canon law. The editors of the *Catholic Mirror* complained that Catholic parents might get the idea that schools with interfaith events were "acceptable places for the education of Catholic children." In the pages of *Columbia*, a Catholic magazine, J. G. E. Hopkins denounced the Festival of Lights. In this "weird performance," Springfield officials "passed on to the children . . . not tolerance and love, but something of their own hazy indifferentism towards principle. . . . A grammar school is no place to preach universal skepticism." These criticisms showed that when the Springfield Plan attempted to radiate out from the schools and into the larger community, it encountered significant barriers—the tropes and teachings of accumulated decades.[14]

The Springfield Plan was about more than changing attitudes. It also aimed to increase equality in employment practices across the city. In each school, job placement officers coordinated with the city's official Placement Bureau to employ recent graduates. The officers kept no records of the race, religion, or nationality of applicants—only their qualifications for potential jobs. If an employer specified that Jews or blacks were not welcome, the Placement Bureau refused to comply with the request. In some cases, that employer received a visit from the local public relations council. The Springfield Plan's program of adult education also spearheaded two investigations. First, it explored the conditions under which domestic workers toiled in Springfield homes and established standards for fair working conditions. In addition, the Springfield Council on Social Agencies launched a probe of the social and economic conditions of African Americans.

The Springfield Plan also waded into the choppy waters of urban politics. Springfield was divided between the Democratic Party—immigrant-based and led by Irish Americans—and the old-line Republican Party, headed by New England Yankees. Local politics was normally a hard-knuckled business. But the Springfield Plan turned the public schools into sites of nonpartisan political meetings. Opposing candidates shared the same stage, spoke about the issues of the day, and fielded questions from the audience. Granrud wrote in 1943 that this "was a true revival of the old New England town meeting." Springfield was trying to become a fledgling crucible of American democracy. As the Plan confronted Springfield's employment patterns and its political tensions, the city waged "total war," Alice Halligan wrote, "on bigotry, and the foes of democracy."[15]

Even in the mid-1940s, the Springfield Plan was still getting off the ground. Its ultimate success would be measured decades hence. "It's a wonderful start," observed a black pastor. "You are determining the social pattern for the future."[16]

THE SPRINGFIELD PLAN WAS NOT THE ONLY EXPERIMENT IN TOWN. With the Plan in its birth pangs, in 1939, a different sort of social investigation commenced.

To reach his New England laboratory, black psychologist Kenneth Clark traveled the 140 miles from New York City to Springfield. He schlepped a briefcase full of dolls, each possessing one of two skin colors: brown or white. These dolls became integral instruments in Clark's attempt to understand the workings of racial prejudice on African American children. The *Brown v. Board of Education* case, decided by the U.S. Supreme Court in 1954, would eventually bring fame to Clark and his dolls. Fifteen years prior, Clark chose two small cities as the main sites for his experiments. Pine Bluff, Arkansas, acted as Clark's southern base, where he measured the effect of segregated schools upon the black psyche. For his northern case study, Clark chose Springfield. As Clark noted, it was "a New England city that had a reputation for good race relations." The Springfield schools stood in for desegregated schools in general. And Springfield stood in for the North at large. It was to present the clearest contrast with the Jim Crow South.[17]

Clark conducted his tests on 119 black children in Springfield's "racially mixed nursery and public schools." He studied sixty-six girls and fifty-three boys, most of whom were between the ages of five and seven. Clark brought each child into a testing room. He asked the child to identify the white doll and the colored doll. More than 90 percent of the Springfield children correctly identified both dolls. Clark then asked each child five different questions: (1) Give me the doll that you like to play with. (2) Give me the doll that is a nice doll. (3) Give me the doll that looks bad. (4) Give me the doll that is a nice color. (5) Give me the doll that looks like you. The tests revealed that the young children in Springfield had already internalized a host of troubling emotions about their own racial identities.[18]

The numbers are instructive. When asked which doll they would like to play with, 72 percent of the Springfield children picked the white doll, against 28 percent who chose the brown one. Fully 68 percent of them chose the white doll as the nice doll, as compared with 30 percent who selected the brown doll. When asked to hand over the doll that looks bad, 71 percent of the children chose the black doll; only 17 percent of them chose the white doll. And when asked for the doll that was a nice color, 63 percent chose white and 37 percent chose brown. Finally, Clark told the children to place themselves in the middle of this experiment—to evaluate their own skin in relation to that of the dolls. When asked, "Give me the doll that looks like you," 61 percent of Springfield children gave the brown doll, and 39 percent of them chose the white one.[19]

For black students in the Springfield schools, Clark's testing room became the site of racial torment. When Clark interviewed a seven-year-old African American, the boy said more than once: "I got a suntan at the beach this summer." He continued to claim that he was actually a "white boy," and that the color on his face was merely the result of a summer at the shore. The boy tried so hard, yet with such futility, Clark explained, "to escape the trap of inferiority by denying the fact of his own race." When required to make this self-identification during the last of Clark's questions, two children sprinted out of the testing room and "convulsed in tears." A five-year-old boy who eventually identified himself with the brown doll offered an unsettling and unsolicited explanation: "I burned my face and made it spoil." One girl demonstrated a consistent preference for the white dolls during the first four questions of the experiment. She described the brown doll as "ugly" and "dirty." When asked the fifth and final question—"Give me the doll that looks like you"—the girl burst into tears. She was one of many children who, in this final act, gazed upon Kenneth Clark "with terror and hostility." Clark's doll experiments showed that if Springfield was to act as some model of pluralism and democracy, for the youngest of African American children it had already become an incubator of self-hatred.[20]

Clark's study unearthed shocking differences between Springfield and Pine Bluff, between North and South. To all five questions, more Springfield children than Pine Bluff children preferred the white doll. Whereas 71 percent of Springfield children picked the brown doll as the one that "looks bad," only 49 percent of the Pine Bluff children agreed. In the final question, 39 percent of the northern children self-identified with the white doll compared with 29 percent of their southern counterparts. The Arkansas testing room held few wrenching conflicts or tortured justifications. "The little Southern children would point to the black doll and say, 'Oh yeah, that's me there—that's a nigger—I'm a nigger,'" Clark observed, "and they say it almost cheerfully." In the Northeast, "the question clearly threw the kids into a much more emotional state." There was no cheer in Springfield.[21]

Clark broke new ground in the field of social psychology, but his interpretation of the results proved highly controversial. To a layman, and even to many a trained psychologist, the results of the experiment seemed clear. Springfield blacks suffered more self-hate than Pine Bluff children; they were more tormented in their racial identities, their personalities more profoundly scarred. But such an interpretation, Kenneth Clark insisted, was "superficial" and "incorrect." Clark argued that the emotional turmoil of the northern children represented an effort "to assert some positive aspect of self." He contended that the southern children had already molded themselves to the ways of an unjust world; as such, they stood defeated. "Adjusting to a pathology is not health. The way the northern kids were fighting it can be seen as a better sign." Two New York University professors came to the opposite conclusion. Clark's tests demonstrated that "the damage is *less* with segregation," sociologist Ernest van den Haag wrote, "and *greater* with congregation." Moreover, Clark had done little to show that a child's identification with a doll could be associated so directly with "personality disturbance." Clark's thesis flew in the face of the existing social science literature. But Kenneth Clark stuck to his guns.[22]

The *Brown v. Board of Education* case brought him renown. Clark first took the witness stand in a lead-up to *Brown*, a case concerning Jim Crow schools in Clarendon County, South Carolina, in May 1951. The NAACP wished to place on the record the basics of Clark's findings in the South: that black children suffered damage from segregation. The lawyers hoped that the statistical comparison between northern and southern schoolchildren would not come up. Clark remembered that Thurgood Marshall "was very worried about that point." As it happened, the results of Clark's experiments in northern schools never made it out of the psychology journals.[23]

And yet for all of Kenneth Clark's work, the torment that raged inside a child's soul was not the primary problem that defined northern race relations in the World War Two era. A more tangible conflict was shaping life in northern cities.

In Springfield, the effort to build a more just and democratic city stood uneasily alongside the reality that racial segregation was determining the city's spatial landscape. After the Springfield Plan was launched, more African Americans flocked to the city. And they clustered in very specific neighborhoods. Out of 750 black families surveyed in 1940, about 630 of them resided either in the Hill section or the North End. As the city's minority population doubled during the 1940s, this pattern of residential segregation deepened.[24]

Before the war, employment discrimination had been the most pressing problem for Springfield's African Americans. According to William DeBerry, pastor of St. John's Congregational Church and the city's preeminent black leader, "the real social tragedy of the Negro in Springfield . . . is the very limited sphere of his industrial opportunity." Three-quarters of African Americans worked as menial laborers. Four out of five black women were domestics. Time would only magnify these employment trends, just as it accelerated segregation in housing and schools. As of 1940, thirteen Springfield schools were all white. The Washington Elementary School, home of the celebrated interfaith Christmas service, was one of them. At Forest Park Junior High, where *Pioneer Spirits* was penned, only two black students attended. Although Springfield did not have total segregation in its schools, its school system was not well integrated. About one-quarter of the schools possessed a meaningful amount of integration. This may have constituted progress when compared with many other American cities, but it raised fundamental questions about Kenneth Clark's study.[25]

The premise of Clark's regional comparison wobbles under the weight of these facts. Clark chose Springfield and Pine Bluff in order to contrast a desegregated educational environment with a segregated one. In Springfield, some black children did attend school with whites. But the city was basically segregated in its patterns of housing, education, and employment. Over the years, these racial divides would widen. But then, this was part of another Springfield story altogether. This story would not make the news.

As WORLD WAR TWO RAGED, THE SPRINGFIELD PLAN BECAME THE subject of feature articles in magazines and newspapers. Two New York publishing houses released books about the Springfield Plan, and Hollywood added a film from Warner Brothers. America's media barons and movie moguls bought into the northern mystique and disseminated it across the country.

When an article appeared in the *New York Times*, Springfield knew it was back on the map. The piece was published under Benjamin Fine's byline on December 7, 1941. The Springfield project, as Fine told New York and the nation, attempted to "inculcate a love of freedom and democracy in the pupils, and to break down artificial barriers of intolerance and bigotry." Fine labeled Springfield a "cosmopolitan" city, "as typical and wholesome a community as can be found anywhere in the land." The tone of Fine's article was exceedingly optimistic, at times even booster-like. He reported that school officials were convincing employers in the city "to discontinue discrimination wherever it was found." The publication of this article not only granted the Springfield program a measure of nationwide publicity, but also bequeathed to it something just as important: a title. Fine's article appeared under the headline, "Tolerance Plan Called Success at Springfield." The program on democratic education would soon go by the name "The Springfield Plan."[26]

Times readers could not have reflected upon the Springfield Plan for too long. On this same day—December 7, 1941—the Japanese bombed Pearl Harbor and the United States plunged into World War Two. Suddenly, America's demonstrations of democracy, and its efforts against racial and religious prejudice, took on added importance. In this changed atmosphere, the Springfield Plan might capture the American imagination. One newspaper would pick up the story about this city's "total war on prejudice," then two more would run similar pieces. Almost every article was positive; several traded in hyperbole. Yet it was not all bluster. Springfield was trying something of significance. Participants in the Springfield Plan sought, at the very least, to create a more equitable and a more democratic city.

That they gained so much attention—and such uncritical media attention—said more about the media itself, and its role in the development of a northern mystique, than it did about Springfield or its Plan. Because World War Two seemed so obviously to pit good against evil, it became easy to blur the lines between propaganda and news. Historically, journalists had become boosters in Chicago—the capital of the Great

West—or in New Orleans, an oasis of commerce and culture nestled in the Deep South. To listen to Atlanta's backers was to believe that the "City Too Busy to Hate" had presided over the birth of many New Souths. But the Northeast had often seemed too secure in its own place in the world, too comfortable in its own self-image, too smug to print such blunt self-praise. Now, during World War Two, the most powerful newspapers and magazines—almost all of them based in the Northeast—began to shine a light on one locale's experiment in tolerance and pluralism. There was a war to win. And a democratic way of life to sell.

Parents' Magazine was one of the first offenders. The New York–based monthly published an article in its December 1942 issue. Jane Butler recounted the story of one Springfield girl whose mother had raised her to fear the "Chinaman." By 1942, "she was cured of her prejudice in the Springfield course." And Butler was impressed by the curriculum. "While listening to the warmth, geniality and spiritual expressiveness of the Negro songs, white students became . . . more appreciative of the Negro's fine qualities." Springfield's "new plan of education," Butler wrote, was "as thorough as the Nazi's for Nazism." If this analogy was taken to its logical extreme, and Hitler represented the world's model of racism, then John Granrud stood as its leading practitioner of racial democracy.[27]

The New York Times published an article by Granrud himself in April 1943. This helped to spread the story farther and wider. Soon enough, out-of-town educators rubbed shoulders with reporters on the trains to Springfield. Pittsburgh officials studied the Springfield Plan over the summer of 1943, and in December that city's Board of Education approved a program to teach pluralism and tolerance.[28]

Boston officials were torn about the brouhaha in the western part of the state. Late in 1943, the Boston School Committee touted the Springfield Plan and its ability to teach the "art of democratic living." But the Boston City Council was unpersuaded. When faced with a measure to adopt a citywide version of the Springfield Plan, Boston's city councilors voted it down. Representatives from Dorchester and Roxbury supported the program, but the other councilmen balked. They stated that the Springfield Plan "implies the existence of discrimination in Boston." This was an implication they could not stomach. Boston would not wage war against racial discrimination, for Boston officials denied discrimination's very existence.[29]

Other northern cities followed Springfield's lead. The upper-crust suburbs of Brookline, Massachusetts, and Great Neck, New York, adopted versions of the Plan in 1943, as did the working-class city of Brockton, Massachusetts. By the fall of 1945, New York City had adopted a "New York Plan," as Benjamin Fine reported, in order to "create better understanding among the various racial and cultural groups of the city." Three New York schools—in Brooklyn, the Bronx, and Jamaica, Queens—instituted this Plan immediately.[30]

Most striking, Wilmington, Delaware, became the first city with formal Jim Crow laws to entertain the Springfield Plan. This highlighted the Plan's strengths and exposed its most glaring limitations. The Wilmington Board of Education concluded that even if the program were adopted, the "existing social patterns may undergo no alterations." That meant the schools could remain segregated. In Delaware, this was a point in the Plan's favor. It could teach new racial attitudes while leaving structures of racial segregation intact. The Plan was attractive to Wilmington more for what it ignored than what it transformed.[31]

By the end of the war, the Plan had stretched all the way to Los Angeles. Versions existed in Denver, Portland, Cincinnati, Milwaukee, St. Louis, Philadelphia, and Kansas City. It even plotted a move from the North to the "True North," as officials from Ontario, Canada, made their way to Springfield early in 1946.[32]

Many black journalists became promoters of the Plan. In the spring of 1944, the Springfield Plan crept into the pages of *The Crisis*, the NAACP publication. Prior to spending a week in Springfield, *The Crisis*'s Noma Jensen had gazed "with skepticism upon the 'Springfield Experiment.'" But she quickly converted. Jensen came to see the Springfield program as "a vital, working plan that was revolutionizing a New England city." Jensen sat in a math class where a black teacher instructed a room full of white children. She saw junior high school students wrestle with the problem of employment discrimination in Springfield, and a fifth-grade history class discuss black soldiers in the Union army. *The Crisis* beamed back to its readership this glowing assessment of the events in Springfield: "As you walk along the corridors and visit the classrooms, you become highly conscious of . . . the 'unity of all peoples' everywhere." *Ebony* magazine's inaugural issue featured an article on the Springfield Plan. In three photograph-heavy pages, *Ebony* recognized the Plan as

"America's hardest-hitting weapon in battling the No. 1 foe of democracy on the home front—race hate." The *Chicago Defender* fixed a steady eye on western Massachusetts. It reported when a black teacher, Rebecca Johnson, was promoted to assistant principal at the Washington School. It also noted that nearby Westover Air Force Base was segregating white soldiers from black. Over the years, the *Defender* continued to evaluate the city's campaign against employment discrimination. The *Defender* held Springfield to its democratic word.[33]

Many writers positioned Springfield at the very center of the "forward-looking" Northeast. In the *Journal of Educational Sociology*, E. George Payne dubbed Springfield "the Mecca for those interested in better human relations." Springfield claimed to represent America at its progressive best.[34]

No journalist did more to create this perception than Benjamin Fine. A native of Attleboro, Massachusetts, and a Jew, Fine became education editor of the *New York Times* in 1941. He kept readers updated on the Springfield story through the early-1940s. Then the *Menorah Journal* liberated him from his word count. In October 1944, he published a twenty-page article on Springfield. "Springfield, Massachusetts, has been the scene of . . . an experiment that may mean more to the growing citizens of the United States than all the history, geometry, Latin or algebra they may learn in school." Fine was often over-the-top. "In five years the impossible has occurred! The program works!" He could not disguise his enthusiasm. "It is a fact that antisemitism has been checked, feelings towards Negroes improved, and all minority groups receive better treatment in the community." The Plan "is a guiding shaft of light to direct us to brighter pastures." One could not imagine a more ringing endorsement from a more prominent reporter.[35]

Up and down Megalopolis, writers touted Springfield. Selden Menefee of the *Washington Post* propagated the image of Springfield as a beacon. "Negroes, Jews, and members of other minority groups probably find less discrimination in Springfield than in almost any other American city." These kinds of messages found a receptive audience. In response to one of Fine's articles, New York City resident Anne Stockton Goodwin penned a letter to the *Times*. "All of us are becoming more conscious of the discrepancies between our ideals of democracy and our performance of them," Goodwin wrote. "In Springfield, Mass., something is being done about this . . . Springfield is overcoming race prejudice. . . . And such plans are the beginning of a new America."[36]

In *Woman's Home Companion*, Helena Huntington Smith not only reported on the workings of the program but also invited other communities to try it on for size. Her article was titled "Your Town Could Do It Too." Springfield students "are learning not only democracy, but something else which might be called democracy plus." Smith reminded her readers that such impulses had a long history in western Massachusetts. "Tolerance on the banks of the Connecticut [River] is not new but goes back to the days when Yankees were Abolitionists and Springfield was a station on the Underground Railroad." Springfield was making good on the promise of its history.[37]

In that spirit, the Springfield schools set about teaching their children to conquer prejudice. Springfield's war on bigotry occupied the pages of many a local newspaper and national magazine, then it floated across the silver screen. As the war ended, the movie house became another forum for the winning of hearts and minds.

The Warner Brothers Publicity Department billed its upcoming movie as "ONE OF THE MOST IMPORTANT FILMS EVER TO COME FROM WARNER BROS.!" The film was "timely," "sensational," and "pulls no punches." According to Henry Warner, *It Happened in Springfield* was produced "out of a feeling of civic responsibility and public service to the American people." Warner's twenty-minute short meant to place the Springfield Plan at the forefront of the American consciousness.[38]

Crane Wilbur, the writer and director, had wished to avoid the feel of a propagandistic tract. To the twenty-first-century eye, he seems clearly to have failed. At the time, however, *Variety* termed the film a "powerful documentary aimed directly at racial intolerance." The *New York Times* cited *It Happened in Springfield* as proof that Warner Brothers held "an ear to the ground." A reviewer in *School and Society* called the film "poignant." He came away "impressed with the vivid portrayal, sans Hollywood 'glamor.'" But in the end, Warner Brothers' attacks on racial and religious prejudice became stale propaganda indeed. The movie would sermonize and sanctify before it would challenge, discomfit, or even engage.[39]

Springfield residents were treated to an early preview. The film opened officially at the Hollywood Theater on April 26, 1945, though NBC had broadcast it on television the previous Sunday. Just as the Germans were surrendering in Europe, Americans ambled into cinemas to observe—at close range—the making of the northern mystique. At the beginning of the film, the Springfield tale was cast as one applicable to all of America. "Here is an American scene familiar to every eye," the narrator intoned. "This street might be found in your town, in my town, in anybody's town." At times, the northern mystique operated by couching the Northeast as normative and universal: what happened here was what happened everywhere. At other moments, the mystique depended upon an understanding of America in which the Northeast was special and distinctive; the kind of progress that took place in Springfield could not occur anywhere else. *It Happened in Springfield* mixed the two modes. In the film, the defining episode of ethnic violence was portrayed as something endemic to any American town. Significantly, this violence took place in a city other than Springfield. But the cure for such violent prejudice was distinctly Northeastern—particular to Springfield and its progressive program.[40]

The victim of the violence is a hapless tobacconist, first pictured outside his shop—in an unnamed city—standing beside a cigar store Indian. Incredibly, his name is not Goldberg or Williams or Suzuki. It is Knudson. John Knudson, a Scandinavian, is attacked because of his ethnicity. In the opening scene, Knudson is asked whether he will back a certain candidate in the local election. When Knudson balks, he becomes a target. A nativist demagogue whips up a crowd. A mob descends upon the cigar shop, bashes in its windows, injures Knudson, and stones a nearby church.[41]

The tobacconist's son happens to be a war hero. Bill Knudson comes home to visit his father in the hospital. He is accompanied by Ann Carter, a teacher in the Springfield schools. Bill Knudson wonders, "How can we talk of understanding and cooperation to the rest of the world unless we practice it in our own country?" Ann Carter responds, "Americans who love their country have been asking that question for a long time, Bill." She assures him, "I think they have found an answer. At least they've found a plan that seems to be working." She brings Knudson and his friend, Sergeant Cliff Stewart, to Springfield, so the veterans (along with the moviegoers) can see the Plan at work. At the Brookings School they glimpse an integrated classroom, though the white students sit up front with the African Americans in the back. "Children of native Americans forget the race consciousness which they might have learned at home," Ann Carter tells her guests. "They accept and understand the children of racial minorities for what they really are: neighbors, friends, and countrymen. . . . They don't talk about it; they simply live it." The veterans are awed by the Springfield Plan; they come away convinced that it holds the key to a future free of prejudice.[42]

Warner Brothers censored the film. The studio cut scenes that pictured black and white students actively learning together. The original version featured a scene in which an African American teacher instructed a classroom full of white students. It was erased from the final cut. Movie industry leaders blamed this omission on the racism of white southerners. In order for the film to play below the Mason-Dixon line, they claimed, scenes with African Americans had to be deleted. "The South just would not permit us to put a Negro teacher in the movie," claimed Arthur DeBra of the Motion Pictures Association of America. When in doubt, northerners faulted the South.[43]

For African Americans, *It Happened in Springfield* was a disappointment. The Springfield chapter of the NAACP had eagerly awaited its release. But, in June 1945, this NAACP chapter condemned the film. *It Happened in Springfield* "side-stepped the real issues of disunity existing in America" and "completely ignored anti-Semitism, which is rife, and Jim-Crowism." The black press agreed. Before the film's release, the *Philadelphia Tribune* had declared that Warner Brothers' "willingness to approach much needed, though controversial, subjects" was "what sets this studio apart." On April 28, the *Tribune* weighed in with disgust. "How then can Warner Brothers eliminate the Negro from its so-called Springfield Plan production and present it as a true picture of what the people of that city are doing to improve race relations?" In January 1945, the *Chicago Defender*—with great anticipation—had cheered the movie as "the finest demonstration of democracy ever to come out of filmland." But in the end, *It Happened in Springfield* was a demonstration of filmland's spinelessness.[44]

As the film played to national audiences, book publishers got in on the act. Viking's *The Springfield Plan* appeared in August 1945, to rave reviews. *Look* photographer Alexander Alland snapped the book's photographs and James Waterman Wise wrote the text. The *Amsterdam News* hailed the book's publication: in a time when "Bilbos and lynchings" were enough to dampen the hopes of African Americans, "progress seems just a word." At that moment, Constance Curtis wrote, "a book like *The Springfield Plan* hits with heavy impact." The book contained numerous photos, and sweepingly hopeful descriptions of the Springfield Plan. Curtis was compelled. "When one has finished reading, there is the feeling that if these things can be done by 150,000, they can be done by 150 million. . . . To say that hope for our country and for the world is beginning to rise in a small Massachusetts community may seem overexuberant—but this factual text brings such hopes forward." Curtis's review was representative of the praise that *The Springfield Plan* attracted.[45]

Barnes & Noble's book, *The Story of the Springfield Plan*, was coauthored by two Springfield teachers: Alice Halligan and Clarence Chatto. To read the two books, to see the prominent advertisements for them, and to gauge the enthusiastic response of reviewers was to understand how the Springfield Plan had gripped the imagination of progressives, intellectuals, and municipal leaders. Ben Burns of the *Chicago Defender* searched for a counterweight to the atomic bomb, and he looked to Springfield. "The secret weapon of death needs to be balanced by a new secret weapon of life, an all-powerful force to conquer the most evil, most dangerous, most destructive enemy of civilization today—the venom of race prejudice and hate." In the postwar world, the depths of evil were clear. Humanity had proven itself capable of genocide, and had built a weapon of unparalleled destruction. The question was where to find a peaceful antithesis. How to build a life force nearly as strong? One *Chicago Defender* writer found it in Springfield.[46]

The books caught the eye of the mainstream media along with the black press. "The school system is actually stamping out bigotry," Sterling North wrote in the *Washington Post*. "Springfield's total war against prejudice is suddenly the biggest news in the postwar world." The *Philadelphia Tribune* concluded its review of *The Story of the Springfield Plan* on a similar note. "This little book . . . would do well to be studied in every State in the Union, so that others, who have not yet learned the better way of life, may be enlightened and understand that democracy can work." One community in the Northeast now practiced a "better way of life." Other cities had to raise themselves to that lofty standard.[47]

In the postwar world, the Springfield Plan still seemed relevant. Atomic bombs had decimated Hiroshima and Nagasaki before articles about the Plan appeared in *Look* and *Vogue*. Proponents hoped the Plan would set the tone for a democratic peace. In May 1946, *Look* featured an article titled, "Prejudice: Our Postwar Battle." Wallace Stegner acknowledged that

"Springfield, Mass., is not Paradise," its Plan "no blueprint for Utopia." But Springfield had nonetheless "welded" Jews, blacks, Poles, Italians, Irish, and Yankees "into a community" and "into Americans." Stegner treated prejudice as a national malady, of which segregation was "probably the most common symptom." In this line of thinking, the fundamental disease of racial prejudice had produced a physical manifestation: segregation. A structural condition was viewed as the result of an attitude. If Americans could only solve prejudice, then they could also stamp out segregation.[48]

To the contrary, Springfield showed that enlightened racial attitudes could coexist quite easily with racial segregation. Or, as school officials in Wilmington, Delaware, had explained, programs for tolerance could work hand in hand with a Jim Crow setup.

The conventional wisdom of the World War Two era had it that white Americans could root out prejudice *and* segregation if only they could win the inner struggle over the demons of racial hatred. Wallace Stegner concluded that the solution to the "Negro Problem," in the North as in the South, resided in the "minds and hearts of white people." The trick was to change white souls; the rest would follow.[49]

The Springfield Plan was most remarkable when viewed in a regional comparison. For all its shortcomings—the questions about whether a focus on white attitudes meant much of anything while racial injustice abounded, the overblown claims about how singing folk songs could foster equality, and the missed opportunity of the Warner Brothers film—the Plan was in a sense revolutionary. Nothing made this clearer than Theodore Bilbo's fury.

Upon reading *The Springfield Plan*, Bilbo penned a letter to its author. The Mississippi senator warned that the "co-mingling of the white children, as in Springfield, Mass., with the Negro race will lead to miscegenation, inter-marriage and then mongrelization." Bilbo was moved to publish a book on the subject. *Take Your Choice: Separation or Mongrelization* appeared in 1947, with the Springfield Plan providing grist for Bilbo's paranoia. Bilbo asserted that in Springfield, "the program adopted in recent years has been aimed at total abolition of all racial distinctions." For its interracial potential, the Springfield Plan made Bilbo tremble. Once the Deep South got hold of it, the program started to seem quite subversive. In that comparative context, the Springfield schools were experimenting with something profound.[50]

As America emerged from World War Two, believers in racial equality and defenders of segregation alike grafted their hopes and their fears onto the Springfield Plan. Theodore Bilbo saw in it the specter of racial amalgamation. Liberal journalists glimpsed the potential for a peaceful and civilized postwar world.

In the pages of the *Chicago Defender*, Eugene Zack testified to the Plan's abiding strengths as well as its deepest flaws. Just after the curtain went up on the movie premiere, Zack delivered a devastating critique. *It Happened in Springfield* "is doomed to failure, for it misses the point of the plan completely." As Zack pointed out, "In its essence, the Springfield Plan is intangible." It was a long-range program, aimed at changing the minds of the city's youth over the course of years and decades. "It is more of a feeling than anything else." Yet racial justice could not primarily be about intangible thoughts and feelings. It was also about actions, laws, social structures, and inequalities. Zack knew how the architects of the Plan might respond to this line of criticism. They would suggest that if a commitment to racial equality was inculcated in young children, those youths would grow up to one day build just cities and democratic polities. "The true evaluation" of the Plan, Zack wrote, thus "belongs to the historians of the future world."[51]

On that score, it would be easy to judge the Plan a failure. Decades hence, who really remembered the Springfield Plan? It slipped silently and suddenly into the dustbin of history. The Springfield Plan went out with a whimper. But the Plan had its moment. In the World War Two era, it was all the rage.

IN RETROSPECT, THE FACT THAT THE PLAN THRIVED FOR FIVE YEARS seems like a healthy life rather than a sudden death. Just to survive, so many forces had to align. The Plan owed its very existence, its debatable successes, and its relative fame to an innovative superintendent, an explosion of human relations organizations, active professors and psychologists, a willing Northeastern city, and, most important, a world war that took a nation of fragmented groups and pressed them urgently together. The Springfield Plan was both of its time and far ahead. The Plan's grand ambitions to batter down prejudice sprung out of a nation's response to Nazism. Its answer to this problem was distinct to the 1940s. It concentrated on folkways more than stateways, on attitudes more than structures, on white more than black, and on prejudice more than segregation.

Springfield residents never unified behind the Plan. One's stance toward the Plan tended to break down along party lines. Wartime unity had kept these political tensions under wraps, but at war's end the antagonisms bubbled to the surface. A Springfield resident later reflected:

> The war years helped the Plan by producing an artificial feeling of cooperation between people. Acceptance of one another was high, and prejudice was low.
>
> Education for democratic citizenship became blurred with the effort to defend democracy. After the war Springfield returned to its old level in human relations. Normalcy surged back and old antagonisms reappeared. The artificial force of the war years disappeared.

The end of the war spelled the death of the Springfield Plan.[52]

Springfield had been a Republican city ever since that party's creation. Republican leaders had first installed Granrud as superintendent and presided over the implementation of the Plan. In November 1945, the Democrats turned the tables. Daniel Brunton became mayor and many Democrats won local offices. They all opposed the Springfield Plan. The incoming Democratic administration ultimately forced Granrud's resignation. By December, Granrud was gone for good. The following year brought a Democratic landslide. In the very beginning, the Springfield Plan had sought to defuse political and ethnic tensions. Those same divisions finally undid the Plan. By 1950, as a member of the Springfield School Committee recalled, "the name of Granrud was never mentioned and the Springfield Plan was a thing of the past. Even to have graduated from Teachers College or Columbia University was to gain a black mark. There was a strong educational conservatism along with the religious and political divisiveness." The home of the extraordinary Springfield Plan became, at once, an ordinary old industrial city with a fractious politics.[53]

Even the Plan's supporters began to wonder what good it had done. In 1950, the NAACP Youth Council pronounced the Springfield Plan a failure. The Plan not only failed to eliminate racial prejudice, the Youth Council charged, but also created the illusion that this very goal had been achieved—thus preventing any further attack on racism and inequality. Racial tensions increased. About 1,500 African Americans had migrated to Springfield during the war, representing a 50 percent expansion of the black population. This added to the unease of white residents. Many blamed the Springfield Plan for the demographic change, claiming that the city attracted black migrants because it was now perceived as a racial haven. Others simply declared that the Plan had accomplished its goal: Springfield had won the war against bigotry, so it could return to a more humdrum everyday life. The new school superintendent subscribed to this view. William Sanders declared, "The principles of the Plan are now embodied in our common practice. The formal outlines of the plan have atrophied with maturity in the same manner that certain lymphatic glands atrophy when the child is well on its way toward adolescence." The Plan had graduated to adulthood, Sanders opined; it needed nurturing no longer. "The Springfield Plan . . . has accomplished its purpose." In the mind's eye, one could glimpse the Boston City Council nodding in agreement. There simply was no discrimination or prejudice. So why enact, or continue, a program to root it out?[54]

One did not have to look far to see this myth dispelled. There were dramatic examples of racial discrimination in Springfield—against local African Americans, against Jamaican workers brought in during the war, and against Japanese Americans who were transported to Springfield from internment centers on the West Coast. Local unions discriminated blatantly against the nonwhite workers in their midst, while Mayor Brunton floated proposals to create low-cost housing for blacks only. During all of these struggles, the local NAACP waved the banner of the Springfield Plan and reminded the city of the reputation that it needed to uphold.[55]

In 1946, the city still had no black policemen or firefighters, no African Americans who served as bus drivers or social workers. The vaunted school system employed but three black teachers. At Smith & Wesson, the city's largest employer, African Americans worked only as floor sweepers, machine oilers, and toilet cleaners.[56]

By 1950, blacks comprised 3 percent of the city's population. By 1956, they counted for 6,500 (or 4 percent) of Springfield's 160,000 residents. Still only ten of the city's teachers were African Americans, out of more than a thousand in all. As an African American leader had reflected in 1946, "prejudice and discrimination do exist here . . . in a subtle form which defies definition but which . . . prevents the advancement of the individual and group beyond a certain point. . . . No, the Negro in Springfield has not gained what might be expected in a locality where the famous 'Springfield Plan' exists." If the African American could not make it there, he would have a difficult time making it anywhere.[57]

THE SPRINGFIELD PLAN WAS A TOUCHSTONE FOR RACE RELATIONS IN the World War Two era. For a moment it became the fancy of the nation. But when the cooperative spirit of wartime was gone, there was less talk of teaching racial democracy in school. Civil rights supporters and racial liberals paid less attention to white attitudes. They focused more on laws and politics. The battle over FEPC (Fair Employment Practices Committee) laws foreshadowed this broader shift.

The Massachusetts legislature defeated one version of an FEPC law, the Curtis Bill, in January 1946. It was placed on the back burner. In March, Springfield representative Ralph Clampit proposed a sort of statewide Springfield Plan. His bill would establish public school courses to combat discrimination. The Plan might have been dying in its own city, but Clampit tried to revive it at the state level. With Clampit midway into his speech on the House floor, Quincy representative John H. Taylor stood up and interrupted. Taylor charged that courses to teach tolerance were "nothing but an attempt to whitewash the nigger." Clampit, taken aback, asked Taylor to repeat himself. "I said whitewash the nigger—with two Gs." The Massachusetts House sat in stunned silence. They expected this type of scene in Tallahassee or Montgomery, but not in Boston. Another representative declared, "I never thought I would see at a committee of this kind a situation I've seen in other sections of the country."[58]

Across Massachusetts, leaders denounced John Taylor. Boston mayor James Michael Curley led the chorus. "At a time when the whole world is endeavoring to create an observance of the Divine Commandment to love thy neighbor as thyself," Taylor's histrionics were "most unfortunate." The editor of the *Christian Register*, Stephen Fritchman, captured the prevailing sentiment: "Massachusetts has no room for a Yankee Rankin." The Boston NAACP called for Taylor's impeachment, and rounded up the support of more than 300 political leaders. Fighting suddenly for his job, and fighting back tears, Taylor spoke days later. He apologized to his fellow House members. The Springfield City Council drafted a motion demanding that Taylor also apologize to the city of Springfield and to all African Americans in the Bay State. John Taylor now found himself an object of unanimous scorn.[59]

It was not that everyone in Massachusetts disagreed with him. From Boston to Springfield, Taylor could find more than a few like-minded souls. The problem was that by airing such attitudes so publicly, he sullied the good name of Massachusetts. Here was a point on which all could agree. As Rev. Emory Stevens Bucke, a Methodist writer, stated, "We feel that Massachusetts should be out to set an example for the nation in its absolute refusal to sanction the use of such remarks by a public official." George Simmons, an adjutant of an American Legion post in Boston, called Taylor's remarks "pro-Nazi" and "un-American." Even worse, Taylor uttered his words "within a stone's throw of the monument erected to the memory of Crispus Attucks."[60]

But all was not lost. Backers of FEPC legislation glimpsed in Taylor's epithet the clearest justification for their cause. Taylor had demonstrated the need for FEPC laws. "When we have reached the place where elected officials express racial discrimination," said Rev. Bucke, "then we can hardly expect that the masses of people seeking employment will ever get justice." The Massachusetts Council of Churches and the Jewish Community Council issued a joint statement in favor of the FEPC. In it they acknowledged the weaknesses of the Springfield Plan. "It now becomes obvious that education for tolerance alone is a watered down and anemic [objective]. We must get on the books of this commonwealth such legislation as the [FEPC], whereby the majesty and strength of our state government will move into the fight against bigotry." They were saying that it was time to press beyond attitudinal transformations and into the realm of legal change. "It is too late to talk in broad terms of brotherhood; the house is here for translating into law the will of the great majority of people, the will to root out discrimination wherever it exists." Changing attitudes was no longer all that important. The key now was to place in the law books protections for racial minorities.[61]

The movement to teach racial democracy lost its momentum, but not its allure. By 1947, there would be a new crucible where culture and institutions collided, where African Americans advanced toward equal opportunity and whites grappled with racial change.

FENWAY PARK COULD HAVE BEEN BASEBALL'S RACIAL TESTING GROUND. In 1945, two years before Jackie Robinson broke the color barrier in Brooklyn, the Red Sox gave him a tryout. But Boston botched its chance to lead.

At the end of World War Two, groups of activists, politicians, and journalists fixed their eyes on America's pastime, pressing for the integration of baseball. In response, baseball owners and general managers promised to hold tryouts for African American athletes—promises that quickly proved empty. They would trot black ballplayers onto major league fields just to alleviate political pressure, without any intent of signing the athletes. Brooklyn was first on this score. In April 1945, general manager Branch Rickey invited two black ballplayers to the Dodgers' training facility at Bear Mountain, New York. Dave "Showboat" Thomas, the first baseman for the New York Cubans, played alongside Newark Eagles pitcher Terris McDuffie. This created an uproar in baseball circles, but brought no steps toward desegregation.[62]

The origins of baseball's integration never really rested in the moral choices of Branch Rickey, or even in the tremendous courage of Jackie Robinson. Neither was integration driven by any truths about the power of the free market, finally cleansed of racism. Rather, this was a story of political power and public pressure. Rickey started to feel the heat in Brooklyn as early as April 1945. In that same month, Boston City Councilman Isadore Muchnick applied a critical amount of pressure in his own city. Boston's municipal laws prohibited businesses from operating on Sundays. Baseball teams needed a special permit to play on the day of rest. Muchnick informed the owners of the Boston Red Sox and the Boston Braves that he would vote to deny them this license unless they gave black players a fair shake. Only when the teams agreed in writing to allow African Americans an opportunity did Muchnick vote to grant them a permit.[63]

The *Pittsburgh Courier* paid for three black players to travel to Boston. On the morning of April 16, 1945, they arrived at Fenway: Sam Jethroe, Marvin Williams, and Jackie Robinson. Robinson dominated the tryout, lashing pitch after pitch deep toward Fenway's green fences. For Wendell Smith, the *Courier* sports editor and longtime warrior for baseball integration, this was a remarkable day. Smith's article of April 21 took on epic tones. "Here Monday on the silken turf of historic Fenway Park . . . deep in the heart of staid old Boston . . . another epochal chapter in the campaign to end racial discrimination in the major leagues was written."[64]

The city that would pioneer baseball integration had to be a place where residents might tolerate—and ultimately accept and embrace—a black player. The city would also have to possess a politician willing to fight for integration. Boston had the second criterion in Isadore Muchnick, even if it was unclear whether in the spring of 1945 "the Hub" possessed that first quality. Boston was not an easy city for African Americans. Many neighborhoods were insular places where racism was deepseated. But Boston still nursed an old abolitionist activism. It had the sense of itself as a beacon—as a place where a racial breakthrough was not only possible but also right.

One Boston journalist kept the faith. Mabe "Doc" Kountze, an African American born in Medford, had written for Monroe Trotter's *Boston Guardian* and then for the *Boston Chronicle*. For Kountze, the tryout generated a feeling of hope. "In Boston, we all expected a fair trial at the Hub's Fenway Park. I . . . was already keenly anticipating the end of the color ban beginning at Fenway Park and Braves Field. Whether Robbie and his mates made it or not, I could see the Sox extending invitations to many others who definitely could." Kountze fully expected the Boston teams to integrate.[65]

Kountze's vision might have become reality, but for Tom Yawkey. A willing and active owner was the third necessary ingredient for the integration of a baseball team, and Boston did not have it. In 1946, Yawkey would passionately oppose integration from his seat on baseball's steering committee. He soon made the Red Sox synonymous with racism. Jackie Robinson, Sam Jethroe, and Marvin Williams never heard a word back from Boston. For Doc Kountze, this counted as "one of the biggest letdowns" of his life. He thought more of the fair Bay State. "I could see it happening in Mississippi, but not in Massachusetts." The Red Sox would ultimately be the last team to sign an African American, in 1959. The great breakthrough happened not in Boston, but in Brooklyn.[66]

TWO

Something in the Air

Jackie Robinson's Brooklyn (1947–1957)

THE AROMA HIT THEM FIRST. THE SMELL OF BREAD RISING FROM the Taystee factory, and cakes baking at the Ebingers plant, greeted the fans when they stepped out of the train station. As the throng pressed closer to the stadium, that scent mixed with roasted peanuts and hot dogs, sweat and grass. Then came the sounds: the excited yells of children, the vendors who hawked scorecards or newspapers. Many Brooklyn natives, such as Joel Berger, recalled Ebbets Field as "a total sensory experience." Nighttime made the stadium a palace, transfixing the eyes. Joe Flaherty remembered the decadent feel "of walking through Prospect Park to see a rare night game." On a balmy evening in midsummer, "all of a sudden the sky would be lit up . . . and as you got closer, you'd pick up your pace, and you'd give your tickets and go charging inside." A Dodger game was the quintessential Brooklyn experience. In the years after World War Two, it became more than that. To those who lived through Jackie Robinson's decade in Brooklyn, Ebbets Field was not only the borough's cultural heart but also the very seat of American democracy. A moral element at once mingled with the magnificent smells and sounds and sights.[1]

Jackie Robinson added this new dimension. That such a racial break-through occurred in this time and place armed postwar Brooklynites with a distinctive claim to progress. As journalist Pete Hamill reflected, "It was about right and wrong . . . we became the most American place in the country." But Brooklyn also held within it all the conflicts of America writ large. It anticipated the changes that would ripple across the Northeast and the tensions that would tear at many more American cities.[2]

Nostalgia for Brooklyn was based on more than a song or a dream, or a romanticized childhood memory. The wide ethnic diversity, the urban neighborhoods that seemed truly to work, the strength of liberal and leftist politics, the foresight of Branch Rickey, and the stoic dignity of Jackie Robinson, Roy Campanella, and Don Newcombe—all of these lent substance to the boasts of Brooklyn residents. But one must pair those factors with others that simultaneously suggested the deepening of inequality: the conflux of black ghettoes, black poverty, and black schools. The two narratives were both very real. Incredible achievements at the ballpark and the flexible racial outlooks they fostered, together with progressive legislation at the municipal and state levels, mingled uneasily alongside housing practices that spelled segregation, planted the seeds of the "urban crisis," and accelerated the growth of more exclusive suburbs. All of these developments occurred at once.

This is the story not just of Robinson in Brooklyn, but of Brooklyn during Robinson's decade there—a place characterized by housing discrimination, segregation, and occasional violence, along with flashes of racial and political progress.

When the history of Jackie Robinson is handed down, it often comes in the language and rhythms of the game—the stuff of hits and runs, stolen bases and brushback pitches. Just as frequently, chroniclers have located Robinson's story within the trajectory of the black struggle for equality—as a first shot in the postwar civil rights movement. But the grand epics of baseball and civil rights look different when wedded to a deeper understanding of the specific place in which the story occurred. Jackie Robinson's achievement must be situated within a broader social, political, and racial history of Brooklyn during a crucial decade. A composite tale emerges; it complicates, and sometimes contradicts, the optimistic narrative about postwar Brooklyn in which Robinson played a starring role.

Nowhere else did the rhetoric of democracy and pluralism proliferate with such power. And nowhere else was its opposite spawned in such close proximity. Housing projects grew on the same Bedford Avenue where the masses huddled to cheer Jackie Robinson and to fume at the epithets slung by his rivals. For every white resident who experienced a change in his or her attitude upon embracing Brooklyn's dark-skinned infielder, another African American family from the South wound up in the burgeoning ghetto of Bedford-Stuyvesant. The two stark stories, and all of their permutations, reveal the region's conflicted character.

In 1948, *Brooklyn Eagle* reporter Ralph Foster Weld set out to articulate Brooklyn's unique spirit through a series of feature articles. He expanded these pieces in a book, *Brooklyn Is America*. "Every great city has a distinctive atmosphere—a something in the air, an essence, a flavor—that belongs to it alone and marks it off from all other cities." Weld found this "essence" in streets and restaurants, beaches and parks. It was every bit as important as other elements that the social scientists could quantify. "That atmosphere is no less real because it is intangible, no less powerful because you cannot define it exactly." Weld was impressed by "the mingling of races in workaday relationships." In Brooklyn, "the discouraged observer of mankind may find some ground for hope. It is the civilized world in microcosm." He emphasized, above all, Brooklyn's process of Americanization—the way it absorbed transplants from so many different places and blended them into a whole without ever disposing of rich cultural traditions. Brooklyn bound all of these peoples together in a web of pluralism. For Weld, Brooklyn symbolized, and actualized, the best of American democracy.[3]

Journalist Jack Newfield was not yet in high school when Weld's series on Brooklyn appeared in the *Eagle*. But Newfield later reached a similar conclusion. He reflected, "There was something about Brooklyn, after the end of World War II—and until the Dodgers left in 1957—that was magical." Working people and immigrants fueled that feeling. It was the "Brooklyn of working-class pluralism. No party platform or political vocabulary has ever been able to bottle the feeling that was in the air of Jackie Robinson's Brooklyn." To many Brooklyn natives, that aura was impossible to miss.[4]

Brooklyn was a polyglot place that housed Catholics and Jews, Italians and Irish, Scandinavians and Slavs, African Americans and Puerto Ricans. One in four Americans traced their family histories through Brooklyn, which swelled to 2.7 million souls in 1947. "Three million people, and hardly a Mayflower descendant among them," mused author Peter Golenbock. "Everyone came as a minority, and they discovered that when they arrived in Brooklyn, everyone was the same: Everyone was poor, everyone was struggling." They lived on the other side of the bridge, away from the lights of Times Square and the riches of Wall Street. Many thought of Brooklyn as a true melting pot. For journalist Thomas Oliphant, Brooklyn "represented a special place that meant and still means melting pot, working families, and a rash pride in a unifying struggle that is mostly hard." It seemed like a sanctuary for the underdog and an interethnic haven.[5]

Brooklyn Jews loomed large in this interpretation. They numbered almost a million and often powered the political Left—in labor movements, in the Communist Party, or as backers of New Deal liberalism. To Oliphant, a Dodger-obsessed Manhattan resident, "Jews made Brooklyn, for all its clannishness and parochialism, a borough with open arms and a visceral, street-level tolerance. . . . Jews in the twentieth century in effect comprised Brooklyn's soul." Gardner Calvin Taylor, the African American pastor of Concord Baptist Church, also credited Jews for Brooklyn's reputation. "Brooklyn itself was for that time the most tolerant and diverse place in America. The key, no question about it, was the large Jewish population, which operated . . . as our collective social conscience." They perched Brooklyn upon the frontier of interracial democracy.[6]

Beneath the surface, Brooklyn bubbled with tension. Ivan Hametz, a Williamsburg Jew who was ten years old when Robinson broke baseball's color barrier, called his neighborhood "a place of diversity"—though there was little harmony. "On certain occasions, Halloween for example, the ugly face of anti-Semitism surfaced. A bunch of thugs would chase Jewish kids with socks filled with chalk and beat us." Racial, religious, and ethnic differences pitted Brooklynites against one another. To Robert Gruber, another Brooklyn native, the borough's ethnic enclaves comprised "a kind of ad hoc segregation. A happy melting pot it was not." Both Gruber and Hametz found comfort and camaraderie in rooting for the Dodgers. Ebbets Field blunted some of the world's sting.[7]

To African Americans, that sting probed much deeper than chalk-beatings on Halloween. World War Two might have intensified democratic feeling at home and buoyed hopes for equality among American blacks and women, but those years also heightened white racial fears.[8]

Brooklyn's black trolley operators bore the brunt of that resentment. The trolleys occupied a hallowed place in Brooklyn's collective heart. The beloved baseball team took its name from borough residents who dodged the trolleys. Black transit workers had struggled to ascend from menial labor into positions as motormen, conductors, and trolley operators. They contended with a fierce backlash. On June 3, 1944, Lillian Oliver admitted a white woman onto her Flatbush Avenue trolley car. Oliver exchanged words with the woman before two white men approached Oliver and struck her in the face. She wielded a switch iron in defense. Police officers arrived on the scene and arrested Oliver. Three days later, workers banded together. Sixteen trolley operators, all of them African American women, went on strike. Trolley cars sat idle on the Nostrand Avenue, Flatbush Avenue, Tompkins Avenue, and Utica-Reid lines. Over the coming weeks, two more trolley operators were assaulted. The NAACP established a fund for the drivers' defense. Oliver was exonerated and the strikers kept their jobs. Black struggle bore fruit even as it exposed a vicious white racism in Brooklyn. And this racism punctured a gaping hole in the Brooklyn mystique.[9]

Tensions ran high on the trolleys through 1944. On the morning before Christmas, William Morris steered his trolley toward the Brooklyn Navy Yard. Four white sailors in uniform, along with two civilian passengers, threatened to beat Morris. The men were outraged because "niggers have no business operating trolleys anyway." Morris spied a Marine Guard stationed at the navy yard's Washington Street gate and, hoping for help, brought his trolley to a halt. The guard offered no assistance. Six men set upon Morris and administered a savage beating, kicking out his front teeth. Morris did not retaliate. He was mindful of a Transit System statute that forbade trolley operators from using force "no matter what the provocation." Earlier that month, two black trolley operators—Gadson Goodson and James Gordon—were sentenced to prison in Sing Sing. Goodson and Gordon had been under attack from white riders, and committed punishable crimes: they fought back.[10]

Beliefs about Brooklyn as a special place persisted despite such racial violence. But when whites and blacks took steps toward a new interracial world, they were halting steps that exposed white unease and insensitivity. There was little interaction between the races, owing to the small black population in the North, the physically isolated black neighborhoods, and the lifestyles that required few maids and cooks. This could produce among white northerners an actual ignorance as well as a willful blindness. As hardware store worker Bill Reddy explained, "There was very little prejudice against blacks because we didn't come into contact with them." If southern whites claimed they "knew their Negroes," then northern cities teemed with so many "invisible men." Joel Martin, who grew up on the border between Flatbush and Borough Park, had few memories of African Americans. "We didn't know of things like racism and prejudice." In this version of northern reality, white Brooklynites barely thought about the blacks who dwelled in their borough. As Robert Gruber recalled, "the only blacks most of us knew were caricatures who visited our homes each week via the airwaves as 'Amos 'n' Andy.'" Realty practices and segregated housing patterns sealed whites off from the black worlds that grew in Central Brooklyn. Whites scarcely gave that universe a thought.[11]

If this appears benign, then it misleads. White Brooklynites, when placed on the defensive, were prone to pounce. Their worldview had a hard edge. "We didn't know we had a race problem," Brooklyn writer Joe Flaherty insisted. "When Robinson was coming up, we liked to think that Negroes didn't need anything, that they were happy in their place." Flaherty took issue with African Americans who deplored that outlook as simple racism. "Don't call my generation racist. . . . I didn't know you people even existed." Flaherty's mindset approximated that of many white Brooklynites, those who toed the perilous line between a lack of knowledge and an odious indifference.[12]

Then there was Jackie Robinson himself. Nothing prodded whites to confront their racial environment like Robinson's arrival. Roger Kahn lived a typical Brooklyn childhood, graduating from Erasmus High and worshipping the Dodgers. As a young man, he became the Dodger beat reporter for the *New York Herald Tribune*. Kahn glimpsed great hope in the transformation that Robinson stirred within white souls. "To disregard color, even for an instant, is to step away from the old prejudices,"

Kahn wrote in 1971. The crowd's new disposition might not extend beyond the baseball field, but then, how couldn't it? "That is not a path on which many double back." Kahn felt these ballpark experiences held deep meaning. "By applauding Robinson, a man did not feel that he was taking a stand on school integration, or open housing. But for an instant he had accepted Robinson simply as a hometown ball player." That was exactly the rub. Issues like school integration and open housing continued to bedevil Brooklyn, even as racial enmity melted in the integrated crucible of Ebbets Field.[13]

New England had its town meeting. Brooklyn had its baseball stadium. As Brooklyn welcomed Robinson, some residents thought, the borough proved itself a working model of the American Dream. Residents recognized the symbiosis between Robinson and Brooklyn. "Without both Brooklyn and Robinson," thought Robert Gruber, Branch Rickey's "'great experiment' would have failed." And because the experiment so clearly succeeded, the mystique about Brooklyn only grew. Jack Newfield pointed out that "in 1947 Brooklyn was seven years ahead of the Supreme Court . . . in rejecting the doctrine of separate but equal and in burying the stereotype of white supremacy." This was an America that had heard of neither Rosa Parks nor Martin Luther King Jr. Newfield's Dodgers were "the national frontier of inclusion and integration." The coming years would show, painfully and repeatedly, that the ideals of inclusion and integration did not always—if ever—mean racial equality.[14]

Robinson was the necessary ingredient in Brooklyn's midcentury mystique. If Jackie Robinson had never played—and thrived—in Brooklyn, residents would have thought differently about their borough. They could still boast that it was a place of many ethnicities, a home for the working class, one with lively storefronts and beautiful brownstones and parks, but it would exist in memory as a different place. "On his massive shoulders," scholars Joseph Dorinson and Joram Warmund wrote, Brooklyn "achieved an apotheosis." Robinson lent Brooklyn its shine. He brought a spirit that infected the ballpark, the borough, the city, even a nation compelled by its own postwar rhetoric of democracy and freedom. Roger Kahn wrote, "A man felt it; it became part of him, quite painlessly." Robinson's glow spread as though contagious.[15]

It was not just about rooting for Jackie Robinson. It was also partaking in the experience of the integrated stands. Ira Glasser, longtime executive

The Brooklyn Dodgers reached the World Series in 1947, Jackie Robinson's first season. Before the first game at Ebbets Field, fans waited to enter the bleachers. This photograph illustrates the degree of racial integration among Dodger fans. STAFF PHOTO, *BROOKLYN EAGLE*, BROOKLYN PUBLIC LIBRARY – BROOKLYN COLLECTION.

director of the American Civil Liberties Union, felt "a sense of community with blacks in that special sanctuary Ebbets Field." The stadium "was for us a common meeting ground in a society that banished almost all other common meeting grounds." White Brooklynites shared with African Americans a mutual aim. Lester Rodney, a sportswriter for the *Daily Worker*, described "those raucous, salty, kidding, good-natured, integrated Ebbets Fields stands, unlike any before or since." For white people who had known blacks only as janitors and manual laborers, this interracial experience at Ebbets Field opened up a whole new world. Here, wrote Rodney, was "the full-blown aura of the magical years."[16]

After World War Two, many Americans searched for the spirit of democracy, hoping to hold it up for the world to see. Ralph Foster Weld believed that he found it in Brooklyn. Jackie Robinson's Dodgers were the defining element in the overall quality that Weld first set out to articulate. Brooklyn's unique version of democracy "can find an impulse in a politely applauding concert audience at the Academy of Music," Weld ventured at first. But this would have been too highbrow for the borough. "It is fed by the chance contacts and byplay of the streets." But this was too easy, too pedestrian. "The teeming beach at Coney, on a hot Summer day, is congenial to it." That was closer, connoting the massive crowds, the outdoors, and the summertime. "That democratic spirit was fully present— unconscious, robust and utterly sincere—in the great commingled shout from 30,000 Brooklyn throats at Ebbets Field when the Dodgers score a run." In a million memories, that sequence ended with Robinson sliding into home plate, creating a cloud of dust, and bouncing back up into the Brooklyn sunshine.[17]

JACKIE ROBINSON DID NOT BEGIN THE MOVEMENT TO INTEGRATE baseball. He was the product of a long struggle. *Daily Worker* sportswriters, Communist Party organizers, *Pittsburgh Courier* reporter Wendell Smith, and the New York City–based End Jim Crow in Baseball Committee all agitated for the integration of baseball. In 1945, the year of Robinson's tryout at Fenway Park, New York State passed the nation's "model law" establishing an FEPC. It would strike at racial discrimination in the workplace. By the end of World War Two, segregated baseball in New York stood on a wobbly foundation.[18]

The Dodgers held a tryout for African American players at Bear Mountain in the spring of 1945. Dan Burley, managing editor of the *Amsterdam News*, believed the tryout's purpose was to muzzle the liberal politicians and quiet the activists. "Branch Rickey and others who set National League policies ought to be ashamed of themselves," Burley wrote. But they could not slow the tide of racial progress. The FEPC bill had passed the New York state legislature in March, by wide margins. Burley thought it "almost a certainty that none of the major league clubs, playing in New York City, in 1946 will get by without Negroes in their lineup." In October 1945, the FEPC pressed the three New York ball clubs to sign a nondiscrimination pledge. Mayor Fiorello La Guardia pushed for a similar promise. The Giants, Yankees, and Dodgers felt "the brunt of the onslaught," Burley wrote. For this was New York, where barring black employees had become illegal:

> If Rickey . . . and [Horace] Stoneham were located in such towns as Washington, D.C., St. Louis, Atlanta, Birmingham, or Chittling

Switch, Mississippi, I . . . would not . . . be too hard on them because that location tells the story. But here they are in the most liberal state in the union and in the biggest, the most important and the most liberal city in the world, setting themselves up as arbiters of who shall make a living and who shall not and making their conditions and findings on the color of a man's skin.

In latitude and in attitude, New York ought to have been light-years ahead of rural Mississippi. Burley used a formulation of the northern mystique as a tool to prod Rickey and others toward integration.[19]

On August 28, 1945, Branch Rickey called Jackie Robinson to Brooklyn for a meeting. Theories abound as to why Rickey decided to integrate the Dodgers—whether he wished to gain a competitive edge, whether he viewed integration as morally right, whether he thought it the best way to swell the Dodgers' coffers, or whether he was, as Dan Burley surmised, "seeking to avoid a head-on collision with the liberal forces fighting discrimination in employment." In that last scenario, Rickey would hold Robinson in reserve and "make a sudden jump" only if the pressure to desegregate "got too hot on brother Rickey." Rickey signed Robinson to a contract during the final week of October. Rickey opened the door, but just a crack. It was left to baseball owners and fans—and Robinson himself—to shatter that racial barrier into a thousand pieces.[20]

Jackie Robinson joined the Dodgers' minor league affiliate, the Montreal Royals, for spring training in 1946. As the specter of baseball integration came closer, whites across America displayed their discomfort.

Sportswriters often reflected the disposition of their readers. Many of them possessed working-class roots and spent their days at ballparks, eating hot dogs, and their nights at bars and pool tables (and hunched over typewriters). They could speak the language of the "common man," right down to his racial stereotypes. On February 3, 1946, the New York chapter of the Baseball Writers Association held its annual dinner and show at the Waldorf-Astoria Hotel. After the speeches petered out, the 1,200 writers in attendance sat back to watch the night's feature performance. The Waldorf stage became an old Kentucky mansion, the home of baseball commissioner Albert "Happy" Chandler. His servant was dressed in the Montreal Royals uniform of Jackie Robinson, who responded, "Yassah massah. Here ah is," to Chandler's entreaties. When the Chandler character called him an "ole-wooly-headed rascal," and asked "Robiee" how long he had been in the family, Robinson replied: "Long time, Kun'l . . . Ebber since Marse Rickey bought me from da Kansas City Monarchs." Guffaws and cigar smoke filled the room. The *New York Times* termed it "a veritable hash" of an evening. Even staunch supporters of integration participated. Arthur Mann, who had become one of Rickey's assistants, performed an impersonation of his boss while four workers in blackface sang "Glory, Glory, Massa Rickey." The *Times* headlined its article "Writers Lampoon Baseball Bigwigs." From that perspective, Chandler and Rickey were the butts of the joke. The crass caricatures of black people seemed scarcely worth a second thought. The *Sporting News*, an opponent of baseball integration, called that year's writers' dinner the "best yet." As Robinson prepared to desegregate major league baseball, this was the racial culture that he confronted—from the box seats up to the press box.[21]

ON THE APRIL DAY IN 1947 WHEN ROBINSON FIRST PLAYED FOR Brooklyn, African Americans composed more than half of the crowd at Ebbets Field. Dodger fans wasted little time in cheering for Robinson. A photograph pictured white hands dangling down into the Dodger dugout, competing for Robinson's autograph. The *Amsterdam News* conducted an informal survey among fans on Opening Day: out of 202 polled, 187 "were rooting for him to make good," eleven thought Robinson "was not big league material," and four voiced no opinion. Joe Bostic, the newspaper's sports editor, calculated a different percentage. The Brooklyn fans were behind Robinson "350 percent. . . . They were with him, not just Jackie, they were with the idea. He became a state of mind."[22]

The story of Jackie Robinson is still told this way—a tale of one community that wholly embraced the ballplayer in its midst. If the truth was otherwise, the media did not let on. In the *New York Times Magazine*, Arthur Daley noted that Brooklyn fans accepted Robinson "without raising a single eyebrow. It's a strange thing but the average spectator is extremely conscious of Jackie the first time he sees him and then the novelty wears off with greater rapidity than anyone would believe possible. Pretty soon he's just a fellow with No. 42 on his back, noticed only when he does something, unnoticed otherwise." In Roger Kahn's retelling, however, every individual fixed on Robinson. He was "the cynosure of all eyes." Baseball fans had come to associate certain colors with the ball game: they expected the players to look white, just as the dirt was brown and the grass green. Bill Reddy, a longtime fan who would become a sportswriter, remembered how "strange" it was "to go out to Ebbets Field and root for a guy of another color." Robinson turned cultural expectations on their head. As Kahn wrote, "Suddenly in Ebbets Field, under a white home uniform, two muscled arms extended like black hawsers. *Black*. Like the arms of a janitor. The new color jolted the consciousness, in a profound and not quite definable way." Douglas Wilder, a young African American from Virginia, journeyed to Brooklyn to take in the sight. (Wilder would become the governor of Virginia in 1989.) Whites at the ballpark "seemed unbothered by their black neighbors," Wilder observed. "You saw something here that was unusual. . . . You saw the acceptance of Robinson by the Brooklyn fans."[23]

Once whites embraced the infielder with the janitor's arms, he worked on them. Robert Gruber marveled, "How quickly did the assertive Jackie Robinson destroy many of our racial stereotypes!" A democratic Brooklyn welcomed Jackie Robinson, and grew even more democratic itself.[24]

The exceptions to this story posed a problem. When paired with the racism and increasing segregation in the borough, they do not appear as anomalies that prove the rule of racial progress. They challenge that assumption. They also show how whites could feel differently about different *types* of racial progress. Many whites could cheer the breakthrough at the ballpark while resisting black advances in housing, schools, and economics.

Some white Dodger fans renounced their loyalties. Brooklyn native Tom "Duke" Bunderick remembered, "When Jackie Robinson came up, there were a lot of adults who dropped their allegiance to the Dodgers. There was a lot of bigotry, among . . . the Irish, the Italians, the Swedes. They said, 'I'm never gonna root for them again, Goddamn it.' It was a lot of union guys saying, 'Sure, first they get into baseball, and then they'll be taking my job.'" The vast majority of letters published in New York newspapers were supportive of integration. Northern newspapers seldom allowed the opinions of bigots to see the light of day. But the existence of a minority spoke volumes. Just as white southerners kept quiet when they *supported* the civil rights movement, white northerners often sealed their prejudices inside. Even in Brooklyn, many opposed integration on the baseball field while they feared its social consequences and corollaries.[25]

In this sense, the popular narrative is false. But it is so ingrained that it stands as the foundational premise in many accounts. Peter Golenbock, author of two comprehensive oral histories, organizes *In the Country of Brooklyn* around a single question: "Why did Brooklynites love Jackie Robinson when everyone else hated him?" The very question distorts. Golenbock's own book includes the reflections of John Ford, an Irish American from Flatbush. "I remember when Jackie Robinson came up to the Dodgers in '47. The Irish were pissed off. When the blacks came to Ebbets Field, they didn't flock there. They came tentatively. . . . They asked, 'Who's going to sit next to all these niggers?'" Ford continued, "The people in the bars where I hung out—the Irish and Italians—were upset when Robinson came to the Dodgers. They were really outraged." Some Brooklynites greeted Jackie Robinson with fury.[26]

Arthur Mann became acquainted with that anger. Mann enjoyed a storied career as a sportswriter, and in 1946 and 1947 he served as Branch Rickey's assistant. Early in 1947, Mann watched as a revolt against Robinson began to brew within the Dodgers' clubhouse. Many Dodgers signed a petition stating that they would not play with Robinson. Mann later published an article about the ordeal in which he criticized Dixie Walker, a southerner who was fingered as the ringleader of the uprising. One white Brooklynite fired off an angry letter to Arthur Mann. The letter writer avowed that he was no southerner, "nevertheless I understand their problems through much reading of the subject." The man was convinced that "Negroes are less than one hundred years out of savagery and slavery yet some want to place them all on an equal plane in all phases." He found this notion absurd. "What a slur on whites, preferring colored over white! . . . You aught [ought] to hang your head in shame!" He was one of many whites who turned against the Dodgers. He signed the letter: "Ex Dodger Rooter."[27]

AFRICAN AMERICANS EMBRACED THE DODGERS EVERYWHERE FROM Peekskill to Pasadena. "Overnight they became Brooklyn fans," Dan Burley wrote. Many thousands had moved north to New York City; thousands of others made the trek just for a weekend, to steal a glimpse of

Jackie Robinson. "They caught trains and planes and buses and autos and came to New York, all at once and together in a great wave of humanity, embarked on a modern pilgrimage to see the new [symbol] of racial advancement." Blacks in Brooklyn at last started to feel the borough was truly theirs. While southern migrants encountered many obstacles to racial equality in the North, they found at least one meaningful difference: that a man as black as them, whose forefathers were Georgia slaves, played baseball for the home team. Some even began to think about believing in the promise of their nation. Willard Townsend, a black union leader in Brooklyn, comprehended for the first time "what was meant by the . . . expression 'as American as apple pie and baseball.'" Wade Siler was a migrant from the South who came to Brooklyn to tend bar and sing in nightclubs. He found himself suddenly "transformed into a Dodger fan." In upper Manhattan, Kenneth Clark allowed sports to interrupt his scholarship. Clark became an instant convert to the Dodgers.[28]

Other racial pioneers saw in Jackie Robinson a kindred spirit. G. Gilbert Smith was a machinist in Jersey City who had integrated the shop during World War Two. "They did all the dirty underhanded things to me that they must be doing to you," Smith wrote in a letter to Robinson. "I came out alright after awhile. Because I developed a thick skin that I had to arm myself with as soon as I entered that shop." This machinist recognized the taunts and epithets that Robinson endured on the field. "I couldn't fight back," Gilbert Smith recalled. "My work had to be better than the other guys but I had to see that there wasn't too much attention drawn to any of the better work I did because I knew I'd never make any friends if they envied me or thought I was a show off." Smith understood the enormous pressure that Robinson faced; he also gained strength from Robinson. "If your batting average never gets any higher than .100 and if you make an error every inning, if I can raise my boy to be half the man that you are I'll be a happy father."[29]

Robinson drafted a response and mailed it immediately to Jersey City. He recognized Gilbert Smith as a kindred spirit indeed. "Maybe the ones, like ourselves, who have to fight hardest for the simple things others take for granted get more out of life in the end." He tried to unload a bit of the burden from his own shoulders. "Don't think your boy could be just as good a man if I don't make an error every inning and bat more than .100? Seriously, I'm sure he will grow up to be a fine man with such a father to guide him." Some African Americans, like Gilbert Smith, looked at Robinson not as a symbol of what they might become but as an embodiment of the struggles they had already waged.[30]

As the 1947 season wound down, the *Amsterdam News* and the *People's Voice* tried to organize a Jackie Robinson Day at Ebbets Field. The prospect aroused concern among Dodger executives and local businessmen. "Many persons believe that violence occurs when and wherever a large group of Negroes assemble," the *Amsterdam News* noted. The newspaper railed against this stereotype and solicited donations in Robinson's honor. On September 23, 1947, all Ebbets Field saluted Jackie Robinson. He was showered with gifts: a white Cadillac, a television, a gold watch from Tiffany's, and an interracial goodwill plaque. Robinson's mother, Mallie, flew in an airplane for the first time to witness the event. More than 26,000 fans came through the turnstiles to join in the celebration; 60 percent of them were African Americans. It was their day in Brooklyn.[31]

For blacks in Brooklyn, the festivities in the baseball stadium comprised only one slice of reality. Just beneath the Jackie Robinson Day editorials and solicitations that the *Amsterdam News* published throughout September, it ran stories about the high prices of groceries in Brooklyn's black areas and the inferior quality of that merchandise. The *Amsterdam News* suggested a grocery boycott. It also exposed and eviscerated slumlords who kept the thermostats off in late September. White Brooklynites tried to separate the two stories of race relations, cheering a black baseball player without thinking about conditions in black neighborhoods. But such distinctions held little meaning for African Americans. They did not divide their lives into categories, setting racial attitudes and sports apart from schools, neighborhoods, housing, employment, and economics. All of these realities together constituted the stuff of life in Jackie Robinson's Brooklyn.[32]

That a Jackie Robinson Day happened at all was testament to the fact that Robinson excelled on the field, exceeding all predictions. In his first season Robinson propelled the Dodgers into the World Series.

The Dodgers faced the New York Yankees in the Fall Classic. The Yankees heaped upon Robinson some of the cruelest epithets of that long season. He had endured the taunts of fans and players in Cincinnati and St. Louis. He had also encountered particularly harsh treatment from the Philadelphia Phillies. The Yankees were more covert. "They holler things at you from the dugout," Robinson reported, "and then when they get out in the open and on the field they don't say anything." From the shelter of the dugout, Yankee players unleashed "the worst razzing" of all. The Yankees thus embodied northern racism. It rarely meandered into the light of day, preferring to cloak itself in the darkness and the seeming anonymity of the sidelines.[33]

The Dodgers lost in the championship. Just as Dodger fans were ultimately left wanting, so were Brooklyn's African Americans. Through the last weeks of October, the grocers in Bedford-Stuyvesant kept their prices 150 percent higher than at other locations in the borough. "It must be remembered that we can stand so much," read an *Amsterdam News* editorial. "There is a limit to our patience." Jackie Robinson's own patience was rubbing against the same limits.[34]

During that first season, Robinson heeded the advice that came from all corners—to ignore his tormentors while he was on the field. His first task was to prove that blacks could succeed in that arena. Dan Burley had implored African Americans "to let him be a ballplayer first and a Negro second." But by the spring of 1948, Burley guessed, "this year it will probably have to be the other way around." Robinson's accomplishments in 1947 only whetted the collective appetite. The integration of baseball deluded few African Americans in Brooklyn into thinking that they had gained full freedom. It shined a light on those inequities that continued to fester. "Once you start succeeding with Jackie Robinson, I think you see increased dissatisfaction," Congress of Racial Equality (CORE) leader Roy Innis later reflected. "Because you become aware of what you have been denied in the past. And you become angry retroactively." To Brooklyn's blacks, that past admitted of much more than weekends at Coney Island and night games at Ebbets Field.[35]

AFRICAN AMERICANS COMPRISED MORE OF BROOKLYN'S POPULATION than ever before. During the Second Great Migration, hundreds of thousands of black southerners had migrated to New York City. Others set sail from the Caribbean. Some even made the move from Harlem to Central Brooklyn. They helped to transform Brooklyn's social fabric. In 1940, 103,000 African Americans called Brooklyn home; the borough was 95 percent white. By the end of the 1940s, 210,000 African Americans lived in Brooklyn. Between 1950 and 1957, Brooklyn welcomed another 100,000 blacks, said farewell to 340,000 whites, and saw its Puerto Rican population rise from 40,000 to 160,000. By 1957, one in five residents identified themselves as racial minorities. If the stands of Ebbets Field became more integrated, it was not just because African Americans flocked to see the Dodgers' black ballplayers; these fans were also living embodiments of the borough's racial transformation.[36]

It was one thing to relate the numbers, and another to see and feel the change. Jimmy Breslin, a legendary local journalist, used dramatic language to tell the story: "Into Brooklyn in the late 1940's they started to come, men with cotton-baling hooks in their pockets, and sad-faced women with arms leaden from hours spent jiggling small children in buses and railroad coach cars from Greenville in South Carolina and Waycross in Georgia." Brooklyn absorbed more than one kind of newcomer. A second migration came courtesy of the airplane. "The late nights at old Idlewild Airport became filled with the poor arriving on cheap flights from Puerto Rico," wrote journalist Jimmy Cannon. He described these migrants from Puerto Rico as "summer people in winter clothes." If the northern metropolis forced them to change their garb, they in turn shaped the city. Brooklyn was becoming a winter place with summer people.[37]

Migrants clamored for jobs in the borough's colossus: the Brooklyn Navy Yard. As America inched into World War Two, the yard teemed with job openings. Soon, the largest employer in Brooklyn was also the United States Navy's biggest shipyard and New York City's center for industry. It counted almost 70,000 workers. The navy yard was a town unto itself. Its streets formed a nineteen-mile labyrinth, with 270 buildings and eight different piers. While the navy yard sucked in millions of federal dollars, it became a hotbed of labor discrimination. In United States Navy yards, more than 85 percent of black employees toiled as menial laborers, helpers, or apprentices—with few opportunities to advance. The Brooklyn yard mirrored this pattern.[38]

When the war drew to a close, the Brooklyn Navy Yard was hit hard. Thousands of workers lost their jobs, and those fortunate enough to remain on the docks faced decreases in their hours and wages. Managers at the Naval Clothing Depot laid off all of the African American women on the night shift, retaining white day-shift workers with lesser tenures.

After the war, the navy yard's workforce declined by roughly 10,000 per year.[39]

While migrants initially came to the navy yard to work, few of them landed stable jobs. And while they had come to Brooklyn to live, fewer still had a choice as to which neighborhood they would call home.

Wherever blacks moved in Central Brooklyn, the lines of the Bedford-Stuyvesant neighborhood followed. Its boundaries "mysteriously change each year," observed a *Brooklyn Eagle* reporter, "as the press of increasing population forces more and more Negroes to find homes in nearby 'fringe' areas." By the end of the 1950s, Bedford-Stuyvesant would house more African Americans than Harlem. Bedford-Stuyvesant's black population grew from 65,000 in 1940 to 137,000 in 1950. In 1948, the *Brooklyn Eagle* described Bedford-Stuyvesant as "one big, continuous slum, largely populated by Negroes. This area is living proof of what discrimination does." This was the Brooklyn that the mystique about democracy, postwar pluralism, and integration so brazenly missed.[40]

Though the *Eagle* had pronounced the neighborhood a black slum in 1948, the transition from white to black was not completed until the mid-1950s. That was when dilapidated buildings crept up alongside historic brownstones, when crime and poverty rose. Bedford-Stuyvesant would eventually extend southward to Atlantic Avenue, touch Myrtle Avenue on the north, and sit on an east-west axis between Vanderbilt and Brooklyn Avenues. In the days before the Great Depression, luxury homes had sprouted on these streets. But whites began to leave the area in the 1920s. They pushed out to Brooklyn's own version of the suburbs: Bay Ridge, Bensonhurst, Flatlands, and Canarsie.

During the 1930s, 30,000 black families replaced an equal number of whites in Bedford-Stuyvesant. Jack Newfield had described the neighborhood in the mid-1930s as "an integrated middle class" place "with tree-lined streets and spacious, solid brownstones." But as homes began to change hands, one black man who moved into the neighborhood recalled an atmosphere thick with racial tension: "Most of the better white blocks hired uniformed foot patrols to keep us from passing through." In 1940, African Americans still comprised only one-quarter of the neighborhood's population. When Rev. Gardner Calvin Taylor came to the neighborhood in 1946, he did not find a devastated black ghetto but a "self consciously middle class, optimistic and hopeful" neighborhood.

Many of the new black residents were professionals and civil servants who had escaped Harlem for brownstone promises. Housing speculators welcomed them to the neighborhood, and realized an awesome return on their investment. The block-busting realtor would become as powerful a symbol of the urban ghetto as the housing project or the brutal policeman. He presided over its creation.[41]

Realtors came from all corners of the five boroughs for a piece of the action. One block at a time, they sought to place a black family in each white area. Some even paid black children to distribute flyers that declared, "I have a buyer for your house," and enlisted black brokers to follow up with house calls. Some realtors sent African Americans to Bedford-Stuyvesant street corners and directed them to feign drunkenness and start brawls. Vague fears among whites would turn to outright panic. "One family just walked out," recalled Margaret Ross Leigh, a longtime white resident. "They left everything. In their haste they didn't even bother to lock the doors behind them." Then came the "truly lower element" of blacks, securing loans for $20,000 homes that the speculators had just scared whites into selling for $2,500. For the rare white who wanted to remain, or the more frequent African American who wished to buy, a world of stonewalling banks and hidden surcharges awaited. Banks gave few loans to whites who wanted to remodel their houses, for they were bad bets to stay. And for African Americans coming into the neighborhood, loans were easy to procure yet impossible to repay. They often wound up with a mountain of debt, advised to slice up and rent out the very dwellings they had just chosen. As black families moved onto one street, white owners on the next were bombarded by the realtors and fliers. Thus Bedford-Stuyvesant grew into the North's largest black community, a place whose boundaries swallowed every nearby street where African Americans dwelled.[42]

African Americans paid high rents for shabby apartments; they endured police brutality; their garbage was sporadically collected; and their streets were rarely cleaned. In the years after World War Two, they began to organize for more playgrounds and swimming pools, for better schools and hospitals. They waged boycotts and sit-ins even as segregation grew more rigid.

Precisely because Jackie Robinson achieved so much in Brooklyn, and because a certain rhetoric developed around the borough's progress, the existing racial inequality seemed so flagrant. Because Brooklynites made such proclamations about interracial democracy, the borough's brand of segregation became that much more insidious.

The two sides were always present in Jackie Robinson's Brooklyn. There were scattered examples that gave life to the rhetoric, and basic social conditions that challenged it. "The best word to describe the situation was *ambiguous*," according to Rev. Gardner Calvin Taylor. "There was no question we had escaped a much more rigid system in the South." Blacks in Brooklyn found "a mobility on the subways and buses" that was unimaginable in Dixie. And still, they had swapped one caste system for quite another. "It is also true . . . that there were many stores in New York where we were not welcome," Taylor remembered. "Residence was strictly . . . segregated . . . only menial jobs were available with very, very few exceptions. At Ebbets Field, nearly all of us sat in the outfield bleachers. In government, there was as yet no opportunities at all." In jobs and housing, in the taverns and restaurants that banned even the most decorated of black war veterans, Brooklyn blacks faced discrimination. In baseball and politics and cultural life, they scored dramatic triumphs. Theirs was not the rigid and enforced inferiority of the South, but a more muddled, yet no less contested, oppression.[43]

BEDFORD-STUYVESANT WOULD TUMBLE TOWARD NOTORIETY IN THE 1950s, showcasing poverty, inequality, racism, and the bankruptcy of urban planning. And yet beneath the signs of outward decay it developed a powerful silver lining. For blacks cultivated a strength in numbers. With every new voter added to the rolls, the potential for black political power grew larger.

In 1946, Brooklyn's elected officials looked like its ballplayers: they were all white. One year after Jackie Robinson broke baseball's color barrier, Bertram Baker won a seat in the state assembly. By the time the Dodgers left Brooklyn, Baker had planted the seeds of a vibrant black politics.

Harlem voters sent Adam Clayton Powell to the United States Congress in 1944. In Brooklyn, however, elective office had eluded African Americans. Myles Paige, who would later become Brooklyn's first black Special Sessions Court Justice, declared, "The Brooklyn Negro is 25 years behind Manhattan politically." Bertram Baker ran for New York City Council in 1941 and 1945, losing both times. When a councilman stepped down in 1947, many believed Baker was next in line. But Baker was passed over. "Each year," the *Amsterdam News* lamented, "we miss by a hair's length and the age-worn 'wait until next time' pops into eminence." The *Brooklyn Eagle* agreed. The story of black politics in Brooklyn "was a history of frustration and impotence."[44]

Yet years of electoral defeat were not synonymous with weakness. Baker built a powerful political organization in the 1930s, one that helped to tip local elections and that backed African American leaders for appointed positions. Impotent it was not.

Bertram Baker grew up on the island of Nevis. He came to the United States in 1915, at the age of seventeen. In 1920, Baker opened a private accounting practice in his home on Throop Avenue in Bedford-Stuyvesant. Four years later, he gained American citizenship.[45]

Baker dove into local politics. He became a fixture at the meetings of the 17th Assembly District Regular Democratic Club, rising to the position of captain. He made contacts in the black middle class—among the teachers and doctors, tailors and barbers—and began to organize a political club of his own. In 1933 Baker founded the United Action Democratic Association of Kings County (UADA). The UADA cut across many fault lines in the black community. Baker gained the support of most every noteworthy group: the local YMCA and the Elks, the Brooklyn branch of the NAACP and the Urban League, Caribbean islanders and native blacks. Baker was a machine builder more than an insurgent. While his organization endured many slights from the regular Democratic Party, Baker counseled a slow and gradual approach.

His patience paid dividends. The UADA helped to elect African American John Coleman to the Board of Higher Education, and Oliver D. Williams to the board of the Brooklyn Public Library. "Every one of these tidbits," remembered UADA member Lawrence Pierce, "was an important step forward and directly attributable to the pressure which was mounted by Bert and his club members." Most important, blacks in Brooklyn were now invested in politics. "I was caught up in the spirit of the whole business," Pierce continued, "which was that blacks were seeking representation." Baker's own campaigns for the city council also helped contribute to a larger "feeling, long before 1948," recalled

Brooklyn resident Franklin W. Morton Jr., "that 'it's about time we got our fair share.'"[46]

In 1946, two black women campaigned for a seat in the New York State Assembly from the 17th District. Maude Richardson was the Republican nominee, and Ada Jackson was the candidate of the American Labor Party. They both lost to the Democratic incumbent, John Walsh. But when the votes of Richardson and Jackson were combined, they surpassed Walsh's total. This highlighted a new electoral calculus in Central Brooklyn. In January 1948, the *Amsterdam News* suggested, "Many feel that this year's election will send a Negro to public office for the first time in the history of the borough." Black Brooklyn was heady with the anticipation of political victory.[47]

After considerable maneuvering, the district boss finally tapped Bertram Baker as the Democratic nominee for the state assembly seat in 1948. Baker's supporters were ecstatic. They unfurled a ditty for the occasion, sung to the tune of the "Battle Hymn of the Republic":

> For many years we've waited for this grand and glorious day,
> To elect our own to office the Democratic way
> He has been in many battles teaching us the civic stand,
> As he goes marching on.
> Forward, forward with Bert Baker
> Forward, forward with Bert Baker
> Forward, forward with Bert Baker
> To the job that must be done.

One black man circled the bases at Ebbets Field while another accepted the Democratic nomination for the assembly seat.[48]

Baker squared off against Maude Richardson, assuring Brooklynites of a black representative. While Richardson secured the nominations of both the Republican Party and the Liberal Party, Baker ran on the tickets of the Democratic Party and American Labor Party. Richardson's campaign committee circulated anticommunist smears. "Loyal Americans want to know whether by this alliance with the 'left' you have subscribed to the principles and the platform of the A.L.P." Baker was well positioned to parry such barbs. When Brooklyn blacks had criticized Baker in previous years, it was because they thought him too conservative, too deeply in league with the Democratic machine, and too pragmatic—in a word, insufficiently radical. The red paint would not stick.[49]

On Election Day, Baker won almost two-thirds of the votes. This ended black Brooklyn's long electoral drought. He did not bury the Brooklyn Democratic machine. He integrated it. As the *Brooklyn Eagle* reported, "the eyes of thousands, Negroes and whites, will follow his progress at Albany." Baker may not have been the cynosure of every eye, but he became the focus of many.[50]

As Bertram Baker took office, the Robinsons prepared to move out of Brooklyn. When Jackie and Rachel Robinson had first arrived in New York, in the spring of 1947, they lived in Manhattan at the Hotel McAlpin. After several weeks, they found a room to rent in Brooklyn. A Bedford-Stuyvesant woman offered part of her home to the couple, and they jumped at the chance. Soon the Robinsons found themselves pressed for space, with only a back bedroom to accommodate Jackie, Rachel, and their first child. To Rachel Robinson, "our living accommodations were a nightmare." Still, Brooklyn grew on the Robinsons. "The feeling in Brooklyn was very supportive, very rich, and we loved it," Rachel recalled. "Some places on the road I hated, their total intolerance; but Brooklyn was the opposite, and Jack loved it, too." Brooklyn stood out for its enlightenment, its tolerance, its welcoming arms. Despite the cramped quarters, the Robinsons would look back on those early days in Brooklyn as some of their best.[51]

In 1948, the Robinsons found a new apartment in Flatbush. They moved into the second floor of a two-story home. A black woman had recently purchased the home, though that acquisition came with a fight. The white (and mostly Jewish) neighbors objected to the idea of African Americans on their block. When they heard that a black woman was attempting to buy the home at 5224 Tilden Avenue, homeowners circulated a petition and attempted to stop the sale. In the neighborhood surrounding Ebbets Field, and even among the supposedly liberal Jewish population, the prospect of one black homeowner excited fears and incited action.[52]

The Satlows were one couple that refused to sign any petitions. Sarah Satlow took several calls from frightened neighbors. When one arrived at her doorstep, petition in hand, Satlow asked, "Are you mad? Are you crazy?" Archie and Sarah Satlow lived two doors down from the Robinsons. The families became fast friends. Sarah and Rachel traded recipes, their children played together, and the Robinsons eventually hired Sarah to handle Jackie's fan mail. The Robinsons enjoyed Flatbush, though the delis, temples, and kosher bakeries seemed foreign. Jack Robinson Jr. eased their transition. The boy was "our ambassador in the community in Flatbush," Rachel remembered. "He would knock at those back doors and ask for cookies, et cetera, and pretzels." As Jackie Robinson recalled, "Jackie [Jr.] . . . was . . . the cause of breaking the ice between us and our hostile neighbors. He would disappear into one of their backyards. . . . Rae or I would go looking for our wandering son only to find that Jackie had enchanted another white person out of his hang-up about their black neighbors." As Jackie Robinson prodded whites toward new ways of thinking with his actions on the baseball field, Jack Jr. did the same in the backyards of Brooklyn.[53]

The general pattern was more troubling. Jackie always wondered how the fine restaurants that treated him so well would have dealt with other African Americans. "One way we knew the answer to that," Rachel recalled, "was by looking at how I was treated when I was not with Jack." She often experienced life in Brooklyn as would any other African American. "Until or unless it came out that I was Jackie Robinson's wife, whites would be as rude to me as they were rude to other blacks." Those everyday encounters revealed the depths of prejudice in Brooklyn.[54]

The Dodgers barnstormed through the South during spring training in 1948. Fans who came to the ballpark that year would find another African American in a Dodger uniform: catcher Roy Campanella. An exhibition game at Dallas's Rebel Field drew 11,370 fans to the ballpark; fully 6,800 of the ticket holders were African Americans. For the first time in memory, blacks sat in the upper reserve section of a stadium in the Lone Star State. While the Dodgers featured two black players, the Cleveland Indians opened the 1948 season with Larry Doby on their roster. The other clubs remained all white. The Dodgers further pressed their competitive advantage, adding pitcher Don Newcombe in 1949. Brooklyn continued to boast that it was far ahead of the rest of the league—and the nation.[55]

The Dodgers' three African American stars occupied three very different places in the white mind. Jackie Robinson always grabbed the headlines. He was a paragon of courage. To Robinson's detractors, how-ever, fearlessness gradually became aggression and aggression turned into viciousness. They alleged that Robinson grew irascible as the years went on. While controversy clung to Jackie, Roy Campanella stayed far away from it. Campanella kept quiet on racial issues. Nobody denied Don Newcombe's talents. But a few poor games in the World Series earned Newcombe the reputation as a "choker." The *Brooklyn Eagle* reported that Newcombe was "just a big Negro kid" before the Dodgers signed him and transformed him into a star. Northern whites fitted all three men into some version of a racial stereotype. Once Jackie was no longer seen as the heroic pioneer, he became the incorrigible black man; Campanella was the effacing appeaser of whites; Newcombe was the dazzling phys-ical specimen who never had the brains or gusto. Such myths became a comfort to their white propagators, a way of keeping in check those black men who were now parts of their lives.[56]

By 1949, upwardly mobile blacks in New York were seeking refuge from the African American neighborhoods in upper Manhattan and Central Brooklyn. Many of them chose St. Albans, Queens, at the Long Island border. Campanella bought a home there and the Robinsons fol-lowed. Rachel Robinson recalled that "housing-hungry Negroes were flocking to this area in such numbers that one can only term it a whole-sale invasion." In turn, "whites were selling fast, so there were many houses to choose from." In the spring of 1949, the Robinsons moved into a home on 177th Street. There they relearned a lesson that the Flatbush experience had taught. It mattered not whether the African Americans in question were famous baseball stars or anonymous labor-ers; whites would still object to black neighbors. Several whites on 177th Street opposed the sale of a home to the Robinsons. Jackie and Rachel thought of their white next-door neighbor as a wonderful man. They learned later that he had served as president of the block association and had harassed would-be black homebuyers.[57]

On the baseball field, Jackie Robinson enjoyed the greatest season of his career. He won the National League's Most Valuable Player award in 1949 and led the Dodgers to another pennant. But the joy in Brooklyn was ephemeral. The Dodgers lost again in the World Series, and again to the Yankees. Then, in the fall of 1951, many Dodger fans experienced the lowest moment of their baseball lives. This was due to Bobby Thomson's

"Shot Heard 'Round the World," a home run that lifted the New York Giants to an epic victory over the Dodgers—and with it the National League pennant. The 1952 team bounced back to recapture the National League pennant. It gained a boost from the right arm of Joe Black, an African American from Plainfield, New Jersey. He became the first black pitcher to win a World Series game.

The New York Yankees were still determined to remain all white. A team executive explained his concern. He was not worried that a black ballplayer would don Yankee pinstripes, but that his presence would attract more black fans. Racial prejudice thrived on such invented distinctions. When a *New York Times* reporter asked Jackie Robinson whether he thought Yankee management was prejudiced against black baseball players, Robinson answered in the affirmative. The Yankee executive admitted as much to Roger Kahn: "We don't want that sort of crowd. . . . It would offend boxholders from Westchester to have to sit with niggers."[58]

Ebbets Field had already experienced what Yankee officials feared. And Dodger fans took those changes in stride. When Robinson, Campanella, Newcombe, and Joe Black brought other African Americans to the ballpark, remembered Brooklyn native Herb Ross, they "changed the whole element of the crowd." By the middle of the 1950s, as Jon Belson recalled, "you go to a Sunday doubleheader, and the dominant smell in the ballpark was bagged fried chicken." It was no longer just the bread baking and peanuts roasting; now, new scents wafted through the stadium.[59]

After Jackie Robinson lost his initial veneer of placidity, public perceptions began to shift. And as Robinson advanced in years, his skills declined. In city after city, white fans unleashed vicious boos. "When it appeared that I was slipping," Robinson reflected, "the people who didn't boo when I was on top felt free to let go, and did." Sportswriter Milton Gross observed that Robinson had been "singled out as the target for official, fan and press criticism." Toward the end of the 1952 season, hostility became "even worse . . . than it was at the beginning." Giants fans relentlessly booed Robinson at the Polo Grounds. Robinson asked a reporter, "Why are they booing me?"[60]

Whatever complex racial attitudes existed in the Northeast, they found their way to Jackie Robinson. He attracted both the scorn and the pride, and saw the progress as well as the backlash. Robinson's stature, and his blackness, made him a magnet for criticism. He came to be portrayed as a hothead. Milton Gross investigated the specific episodes for which Robinson earned the most enmity—spats with umpires and opposing players—and found the charges against him unjustified in each instance. Baseball fans had been waiting for Robinson to fail, ready to place this transcendent figure back into the straitjacket of racial stereotype. Many Dodger fans stuck by Robinson. But for those who turned against him, Robinson had a straightforward explanation: "Those who have become opposed to me resent my success deep down inside only because I am a Negro."[61]

In 1953, Junior Gilliam took over at second base and chased Robinson across the diamond to third. One year later, the Dodgers signed Sandy Amoros, a native Cuban. On the days when Newcombe or Black pitched, the Dodgers' lineup featured five racial minorities and four whites. For Robinson, the extraordinary fact was that this all came to feel natural:

> The one thing about it that impressed me most was the lack of comment.
>
> Here was a major league club which had created an uproar only eight years ago by signing one Negro. Now, its Negroes in some games outnumbered its white players, and nobody in the ballpark seemed to be giving it a second thought. I couldn't help thinking that maybe democracy in the U.S.A. is doing better right now than many people are willing to believe.

Silence was progress, and it spoke volumes.[62]

The Dodgers lost again to the Yankees in the 1953 World Series. During that season, the Robinsons began to look at houses outside of New York City. They discovered, with frustration but not shock, that one Yankee executive had accurately described the racial behavior of his Westchester County ticketholders. Those families wanted African Americans neither in their box seats nor on their suburban streets.

MANY BLACK NEW YORKERS WOULD HAVE ENJOYED THE THEORETICAL possibility of house hunting in the suburbs. They would have been happy just to forsake Bedford-Stuyvesant for other Brooklyn neighborhoods. But few realized their dreams of mobility.

Martha Brown spoke for thousands of blacks in Bedford-Stuyvesant when she penned a letter to the NAACP's Brooklyn branch on April 12, 1955. "I am so disgusted and worried till I just don't know what to do." A single mother with three children, Brown had tried several times to secure adequate housing for her family. "I live in one room in which I cook, eat, and sleep," in an apartment at 1094 Myrtle Avenue. "It is heated by an oilstove. . . . We really need a larger place to stay." Brown was turned away from several apartments. "I've also filled out an application for the Project and was never interviewed. I've filled out three . . . I've also written letters asking for an explanation; so far I haven't heard from them." Brown concluded on a note of desperation: "I can't really explain everything as I am so worried, not knowing what will happen next. So won't you please try to help." Brown's plight symbolized that of the ill-housed in Jackie Robinson's Brooklyn.[63]

With each passing year, more housing projects kissed the sky. Between 1936 and the end of World War Two, New York City erected 14,000 low-rent and middle-rent apartments. The Farragut Houses, with 1,400 apartments, abutted the Brooklyn Navy Yard. The Gowanus Houses rose along Wyckoff Street at the mouth of the Gowanus Canal, providing the public with 1,140 more units. Yet the building of apartments failed to keep pace with the rapid influx of migrants and returning veterans. Between 1946 and 1954, the city built another 54,000 units of public housing. Most of them were reserved for veterans and those displaced by urban renewal projects. Martha Brown fitted neither criterion.[64]

Segregated housing was the scourge of the North. Housing was the most intractable of all racial issues, the fault line fraught with the most tension. The act of moving into a home brought with it a sense of physical fixedness and seeming permanence. Where a mother lived dictated which school her child attended and for whom she might vote; it was also closely bound with her economic class. And in the 1950s, one's home became intimately tied to one's understanding of the American Dream.[65]

Housing discrimination was alternately subtle and overt. "Nobody said where you could and couldn't live," recalled William Thompson, Brooklyn's first African American state senator, "but where a bank might give a black person a mortgage on Hancock Street, it would never give him a mortgage in Bay Ridge. Blacks could only move out in concentric circles: to Crown Heights, then to East Flatbush, Flatbush." Blacks who ventured beyond those circles paid the price. It was often the well-off African Americans who learned that lesson firsthand. In 1952, a cross was burned in St. Albans. Count Basie, Roy Campanella, Ella Fitzgerald, and Jackie Robinson all owned homes in the vicinity.[66]

In 1954, New York City's Board of Estimate considered proposals to build housing projects in Bushwick, upper Manhattan, and Castle Hill in the Bronx. The Board convened open hearings on March 11. It immediately approved the Jasper Houses, at the border of Morningside Heights and Harlem. But the Castle Hill and Bushwick plans spurred "extended and acrimonious hearings" because those projects would abut white neighborhoods. Thomas Canning, executive secretary of the Real Estate Board of the Bronx, declared, "We are opposed to all public housing. Keep it out of the Bronx and keep it out of New York City!" Supporters of the projects characterized such arguments as blatant racism. Caught in the crossfire, the Board of Estimate postponed its decision for two weeks. State officials then denounced the delay. New York State Housing Commissioner Herman Stichman accused New York City leaders of "yielding to racial bigots."[67]

Cries for "states' rights" filled the halls of southern legislatures. But in the Northeast, when it came to policies regarding race, there was little tension between federal and state bodies. The more common conflict pitted state governments against officials from racially mixed cities.

In New York City, the good liberals were outraged by criticisms from Albany. Before Abe Stark served as City Council president, he had built a famous clothing business in his native Brooklyn. Stark's advertisement underneath the Ebbets Field scoreboard—"Hit Sign, Win Suit"—was a fixture at the ballpark. Stark championed New York City's progressive tradition. In a press release dated March 25, 1954, he noted, "There is no . . . governmental body in the country which goes so far in trying to prevent discrimination as we do here in New York. This Board of Estimate has members who would be the first to fight any semblance of bigotry and intolerance." Stark was baffled by the state's charges. "My whole life has been devoted to a fight against discrimination. As the sponsor of a City Council resolution calling for a permanent Council on Intergroup Relations, I bitterly resent and repudiate Herman Stichman's insinuations." Stark then challenged Stichman to pinpoint the supposed bigotry. Every New York City agency, Stark asserted, was "administered without regard to race, color, creed, or national origin. . . . Where is the 'discrimination' or 'segregation'?"[68]

It was a question that white northerners would continue to ask. In response, African Americans could point to the obvious examples of segregation: in the growing black ghettoes, the underfunded black schools, the exploding white suburbs, the gerrymandered districts with white elected officials. Where was the segregation? In Harlem and Bedford-Stuyvesant. Yet again and again, whites like Stark would deny the claims of discrimination as they invoked a liberal mystique about their city. They would meet those charges with shaken heads and rolled eyes, in postures of innocence and defensiveness. They would point at the South, then back at themselves, boasting of New York City's traditions of liberalism and democracy, its councils on intergroup relations, its fair employment laws, and the examples of Jackie Robinson and Roy Campanella. And they would repeat the question: Where was the segregation?

The NAACP's Walter White had spoken out on the public housing proposals. "We cannot afford to indulge the prejudices of benighted peoples in New York any more than in Mississippi." He hit white northerners where it hurt, wielding the region's mystique as a spur to action. At a March 25 meeting, the Board of Estimate finally approved the housing plans for Bushwick and Castle Hill.[69]

Two months later, the United States Supreme Court handed down its ruling in *Brown v. Board of Education*. The Court's decision "caused many persons in Brooklyn to look with new interest at his Negro neighbor," Sid Frigand wrote on page one of the *Brooklyn Eagle*. "Who is he? Where did he come from? What is he doing?" To whites in the Northeast, these were open questions.[70]

Frigand wrote a series on "The Negro in Brooklyn"; the *Eagle* printed one article per day for a fortnight. Frigand tackled the issue of segregated housing in three of those articles. He stated the blunt truth: "A Negro, for all practical purposes, still can't purchase a new house in Brooklyn." Yet there were cracks in this wall. Frigand detailed the "hardy little bands of 'ambassadors' in so-called white neighborhoods," living "in happy anonymity." The very existence of such ambassadors set Brooklyn apart from cities like Chicago and Detroit—places that were more thoroughly segregated at the time, and less consumed with laying claim to a mystique about racial progress.[71]

In May 1952, the color barrier fell in one part of Crown Heights. Geoffrey Lawrence, an African American clerk at a Flushing grocery, pooled his money with his brother-in-law to purchase a brick house on Carroll Street. It cost considerably less than similar homes in black neighborhoods. The Lawrences, initially expecting the worst, came away "happily disappointed." The day after moving, their next-door neighbor invited the Lawrences over for coffee. "Since that day," wrote Frigand, "the 'novelty' of a Negro neighbor has worn to a point where the Lawrences and the Farleys are just two more families on the block." This was not a fluke, but the result of sustained activism. The Crown Heights Owners Association, along with the Brooklyn NAACP, the Community Association of Districts 25 and 27, and local parent-teacher groups, had worked to educate homeowners in the area—informing them that the connection between African American homeowners and plummeting real estate values was an illusion. Crown Heights became a testing ground for integration. Some interracial couples looked for homes specifically in Crown Heights, citing its "hospitable environment." Surprisingly, the feeling at its baseball stadium seeped onto some of its city blocks.[72]

White Brooklynites were divided in their response to Sid Frigand's series. One liberal reader declared, "the articles presented in the *Eagle* will do more than all the conferences ever held over a dinner table to foster race relations." Taking stock of the overall reaction to its series, the *Eagle* proudly reported, "the praise predominated by far." But it had to acknowledge that this exposé on black Brooklyn led twenty-seven businesses to withdraw their advertisements.[73]

In 1955, a black Democrat from Brooklyn and a white Republican from the Finger Lakes region of the state came together to craft a law against housing segregation. The Metcalf-Baker bill, named for State Senator George Metcalf and Assemblyman Bertram Baker, would vest the State Commission Against Discrimination with the authority to enforce all nondiscrimination laws in public housing. The bill would also outlaw discrimination in multiple-unit dwellings financed by the Fair Housing Administration (FHA) and the Veterans Administration (VA).

The policies of these federal agencies—the FHA and the VA—had helped to create exclusive white suburbs and struggling brown cities. In the instance of the Metcalf-Baker bill, the state of New York fancied itself more enlightened on race than the federal government. Early in 1955,

Metcalf and Baker began to drum up support for their bill. An audience of 120 gathered at the Hotel Schenectady where Metcalf proclaimed that "an end to housing segregation is the final requisite to halt discrimination throughout the state." Baker called housing the last bastion of northern segregation. "We learned to work together, we learned to play together and so now the purpose of these bills is that we learn to live together." Metcalf and Baker proclaimed that their bill would finally substantiate so many northern promises.[74]

On April 1, the Metcalf-Baker bill passed the State Senate and the State Assembly by unanimous votes. "This law will enable anyone to go into the open market and purchase the home of his choice in any location he chooses," said the NAACP's Madison Jones. Only four other states had similar laws: Connecticut, Massachusetts, New Jersey, and Rhode Island. On April 15, 1955, Governor Averell Harriman signed the Metcalf-Baker bill into law. Martha Brown had penned her letter to the NAACP three days prior.[75]

EVEN FOR THE RARE AFRICAN AMERICAN WITH CASH TO BURN, A HOME in the Connecticut suburbs proved elusive. Lemuel Rodney Custis found it much easier to earn a medal in World War Two than to build on his own property near Hartford. Custis was a fighter pilot and a captain with a master's degree from Howard University. He had been a member of the famed Tuskegee Airmen. In 1951, Custis and his wife, Ione, bought a lot on Nott Street in Wethersfield. They filed plans to build a house, making sure to meet the square-footage requirements for their street. Before they started to build, the area's zoning grade was changed, requiring an additional amount of square feet for each new home. Custis applied for a variance to proceed with his plans; the Wethersfield zoning board granted this variance. Then the neighbors on Nott Street mobilized. They filed an action with the Wethersfield Zoning Board of Appeals and obtained an injunction to halt construction of the Custis home. Two years after Custis bought the property, he still could not build on it.[76]

Custis's story had a happy ending. In June 1953, a local court ruled in his favor. He reported to the NAACP's Walter White that "our long fight to build a house in Wethersfield has been successful. Immediately upon the court's decision . . . we lost no time in 'breaking ground' and now our little house is rapidly taking shape." Custis was sobered by the amount of sweat needed to gain an inch. He only hoped that his long struggle would make the next man's shorter. "Because of our experiences, perhaps another Negro family in Connecticut will not have to battle nearly two years to have their basic rights affirmed." Yet at that moment, in the summer of 1953, another African American veteran encountered manifold obstacles during his own quest for a home in the Connecticut suburbs.[77]

Jackie and Rachel Robinson envisioned New England as a step up. "I started thinking about Connecticut," Rachel Robinson said, "about fresh air and ponds and lovely stone walls. The whole notion of New England seemed good to me." Of course, all-white towns did not seem ideal. But "where in the countryside of Westchester County . . . or in Connecticut could we find a Negro neighborhood?" Jackie noted, "There just isn't any." The couple made a conscious decision. They chose the white world of the Connecticut suburbs over its alternative. Rachel Robinson explained that very few neighborhoods in New York City were actually integrated. "You know that the ideal of finding a community with the type of housing that you desire, which is integrated, is almost impossible." The schools in St. Albans were overcrowded and on their way to becoming all black. The Robinsons weighed all the factors and opted for suburbia. "We were convinced that the disadvantages of bringing our children up in a predominantly white community would be far less than the disadvantages of bringing them up in an all-Negro community. We also felt that someone had to lead the way in this struggle for integrated housing." They had been pioneers before, and they would be pioneers again.[78]

With "great zest," Rachel Robinson scrutinized the real estate listings in the *New York Times*. "I could hardly wait for the papers to be delivered on Sunday." She devised floor plans for the home of her dreams. Then reality intervened. The Robinsons attempted to buy land in New Canaan but were rebuffed. Rachel called about one house in Greenwich and, after giving her name, the owners refused to show it. The Robinsons answered ads for a number of other homes in and around Greenwich. "When the brokers saw us, the houses turned out to be just sold or no longer on the market, phrases like that. The brokers said they themselves didn't object. It was always other people." The couple settled for a property just across the state line in New York. Jackie recalled that in autumn 1953, "we finally found a piece of land in New York's Westchester County that was just what we wanted." The Robinsons offered the asking price, waited for weeks, and were told that the price would be raised by five thousand dollars. This was standard practice in housing discrimination, a surefire way for whites in exclusive towns to claim that they had nothing against African Americans—it was just that blacks could not meet the asking price. This was hard economics, they would say, not racism. So the Robinsons promptly kicked in the extra five thousand dollars. "There was another period of confused silence," Jackie recalled. "At last, we were told that the land had been sold to somebody else. It was this way everywhere we went." Rachel became enraged at her broker, who preselected areas where the Robinson children would feel "comfortable." Rachel recalled, "I wondered how she knew where my children would be comfortable. I suspected not in her backyard." Whites in Connecticut's Fairfield County—like those in New York's Westchester—did not want an African American for a neighbor, even if it was Jackie Robinson.[79]

Stamford, Connecticut, was a small city of 80,000 residents, 5 percent of whom were African Americans. The North Stamford section of town resembled many exclusive Fairfield County suburbs. "The events leading to our coming to Stamford," Rachel Robinson recalled, "were put together as if they were part of a great plan for us." First, she received a call from a reporter at the *Bridgeport Herald*. Rachel recounted the indignities of her home-buying search. The resulting article appeared on October 25, 1953, under the headline, "No. Stamford Nixes Jackie Robinson." It detailed the "runaround from brokers" that the Robinsons endured in the "exclusive backcountry" of North Stamford. During the interview, Rachel had described her experiences in nearby Greenwich, Pound Ridge, Purchase, and Bedford Hills. When the reporter asked local real estate brokers for their response, realtors told the *Bridgeport Herald* "that I wasn't a serious buyer, that I was trying to start trouble—just like Jackie Robinson, I guess." The newspaper also noted that the Greenwich Real Estate Board's bylaws prohibited brokers from "selling or renting to 'any race or nationality' that would tend to bring down real estate values." Greenwich brokers identified such groups as "Jews, Italians, and Negroes." The realtors promptly blamed the bylaws on "property-owning 'bigots.'" In the Connecticut suburbs, the real racist was always the next guy.[80]

This exposure in the *Bridgeport Herald* moved Stamford residents to outrage. "I don't know whether they were trying to get a reaction out of North Stamford or what," said Rachel, "but that's the way it came out." Five ministers drafted an antidiscrimination statement and circulated it among homeowners and church members. It read: "Exclusion of any persons solely for reasons of race, creed or national origin could lessen the spiritual, economic and social development of our area." The community was divided. Many residents signed the antidiscrimination petition. Others argued that the clergy had "blown up the issue." Some parishioners complained that their ministers' actions would jeopardize their investments.[81]

Public opinion swung to the Robinsons' side. As Jackie remembered, "the town practically urged us to live there." Ministers and homeowners requested an audience with Rachel Robinson. Richard Simon, head of the book publisher Simon & Schuster, and his wife Andrea hosted a meeting at their North Stamford country house. The ministers assured Rachel Robinson that good would prevail in Stamford. As they all rose to depart, Andrea Simon asked Rachel to stay behind. Simon had called a broker to bring them house hunting. Rachel took to a property they viewed at 103 Cascade Road. It had five acres of land with a foundation for a lakeside house. The Robinsons reached an agreement with the owner and builder, a native Russian named Benedict Gunnar. "I don't know that I ever have felt closer to being a real American," as Rachel Robinson recalled that moment, "closer to having lifted from my shoulders the nagging doubts and insecurities that are the heritage of the American Negro." For her, the ability to buy a home was the true test of American freedom.[82]

The Robinsons finally moved to Cascade Road in the summer of 1955. One neighbor across the street sold his house at a "sacrifice price" almost immediately after the Robinsons moved in.[83]

A black family confronted everyday frustrations in the Connecticut suburbs. The Robinsons attended the otherwise all-white North Stamford Congregational Church. Jack Jr. entered the North Stamford public schools in 1955, the only African American in his class. And the High Ridge Country Club rejected Jackie Robinson's membership application. It was particularly difficult, Rachel recalled, "to explain to Jackie [Jr.] why this great man that he calls Dad wasn't good enough to play at a country club owned by the father of one of his classmates." Just as painful, Sharon Robinson lost a white friend when she and her friend became old enough to see the racial barrier that stood between them. David

Jackie Robinson, Rachel Robinson, and their children at home in North Stamford, Connecticut, in 1956. The Robinsons moved into this house in 1955, after many years of struggling to buy a home in the all-white suburbs. GENEVIEVE NAYLOR/CORBIS.

Robinson, the youngest of the three children, endured taunts of "nigger" at the New Canaan Country Day School. "We don't want our children growing up not knowing Negroes of their own age," Jackie Robinson lamented. That seemed to be the price of ice-skating on his own lake, playing touch football in his wide front yard, and riding the lawnmower across it each week.[84]

Just as the Robinsons were moving into their North Stamford home, the neighboring town of Darien confronted its own group of black New Yorkers. Darien's ordeal began when the St. Thomas Liberal Catholic Church of New York City bought a twenty-one-room house on Middlesex Road. The congregation counted one thousand blacks, and Rev. James Roberts planned to use the estate as a summer camp. Darien's Planning and Zoning Commission proposed an amendment that would require permits for "uses other than residential in residential zones." On June 14, 1955, residents packed into Town Hall and participated in that most democratic of New England rituals: the town meeting. "The issue was both simplicity itself and complex beyond belief, everyone agreed," according to David Anderson of the *New York Times*. "The consensus from the beginning was that merely town zoning and not a racial problem was under discussion." Darien residents told themselves that the prospect of 500 black youngsters descending on their town had nothing to do with race. After two hours of discussion, the amendment passed. Planning and Zoning Commission chairman Richard Tweedy captured the prevailing sentiment:

> I think I can say in all truthfulness that our action in calling this hearing was in no way motivated by the fact that a Negro group was immediately involved. These amendments have nothing to do with race, religion, color, or creed. They are designed to protect our homeowners whoever they may be.

Darien residents thus participated in two long-standing American traditions: democracy and discrimination.[85]

WHILE SUBURBANITES FENDED OFF RACIAL CHANGE, MANY WHITES FLED Jackie Robinson's Brooklyn. Brooklyn changed so thoroughly that the borough of 1950 was barely recognizable ten years later. Brooklyn native Bill Reddy remembered 1957 as the year when "everyone who could was running to Long Island." African Americans and Puerto Ricans were not themselves responsible for the larger economic, social, and demographic forces at work, but they were the faces of those transformations. Corner candy stores turned into bodegas; polkas metastasized into rumbas; potatoes became plantains. Reddy recalled it all as a trauma:

> The language changed, the customs changed. Groups began to take over that hadn't been there before. . . . Food stores began to display different types of vegetables and fruits. Brooklyn was changing slowly from the solid Italian, German, Irish, Jewish that it had been to a tropical flavor. Who the hell ever heard of frying green bananas?

The rueful question exposed a deep anxiety.[86]

The Dodgers stood as both cause and effect of these changes. They brought the borough its greatest triumph in 1955, and plunged Brooklyn to its nadir two years later.

The 1955 World Series would live on in the memory of every Brook-lynite as the definition of bliss. The Yankees won the first two games, bringing the familiar sense of doom. But the Dodgers won the next three, all at Ebbets Field. Back at Yankee Stadium, the Yankees drubbed the Dodgers in game six. In the deciding contest, Johnny Podres shut the Yankees out through the first five innings as the Dodgers nursed a 2–0 lead. Yogi Berra came up to bat with runners on base in the sixth inning. He drove a pitch into the left-field corner, seemingly beyond the reach of Sandy Amoros. But Amoros sprinted, speared the ball, twirled, and fired it back to the infield for a double play. Podres silenced the Yankee bats for the last three frames. Years of melancholy turned to shock, then to joy, then to ecstasy. For a decade, they had called Brooklyn the center of the postwar universe. Now, for a night, they were on top of the world.

Victory did not place more spectators in the seats. Ebbets Field was cramped to begin with. While Yankee Stadium seated 75,000 fans and the Giants could fit 56,000, Ebbets Field housed 33,000 at the most. For owner Walter O'Malley, the team was a losing proposition. O'Malley needed to make Ebbets Field more attractive to the new suburbanites, those who may have left Brooklyn physically but remained psychically attached to the Dodgers and to the borough. O'Malley wanted a new stadium in Brooklyn with a parking lot. He eyed a site at the confluence of Flatbush and Atlantic Avenues, requested permission to build, and asked New York City to finance the parking lot. Robert Moses, the seemingly omnipotent developer of public works, refused to condemn the buildings at that corner. In December 1956, the Board of Estimate declined O'Malley's request. Moses offered to lease a site for stadium construction (at enormous profit to his own city authority) at Flushing Meadows, Queens. Denied the chance to build a new stadium in downtown Brooklyn, O'Malley took the Dodgers far from the five boroughs. They moved west.[87]

The Dodgers' departure filled Brooklyn with a deep sadness. The final game at Ebbets Field was played on September 24, 1957. "On that last day," remembered Marvin and Walter Rosen, proprietors of Junior's restaurant, "an entire way of life was eradicated." White residents decried the loss of a specific borough that had spawned their nostalgia, the one where egg creams flowed generously, where children played stickball on the streets, and their beloved baseball team embraced a black man. But there was tragedy in the fact that many of these individuals could not find reasons to stay on their block when an African American family bought a home, or to keep their kids in school when Puerto Ricans sat next to them. There was also tragedy in the way they saw a hero in one black ballplayer but ruin in a thousand black migrants. Whites did not take the soul of Brooklyn with them to the suburbs. Instead, those who fled failed to adjust to Brooklyn's new soul. They had once boasted that their borough was so inclusive, able to absorb any group in its mélange. But somewhere in that process, white Brooklynites lost patience with the larger vision. Indeed, it had always existed more as a fanciful aspiration than a description of their lived experiences. The suburbs, the Sunbelt, and the "urban crisis" loomed on the horizon. Jackie Robinson's Brooklyn was yesterday.[88]

THREE

"If We Were Segregationists"

The Struggle to Integrate Northeastern Schools (1957–1965)

T HE DODGERS PLAYED THEIR LAST GAME AT EBBETS FIELD ON September 24, 1957. That same day, President Dwight Eisenhower dispatched the 101st Airborne to desegregate Central High School in Little Rock, Arkansas.

In the late-1950s, the schoolhouse became the seat of racial drama. White mobs did not mill in front of northern schools—at least not yet. But these schools were no bastions of integration. Neither were white northerners interested in making them so.

When the *Brown v. Board of Education* ruling came down in 1954, African Americans in northern cities glimpsed an opening. They sensed that the Supreme Court's mandate might extend to all forms of school segregation, not just the version of Jim Crow that lived in southern laws.

Most northern whites dismissed any connection between *Brown v. Board of Education* and their own schools. New York City superintendent of schools William Jansen spoke for them: "It is well known that no form of segregation within the meaning of the historic decision of the Supreme

Court is practiced or sanctioned in New York." The editors of the *New York Times* agreed. They explained that "the more subtle forms of segregation . . . create, as if by accident, a school almost wholly white, Puerto Rican or Negro in its student body." While the editors acknowledged such segregation, they claimed that it "has never had official sanction in New York." To the NAACP, this was pure fiction—for such arguments neatly distinguished between intentional and adventitious segregation. These arguments often overlooked the policies that helped to build ghettoes abutting Central Park, the way many suburbs positioned themselves beyond the grasp of the black middle class, or the redistricting and student-transfer policies that sifted white children and racial minorities into separate schools across the North. The NAACP's lawyers sought to expose and destroy school segregation's northern incarnations. More than a decade before Boston confronted busing, the NAACP waged battles in the courtrooms of the Northeast's small cities.[1]

The irony was that in order for the NAACP to fight school segregation in the North, it had to also fight against the ideology of color blindness. This doctrine had a hallowed place in civil rights history. It stretched back to Justice John Marshall Harlan's dissent in *Plessy v. Ferguson*. In 1896, Harlan had written: "Our Constitution is color-blind, and neither knows nor tolerates classes among citizens." In the 1954 *Brown v. Board of Education* decision—the greatest triumph in the NAACP's history—the Supreme Court had relied upon the same idea. Then, in 1963, the nation stood enthralled by Martin Luther King's appeal to color blindness on the Washington Mall. King dreamt "that my four little children will one day live in a nation where they will not be judged by the color of their skin but by the content of their character." It was a stunning vision, and African Americans and white liberals rallied around it. Yet in that same period, the white leaders of the North were claiming the ground of color blindness as their own. When northern school boards were challenged for the "de facto segregation" that they harbored, white leaders fell back on this ideology. They asserted that they had not considered race when assigning children to schools, that any patterns of segregation were the unavoidable results of geography, neighborhood, and economics. In turn, the NAACP took aim at the doctrine of color blindness. This marked a seminal shift in the civil rights era.[2]

In the hands of white northerners, color blindness was so powerful because it was malleable. To see the different ways in which they deployed this ideology is to understand, in part, the apparent contradiction that rested at the heart of Northeastern race relations. The ideology of color blindness helped explain how one could vote for a black politician (because one did not consider race when stepping into the voting booth), and how one could at the same time countenance segregation in schools (because white leaders supposedly did not pay attention to race when assigning students to schools). In two different realms—electoral politics and school integration—whites' commitment to color blindness produced two very different results.

FROM A CASE INVOLVING NEW ROCHELLE, NEW YORK, THE NAACP gathered important inspiration—if not a lasting legal precedent. New Rochelle was dubbed the "Little Rock of the North." Controversy there centered on the Lincoln Elementary School, which had educated almost all of the city's African American youths. When blacks moved to New Rochelle during the years of the Great Migration, the Board of Education redrew district lines time and again, keeping African American children within Lincoln's district. This gerrymandering ended in 1934, but the Board instituted a new practice: white children who lived in Lincoln's district could transfer to other schools. Many white youngsters were bused past Lincoln each morning to attend the Mayflower School, one-half mile away. By 1960, the Lincoln School contained 29 white children and 454 African Americans. If New Rochelle's African Americans lived north of Jim Crow, their schools seemed wholly of it.[3]

Black parents filed a lawsuit known as *Taylor v. New Rochelle Board of Education*. Judge Irving R. Kaufman's New York District Court took up the case in 1960. Kaufman had previously sentenced Julius and Ethel Rosenberg to the electric chair. The judge appeared quite a bit more humane in this trial. Kaufman's ruling debunked notions of northern progress. "I see no basis to draw a distinction, legal or moral, between segregation established by the formality of a dual system of education, as in *Brown*, and that created by gerrymandering of school district lines and transferring of white children. . . . The result is the same."

Kaufman thought New Rochelle could abolish segregation, if only the will existed:

> I cannot accept the proposition that in this relatively small community in the north, men of good will, wisdom and ingenuity could not have devised a plan for the orderly desegregation of the Lincoln School. . . . It is of no moment whether the segregation is labeled by the defendant as 'de jure' or 'de facto,' as long as the Board, by its conduct, is responsible for its maintenance.

The schools of the North stood well within *Brown*'s grasp.[4]

School segregation could appear intractable in mammoth cities like New York and Chicago. In contrast, the small cities of the Northeast seemed like relatively manageable cases—places like New Haven, Hartford, Bridgeport, Providence, New Rochelle, and Springfield. NAACP lawyer Lewis Steel admitted that it would have been difficult for a court to implement system-wide desegregation in a metropolis as large as New York City. But "in a lot of the small cities, something could have been done about it." In Springfield, where Steel worked on two cases for the NAACP, "you could do it with—not a snap of the finger—but people of good will could have easily figured out a workable way of desegregating the schools and opening the society up." In 1964, black parents in Springfield sought to begin that process. They filed a lawsuit against the Springfield School Committee. The NAACP took up their case, believing that if it broke the back of school segregation in this small city, the North's version of Jim Crow might crumble.[5]

SKATING RINKS AND SCHOOLS NOW BEAR THE NAMES OF THE DEFENDANTS. Hundreds of students currently attend the Mary L. Lynch and Alice B. Beal elementary schools. Theodore Dimauro became the mayor of Springfield in 1978, and later lost a close race for the United States Congress. Charlie Ryan served two terms in City Hall during the 1960s, took a thirty-year hiatus from local politics, then rode back into the mayor's office in 2004. The Romeo J. Cyr Arena sits smack in the middle of Forest Park, an Olmsted-designed park that remains the jewel of Springfield. The names Ryan, Cyr, Dimauro, Beal, and Lynch still carry weight in the city. In 1964, they were accused of creating, upholding, and justifying a Jim Crow system of education.

In the way that the Springfield School Committee drew lines, the northern model of segregation came to life. In 1955, the School Committee created optional-attendance areas within three school districts: Tapley, Brookings, and Hooker. All three districts had black majorities. The optional areas encompassed streets where white families resided. White children were given the option of attending the Armory Street School (99 percent white) or the Acushnet School (95 percent white) instead of Tapley, Brookings, or Hooker. All of these students chose the white schools. The School Committee then reapproved the optional areas in 1961. Two years later, the committee shifted more white students from the Tapley district to the Armory Street School. And after some black students from the Hooker School moved with their families to a new housing project in another part of the city, they were bused back to Hooker.[6]

DeBerry was the only school in the city with an African American enrollment that exceeded 90 percent. In 1963, the School Committee redrew the DeBerry district to include Northampton Avenue, a street with many black children. The School Committee also changed the line between Buckingham and Duggan Junior High Schools. Buckingham's district previously included Dorman Elementary School, with its 180 white students. In 1963, the district line was redrawn at Roosevelt Avenue; the Dorman students would then attend Duggan. This left Buckingham with six feeder elementary schools that all had black majorities. The School Committee thus funneled black children into specific schools and transferred white students out of them. These were policy results, not just accidents of geography.[7]

African Americans comprised 8 percent of Springfield's population and 16 percent of the public school enrollment. Both figures were rising. Almost all of Springfield's black students were clustered in seven of the city's fifty public schools. A report would later conclude, "School segregation in Springfield was as severe as in Boston." While dramatic student boycotts in Boston, New York, and Philadelphia exposed the issue of segregation in northern schools, the plight of African Americans in small cities like Springfield lurked beneath the national radar.[8]

The events of June 1963 altered America's racial landscape. On June 11, Governor George Wallace stood in the schoolhouse door at the University of Alabama, symbolically blocking African American students from enrolling. In a televised address that evening, President John F. Kennedy endorsed the cause of black civil rights—an issue "as old as the scriptures and as clear as the Constitution." Hours later, an assassin's bullet felled Medgar Evers, the civil rights leader, in Jackson, Mississippi. Against this national backdrop, the Springfield School Committee convened to investigate the issue of segregation.[9]

On June 27, 1963, the School Committee met with representatives from the local and national NAACP. The School Committee agreed to form an ad-hoc commission that would study the problem of "racial imbalance"—a term that became shorthand in the North for segregation. The committee met again on the night of September 19 to examine the results of this study. At that point, it considered a resolution recognizing "that racial concentration exists in some schools" and "that integrated education is desirable." The resolution pledged to "take whatever action is necessary to eliminate to the fullest extent possible, racial concentration in the schools." This measure sparked intense controversy, though eventually it passed. School Committee member Dorothy Robinson then offered another proposal. She urged the committee to adopt an integration plan effective in September 1964. Mayor Charlie Ryan seconded that motion, but the other School Committee members voted against it. Romeo Cyr wondered where the money would come from, and Theodore Dimauro thought that implementation by the following September would not be feasible. Superintendent of Schools Thomas McCook noted that an integration plan "might not be agreeable to other parts of the community," a reference to the brewing white opposition. Twice the committee considered Dorothy Robinson's proposal, and twice voted it down. When Robinson tried to put it up for vote again, nobody would second her motion. The meeting adjourned at one o'clock in the morning.[10]

The issue of school integration began to influence local politics. Mayor Charlie Ryan, in his bid for reelection in 1963, ran against John Pierce Lynch. And Lynch attacked Ryan for the small steps toward integration that the School Committee had taken. Lynch ran a full-page advertisement in the Springfield newspaper. It depicted black students trickling out of a school bus and into a school. The ad listed fifteen schools in white neighborhoods and warned: "Ryan and the NAACP . . .

made a secret deal. Is your school next?" The School Committee's mere acknowledgment that integration was desirable seemed too much for some Springfield residents. Vincent DiMonaco and Rosemarie Coughlin ran for seats on the School Committee in the fall of 1963. Both of them campaigned against desegregation. As Charlie Ryan remembered, "Rosemarie . . . kind of copied" Louise Day Hicks—the infamous head of the Boston School Committee. Charlie Ryan won election in November; so did Coughlin and DiMonaco. Dorothy Robinson resigned her seat in frustration, leaving the School Committee with a majority that opposed integration.[11]

African Americans swung into action. Nine families, representing sixteen children, brought a lawsuit in United States District Court against the Springfield School Committee.

For Roger Williams, the civil action was a long time coming. Williams had three children in the Springfield schools. In 1962, he had written a letter to the Springfield School Committee asking for more teaching of black history in the schools. He received no response. Williams decided that his daughter Debra Ann would fare better at Duggan Junior High School than at the majority-black Buckingham. Williams tried, and failed, to secure a transfer for his daughter. He was not the only black parent who wanted a transfer out of Buckingham. A group of parents mobilized. They resolved to hold a sit-in at the opening of school, in September 1963. The local NAACP got wind of the plan and discouraged the sit-in. The NAACP "came to us and told us they felt this was not the right attitude," Williams recalled. Instead, the parents filed a lawsuit.[12]

The plaintiffs charged that the City of Springfield "maintained on a segregated basis" some thirty-six public schools. Six of these schools had large black majorities; the rest were almost entirely white. The complaint alleged that the School Committee had "created arbitrary attendance districts and zones in such a manner as to establish and perpetuate a racially segregated school system." The School Committee was "thereby ensuring the entrenchment of segregation in the Springfield school system." The connection of the very term "segregation" with this small New England city proved jarring at the time. Many Springfield residents associated "segregation" with faraway places, like the Jim Crow South or big-city ghettoes. Black parents in Springfield asserted that their city was qualitatively no different. They not only posited that segregation existed in the schools, but that it had been created—and maintained—by a set of policies, decisions, and regulations. They requested an injunction to restrain the School Committee from enforcing such procedures, and asked the School Committee to finally submit a desegregation plan.[13]

In response, the School Committee could have developed an integration plan. Instead, on January 30, 1964, the committee voted unanimously to cease all actions toward integration. It halted all plans to conduct further studies or investigations on the subject. Moreover, committee members resolved "not to confer with persons or groups on the racial issue."[14]

If the city had taken any concrete steps toward desegregation, it could have avoided the lawsuit. So said Frank Buntin, a teacher at Buckingham and chairman of the education committee for the NAACP's Springfield branch. Instead, "there has been absolutely no evidence of progress on this desegregation plan since it was first proposed last October." Buntin viewed the lawsuit as a kind of insurance. It was meant to prod the committee into action and to serve as a fallback if it failed to move. "What we want is action for the present generation of schoolchildren—not some remote plan for the distant future."[15]

On behalf of that generation of schoolchildren, Robert Carter traveled from New York City to Springfield, Massachusetts—precisely twenty-five years after Kenneth Clark had made the same trek. As General Counsel for the NAACP, Carter believed that "separate and unequal" went "hand in hand, no less in the North than in the South." Carter was born in Florida and raised in Newark, New Jersey. He earned law degrees from Howard University and Columbia University, and in November 1944 he joined the legal staff of the NAACP. Those were heady times at the nation's leading civil rights organization. Carter suddenly found himself in the thick of school integration cases like *McLaurin v. Oklahoma* and *Sweatt v. Painter*. In the *Brown v. Board of Education* case, Carter worked as Thurgood Marshall's second-in-command. He wrote the brief for the Supreme Court and engaged in every strategic decision along the way. After the *Brown* case, Carter began to focus his energies on segregation outside the South. He viewed school segregation as "one of the most frightening issues facing blacks in northern areas." It "was a field in which our resources would do more than any other single issue to solidify support for the NAACP." In the fall of 1963, Carter and two Boston activists met with the Massachusetts education commissioner regarding segregation in Boston schools. At that moment, African Americans in Springfield reached the breaking point. Carter was already with them in spirit—and very soon in body.[16]

Carter and his staff joined forces with two Springfield attorneys, Henry Weissman and Clifford Clarkson. Together they drafted the civil action. It took on the name of the black student who appeared first in the alphabet: Abraham Barksdale Jr.

ROBERT CARTER AND ED BROOKE COULD HAVE RUN INTO EACH OTHER in downtown Springfield on the morning of October 21, 1964. Brooke, the state's attorney general, was at his local headquarters on Main Street to work on his reelection campaign. A few blocks away, at the federal courthouse, Robert Carter stood before Judge George Sweeney to deliver his opening statement in *Barksdale v. Ryan*. "We intend to show that the concentration of Negroes and other nonwhites in these nine schools is not innocent but is by design." And whether innocent or by design, whether that segregation was labeled "de jure" or "de facto," "the Constitution requires that the resultant inequality be remedied." City Solicitor James Allen spoke for the defense. "I don't, frankly, know what de facto segregation means," Allen announced. "We categorically deny, and I assume the evidence will show, that there is no intentional plan to segregate anybody in Springfield." He acknowledged the existence of racial imbalance. "Some schools do have more colored people than other schools, but this is because of living patterns." Any instance of segregation was the simple by-product of neighborhood schools. There was "nothing unconstitutional" about it.[17]

The defendants in *Barksdale* invoked northern myths of racial equality in order to ignore the rampant segregation in Springfield's schools. The ruse began on the first day of the trial, when School Committee member Mary Lynch was asked about the logic of student assignments. Lynch insisted that the School Committee used only one criterion: that students attend school in their neighborhood. Henry Weissman, an attorney for the plaintiffs, asserted that the meaning of "neighborhood" was anything but self-evident. "What is a criterion for describing a neighborhood? Is it geographical . . . or is it racial, or is it God knows what?" Weissman pressed Lynch: "Would you know where the Negroes of Springfield live, generally?" Lynch responded, "No, I would not." Had Lynch observed the color of the students at DeBerry School? "White and non-white, sir," was all she would say. Lynch denied that she knew the racial identity of students in various schools, in optional areas, or of those who were bused. She previewed the School Committee's strategy: to trumpet its own color-blind bona fides at every opportunity.[18]

Vincent DiMonaco denied the premise of every question, turned it on its head—or, when necessary, he played the fool. When Weissman asked what steps the School Committee had taken to reduce racial imbalance, DiMonaco replied, "I don't know if there is racial imbalance." Weissman then asked DiMonaco whether he was aware that Springfield contained some predominantly black areas. "I never took a head count," DiMonaco shot back. This member of the School Committee came off as ignorant at best and malevolent at worst.[19]

Thomas McCook, the superintendent of schools, employed the same color-blind defense. McCook was examined by Barbara Morris, an NAACP lawyer. She asked about the students at DeBerry School. Mc-Cook answered, "I didn't think of them in terms of race. I just thought of them in terms of students." Morris asked with incredulity, "And you were able to look at that great number of students in DeBerry, and wipe completely from your mind the fact that they were Negroes?" McCook allowed, "I wouldn't say wipe completely, but I just regarded them as students." The longer the School Committee persisted in this strategy, the odder it seemed.[20]

Frank Buntin, a teacher at Buckingham and local NAACP leader, testified about his dealings with two members of the School Committee. He recalled confronting Dr. Helen Theinert about the proposed zone changes to the Buckingham and Duggan school districts. Theinert was director of research and public information for the School Committee. She had appeared at Buckingham in 1963 for a Parent Teacher Association meeting. She told those assembled that the district line would be redrawn at Roosevelt Avenue. The parents and teachers informed Theinert of that area's racial composition: "You can name the number of Negroes who live east of Roosevelt Avenue." Before Theinert departed, one parent asked whether she had any ideas to help alleviate segregation. Theinert offered one suggestion: "If you people didn't move together, there wouldn't be such a problem." In the courtroom, Robert Carter presented Theinert with a map that detailed the racial implications of the rezoning. She denied any previous knowledge of this. "You didn't know that the effect of rezoning," asked Carter, "was to take out many white families and keep the heavy concentration of Negroes in?" Theinert responded: "I wasn't aware of that until I looked at this map." These white northern leaders clung desperately, and disingenuously, to the doctrine of color blindness.[21]

Frank Buntin was further disturbed by his interaction with Superintendent Thomas McCook. That controversy began in January 1964, when Buntin's comments about the *Barksdale* lawsuit appeared in the *Springfield Union*. Buntin's principal informed him that McCook wished to speak with him. One April afternoon, Buntin dismissed his class early in order to accommodate McCook's request. At the meeting, McCook "mentioned the fact that the School Committee had voted . . . to curb my activities." McCook asked Buntin to "take a less active part" in the NAACP. "I told him that I couldn't do this, because I felt that this was the attitude being reflected in such places like in South Carolina or Mississippi, where they do not allow Negro teachers to belong to NAACP." The Springfield School Committee's bylaws prohibited teachers from criticizing the school system. Buntin asserted that he had made no statements about administrators, faculty members, or the schools themselves. He only pointed out that segregation existed in Springfield, and that the School Committee ought to do something about it. If that was an actionable offense, then Springfield was sliding ever closer to South Carolina and Mississippi.[22]

Thomas McCook and Helen Theinert were not Ross Barnett or Lester Maddox. Unlike those segregationist southern governors, McCook and Theinert relied on neither violence nor its threat. They did not dedicate their careers to the maintenance of white supremacy or the assurance of black oppression. Yet in many of their utterances and actions, they defended segregation. These individuals presided over a school system that thoroughly separated the races. If neither of them thought this state of affairs to be just or blessed, they also saw no reason to disrupt it.

To combat the color-blind defense, Robert Carter and his team entered into evidence exhibit after exhibit: maps of city neighborhoods, charts with racial breakdowns of each school, photographs of classrooms, lists of students' test scores, and minutes of School Committee meetings. It was an illustrated history of the workings of segregation.

In *Brown v. Board*, Robert Carter had used the testimony of social scientists to great effect. Kenneth Clark and his doll tests had stolen the show. If *Barksdale* had a star witness, it was Thomas Fraser Pettigrew.

A professor of social psychology at Harvard, Pettigrew was an expert on racial prejudice and desegregation. *The Harvard Crimson* called his course on these topics—Social Relations 134—the "academic stronghold of the Harvard civil rights movement." But Pettigrew was no typical Cambridge intellectual. Pettigrew was born in Richmond, Virginia, in 1931. He attributed his own liberalism to the lessons about racial justice that he had absorbed from Mildred Adams, his family's black cook. Pettigrew took that mindset with him to the University of Virginia, then to graduate school at Harvard. Early in 1964, he testified before the Boston School Committee. In anticipation, Pettigrew sorely hoped that Louise Day Hicks would label him an "outside agitator." That would have produced the rarest of scenes: "the first time that a Northern racist ever called a Southern liberal an outside agitator." In the Springfield courtroom, Pettigrew got his wish.[23]

Pettigrew sported a crew cut and he moved in and out of a light southern drawl. Responding to Robert Carter, Pettigrew explained that while an integrated school system was not an end in itself, it served as a necessary prerequisite to a quality education. "Without it, you can't hope to have excellent education for Negroes or whites," Pettigrew said. He concluded that school segregation inflicted the same damage upon African American students in the North as in the South.[24]

James Allen questioned Pettigrew about his specific knowledge of Springfield. Pettigrew testified that he had studied in detail only one New England city: New Haven. Pettigrew said he had been refused entry when attempting to study segregation in other Massachusetts schools. So Pettigrew knew nothing in particular about the Springfield schools, Allen asserted. Allen believed that this rendered Pettigrew's testimony meaningless. Allen's thinking was premised on a kind of Massachusetts exceptionalism, even a Springfield exceptionalism. Allen summoned the ghosts of the abolitionists, and the more recent example of the Springfield Plan, to argue that Pettigrew's generalizations about segregation and prejudice applied not to this fair city.[25]

But James Allen's tongue slipped. He was midway through a sentence when he uttered the term "nigger" instead of "Negro." A hush fell over the courtroom. The epithet stripped any veneer of respectability from Allen's arguments. He had been contending that although segregation, racism, and inequality plagued the country, things were better in Springfield. A single slip of the tongue proved as fatal to his argument as all of Robert Carter's evidence.[26]

Thomas Pettigrew relished the chance to spar with Allen, whose words he would remember almost half a century later. "'Just because my generalizations held true throughout the nation, why,' he asked, 'would these processes be necessarily valid in Springfield?!'" Pettigrew rejected this logic, and he said so on the witness stand. "We don't really have to repeat these things in every single place to believe that the phenomena operate. It is a little like if you dropped an atomic bomb on Springfield, although it has never been done before, you could predict with a high degree of certainty that it would explode as it does in Nevada." He was an expert social scientist, supremely confident in his methods. "We feel that things we have learned in New Haven will operate in Springfield, Boston, in any community with a population of non-whites roughly of this order." Springfield was thoroughly representative in its patterns of segregation.[27]

Allen was happy to engage the analogy of the atomic bomb. Because Pettigrew had never studied Springfield, Allen suggested, "you wouldn't know if we had . . . special conditions in this city, for example, bomb shelters, the inference would not be correct, would it?" Allen accepted, just for the sake of argument, the proposition that racial imbalance harmed black children. But "have you considered whether we have any special programs here that tend to cure this social damage?" Pettigrew knew what he was driving at. "There was a plan in the forties which Springfield had called the Springfield Plan, which is rather famous . . . and race relations specialists took great interest in it." Earlier in the 1960s, Pettigrew tried to explore what had become of the children of the Springfield Plan. Little did Pettigrew know that he was staring right at one of those children. "I was under it," Allen volunteered. And Allen asked, "Can you tell us what the plan involved that appealed to you and other sociologists and psychologists?" Pettigrew was interested in the Springfield Plan's "special attention to race, which many school systems in the United States have attempted to repress." The Plan was remarkable because it taught students to see racial differences and to begin to deal with them.[28]

Pettigrew finally pierced the shield of color blindness. He explained one of the problems in Boston's schools: "Conscientious and sincere teachers believe that they are doing a good job in an interracial classroom by ignoring race, and they tell you with great pride that they just don't treat Negro children any different than white children." This was the wrong approach. In contrast, "the Springfield Plan in the 1940s interested us because it explicitly took up race as an issue, the history of Negro-Americans . . . which most public school systems absolutely ignore." In most school systems, race "was repressed and denied, and we think to the detriment of the children involved." Pettigrew was saying that Springfield leaders could not tout the legacy of the Springfield Plan in one breath and position themselves as color-blind in the next. The Springfield Plan's genius was to acknowledge color, to see it, and to attempt—albeit in a limited fashion—to grapple with it. The Plan of the 1940s and the color-blind ideology of the 1960s stood in direct opposition.[29]

True to the outside agitator storyline, Pettigrew received a rude farewell. After a long afternoon on the witness stand, he walked out of the courthouse and toward his car. Forty-six years later, he held on to the bitter memory. "Some good citizens of Springfield took the air out of all four of my car tires."[30]

JAMES ALLEN BEGAN HIS CLOSING ARGUMENT IN UNORTHODOX FASHION. He praised his adversary to the heavens. He rejoiced in the Supreme Court's 1954 *Brown* decision, "which finally held . . . that segregation is legally wrong." Robert Carter had "accomplished as much . . . in ridding our society of a poison which had existed, as many of the battles of the Civil War." Allen agreed that segregation was legally wrong and morally indefensible. "Should your Honor find that in the City of Springfield we are practicing segregation, then we are entitled to every censure and rebuke that is possible." But that conclusion would be hard to sustain, he insisted. "There is not one shred of evidence in this case of any policy or practice of deliberate segregation." Allen's argument still depended upon a distinction between "deliberate segregation" on the one hand and "racial imbalance or de facto segregation" on the other. He argued that the latter was the unavoidable result of neighborhood schools.[31]

Allen thought it his duty to restore Springfield's good name. Against the plaintiffs' charges of segregation in the Springfield schools, he employed a rhetorical tactic that mixed outrage, innocence, and condescension. Allen declared, time and again, "If we were segregationists. . . ." This was a hypothetical so far removed from reality that no thinking judge could believe it. "If we were segregationists," Allen mused, Springfield's leaders would have created far more blatant patterns of segregation. "If it was our policy to segregate students . . . at the time the Duggan School was built . . . we could have built it a little bigger and originally established the boundary line down at Roosevelt Avenue." But the School Committee had "no policy to segregate." Allen thought the allegation ridiculous. "If we were segregationists, why would we pick the very year in which a suit was pending to make this kind of change? We would have to be very stupid." Allen's answer was simple. "We are not trying to segregate. We are trying to run a school system."[32]

Allen also revisited the Springfield Plan. He pointed out that the Springfield schools still taught the histories and cultures of many different racial and ethnic groups. The Plan had become "a part of the fiber of our system." Far from a den of segregation, James Allen's Springfield remained an interracial frontier.[33]

He acknowledged that the School Committee members "may have appeared a little bit strange . . . when asked, 'Do you know if this is a Negro school, a white school.'" But their responses actually reflected well on them, Allen said. "In this system there are no records kept on a racial basis . . . the district lines are drawn without regard to race, special transfers are made without regard to race, bussing if bussing is needed is done without regard to race." Of course the School Committee was taken aback when questioned about race. "Suddenly you ask a person who is in a system that is color-blind, 'What is the color of this area, or that area?' . . . And he says, 'I really don't know,' because he has never been trained to look at it that way." Allen paid tribute to the defendants, who presided over a school system that was truly blind to color.[34]

Robert Carter found that argument beyond bizarre. "The defense in this case attempts to argue and present evidence as if this were a case on Mars." It acted "as if the Court were not familiar with the normal practices and customs in the United States and came here from some foreign planet, viewing the situation afresh." In the middle of the 1960s, segregation permeated the land—and everywhere African Americans waged struggles against it. This was a battle for America's soul. To think that the defendants were unaware of race, or that they knew not where black families lived, was absurd.[35]

Carter struck at the defense's most sacred concept: the "neighborhood school." He conceded that the idea of the "neighborhood school" might have held meaning in the 1930s, at least in small cities like Springfield. But the Second Great Migration altered that forever. Northern cities had become shaped by residential segregation. Neighborhoods were defined by race. In this relatively new spatial landscape, a neighborhood school amounted to a segregated school. And although the School Committee supposedly held the "neighborhood" as a sacrosanct entity, it drew and redrew school district lines through the middle of neighborhoods, and transferred and bused students in and out of such neighborhoods. The School Committee had defiled the neighborhood and then reinvented it in order to perpetuate school segregation.[36]

Still, Carter needed to find a way out of his main dilemma. From Justice John Marshall Harlan's dissent in *Plessy v. Ferguson* to the Supreme Court's ruling in *Brown v. Board of Education*, the best argument against segregation lay in the claim that the Constitution was color-blind. Now, at the high point of the civil rights movement, Robert Carter turned around and fought against the color-blind doctrine.

Carter crafted a brilliant argument. While one could not use race in order to create or uphold segregation, he maintained, one had to consider racial factors in order to *eliminate* segregation where it already existed. The difference was that the latter strategy gave life to the Fourteenth Amendment, while the former violated it. Carter then flipped the claims to color blindness upside down. He posited that if "you have to act color blind," then school boards could not use geographical factors at all. For geography was itself inflected with color. Given that so many American cities were spatially segregated, any drawing of district lines in a geographical manner would be "effectuating a racial result." In the cities of the North, there was no way *not* to deal with race. If one assumed a guise of neutrality, he or she acceded to the prevailing patterns of housing segregation.[37]

Carter continued the assault. To claim "that the ground is limited to formal segregation" was to offer "a sterile argument." One could not tell a child in the DeBerry School "that the infirmity which you feel, the educational detriment that you receive, is somewhat different than the child in Alabama . . . because . . . you are being sent here not by law but by Board regulations, and this is different." Either way, this amounted to racial segregation. Either way, it caused harm, and either way, it violated that child's constitutional rights.[38]

James Allen's hypothetical had little to do with the crux of the case, Carter said. "I am not trying to show that the . . . School Committee in Springfield is made up of rabid segregationists, because as a matter of fact I don't believe that they are." The problem was that they failed to concern themselves with segregation. "They really didn't think about this problem until . . . last year . . . and now that they have a lawsuit they want to be less open and frank about what they really feel." Carter could agree with Allen: "I don't feel that these people are segregationists." But they were public officials who had abdicated their duties by allowing segregation to deepen. "We think that these children have been denied equality of educational opportunity," Carter concluded. "The Constitution demands" that the Springfield School Committee "secure their intended relief."[39]

As the two sides awaited Judge George Sweeney's decision, Springfield residents seemed uncertain about whether the city should bask in the publicity it had garnered, hide its face for shame, or battle to defend its reputation. The *Springfield Union*'s editors remained boosters through and through. They took satisfaction in the empty conclusion that despite the trial, "an excellent school system has been done no harm." Thus they evaded and obscured the issue. For how could an "excellent school system" possess such racial segregation?[40]

It could not, George Sweeney ruled. The new year was eleven days young when Sweeney issued his decision. He began his opinion with a nod to the Springfield School Committee. "I find that there is no deliberate intent on the part of the school authorities to segregate the races. If segregation exists, it results from a rigid adherence to the neighborhood plan of school attendance." Sweeney also praised the School Committee for its 1963 resolution in favor of school integration. In addition, he ruled that the committee did not intend racial segregation when it drew and redrew district lines. At first, all of this boded well for the defendants.[41]

Sweeney noted that "segregation, in the sense of racial imbalance, exists in the Springfield school system." Even the defendants had admitted this. Then he listed every Springfield school, along with its racial breakdown. He recapped the evidence concerning low test scores in imbalanced schools, and revisited Thomas Pettigrew's testimony about the effects of those schools upon black children. In light of all the evidence, Sweeney could not swallow the defendants' argument. "The question is whether there is a constitutional duty to provide equal educational opportunities for all children." Sweeney found that such a duty existed, and that Springfield had failed to fulfill it. "While *Brown* answered that question affirmatively in the context of coerced segregation, the constitutional fact—the inadequacy of segregated education—is the same in this case, and I so find" School Department leaders "must deal with inadequacies . . . as they arise." When the neighborhood school policy resulted in "segregation in fact," it "must be abandoned or modified." Sweeney's conclusion was simple and powerful: "There must be no segregated schools."[42]

Sweeney sought to avoid an error that the Supreme Court had committed in *Brown II* (1955). In its follow-up decision to *Brown*, the Supreme Court had ordered desegregation "with all deliberate speed"—but it set no firm date for integration. In response, southern leaders had dragged their feet for years. George Sweeney closed off all avenues for delay. He ordered the Springfield School Committee to present an integration plan by April 1965. In an opinion that numbered less than five pages, Sweeney emboldened black parents, inspired civil rights activists, and jarred the white leaders of Springfield.

Celebrations broke out at the NAACP offices in New York City. The NAACP issued a joyful press release: If "there must be no segregated schools," then the conditions in virtually every urban school system invited a legal challenge. Robert Carter hailed the ruling. For a moment, he could ponder as a real possibility the crumbling of "segregation, northern-style."[43]

African Americans in Springfield also rejoiced. Oscar Bright, chairman of the local CORE chapter, was "tremendously pleased and gratified" by Sweeney's decision. Frank Buntin declared that the ruling vindicated the NAACP. He prayed that the School Committee and the "whole community" would act with speed and in good faith. NAACP leaders hoped that the *Springfield Union* was right when it foresaw in Sweeney's opinion "far reaching" effects for urban schools across the country. As Professor Herbert Reid of Howard University Law School put it, Sweeney's decision "sounds like a landmark."[44]

Members of the Springfield School Committee were shocked and chagrined. To Romeo Cyr, the ruling came as "a real surprise." Rosemarie Coughlin made no effort to conceal her disgust. "I am sick over it. We are giving them every opportunity for equal education." During the trial, Coughlin had claimed that she knew nothing about school segregation except for what she read in the newspaper. On the morning of January 12, 1965, her own quotation appeared on the front page of the *Springfield Union*. Coughlin imagined that compliance with the court order would bring widespread busing. The School Committee "may as well buy the bus company." She warned of white disaffection and white flight. "The taxpayers will only take so much . . . many residents will attempt to move out of the city." Springfield's white leaders viewed Sweeney's decision not as a pill to swallow but as an affliction to treat—and ultimately to overcome.[45]

The editors of the *Springfield Union* denied that there was anything wrong with mostly black schools in the middle of a mostly white city. A century prior, the *Springfield Union* had been one of the first major newspapers to cheer Abraham Lincoln. Now it raised the banner of white resistance. "Springfield is in the position of being pushed into a most questionable venture in school integration. . . . The city can do no less than appeal the decision of Judge Sweeney." The newspaper portrayed Sweeney as a rabble-rouser rather than a reasoned jurist. Its lead editorial was titled, "Bombshell From the Bench."[46]

Springfield whites grew more hostile. Fears ran rampant at Parent Teacher Association meetings, where visions of crosstown busing danced in parents' heads. Hundreds of citizens jammed the hallways of the School Department offices on Thursday night, January 14, when a record number of people turned out for a meeting of the Springfield School Committee. The audience was so large that the committee moved the proceedings to the nearby Technical High School auditorium. There, James Allen argued that the committee should appeal Sweeney's decision. Allen stated that Sweeney had created "a new rule of law." Mary Lynch then motioned to appeal Sweeney's ruling. The vote was unanimous. They would file an appeal with the United States Circuit Court of Appeals in Boston. If that court sided with Sweeney, the School Committee declared itself ready to take the case to the United States Supreme Court. As the crowd trickled out of the auditorium, Rosemarie Coughlin explained her vote. Sweeney's decision "required the city of Springfield to do something that no municipality in the United States has previously been required . . . to abandon a long-established neighborhood school system that . . . is free from any intentional segregation." Springfield stood as a trailblazer in education again.[47]

African Americans in Springfield blasted the school board. To Frank Buntin, the unanimous vote to appeal served as "further proof that the members want to continue segregation in Springfield's schools." The city could just as easily have pledged itself to desegregation. Instead, "Springfield . . . took a step backward. The committee members had the opportunity to lead the whole nation along the road to equal education by working to abolish de facto school segregation, but they failed miserably." Oscar Bright noted that the School Committee had itself resolved that integrated education was desirable. Now these "incompetent officials" were ensuring Springfield's "continued" place as a "second-class city for both Negro and white."[48]

The local NAACP convened at the Dunbar Community Center to plan its response. On January 19, NAACP members drew up three demands. They agreed to take formal action that would attempt to block federal funding for the school system, so long as city leaders failed to propose an integration plan. The NAACP also resolved to try to block funding from the Commonwealth of Massachusetts. Finally, the NAACP asked for official representation on a local organization called the Springfield Action Committee.[49]

To the *Springfield Union*, the NAACP's demands felt like dollops of salt on an open wound. The editors noted that during Charlie Ryan's 1963 bid for reelection, he had been attacked as an integrationist. Ryan easily won that election. This showed that "Springfield obviously was preparing to accept change." Moreover, the School Committee's initial steps toward integration had obviated the need for the *Barksdale* case. The editors allowed that *Barksdale* had posed the all-important question for northern cities: "When the Supreme Court ruled in 1954–55 that school segregation by state law had to end, did it mean that school integration everywhere had to begin?" Sweeney had decided that question incorrectly. Only the most "vigorous champions of integration" agreed with him. School integration was not a goal to seek but a scheme to contest.[50]

For the *Union*, Springfield could save the rest of the country from the difficult reality of school desegregation. "Springfield had to appeal to resolve these questions for the rest of the country." Springfield undertook a noble endeavor, sheltering so many lesser cities—with weaker stomachs—from this ordeal. "The city is doing the nation a service by keeping the case alive." The School Committee, in its refusal to submit an integration plan, was pictured as the defender of high ideals.[51]

The overwrought rhetoric and the tortured logic showed something. It showed the city's white fathers and mothers on the defensive. They twisted a court appeal into an act of noblesse oblige while fuming at the decision of George Sweeney and gaping at the rising pace of local black activism. They had lost this round, and had lost it decisively. Robert Carter's vision carried the day. The court spoke for a nation, and a city, in which "there must be no segregated schools."

As QUICKLY AS ONE COURT RULING OPENED THE DOOR FOR AFRICAN Americans, another closed it shut. On July 12, 1965, the United States Circuit Court vacated George Sweeney's decision.

Judge Bailey Aldrich believed that Sweeney's order would have amounted to a "radical correction" of the school system—which was indeed Sweeney's intent. Aldrich worried that Springfield would be turned upside down in the name of abolishing segregation. Buses would wrench children from their neighborhoods and carry them across the city. First graders would have to traverse dangerous intersections. The game would not be worth the candle.[52]

Aldrich was saying that a school system ought not have as its highest priority the elimination of segregation. To agree that "there must be no segregated schools" would be to accept that African American students possessed an "absolute right" to integrated schools. "We can accept no such constitutional right," Aldrich concluded. The long road toward integration would stretch even longer.[53]

School Committee members were ebullient. The ruling restored Rosemarie Coughlin's faith in the judicial system. And it increased her resolve. "I will never bend to any pressure groups. I believe that Judge Sweeney's ruling did more harm than good to the Negro people." Similar sentiments were uttered in Albany, Georgia; Jackson, Mississippi; Plaquemines Parish, Louisiana; and across America. Coughlin hoped African American leaders and parents in Springfield might now see that the Springfield School Committee was "discriminating against no one."[54]

Other members of the School Committee were of the same mind. Vincent DiMonaco remarked that the Circuit Court could have reached no other conclusion. "Springfield has always taken pride in its fair treatment of minority groups." Romeo Cyr commented that the committee had always displayed "good faith" on the integration issue. To members of the School Committee, the circle now seemed complete. Their ordeal had begun in George Sweeney's district court, at pains to prove that they were not segregationists. Sweeney's ruling forced indignation, if not soul-searching. Now the School Committee celebrated. For they were not segregationists after all.[55]

On July 14, Henry Weissman announced that the NAACP would appeal the ruling to the United States Supreme Court. He noted that Bailey Aldrich had approved of the School Committee's steps toward integration in 1963. Aldrich stated that he was merely waiting to see whether Springfield would propose a workable desegregation plan. If the School Committee failed to do so, Weissman warned, those officials would invite "further court action, as well as demonstrations, sit-ins, civil disobedience, and other nonviolent action." The streets would flow with disaffection.[56]

THAT PROPHECY ARRIVED WITH STUNNING SPEED. IN FACT, AFRICAN Americans had begun to wage sit-ins well before Bailey Aldrich's ruling. On June 4, 1965, twelve members of CORE organized a protest in the office of the superintendent of schools. They locked arms, sang freedom songs, and criticized the inaction of local officials. Police officers dragged the protesters into a waiting patrol wagon. After Aldrich's decision, anger continued to mount. And it fused with outrage over police brutality.

On Friday night, July 16, police officers descended upon the Octagon Lounge. This nightclub stood on Rifle Street in Winchester Square, a black part of Springfield. By the middle of the night, officers had arrested eighteen individuals—including seventeen African Americans—and had used excessive force. Lester Williams, a disabled Korean War veteran and a doorman at the Octagon, found himself among the arrested. Charges of police brutality galvanized the black community. Civil rights leaders called a meeting at Oscar Bright's home on Saturday, July 17. The brutality at the Octagon quickly eclipsed *Barksdale* as the most pressing concern for African Americans in Springfield.[57]

On Saturday afternoon, local CORE and NAACP leaders drafted a list of five demands. They requested an immediate suspension of all police officers involved in the Octagon incident; an investigation conducted by a neutral party from outside the city; a mandatory six-month course on human relations for all Springfield police officers; the institution of a civilian review board; and the assignment of more black police officers to Winchester Square. The leaders immediately scheduled a community-wide meeting at the Dunbar Community Center for that same Saturday night.[58]

The anger surged openly at Dunbar. Four hundred people attended, including several who had been arrested at the Octagon and subsequently released. Those individuals recounted the brutality they had endured. Audience members called for violent retaliation, though Oscar Bright talked them down. They agreed to send a delegation that would speak with the mayor. Bright, Juanita Griffin (a PTA leader whose husband was president of the local NAACP), Ben Swan (vice-chairman of CORE), and the Reverend Charles Cobb took the demands to City Hall.[59]

That was when Charlie Ryan's nightmare commenced. A Springfield native, Ryan lived in an old colonial house near the entrance to Forest Park. He had attended Classical High School, then went on to Georgetown University and law school at Boston College. Ryan returned to Springfield and joined his father's law firm. He became mayor in 1962, at the age of thirty-four. Ryan had no inkling of the racial tumult to come. "1960 and '61 was more like the fifties," he remembered. Race and civil rights "really wasn't an issue. And if something was happening in the South, it was not provocative enough to have caught the attention of the country." When Ryan took the oath of office in January 1962, the racial upheaval was nowhere in sight. Three years later, Ryan would find himself at the center of a storm.[60]

The Ryan family had rented a cottage on the Rhode Island shore for two weeks in July 1965. Ryan would leave City Hall at noon on Fridays, drive to the cottage, and travel back to Springfield early on Monday mornings. He pulled into City Hall at about 8:45 on the morning of July 19 and noticed some seventy-five African Americans milling outside. He realized, "I know all these people—I know every single one of them . . . they're my friends!" Ryan had worked closely with Cobb, Bright, and Swan. In the 1963 mayoral election, Ryan carried the black wards of the city by a margin of ten-to-one. "No white guy ever won the black community like I did," Ryan asserted. "I was way ahead of my time as to black people being in the administration." Ryan had also been the only defendant in the *Barksdale* case who acknowledged the extent of segregation in Springfield schools. Ryan had built up a reservoir of goodwill with African Americans. But in the summer of 1965, the atmosphere was changing.[61]

Ryan invited the delegation into his office and listened to their stories of the Octagon incident. It was a tense meeting. Ryan expressed "shock and concern" over the events, and declared himself sympathetic to the proposed demands. So the group outside of City Hall dispersed.[62]

One demand had troubled Charlie Ryan from the beginning. He insisted that he did not have the authority to suspend the police officers. Both the union and the police commissioner had a say in their fates. Ryan relayed this to Rev. Charles Cobb on Tuesday, July 20. That night, African Americans assembled at Dunbar for another mass meeting. On July 21, more than 100 marchers returned to City Hall. Ryan explained that he was not about to suspend the police officers. Moreover, he expressed "great rancor over the use of the term 'demand.'" CORE and the NAACP responded in kind. They formed a new organization called the Council of Organizations of Civil Rights (COCR), and elected Juanita Griffin as chairperson. Mass protests became everyday events. A long and hot summer settled on Springfield.[63]

Across America, the middle of the 1960s witnessed sit-ins and boycotts, kneel-ins and walkouts and wade-ins. On Thursday, July 22, Springfield demonstrators waged the most peaceful of endeavors: a "sleep-out." But the moment did not begin in tranquility. Early that evening, more than 200 people gathered at Dunbar, ready to head downtown. Ben Swan told the crowd, "I don't think [Ryan] is taking us seriously." One audience member shouted back, "I'll tell you when they will take us seriously.

When everybody gets a shotgun and shoots every cop in sight." There were no shotguns in Court Square that night, only singing and chanting and even "snake-dancing." The demonstrators eventually set up beds on the front steps of City Hall and drifted off to sleep.[64]

The incipient leaders of COCR met with Charlie Ryan on Friday, July 23. Ryan stated that he had decided to reassign all seven police officers in question. He asked that COCR members keep this information private, for he would announce it at a meeting with the police commissioner the following Monday. But on Friday, Police Commissioner James Bulkley referred to the reassignment of police officers as an unreasonable demand. At the Monday meeting, neither Bulkley nor Ryan mentioned reassignment. Charlie Ryan was caught between dueling impulses and between rival constituencies. He believed in black civil rights. Yet nine in ten city residents were white. Many of them thought the mayor was already "too good" to African Americans. At the same time, Ryan had begun to lose favor with the black community.[65]

Between July 27 and August 8, two more African Americans were arrested by police officers who had been involved at the Octagon. In response, civil rights leaders boiled their original list of demands down to one: they wanted the seven police officers from the Octagon assigned to desk jobs. Several hundred people marched two miles—with signs and songs and in muggy heat—from Dunbar to the center of downtown. The demonstrators vowed to remain on the steps of City Hall until seven police officers were taken off the streets.[66]

Then Los Angeles exploded. On August 11, police brutality in the Watts neighborhood incited an uprising. Buildings and stores burned for the better part of five days. The Los Angeles sky was thick with smoke. Thirty-four people died and more than a thousand were wounded. Watts became the very picture of black insurrection, the sum of all white fears. It also sent an unmistakable message—that national civil rights laws had failed to address conditions in cities outside of the South. President Lyndon Johnson had signed the Voting Rights Act just five days before the Watts riots.

In Springfield, Charlie Ryan stationed at City Hall police officers who were both black and white. He was careful not to antagonize the protesters. Still, Ryan would not budge from his position. He wanted the Octagon victims to file formal charges of brutality and to let it play out in the courts. On August 13, the police chief informed the black demonstrators that the city would permit peaceful assembly from 8:15 a.m. to 4:45 p.m. only. At 4:55, riot squad officers emerged from City Hall, rushed the demonstrators, and dragged fourteen of them to a van. Later that night, Oscar Bright led another march to City Hall. Police officers threw Bright and nine others in jail. While the nation's eyes were still riveted on Watts, Springfield's Winchester Square burned. Black youths firebombed two white-owned businesses. Springfield had better fortune than Los Angeles. A slow rain quickened into a downpour, extinguishing the blazes.[67]

The arrests further galvanized the black community. On the evening of Saturday, August 14, marchers trooped from the Octagon to Court Square and joined in song. These were the verses of the classical civil rights movement, the verities of nonviolence. Policemen arrived at Court Square and the two sides struck a compromise: the demonstrators could carry on if they ceased with the singing. But at two o'clock in the morning, sixty helmeted police officers surrounded the protesters and arrested forty-four of them. This brought the weekend arrest total to sixty-eight in a place the *New York Times* was terming a "racially troubled industrial town."[68]

Robert Carter decided that the NAACP needed a legal presence in Springfield. He had Lewis Steel in mind. Steel was a New York City native and a Harvard graduate who hailed from a prosperous Jewish family. He began to work for the NAACP in the early 1960s. He was on a family vacation in the Hamptons when Carter telephoned him. Steel agreed to go to Springfield, and he quickly found his way to the local NAACP office: a small room on the second floor of a building near Winchester Square. The window had a bullet hole in it. Steel would remember his months in Springfield as "an intense period of time." Decades later he recalled the uncertainty of it all: "You weren't sure how this would escalate. And it was not because of the demonstrators. It was because of the police. . . . Were the cops a danger to them? Absolutely. Any demonstration could lead to more injury, more people being hurt, more arrests." In August 1965, Steel filed a lawsuit that charged the police with civil rights violations. He later returned to the Hamptons, vacationing "with these perfectly fine white people, who didn't care." This was what Lewis Steel called his "double life," and it was "absurdly painful." He traveled uneasily between these two worlds.[69]

The continued protests and arrests raised Springfield's profile. Members from the eleven other CORE chapters in New England planned to travel to Springfield on Saturday, August 21. Police Chief John Lyons denied them a parade permit, but the activists vowed to march regardless. Clifford Montiero, head of the Rhode Island CORE chapter in Providence, declared that Springfield "may become the Selma of the North."[70]

The *Washington Post* and the *Los Angeles Times* both reported that a "Selma-type" march was coming to Springfield. Charlie Ryan pondered this notion. "I knew that several people had been shot and killed in Selma, not too long ago." Governor John Volpe had Watts on his mind. Volpe called a summit meeting in Boston to try to defuse the situation. Ryan drove across the state on Thursday, August 19, to caucus with the governor and lieutenant governor as well as Attorney General Edward Brooke. Ben Swan and Oscar Bright also traveled to Boston to attend the meeting. After seven hours in a room without air-conditioning, the two sides reached an agreement. The city would reassign the police officers—among other measures—and the leaders would call off the march.[71]

Ryan went on television to explain the situation. He told Springfield residents that a compromise had been reached, but that he had not granted all of CORE's original demands. For instance, there would be no civilian review board. As Swan and Bright watched Ryan's speech, they believed the mayor had reneged. Reverend Charles Cobb called Ryan's description of the Boston agreement "absolutely false." The march was back on, they declared, scheduled for Sunday, August 22.[72]

Springfield seemed to be tearing at the seams. Newspapers reported that shots had been fired near Charlie Ryan's home. In another televised address, Ryan warned that outside agitators were hurtling toward Springfield by the carload. He began to prepare for the impending march, knowing full well that his own police force was at the center of the trouble. As Ryan later recalled, "Our police department had been under the gun ever since the night of the Octagon Lounge! . . . The Springfield police department on the street is kind of a red thing to a bull." So Ryan asked Governor John Volpe to mobilize the National Guard.[73]

One thousand National Guardsmen arrived in Springfield on Sunday morning, their bayonets aloft. They were there to keep order, and to ensure that the demonstrators could exercise their right to protest peacefully. More than 1,000 marchers walked a two-mile route, with 4,000 spectators lining the streets. They walked three abreast, women in the middle and men on the sides, as John Fenton reported on the front page of the *New York Times*. At the end of the march, 5,000 people congregated in Court Square. Every marcher had signed a pledge of nonviolence. But George Wiley, CORE's associate national director, had a different message for the Court Square crowd. Said the Rhode Island native, "The civil rights struggle in the North will be longer, bloodier, and more bitter" than it had been in the South.[74]

From the vantage point of the Springfield civil rights struggle, that was starting to seem possible. The "Selma-type" march helped little to achieve the demonstrators' specific goals. None of the officers were reassigned. School segregation would deepen in the coming years, residential segregation would increase, and nothing would be done to address police brutality. On August 26, those who had originally been arrested at the Octagon were placed on trial. Eleven black men and one white woman were found guilty of breach of peace. Insult was added to injury.[75]

Unwilling to let the issue fade into the background, civil rights activists planned another demonstration. They filed for a parade permit, but the request was denied. On September 11, picketers took to the streets nonetheless. The police arrested all forty-five of them. COCR filed a lawsuit, known as *Griffin v. Ryan*, alleging numerous civil rights violations on the part of the city. In the ensuing trial, which began in 1966, Lewis Steel offered witness after witness who detailed the repressive tactics of the police. Ben Swan testified that "the fear of arrest and brutalization has virtually brought all COCR activity to a halt." African Americans were cowed into a kind of submission. Steel argued to the court: "The methods the defendants have used in quashing public dissent are indistinguishable from those fashioned by municipal authorities in southern communities. . . . Indeed, the success defendants have achieved in stifling public dissent is greater than that achieved in many southern communities." Neither the police chief nor the mayor took the stand in their own defense. One police officer testified that he saw demonstrators performing an "African chant," similar to what he had seen in movies. If this was the best the defense could do, Steel thought, he had the trial won. "We put in credible, believable testimony against them. And they literally put up no defense." But the judge ultimately ruled in favor of the city.[76]

"Was it like Birmingham or Selma?" Lewis Steel asked half a century later. "No." But "was there danger in the streets? Were they frightened? Was there repression? Absolutely. . . . Law enforcement was committed on suppressing this movement." If the Springfield police had been violent segregationists, they would have breathed fire or sported billy clubs. As it was, they merely arrested the protesters, denied them parade permits, and broke their spirit.[77]

IN THE NORTH, RACIAL PROGRESS ADMITTED OF NO EASY MEASURE. IT depended which level of society one examined: the legislature, the courts, the ballot boxes, and the streets all revealed different truths. As one pendulum swung high toward victory, another sagged toward defeat.

In August 1965, the Massachusetts state legislature passed the pioneering Racial Imbalance Act. Mere weeks after Bailey Aldrich's courtroom reversal, state legislators overrode him. Governor John Volpe quickly signed the bill into law.

A 1964 state task force had found 55 racially imbalanced schools in Massachusetts, including 45 in Boston and 7 in Springfield.* The Racial Imbalance Act formally outlawed segregation in all Bay State schools. Yet it would take a decade for the Springfield School Committee to lift a finger. In part, this was because School Committee members clung to the fiction that they were not segregating.[78]

In the South, civil rights victories were also fragile and incomplete. But in Dixie, change could arrive suddenly and it could feel profound. A whole way of life could appear to crumble in the blink of an eye. When a sharecropper marched from Lowndes County, Alabama, to Montgomery, or cast a ballot for the first time in his life, epic transformations seemed afoot.

The stakes in the North were messier, harder to see and to articulate. The protests and the boycotts, the litigation and the legislation rarely brought the same sense that an entire era had passed in the night. There were few individual epiphanies on the part of white northerners, no searches for collective catharsis. And for African Americans in northern cities, the targets often proved elusive. Many of the same problems

---

*For purposes of the law, racial imbalance existed in any school where more than half of the student body was nonwhite.

still exist half a century after the *Barksdale* case: entrenched patterns of housing and school segregation remain, though they have no sanction in the law. Because the targets were at once more obscure and so deeply entrenched, the struggles could be longer, more protracted, more contradictory in their ultimate results.

The northern school integration lawsuits—of which there were many—rarely went anywhere. As Lewis Steel pointed out, had one of these cases reached the United States Supreme Court, and garnered a favorable ruling, this "would have given the movement its moral and legal authority"—the kind of widespread authority that northern struggles never fully gained.[79]

The Springfield story also illuminated the racial ideology of white northerners. If African Americans in northern cities *had* all been up against violent segregationists, the fight might have been more straightforward and more dramatic—more likely to grip the popular imagination. In Springfield, the supposed enemies denied that they were adversaries at all. The upholders of "racial imbalance" stated that they were color-blind. White northerners developed a whole worldview that refused to see, or to take responsibility for, the patterns of segregation that defined their cities. James Allen summed up this worldview in his hypothetical: "If we were segregationists." It was a worldview that became very difficult to combat. The North had few Bull Connors or Jim Clarks, few swaggering sheriffs who had built entire careers out of brutalizing black people. The dearth of such villains made for an absence of moral absolutes. There would be no Selmas in the North.

Although the North had no terrible bridges to march across, and no mass protests that riveted the nation, it came to possess something almost as incredible: a black senator.

While the ideology of color blindness enabled white northerners to defend and perpetuate segregation in neighborhoods and schools, it would also encourage them to vote for a black leader. Whites' commitment to color blindness helped to bring segregated schools as well as a black senator. Nobody understood that complexity better than Ed Brooke.

This chapter was about the more subtle Northern attain on segregation, and the idea of "colorblindness" that refused to acknowledge/take responsibility for/fix the issue of segregation/racial inequality because so many white people bought into the idea that bec. they didn't see color there was no segregation/problem + they couldn't do anything about it.

PART II

FORERUNNERS

FOUR

The Color-Blind Commonwealth?

The Election of Edward Brooke (1966)

"I NEVER SUCCUMBED TO THE REALITY," EDWARD BROOKE REFLECTED some forty years later. By "the reality," he meant the fierce opposition to racial integration that existed in Massachusetts during the 1960s, the riots that exploded across urban America, and an emergent white backlash. "I never let that deter me." Instead, Brooke offered Massachusetts voters an alternate reality—a place where race was no political object, where issues of segregation and racial violence had little impact on the campaign for a United States Senate seat. "I was also asking the voters to *rise above* that," Brooke recalled. *"Rise above* that and vote for me."[1]

Ed Brooke made for an unlikely Massachusetts senator. He was an Episcopalian and a Republican in a state where Protestants constituted less than one-third of the population and where only one-in-five voters were registered as Republicans. More to the point, 97 percent of Bay State residents were white. Ed Brooke was an African American.

Brooke announced his intention to run for the Senate in December 1965. At that time, he was serving his second term as state attorney general. Brooke held the highest statewide office of any African American in the country. Between 1962 and 1972, he would win four statewide contests in a row—including election as the first African American senator since Reconstruction. He remains the only black senator ever to be reelected.

Brooke walked a fine line throughout his political career. During twelve years in the Senate, he fought hard for civil rights legislation. Yet Brooke was uneasy with the insistent focus on his race. He felt that his racial identity could hem him in. "To be defined as a historical first," Brooke staffer Richard Norton Smith recalled, "is ironically enough in some ways restrictive. For Brooke, that was a greater challenge." Brooke would strive to perfect this balance—willing and able to embrace his black identity and the historical dimensions of his own achievement, while at the same time urging the electorate to discard those very facts when they stepped into the voting booth.[2]

Ed Brooke was all of these things, all at once. He was a black man committed to civil rights and a leader who downplayed his own race, a politician acutely aware of the toxic racial atmosphere gathering around him and yet completely unruffled by it. That he could be all of these things, all at once, was at the heart of his political genius. It helped explain how he convinced one million whites in Massachusetts to rise above race by voting for a black man. It accounted for his success as a liberal Republican in a state with many conservative Democrats. And it showed how he could resist the temptation to succumb to the more unsavory parts of reality.

During the same years when Brooke was winning elections, blacks were flocking to Boston. School and housing segregation intensified while black poverty and black unemployment worsened. Bay State voters achieved racial progress in the realm of electoral politics, just as racial inequality deepened by almost every other measure. Massachusetts during the 1960s laid bare the duality at the heart of Northeastern race relations.

ED BROOKE WAS BORN IN THE NATION'S CAPITAL IN 1919. HIS FATHER was a lawyer for the Veterans Administration, and a lifelong Republican. Brooke's grandfather had been a Virginia slave. Brooke attended all-black schools, including Washington's Dunbar High School, and passed his days in a segregated neighborhood. "I never interfaced with white people at all when I was growing up," he recalled. Brooke graduated from Howard University, and in 1942 he joined the army. He became a member of the 366th Infantry Combat Regiment and reported for training at Fort Devens in Ayer, Massachusetts. At segregated Fort Devens, white soldiers enjoyed exclusive access to the swimming pool, tennis courts, and social clubs. Black soldiers traveled to Roxbury for social life. Brooke found "a wonderful sense of freedom" in the city of Boston—a freedom that had existed neither in Washington nor on the base. He then shipped off to Italy, rose to the rank of captain, and eventually earned a Bronze Star. He also met and wooed an Italian woman named Remigia Ferrari-Scacco.[3]

At war's end, Brooke moved back to the Bay State. He enrolled in law school at Boston University, then married Remigia in June 1947. After earning his law degree, he opened a practice in Roxbury and bought a home nearby on Crawford Street. Brooke was cementing his place in Boston's black community.

In 1950, Brooke delved into Massachusetts politics. That world would consume him for the next three decades. He ran to become the state representative from Roxbury's Twelfth Ward. It was common practice for candidates to "cross-file"—to seek the nominations of both the Republican and Democratic Parties. Brooke finished far off the pace in the Democratic primary, for the old Irish machine still dominated this party. But Brooke won the Republican nomination. In the general election, he finished third in a field of six. By 1952, when Brooke ran again for state representative, the practice of cross-filing had been banned. So he declared himself a Republican at the outset.* He lost, but came closer than before. He expanded his law practice and became active in veterans' organizations. Brooke was retooling, networking, and biding his time.[4]

Although the Bay State was deeply Democratic, party meant little in terms of ideology. The political rivalries in Massachusetts involved ethnicity, nationality, class, religion, and geography—not policy. Democrats congregated in the cities and built their strength in Irish Catholic neighborhoods, while Republicans drew their electoral power from suburban Yankees. According to the *Boston Globe*'s Martin Nolan, "'Liberalism' and

---

*Brooke was not the only black Republican running for office. In Malden, Massachusetts, Herbert Jackson won election to the state legislature in 1950. In a sense, Jackson was the forerunner to the forerunner.

'Conservatism' have been mentioned as issues in Massachusetts politics as often as, say, the agricultural parity on soybeans."[5]

Personality proved a more valuable tender. Since United States senators were first elected by popular vote in 1913, eight men had represented Massachusetts: two Kennedys, two Lodges, a Saltonstall, and a Coolidge among them. It was a close-knit world of powerful political families. Breaking in could seem impossible.

In 1960, Republican governor Christian Herter encouraged Brooke to seek the open office of secretary of state. At the Republican convention in Worcester, Elizabeth McSherry of Newton seconded Brooke's nomination. She highlighted the gravity of the moment: "Massachusetts has a great heritage in equal rights that started before the Civil War, but that was over a hundred years ago and we need to be reminded that we are still in the forefront of civil rights and must practice what we preached." Republican delegates cloaked themselves in the Bay State's progressive mystique as Brooke became the first African American nominated for statewide office. This invocation of history, and the spirit of self-congratulation, would recur in many of Brooke's later campaigns.[6]

He faced a steep uphill climb. "I wanted to prove that white voters would vote for qualified Negro candidates," Brooke wrote in his 2006 autobiography, "just as Negroes had voted for qualified white candidates." African Americans numbered 95,000 in a state of almost five million. When Brooke campaigned in small towns, he was changing the color of voters' worlds. "Some of our voters haven't even seen a Negro," Brooke mused to a journalist. "They will have to meet me and be reassured that I'm not an ogre."[7]

Brooke's opponent was also an ambitious young politician: Kevin White. White would later become the mayor of Boston. At the time, he traded on the racial issue. His 1960 campaign used a deceptively simple slogan: "Vote White." Brooke later admitted that he was "surprised and hurt," terming the slogan "a blatant appeal to people to support him—and reject me—on the basis of race." When Brooke pressed the issue, White proclaimed innocence: he had only used his own surname on a bumper sticker. Brooke remained unconvinced. But in public he never broached the subject.[8]

The battle for secretary of state was hardly the most important race on the ticket that year. John F. Kennedy, the Bay State's junior senator, had emerged as the Democratic nominee for president. He tried to persuade Americans to vote the first Roman Catholic into the Oval Office. At the same moment, Brooke was asking the Massachusetts electorate to look past his racial identity. Kennedy eked out a victory over Richard Nixon. The Republican Party struggled in the Bay State, but Ed Brooke almost pulled off an upset. Kevin White won 1,207,000 votes to Brooke's 1,095,000. Brooke reflected, "I proved that I could overcome the racial and financial handicaps." Some Massachusetts voters were proud to support a black man. For others, race remained a barrier. Brooke's race functioned alternately as an obstacle or an allure.[9]

From 1961 to 1962, Brooke headed the Boston Finance Commission. He went after the corruption and bribery that seemed endemic to Boston politics. This experience helped Brooke to fashion himself as a crusader for good government. And when the office of state attorney general opened in 1962, Brooke considered pursuing it. Elliot Richardson, a wealthy lawyer, also desired that position. He encouraged Brooke to seek the office of lieutenant governor instead. Brooke declined the offer and advised Richardson to prepare for a fight. Richardson "had planned that he would be elected attorney general," Brooke remembered, "and then governor, maybe the Senate and then on to the White House." Brooke threw a wrench into those plans. "This unknown person came up from the South, that had never been elected to any public office. . . . Sort of upset the apple-cart."[10]

It was a time when politicians learned their fate in convention halls. At the Republican convention in Worcester, Richardson and Brooke engaged in a nasty battle. Brooke's father, Edward Brooke Jr., made the trek to Worcester. In the first order of business, the delegates selected Senator Leverett Saltonstall as the convention's chairman. The Saltonstall name was gold in Massachusetts politics: Four generations of Saltonstalls had held office. Leverett Saltonstall served three terms as governor and twenty-two years in the United States Senate. He was the very definition of a Yankee Brahmin. And Elliot Richardson had previously worked on his staff.

By early evening, Brooke recalled, the auditorium had turned "hectic, hot, and steamy." After every delegation but one had announced its votes, the candidates were deadlocked at 839 delegates apiece. Then Middlesex First District went for Richardson, giving him 854 delegates—the minimum required in order to claim a majority. Richardson supporters celebrated. Some headed out of the convention hall and made for the

Massachusetts Turnpike, motoring back toward Boston. But one Middlesex delegate, Francis Alden Wood, stepped to the microphone and asked to be recognized. Wood charged that the votes had been counted before he made his choice. He wished to vote for Brooke. Now Richardson appeared one vote shy of victory. Leverett Saltonstall ordered a second ballot. Chaos gripped the hall. Brooke and Richardson tried desperately to locate their supporters. When the voting commenced, Brooke's father retired to the balcony to sit by himself. The delegates now saw that neither candidate was necessarily the favorite. On the second ballot, Brooke garnered 792 votes to Richardson's 673. As Brooke claimed victory, his father wept with joy.[11]

In the general election, Francis Kelly opposed Brooke. A former lieutenant governor and attorney general, Kelly embodied the stereotype of Boston's Irish Democratic machine. Days before the election, radio host Jerry Williams invited each candidate on the air—one after the other. "If I were not a gentleman," Kelly sniped, "I'd say that my opponent is a Negro man who has a white wife." Brooke followed. And he began to turn the racial issue. "Kelly's statement is sad," Brooke said. He insisted that Massachusetts voters were above racism—that they could, and would, elect him in spite of his race. The electorate would prove itself to be color-blind. But there was also another dynamic at hand. Brooke's race added resonance to an argument about political novelty. Kelly was a politician of the old school; Brooke was the agent of change. Brooke promised to transcend partisan and ethnic divides, and to transform the prevailing culture of political corruption. Everything about Brooke seemed new. He *looked* like the political future.[12]

This strategy appealed to a specific segment of voters. It was about generation, geography, and class as much as race. Brooke wooed World War Two veterans and new suburbanites. Many of these voters had long felt under the thumb of Boston's Irish Democrats. "The Hub," known for its corruption and its insularity, had become an embarrassment to them. For them, Brooke was the harbinger of a brighter future—a vehicle that would whisk them away from the dreary present. The younger generation of Massachusetts voters, those who had escaped Boston, became his core constituents.[13]

The 1962 election was cruel to the Republicans nationwide. In Massachusetts, a Democratic groundswell swept Ted Kennedy into the United

States Senate in a special election. But Brooke pieced together a decisive victory. He had encouraged Democrats to cross party lines. Thousands of bumper stickers across the commonwealth advertised: "Another Democrat for Brooke." Racking up large majorities in the suburbs, Brooke won by a margin of 56 percent to 44 percent. When one of President Kennedy's aides told him of Brooke's victory, Kennedy remarked, "That's the biggest news in the country." Brooke was the only Republican to win constitutional office in the Bay State that year. Brooke seized on this as more evidence to bolster his argument about color blindness. "The voters had ignored race," he explained.[14]

BROOKE COULD NOT IGNORE RACE DURING HIS FIRST TERM AS ATTORNEY general. He quickly found himself at the center of a fight over school inte-gration in Boston. The city's schools were almost completely segregated. In 1963, Boston's NAACP requested a hearing with the Boston School Committee. Louise Day Hicks presided over the June 11 meeting. She refused to acknowledge the existence of de facto segregation. In response,

On February 26, 1964, twenty-thousand students in Boston boycotted the public schools to protest segregation. Activists gathered at the Tremont Street Methodist Church, and joined in song. ASSOCIATED PRESS.

on June 19, more than one quarter of Boston's African American students boycotted the schools. Both sides hardened their stances during the ensuing months, and Hicks won reelection in November with almost 70 percent of the vote. Boston had fast become an incubator of the "white backlash" as well as a crucible of the northern black freedom struggle.[15]

African Americans drew up plans for another boycott of Boston's schools. They set the date for February 26, 1964. The state commissioner of education asked Brooke to rule on whether the boycott was legal. Brooke lost sleep over the decision. "I labored with it, I prayed, I did everything I could. But mostly what I did was research and have my staff work with me on that." Brooke kept asking himself one question: "What does the law say about it? It says that you can't keep children out of school to protest." In the end, Brooke outlawed the boycott. He questioned its legality and its wisdom. "Boycotts, sit-ins, and demonstrations don't achieve the desired consequences in this Commonwealth. On the contrary, they merely intensify the resentment of the population at large and undermine the best interests of the Negro community." Less than a year earlier, deep below the Mason-Dixon line, Martin Luther King Jr. had also ruminated about civil disobedience. He reached the opposite conclusion. In his famous "Letter From Birmingham Jail," King wrote of those moments in which Americans were compelled to reject state laws in favor of a higher law. Despite Brooke's ruling, the boycott occurred as planned on February 26. Twenty thousand students, black and white, boycotted Boston's public schools. Interracial groups of activists staged protests and gathered in mass meetings throughout the city. For Brooke's stand, he lost several allies in Boston's civil rights community. "That cat can't help us," said Cornell Eaton, an African American and chairman of the Boston Action Group. "He's too involved with the white power structure." This kind of criticism would dog Brooke throughout his career.[16]

Brooke took the criticisms to heart. During an interview in 2009, he could still feel the sting. "To this day there are critics. They will never forgive me for that." At root, Brooke did not view himself as a civil rights leader. He was a politician, a lawyer, and a policymaker. "I was not known as a big civil rights leader, and I never wanted to be a great civil rights leader. I said you've got them out there . . . thank God . . . but I'm not that one." For Brooke, the distinction between civil rights and electoral politics was crucial.[17]

In 1964, Ed Brooke ran for reelection as attorney general of Massachusetts. These supporters held a sign that read, "You Can Believe in Brooke." FROM THE EDWARD W. BROOKE III COLLECTION, HOWARD GOTLIEB ARCHIVAL RESEARCH CENTER AT BOSTON UNIVERSITY.

At the level of national politics, the Republican Party lurched to the right. The party's 1964 convention, held in San Francisco, was one of the low points in Brooke's political life. The party chose as its presidential nominee Senator Barry Goldwater of Arizona. Goldwater opposed the 1964 Civil Rights Act and railed against government spending. Brooke still wanted to believe that the Republicans were the party of Lincoln, that they could stand for innovation and progressivism—for more than just opposition to government. But the events in San Francisco's Cow Palace made him feel like an outcast.[18]

In November, Lyndon Johnson defeated Goldwater in a landslide. For the first time in American history, a Democratic president won every New England state. Johnson carried Massachusetts by a percentage margin of 76 to 23. Ted Kennedy was elected to a full term in the Senate, winning by one million votes. Still, Ed Brooke won reelection by 800,000 votes. He carried 349 of 351 Massachusetts towns; Blackstone and Millville, on the Rhode Island border, stood as the only holdouts. As the *Newark Sunday News* reported, Brooke was "at a new zenith."[19]

Through the summer and fall of 1965, speculation swirled about whether Senator Leverett Saltonstall would step down at age seventy-three. Indeed,

Brooke was thinking about higher office. He had already enlisted a polling organization to analyze his prospects for the United States Senate as well as the governorship. By Brooke's own reckoning, he had amassed "the most powerful . . . political organization in the state." He was prepared to turn it loose.[20]

Saltonstall scheduled a press conference for December 29, 1965. Brooke pounced. Although he did not know Saltonstall's intentions, Brooke quickly announced a press conference of his own for the following day. Brooke devised three possible courses of action. If Saltonstall announced for reelection, Brooke would launch his own reelection bid for attorney general. If Saltonstall retired, Brooke would ask Republican governor John Volpe whether he planned to pursue the Senate seat. And if Volpe fancied the Senate seat, Brooke would declare himself a candidate for governor. If Volpe stood pat, Brooke would run for the Senate.

On December 29, Leverett Saltonstall announced that he would not seek reelection. Brooke set his plan in motion. He phoned Volpe and asked his intentions, but the governor was noncommittal. Brooke pressed Volpe, noting that he had already scheduled a press conference. In multiple conversations, Volpe pleaded with Brooke to take his time. Volpe never did commit one way or the other, so Brooke forged ahead. On the night before New Year's Eve, in Boston's Sheraton Plaza Hotel, Brooke shared the stage with his wife Remigia and their two teenage daughters. He declared his candidacy for the United States Senate: "I have a deep and abiding faith in the ability and desire of the people of Massachusetts to make their choice on the basis of qualifications and programs." Although the announcement itself came as no shock, the prospect that Brooke raised was no less enchanting.[21]

BROOKE RUED THE EMPHASIS ON HIS SKIN COLOR. HE SAID IN APRIL 1966, "The racial issue has been beaten, beaten, beaten. I'm born what I am so you take me as I am." Two months earlier, Brooke had insisted, "The voters of the state are so racially blind, they reelected me by 800,000 votes." *Life* duly heralded him as the "Bay State's Color-Blind Candidate."[22]

Brooke entered the Senate contest with a clear advantage. One early poll pitted Brooke against Endicott "Chub" Peabody, the eventual Democratic nominee. It revealed a 67 to 21 percent advantage for Brooke. He maintained a commanding lead in the polls through the spring of 1966.[23]

During the summer, riots flared in some thirty-six American cities—from the Hunters Point section of San Francisco to Cleveland's Hough neighborhood. African Americans clenched their fists and cried "Black Power." The white backlash mounted. Martin Luther King Jr. took his civil rights campaign to Chicago, where he was struck with a rock in Marquette Park. It was an unseemly time to talk about color blindness. When voters looked at Ed Brooke, they surely registered his race.[24]

Brooke's campaign slogan acknowledged this reality and played on it. In blue letters set against a white backdrop, his bumper stickers and pins proclaimed: "Proudly for Brooke." The slogan summarized, somewhat implicitly, the relationship between the black attorney general and those millions of white voters upon whom he depended. "Proudly for Brooke," as the *Boston Globe*'s James Doyle suggested, was "faintly suggestive of the so-called 'conscience backlash,' that political urge to vote for Brooke in order to place a Negro in the United States Senate and expiate the everyday discrimination members of that race suffer." Parents in Newton, laborers in Holyoke, professors in Williamstown, and bar-backs in Brighton could display their own enlightenment on their bumper or their lapel. They need not support school integration or open housing; they could simply proclaim that they backed Brooke, with pride in their African American attorney general and in their great state.[25]

"Proudly For Brooke" sparked internal debate from the beginning. Brooke's campaign manager, Al Gammal, wrote to him on May 9, 1966: "I do not like the word 'proudly,' and certainly not in this context." Gammal detected in this phrase emotional affirmation more than political substance. "If the salient implication, and it may be taken that way, is that we are proud because you are a Negro from Massachusetts, then I resent it and so will the people, and for that matter, so ought you." Gammal found emptiness in the very syntax, and suggested a number of alternatives. "Believe in Brooke—Vote for Brooke—Elect Brooke—Love Brooke—Hate Brooke—are all affirmative verbs, but 'proudly' . . . is sterile and meaningless. 'Proudly for Brooke' on the bumper sticker says nothing." Al Gammal held out hope for a color-blind campaign. "It seems to me that the advertising firm is not looking at Ed Brooke, the *man*, but Ed Brooke, the Negro." Gammal thought that if Brooke truly wanted to wage a campaign above and beyond race, his slogan ought to reflect that. Gammal lost this battle, at least initially. "Proudly For Brooke" continued to adorn bumpers and billboards across the state.[26]

Whites in New England exhibited two disparate impulses when it came to race, and both of them found expression in Ed Brooke's Senate campaign. On the one hand, they quaked with fear at the prospect of urban violence and Black Power—two entities that became increasingly linked in white minds. On the other hand, many in Massachusetts were eager to support an African American for high office. It was not that white northerners were all either bleeding-heart racial liberals or charter members of the white backlash. For many individuals, the fear and the pride mingled together.

By the end of the summer, the pride still seemed to be winning out. Brooke was juggling the impossible. He waged a color-blind campaign while at the same time encouraging those voters who were happy to bash the racial barrier. The August polls found him well ahead of every potential Democratic nominee.

THAT WAS BEFORE STOKELY CARMICHAEL CAME TO BOSTON. ON THE last Saturday in August, Carmichael—the Black Power leader—traveled to Roxbury. This was the old stomping ground of Malcolm X. Approximately one thousand African Americans gathered to hear Carmichael at the Jackson-Reeb Memorial Playground. "It's time for all black people in Boston to get together," Carmichael told the crowd, and "move to gain control over your communities." He also spoke at Estelle's Restaurant, and at Harvard several days later. The Nation of Islam's Louis X joined Carmichael at the playground, then appeared before an audience of 1,500 at the Patrick Campbell School. There, Louis X spoke for ninety minutes amid spirited encouragement from the crowd, a scene one audience member called "the most remarkable thing I've seen around here in years." Carmichael held nothing back at Estelle's Restaurant. "This country is antiblack, racist, and rotten through and through and I, personally, don't want any part of that kind of system," Carmichael said. Brooke's Senate campaign was an effort to integrate that very "system."[27]

Carmichael's words reflected the tense racial dynamic on the horizon. One of Brooke's field directors assessed the climate in Springfield. "Will certainly be tougher than '64," Evan Dobelle wrote. "The bloom is off the civil rights movement." Shortly after Carmichael brought his Black Power message to Boston, Brooke's support in the polls dropped to the 50 percent mark for the first time in the campaign. He was losing voters with each passing day, and his race seemed to be the reason.[28]

Brooke began damage control. On September 4, he appeared on television's *Issues and Answers*. ABC's Bill Lawrence jumped into the breach with his first question: "Mr. Brooke, do you feel that the militant Negro slogan of 'Black Power' is hurting you politically in Massachusetts?" Brooke clarified his message. "I don't really think it is hurting me," Brooke began. "It is a term which many people don't understand. . . . If Black Power means economic and political power of the Negro in order that they might improve their lot, I think Americans will accept it." Brooke explained that Black Power admitted of many different meanings; the problem was that it had come to be equated with violence. "But if it means militancy and violence, of course, then I think it has to be rejected and I don't think, frankly, that it is going to have an impact in so far as my candidacy is concerned." Brooke went on to highlight his own membership in the NAACP and his strong support for further civil rights legislation. Bill Lawrence noted that while many parts of America had exploded in racial violence, Massachusetts remained quiet. This provided Brooke with an opening to invoke a mystique about the Bay State's history:

> I think historically Massachusetts has stood for equality and justice. . . .
> I think we have had enlightened leadership. Our governor and our legislature has been far ahead of most states in the country in civil rights legislation. . . . I don't want you to believe that Massachusetts is so unique that it doesn't have its problems. It does. We have a problem of de facto segregation of the Boston school systems. . . . But . . . our people . . . understand that the Negro should be given his equality under the law and his civil rights and he is given them in Massachusetts in the main.

In Massachusetts, Brooke suggested, it was possible for an African American to rise higher than he could anywhere else.[29]

Brooke developed a line of appeal in which he himself stood as the picture of the American Dream. He tried to engineer a scenario in which a vote against him became analogous to a vote against the very promise of the nation. He denounced black radicalism while championing a vision of interracial democracy. He accomplished the former in a speech in Springfield in September 1966. "I reject black supremacy, white supremacy, 'black power,' or 'white power,'" Brooke said, testing out a message that he would perfect in the campaign's last months. "We must reject the idea of pitting one group against another." Brooke's staff then outlined a number of points for prospective speakers. "Ed Brooke embodies the American dream," speakers should feel free to suggest. "He is a living, breathing example that if you . . . work hard enough, if you have the ability, character and integrity regardless of your race, color or creed, you can achieve that American dream." And it was essential to distinguish Brooke from other prominent African Americans of the day. "He is in answer to the Carmichaels and the Adam Clayton Powells." Finally, speakers were asked to conjure the horrible specter of a Brooke defeat. "It would be tragic if the man who is acknowledged as the most competent, the most able, the most deserving is rejected because of his color. If Ed Brooke loses, it would set the Republican Party and the nation back 100 years. If we lose this seat, we will never recover it in our life time." In this version of the campaign narrative, an Ed Brooke loss would kill the cause of democracy.[30]

This message never resonated with one segment of the electorate: the white working class. Brooke's pollsters frequently asked voters which qualities best described Brooke. In the fall of 1965, even while Brooke was at the peak of his popularity, only 18 percent of Massachusetts residents termed him "on the side of the working-man." In 1966, that number fell into the single digits. Ed Brooke was many things to many people, but rarely a hero to lower-income whites. Nor did he vie for their votes. "I never got down and had to roll up my sleeves and try to be a populist," Brooke recalled. Within Boston, he always fared worst in South Boston and Charlestown—two bastions of working-class Irish Americans. As one anonymous voter told a pollster, "I prefer the Democrat because he is more for the working man." If the Democrats had a chance to defeat Brooke, these voters would have to carry them.[31]

The Democratic primary pitted John Collins against Chub Peabody. Collins, the mayor of Boston, had presided over the city's ordeal with urban renewal. Peabody was a Yankee suburbanite and former governor who hailed from a prominent Massachusetts family. Peabody enjoyed high standing among civil rights activists in Massachusetts, due in part to the actions of his mother—who was famously jailed during a protest in St. Augustine, Florida. Peabody had also been a driving force behind the state's Racial Imbalance Act.

Conventional wisdom had it that Collins would play to racial fears against Peabody's racial liberalism. In a potential campaign against Brooke, Collins's research team advised him to play the race card. Ingalls Associates offered a few possible campaign slogans: "Don't discriminate against accomplishments. Vote Collins." Or, "Be honest with yourself—Vote Collins." As the September primary election approached, Collins hit the racial issue more forcefully. He denounced "civil disobedience as a means of attaining democratic objectives," a way to criticize the Peabody family as well as civil rights activists and antiwar protesters. Five days before the primary, Collins declared, "I also reject the George Rockwells and the Stokely Carmichaels of this nation. I repudiate their doctrine of power, white and black." Ironically, Ed Brooke had also deplored "white power" and "black power." But Brooke never went so far as to compare Carmichael with the head of the American Nazi Party. While Collins spoke these words to whip up the white backlash, Ed Brooke used similar language to soothe those fears.[32]

Peabody surged to victory in the primary, beating Collins by a percentage margin of 50 to 42. The other 8 percent, about 52,000 votes, went to a man who ran on an anti–Vietnam War message: Thomas Boylston Adams.[33]

Brooke had no competition for the Republican nomination. The party's convention was a toast to him. As the Massachusetts GOP stood "Proudly for Brooke," the controversy over that slogan seemed a distant memory. The first nominating speech, whose text was approved by Al Gammal, asked party members "to stand up proudly, tonight and in November, for Edward W. Brooke." In Brooke's acceptance speech, he recalled the atmosphere when he first took office in 1963: "Our state was plagued with graft and corruption . . . the political climate was such that industry did not want to come to Massachusetts, and where people were ashamed of being a Massachusetts resident." Brooke asserted that he had cleaned up the state, and he promised to replace the shame with pride. "I ask you never to lose faith in this great Commonwealth . . . because

On September 14, 1966, Brooke accepted the Republican Party's nomination for a seat in the United States Senate. He would go on to win the election in November. FRANK C. CURTIN/AP/CORBIS.

Massachusetts has an illustrious history." By electing Brooke, voters could help the Bay State live up to its glorious past.[34]

Ed Brooke stood as the Bay State's "showpiece of racial tolerance," as *The Nation* observed. In the general election, Chub Peabody would have to fight Brooke for the vote of every last civil rights supporter. For all of the candidates' similarities on policy, the Peabody-Brooke contest presented startling personal differences. As Brooke later mused, "If the grandson of slaves could defeat the grandson of the headmaster of Groton, that was a man-bites-dog story."[35]

FEARFUL WHITES HAD NO OBVIOUS CHAMPION IN THIS CAMPAIGN, BUT their presence would still be felt. Based upon telephone interviews, pollsters classified each voter as either "least prejudiced," "less prejudiced," or "most prejudiced." More than 60 percent of voters fell into the middle category. About 20 percent were at the most enlightened end of the spectrum, with 15 percent classified as the most prejudiced. Even among the "most prejudiced," Brooke had maintained a 51- to 26-percent lead over Peabody in May 1966. But after Stokely Carmichael's visit, an enormous swing occurred. Peabody came to enjoy a 46-to-38 advantage among these voters. Brooke clung to a small lead among the middle sector of the electorate, but Peabody had narrowed that gap by 27 percentage points. The "least prejudiced" voters remained committed to Brooke throughout, though there again he experienced slippage.[36]

Voters voiced their prejudices to pollsters. "I think I'm bigoted in this," one individual acknowledged. "I don't think I'd want to vote for a colored person." A Peabody supporter cited his own family history in order to explain his vote. "The only reasons I'm for Peabody is I don't want Brooke. I'm angry at his people. My parents came here from Europe with nine children and my father went out to shovel snow and support us. I worked days, went to school at night . . . but his people don't work like we did. They want everything handed to them." Few poll respondents were as verbose, but their views proved no less alarming. Said one, "Brooke is a good man, but I have personal views I would not like to discuss." Brooke could no longer elude or elide the fact of his race.[37]

While voters in Massachusetts reconsidered their support for Brooke, the national media continued to churn out glowing articles. The *Saturday Evening Post* predicted that if Brooke were elected in November, "he would become, automatically, as visible to the rest of the world as Bobby Kennedy is." The press also brought the backlash into the light. The *National Observer* reported that "anyone who wanders into his headquarters can overhear conversations among his workers speculating on the possibility of a 'backlash.' One worker last week, in a typical remark, said: 'Those riots can't help but hurt old Brookie.'" The campaign would turn on how Brooke handled rising white resentment.[38]

Reports of backlash, frontlash, and "counter-lash" rolled off the presses. "Brooke can scarcely get his name in the paper," the *Boston Globe*'s David Wilson wrote on October 1, "without finding it flanked by a portrait of Stokely Carmichael or Adam Clayton Powell or an account of collision between police and Negro rioters." Brooke told a reporter that the race issue "seems to take precedence over the candidates themselves. It clouds my purpose for running, even my programs and proposals." Racial tensions were defining the American political landscape. In California,

Ronald Reagan mounted a bid for the statehouse on a platform that denounced urban rioters and warned, "The jungle is waiting to take over." In Alabama, Lurleen Wallace (the wife of George Wallace) hinted at another term of family-style segregation forever. City streets could barely contain the anguish of African Americans. More than a few politicians exploited white anger and fear, offering themselves as the leaders who could extinguish the fire this time.[39]

In all of Brooke's previous campaigns, he had successfully de-emphasized the issue of his race. He had even turned it into a subtle advantage among a segment of voters. But this time, there was no avoiding it. In an interview decades later, Brooke acknowledged as much: "I was running against a backlash. Racial issues were never as flagrant in this country as they were when I was a candidate, and I knew that." Brooke's race seemed to stand between him and the Senate. In a rare moment, he appeared unsure which way to go.[40]

The "color-blind candidate" confronted his own color. Brooke launched an advertising blitz. In the last month of the campaign, voters became intimately familiar with his visage and his voice. Between October 1 and Election Day, he bought 3,291 radio spots and 264 television ads. Fourteen times he broadcast a campaign film. He appeared on eleven question-and-answer shows, entitled "Ask Ed Brooke." He aimed his message straight at the hearts and minds of fearful whites. In a televised speech, he lumped Stokely Carmichael together with segregationist icon Lester Maddox, denouncing the pair as "extremists of black power and white power." Then he turned the screw. "A vote against me," Brooke declared, "is a vote for Stokely Carmichael."[41]

Always the juggler, Brooke pivoted quickly and tried the opposite tactic as well. He declared that there was no backlash—that it was a confection of the media. "When I go into the factories and shake hands with the workers, I watch them carefully. They look at me. Their eyes don't turn away. They don't turn their backs on me. They could." Brooke employed an impressionistic test to measure the existence of backlash. In the bars and on the streets, "I get a warm response; I don't get just a perfunctory, polite reception." Brooke parried reporters' perpetual inquiries. He stated, "I see more in your writing on it than I see among the voters. . . . The backlash has nothing to do with this campaign." Brooke's findings notwithstanding, "the white backlash is there," *Globe* political editor Robert Healy wrote on October 2. "It may be still in November and it may not. There is no measuring device for it."[42]

In an attempt to excise any rhetoric that dealt in racial innuendo, Brooke decided to dispose of his campaign slogan. On October 8, he ditched "Proudly for Brooke." A different slogan appeared: "Brooke, A Creative Republican."

A more combative opponent might have fanned the flames. But Chub Peabody was not that man. Peabody declared, "Backlash is just so much baloney." Two days before the election, Peabody would confess publicly, "I am shocked and ashamed that any person or publication would strive to inject this issue into the present senatorial campaign." Similarly, Brooke told his supporters: "I'm tiring of hearing about backlash, sidelash, or any other kind of lash." In the fall of 1966, the white backlash was on everyone's lips—everyone, that is, except for Ed Brooke and Chub Peabody.[43]

When poll results were released in the last week of October, Brooke had reason to believe his strategy was paying dividends. He had arrested his decline. He possessed a two-point lead among the "most prejudiced" voters, though another 24 percent of those voters were undecided. There was much in the poll results to give Brooke pause. The pollsters had asked voters whether they personally knew anyone who had claimed that they would support Brooke, but once in the voting booth, would actually vote against him on the basis of race. Eleven percent of voters knew such an individual. In the city of Boston, one in five voters admitted knowing such a person.[44]

This round of polling also suggested that frontlash and backlash were both alive. "He's magnetic," said one Brooke supporter. "Feather in our cap to send a Negro to Washington." Another voter had long been undecided, but finally switched to Brooke—largely *because* of his race. "It is a step forward because of his race and it is about time that a step forward was taken. . . . Sometimes I think that he should speak up about Civil Rights more." For others, Brooke's race had the opposite effect. "I was for Brooke, but now I have changed. It's hard to put into words. Right now I can't see a colored man as Senator." This Brooke-turned-Peabody supporter stated, "This rioting is too much." Another voter, who switched from undecided to Chub Peabody, had a straightforward reason. When asked to explain the switch, this individual replied, "Our own race." The reason for opposing Brooke: "Negro."[45]

The white backlash continued to enthrall. A front-page article in the *Wall Street Journal* noted that the election changed when "the shade of Stokely Carmichael entered the contest." Reporter Cal Brumley traveled with Chub Peabody past a firehouse in Marblehead, where a fireman assured Peabody, "We're with you." By way of explanation, another fireman added, "Black Power." One telephone operator from Reading fretted that if Brooke won, "there would be no holding 'them' down; we'd have a Negro president, and you've got to believe it." In central Massachusetts, the owner of a liquor store worried about how a Brooke victory might influence the African American population. "'They' are so damned arrogant now . . . can you imagine what it would be like if he was elected?" To these voters, the prospect was not pretty.[46]

Ed Brooke's Senate campaign invited the gaze of the world. Paris's *Le Monde* published an article on October 28; the *London Times* followed with a story four days later. As racist quotes from Massachusetts voters began to fill the pages of national and international publications, something more profound seemed at stake. The world was watching the Bay State to see whether it would vindicate the American Dream or cave to the vagaries of prejudice.[47]

ALONGSIDE THE BACKLASH, ANOTHER ISSUE SHARED CENTER STAGE: THE Vietnam War. While Peabody toed the Democratic Party's line on Vietnam, Brooke called for a reevaluation of Lyndon Johnson's strategy. On October 21, the candidates appeared at Faneuil Hall before 250 supporters of Thomas Boylston Adams. Peabody placed the burden on North Vietnamese leaders. Peace would be possible only when those men "begin to realize that we will not permit their aggression." At such jingoism, thirty-five audience members stormed out of the hall. Brooke warned that if the war grew in intensity, its consequences would be dire. "Further escalation will make it impossible to end without triggering a war with Red China or a nuclear holocaust on earth." That line drew enormous applause. The audience was Brooke's.[48]

He proceeded to sew up the antiwar vote. On October 28, Massachusetts Political Action for Peace endorsed Brooke. In a letter to 10,000 supporters, it called Brooke "the best available choice." While "Mr. Brooke is by no means now a 'peace candidate' . . . we rate Mr. Brooke as fair and Mr. Peabody as unacceptable." On November 1, two more groups endorsed Brooke. The Committee of Religious Concern About Vietnam mailed its endorsement letter to 2,500 clergymen. And a group of college professors, headlined by scholars at Harvard and M.I.T., sent its endorsement to every faculty member in the state. Brooke had long targeted what he called the "thinking electorate" of Massachusetts. With his stance on Vietnam, he found the way to their hearts.[49]

The *Boston Globe* bestowed its prized endorsement upon neither candidate—at least not explicitly. The *Globe* hoped that no voter would evaluate the candidates on the basis of race. The white backlash "has no place in Massachusetts. It should have no part in the election." The editors repeated Brooke's syllogism in which a vote against him was a vote for Stokely Carmichael. "It is essential that people vote either FOR Edward Brooke or FOR Endicott Peabody. Not AGAINST Brooke." The editors found no differences between the candidates on civil rights. But the candidates' disagreement over Vietnam was substantial. "There are honorable differences on Viet Nam. There is no honor in a 'white backlash.'" Reading between the lines, there seemed only one legitimate reason to oppose Brooke: he might not be hawkish enough for some voters. This painted Peabody into a corner. The editorial was not an outright endorsement of Brooke, but it provided no good reason to vote for Chub Peabody.[50]

THE ELECTION GREW LARGER AS IT DREW NEARER. "NOWHERE IN THE 50 states of the Union is there a more important political contest," the *Fitchburg Sentinel* proclaimed. The very idea that a backlash might derail Brooke was an insult to the Bay State, "a libel . . . against the decency and democracy of Massachusetts voters." The Massachusetts electorate would see through any attempts to link Brooke with Stokely Carmichael, thought the Fitchburg editors. The election of Brooke, "an erudite and cultured Negro," would "prove a balm to the ailing Republic." The language varied from newspaper to newspaper, but the thrust was often the same. To many journalists, a Brooke victory could act as a salve.[51]

Massachusetts's prominent place in the nation loomed large in these observations. The editors of Boston's black newspaper, the *Bay State Banner*, recalled how Massachusetts had "swelled with pride" when John F. Kennedy was elected. And they remembered the glow of 1962, when

Brooke became attorney general. Now in 1966, "the people of Massachusetts are again being asked to write history. . . . The BAY STATE BANNER stands proudly for Brooke." The *Holyoke Transcript-Telegram* also invoked the commonwealth's grand history: "Massachusetts has produced giants in national affairs. We have an opportunity to continue this tradition of leadership with the election of Edward W. Brooke. He is worthy of the heritage." Such pronouncements were bright harbingers for the Brooke campaign. Evan Dobelle was giddy in his November 4 report from the field: "All signs are *up*. . . . Definitely we will win overall."[52]

When Brooke appeared on WBZ Radio a night before Halloween, he had told Massachusetts voters that they could stand above appeals to color: "I don't think anyone in Massachusetts is going to vote against me because of a riot that took place in Chicago." As proof of the voters' color-blind capacities, Brooke referenced his last electoral victory. In 1964 he had carried the city of Boston, on the same day that Louise Day Hicks won 70 percent of the vote.[53]

Boston's simultaneous support for Hicks and Brooke showed the complex racial thinking of the electorate. The potential for racism and for tolerance so often existed within the same person. Brooke needed to bring out the voters' better angels while making sure not to awaken their racial fears. It was a balance that would become impossible to strike a decade later, amid the fires of the Boston busing crisis. But in 1966, Brooke could yet pull it off. Northeasterners still saw themselves as leaders in terms of racial progress. Voters remained vulnerable to any campaign able to mobilize that powerful belief.

The *Boston Sunday Herald* proclaimed this "the most important election in state history." Massachusetts would either give America its first elected black senator, or would offer itself as a pacesetter for the white backlash. No third way existed.[54]

One political cartoonist sounded a note of alarm. On the final Sunday before the election, the *Herald*'s editorial page featured a drawing by James J. Dobbins. It pictured Ed Brooke with a bare torso. Blood dripped from his back, as though lashed by a whip. Across his back was stenciled the word, "Backlash." Peering out from the bottom right corner of the cartoon, a tiny creature held a sign that warned, "It Can Happen Here." Massachusetts might display the ferocity of white racism. Yet Dobbins's cartoon had an ambiguous title: "Innocent Victim?" The question mark was haunting. If Brooke was lashed by racism at the polls, was he not an innocent victim? The *Herald* cartoon hinted at a dark undercurrent: the belief that if the backlash surfaced, Brooke would have somehow brought it upon himself.[55]

Brooke knew that the larger atmosphere of racial tension provided an unavoidable backdrop for his campaign. "At that time of racial unrest in the country, you would have thought that Peabody would have been a shoo-in," Brooke recalled many years later. "We played down everything we could which might cause racial unpleasantness. You had race riots, and everything going on at that time. . . . And here I'm right in the middle of it." Brooke attempted to elevate the election to a higher plane. "I was asking the voters to *rise above* all that." He was suggesting that the dignified campaign for the Bay State's Senate seat could—and should—exist on a level apart from racial hostility, violence, and controversy over segregation. Pulling the lever for him was a way for voters to rise above it all.[56]

Days before the election, Brooke issued a press release. He criticized Black Power just as he highlighted themes of common humanity and America's unique promise: "We are all, together, citizens of one nation. We are many races and many creeds, brought here by hope or chance, by faith or fear or by necessity. We have a common responsibility, to ourselves and to the world, to prove that our way of life is more than a few words inscribed in the Declaration of Independence or on the base of the Statue of Liberty." There was one way to breathe life into the claims of America's founding documents: vote for Brooke on Tuesday.[57]

After a long campaign, it was all over in a flash. On Election Day, November 8, both candidates worked full days on the trail and cast votes at their polling places. A crowd of 1,500 Brooke supporters huddled at the Sheraton Plaza Hotel in Boston's Copley Square, tense with anticipation but bubbling with hope. At 7:30 in the evening, the contours of a Brooke victory began to take shape. Holyoke reported a win for Peabody, but by a margin of only 302 votes. In that staunchly Democratic city, Brooke fought Peabody to a virtual standstill. The crowd exploded in cheers. By nine o'clock, Brooke's internal figures showed that he would win handily. It was midnight when Chub Peabody delivered his concession speech.[58]

In the end, Brooke had persuaded the Massachusetts electorate to rise above all the racial unrest in the land. Brooke encouraged white voters to think of themselves as color-blind—the very thing that Robert Carter and NAACP lawyers tried to combat. Voters "didn't consider" the Senate campaign "a racial issue," Brooke asserted. "I think we were somewhat successful in getting them to come around to that thinking. . . . I think they just looked beyond race."[59]

Brooke pounded Peabody throughout the state. He built his strength in the suburbs, where he won 65 percent of the total votes. Statewide, black voters supported Brooke at a clip of 86 percent. Then there was Boston. Out of 193,000 votes in all, Brooke lost the city by 23,000. Brooke won two-thirds of Roxbury's votes, and in the Back Bay he won almost seven out of every ten. The working-class Irish American wards told a different story. Peabody bested Brooke by a 75 to 25 percent margin in South Boston; in Charlestown, the damage was 77 percent to 23 percent. These voters were not *for* Chub Peabody, the Yankee from Cambridge—they were *against* Ed Brooke. On this night, it did not matter. Brooke won by an overall margin of 61 percent to 39 percent.[60]

Shortly after Peabody conceded, Brooke appeared in the hotel's main ballroom. The orchestra struck up "Happy Days Are Here Again." Brooke waded through the crowd, feeling "elated, overjoyed, overwhelmed." In his victory speech, he termed this triumph "the supreme moment of my life." Brooke continued, "This is the answer the world has been waiting for. It proves that the people of Massachusetts judge you on your merit and worth." Those words brought with them "the longest and loudest applause of the evening," the *Boston Globe* reported. Audience members clapped and thundered for Brooke and for themselves: citizens of the color-blind commonwealth.[61]

MASSACHUSETTS OFFERED ITS NEW SENATOR AS A GIFT TO THE NATION. Half of the story was that a black man would be integrating the United States Senate. The other half was that the old Bay State had done it again. Speakers invoked the example of the Pilgrims and the words of Daniel Webster; the ghosts of abolitionists and Radical Republicans danced across the pages of magazines and newspapers. In the afterglow of Brooke's victory, leaders and citizens alike summoned the northern mystique.

Elsewhere in America, racial fears continued to shape politics. Lurleen Wallace became governor of Alabama. In California, Ronald Reagan's "law and order" message carried the day. In the Midwest, two liberal Democrats were stung by defeat: Illinois Senator Paul Douglas and Michigan's G. Mennen Williams. And in New York City, the backlash scored an electoral victory: New Yorkers voted down the Civilian Complaint Review Board, a body that focused on the issue of police brutality. But Massachusetts was different. There the backlash was declared dead on arrival.[62]

Massachusetts citizens saw in Brooke's Senate run an opportunity to realize a triumphal version of their past. A lofty historical image was something to strive toward. It helped to knit the fabric of the Bay State's political culture; it provided the setting for Brooke's campaign. One could no easier tear this historical sheen away from the Bay State than remove collective memories of slavery and segregation from Mississippi or Alabama. The past breathed with life in Ed Brooke's Massachusetts.

In his victory speech, Brooke praised "this great Commonwealth, founded by the Pilgrims," which had "given the country and the world" so many of its political leaders and its heritage of freedom. The day after the election, the *Boston Globe* titled its lead editorial, "There She Is." Brooke's victory "has significance for the world," the editors began. "For it tells all persons on this earth, two-thirds of whom are nonwhite, that in our democracy a Negro can be elected to any public office despite the color of his skin." The *Globe's* editors succumbed to the drama of the moment. "The Bay State today can hold its head high and proudly recall the words of Daniel Webster in 1870: 'I shall enter on no encomium on Massachusetts; she needs none. There she is. Behold her, and judge for yourselves. There is her history; the world knows it by heart.'" Massachusetts elected a black senator, and reveled in its historic claim as the home of the city upon a hill.[63]

One specific historical era was the subject of more than a few analogies: the Civil War and Reconstruction. According to *The Crisis*, "Mr. Brooke will assume the mantle once worn with honor and distinction by . . . Charles Sumner, who brilliantly and uncompromisingly espoused the Negro cause both on and off the Senate floor." The parallel seemed uncanny. The first civil rights bill was passed in 1866. Exactly a century later, Ed Brooke won election to the office that Sumner had occupied. The editors of the *Silver Lake News* certainly hoped that these historical correlations held meaning. From Pembroke, a small town on the South Shore, they wrote, "We can hardly wait to see [Brooke] in action in Washington. It may be the dawn of a new era of Reconstruction." In Massachusetts, it was cause for joy if this bit of history happened twice.[64]

The Boston *Pilot*, a weekly Catholic newspaper, had at least enough perspective to set the story of Brooke's victory within the larger context of race in Boston. The segregation that beset Boston's schools, "and our reluctance to do something positive about it, have been widely exposed in the mass media across the country." The Bay State's good name was dirtied. "It has been easy to believe that racism and bigotry were prevalent here." Such circumstances made Brooke's victory all the more urgent. The Bay State had restored its reputation. There was "something appropriate in the leadership our state has taken." Massachusetts was fulfilling its history:

> The history of this Commonwealth and its people, so proudly recorded in abolitionist times, is a consistent story of concern for the Negro and his problems. In recent years, we can claim to have written on the law books of this state the most advanced legislation protecting civil rights, from the first fair employment laws to the latest imbalance statute. Some people have accused us of passing the laws but not really believing in them, of posturing rather than acting with sincerity. If we needed an answer to this charge, we have it now in unmistakable terms.

More than a million white voters had chosen a black man as their senator. For this feat, "We ask no accolade, and deserve none." Here was Massachusetts being Massachusetts, no more and certainly no less.[65]

Other New Englanders exhibited the natural reaction of one neighbor to the achievement of another. They alternated between pride and envy. Maine's *Lewiston Evening Journal* called Ed Brooke's victory a "refreshing breeze" that gusted along the Atlantic coast. Further inland, the *Monitor & Patriot* of Concord, New Hampshire, cheered the election as "a tribute to Massachusetts voters." Brooke's victory showed how racial politics in New England had changed. It constituted "a hallmark in American political history." In the *Woonsocket Call* of Rhode Island, columnist Edward Berman did not begrudge the Bay State its moment. "Massachusetts voters have a right to be proud," Berman wrote. The election would have lasting import. "What discriminating Massachusetts voters did on Election Day will be long remembered."[66]

THE REACTIONS OF MASSACHUSETTS VOTERS WERE MORE COMPLICATED. One Boston woman criticized media portrayals of Brooke's election. "I voted for Edward Brooke not because he is a Negro but because I felt he was more his own man than Peabody," Carolyn Nemrow explained in a letter to *Time*. She resented the insinuation that the 1966 campaign had pitted racial progressivism against the white backlash. "Newsmen cannot grasp the fact that we are not all liberals with Socialistic tendencies like themselves, but just plain conservatives who still believe in people doing for themselves." Nemrow supported Ed Brooke because she perceived him as more conservative. Indeed, Brooke relied upon Massachusetts conservatives as much as he did civil rights liberals.[67]

Brooke's ambiguity on racial issues helps to explain his broad support among white voters. Boston resident Alyce O'Sullivan demonstrated this with an odd but revealing statement. "In furthering the Negro cause, Senator Edward Brooke is worth a thousand militant civil rights workers. We in Massachusetts are very proud of him." O'Sullivan felt neither threatened nor challenged by Brooke. She expressed pride that Brooke was an African American *and* that he was no "militant." In this light, Brooke's efforts to distance himself from Stokely Carmichael seemed quite successful.[68]

Among African Americans, Brooke gained strident supporters as well as staunch critics. Ben Swan, a leader of Springfield's CORE chapter, counted himself among the latter. "I don't think of him as a humanitarian," Swan said of Brooke. "I think of him as a person primarily interested in winning elections." Swan spoke from his own recent experiences with civil rights struggles in Springfield. He saw Ed Brooke's plight as something quite separate. Swan thought Brooke had sacrificed the larger racial cause on the altar of political victory. To Swan, winning elections was very different from winning freedom and equality. Others did not make such a sharp distinction. Kenneth Guscott, president of the Boston NAACP, saw mass protest and high politics as part of the same broader quest: "We're not stupid enough to think he should be marching on the streets; there's more than one way of advancing the cause." These differences of opinion posed the question of whether electoral politics was part of the larger "cause." Brooke himself tried to have it both ways. He refused to run as a black candidate, and he tried to sidestep racial issues. Yet he never denied that his career was bound up with the long struggle for black equality.[69]

At the time of his election, many observers placed Brooke squarely in the main narrative of the civil rights struggle. They drew a straight line from Jackie Robinson to Ed Brooke. Robinson integrated the national pastime; Brooke desegregated the corridors of power. To *Globe* sportswriter Harold Kaese, Brooke's election was "as inevitable as the next wave breaking on the beach. . . . Because we have learned that talented Negroes will rise to the occasion. Who taught us? Nobody more than the Negro athlete. . . . Hats off to . . . Jackie Robinson and other Negro athletes who did so much blocking out in front of the man now carrying the ball, Edward Brooke." The link between Jackie Robinson's Brooklyn and Ed Brooke's Massachusetts was plain.[70]

Jackie Robinson himself weighed in on Brooke's victory. "Here is a man of whom we can be truly proud," Robinson wrote. He dismissed the suggestions that Brooke was too conservative on racial issues. Robinson had endured the same criticisms; they were standard for the interracial pioneer. "Perhaps he has not done some of the drum-beating and flag-waving that some people would have had him do. There never was any doubt in my mind about Ed Brooke's devotion to his race." Both men had been longtime Republicans; both had scored racial breakthroughs while downplaying the fact of their own race. Both became prominent symbols of black equality.[71]

To so many individuals at the time, Ed Brooke's election was a major event. The Concord, New Hampshire, newspaper called it a "hallmark in American political history." *Amsterdam News* columnist Poppy Cannon White wrote on November 26, "the sweeping victory of Edward Brooke is Topic A across the country." White invested Brooke's election with a transformative power: "The world has moved."[72]

The editors of Boston's *Jewish Advocate* also saw profound meaning in Brooke's election. "We are encouraged by Mr. Brooke's victory, by the lesson it offers the nation and by the hope it can communicate to the tortured soul of some Negro child." The *Advocate* placed Brooke's triumph within a longer historical perspective. "It does not take a seer to know that long after such [men] as [Lester] Maddox and [George] Wallace are forgotten, the nation will remember the day that Attorney General Edward W. Brooke was elected by Massachusetts."[73]

From the vantage point of the twenty-first century, the outstanding fact is that many Americans do remember George Wallace—the Alabama segregationist who stood in the schoolhouse door. Very few, including Massachusetts natives and residents, know the story of Ed Brooke. If this event was such a landmark, if it so moved the world, why is it so little remembered?

Though Brooke compiled a substantial legislative record, he did this quietly. He championed fair housing and school integration. But he was a moderate in a time of tumult, and a liberal Republican during the heyday of the "Southern Strategy." He does not fit with the dominant stories of that era: civil rights, Black Power, white backlash. This very ambiguity often allowed him to float above controversy at the time, and made him attractive to many Massachusetts voters. It also left him out of the main narratives of America in the 1960s and 1970s.

In addition, one must consider the specific racial history of Massachusetts. What many remember about race in Massachusetts during Ed Brooke's career is the Boston busing crisis. They recall white resistance, not interracial politics. When Boston exploded in violence during 1974, this had a way of overshadowing all that had come before.

By the middle of the 1970s, the old promise of interracialism—whether embodied by Jackie Robinson or Ed Brooke—seemed but a distant dream. Whites opposed busing as African Americans struggled for power. The middle ground washed away. Ed Brooke would have been a bizarre totem of this time. An African American would not win another election at the top of a statewide ticket until Douglas Wilder in Virginia in 1989. Another African American would not join the United States Senate until Carol Moseley Braun (from Illinois) in 1992. For decades, Brooke stood as the one great exception.

That is also why he was, for a moment, the bearer of so many hopes: hopes for black equality, for democracy, for an interracial vision of America, for progress in the Northeast. *Pittsburgh Courier* columnist Adolph Slaughter explained the aura that came to surround Ed Brooke. In December 1966, as African Americans anticipated Brooke's entrance into the

Senate, they "ushered in a 'mystique' about a Negro Senator." Slaughter observed that Brooke faced "herculean" expectations, for he carried a race on his shoulders. "All of the divergent views" held by African Americans "would have coalesced into a vote for Brooke had they all lived in the state of Massachusetts." That Brooke tried to downplay his blackness was im-material. "Who really cares—or believes—when Brooke insists that he is a United States Senator who HAPPENS to be a Negro. To the Negro, he is a Negro." His symbolism now outweighed his actions and words. "Like the image and imagery of John F. Kennedy, he can be touched; he can be seen. He, like Kennedy, lives! Furthermore—'he is ours.'" A mys-tique grew around Ed Brooke himself.[74]

TWO DECADES PASSED BETWEEN BROOKE'S DISCHARGE FROM THE ARMY and his election to the United States Senate. His ascent served as a par-able of progress. Brooke showed how high an African American could rise in Massachusetts. But in those same twenty years, a social history of blacks in the Bay State told the opposite tale. This was a story of in-creasing segregation, solidifying ghettoes, deepening black poverty, and endless battles against a resilient white prejudice.

Before the United States entered World War Two, Boston was a city of 770,000, only 3 percent of whom (23,000) were black. By 1967, blacks numbered 90,000, comprising 13 percent of the city's population. They filled up Lower Roxbury and pushed to the edges of many historically white neighborhoods. For thousands of whites, African Americans could no longer loom as an abstraction.[75]

Boston was an insular place, populated mostly by working and middle-class white people. They were not the enlightened purveyors of the northern mystique, but lived paycheck-to-paycheck and shuddered at the prospect of integrated blocks, competition for employment, and challenges to their "neighborhood schools." This was the Boston that came to mind for basketball star Bill Russell. "I realized in my first year" with the Boston Celtics (1956) "this town was basically a racist town, and not very subtle about it." Russell would recall Boston as "a flea market of racism." In June 1966, Roxbury's Patrick Campbell Junior High School invited Russell to speak at graduation. He brought not just congratulations for the graduates, but a warning for their fellow city dwellers. "The fire that consumes Roxbury consumes Boston. The fire will spread."[76]

For many African Americans in Massachusetts, conditions appeared to be getting worse. In Boston, the most prominent marker of racial inequality—and the most contested—was segregation in the schools. One year after the Racial Imbalance Act was passed, the number of imbalanced schools in Boston rose to 46. Campbell Junior High, where Bill Russell spoke, had 16 whites in a student body of 663. At the Gibson School, which gained prominence through Jonathan Kozol's book *Death at an Early Age*, 91 white students attended alongside 535 racial minorities. By 1972, Boston would have 75 imbalanced schools. In violation of the Racial Imbalance Act, the Boston School Committee did nothing.[77]

The Boston School Committee spoke for the Bay State's white majority. An August 1966 poll showed that only 23 percent of Massachusetts residents approved of the Racial Imbalance Act; 60 percent disapproved. In the city of Boston, only 13 percent approved of the law; fully 82 percent disapproved. The percentage of Boston residents who approved (13 percent) approximated the percentage of African Americans in the city. White Bostonians stood uniformly against it. Support for open housing laws was even weaker. Only 17 percent supported open housing laws. Sixty-eight percent of respondents believed that a white owner should be able to refuse to sell his home to an African American. Most Massachusetts residents sided spiritually with the white citizens of Fairfield County, Connecticut, rather than with Jackie Robinson.[78]

Here was the postwar Northeast in miniature. It was a place where African Americans could achieve epic advances in the realm of electoral politics, but where whites seemed unwilling to abide racial equality in everyday life.

ED BROOKE RETURNED TO HIS NATIVE WASHINGTON WITH MORE THAN a little fanfare. On January 10, 1967, Ted Kennedy escorted him down the aisle of the Senate chamber and Brooke was sworn in as a United States Senator. Ninety-one years had passed since Blanche Bruce, an African American from Mississippi, took the Senate oath.

Well-wishers had started to gather at the Senate Office Building at ten in the morning. By one o'clock, more than a thousand people jammed the reception area, spilling into the corridors. Ed and Remigia Brooke arrived at two o'clock and shook hands for the better part of three hours. On February 17, Brooke had the cover of *Time* to himself.

One month later, *Bay State Banner* columnist Mark Grimes probed the underbelly of race relations in Massachusetts. Millions of migrants "have left hostile territory in the South and come to an even more hostile territory, the North," Grimes wrote. They experienced the region at its worst:

> Those poor folks who came North expecting things to be better have discovered the horrible truth, it's no better up here than it was down there . . . but there has been a change in these people . . . they came North prepared to do battle with city governments . . . and scared hell out of the bigots who now realize the black man is a force to contend with . . . one way or the other. The showdown is coming, and in the not too distant future.

Grimes warned of the racial cataclysms that would shake Boston.[79]

A showdown came to Roxbury on June 3, 1967. That day, a group of black mothers staged a sit-in at the Grove Hall Welfare Center. Their grievances had been simmering. In June 1966, a group called Mothers for Adequate Welfare had met with Boston welfare commissioner William Lally. They requested extra money for Thanksgiving and Christmas dinners, and asked that their children not be labeled "illegitimate." Lally demurred. The mothers sought meetings with other municipal officials; they were repeatedly treated with indignity. So on June 3, 1967, once inside Grove Hall, the mothers chained themselves to various parts of the building. Police officers removed their badges, entered the welfare office, snipped the chains, and dragged the women out to the sidewalk. Crowds formed. Stones and bottles were thrown, and by the time darkness fell, about one thousand people had gathered. Soon they were "at war with 1,700 blue-helmeted police," the *Amsterdam News* reported. A riot raged on Blue Hill Avenue for three days.[80]

The upheaval did not come out of nowhere. In March and April of 1966, the Massachusetts Advisory Committee to the United States Commission on Civil Rights had convened open hearings on the state of Boston's black neighborhoods. The committee concluded: "Feelings of alienation, bitterness, discouragement, and hopelessness were evident in the statements of almost every person" who spoke. They told of "deplorable conditions" in housing, employment, and education. It was "impossible to overstate the indignation and despair" expressed by blacks who testified. The larger statistical portrait reinforced that testimony. The 1960 census showed that one-half of Boston's African Americans lived in dilapidated housing; infant death rates were high; and the black unemployment rate was twice that of whites. "The Negro in Boston is caught in a vicious cycle," South End resident Rowena Stewart testified. "It starts when he comes into the ghetto where a rental agency refers him to a landlord who thrives on newcomers." It continued on to the "broken-down" room that he rented, one "that is rat infested and has cockroaches," with "holes in the ceiling." It was a cycle with no end. Poor housing combined with low incomes and inferior education to keep Boston's black population on the bottom rung.[81]

African Americans lamented the fact that they had no outlet for their disaffection. No officials would listen, nor would any local politicians act on their behalf. Reverend Gilbert Caldwell charged that "much of the energy being expended in Boston in the area of race relations seems to be concerned with devising ways in which to say that there is no problem." A. Robert Phillips, a longtime Roxbury resident, found himself "shocked at the blatant disrespect and disregard the city of Boston has shown for the citizens of Roxbury." Boston was "the only major city in the nation whose School Committee boasts of its inability to recognize a badly deteriorating school system." If School Committee members and city councilors would not acknowledge the existence of segregation or the presence of inequality, there was no discussion to be had. "You have no way to communicate with anybody," testified Charles Evans, an unemployed resident of the South End. "You can't find a decent job or a decent place to live." Evans concluded: "Being a Negro in Boston is the worst thing in the world."[82]

Except, of course, if that individual happened to be a United States senator. In Massachusetts, and there alone, both realities were possible.

FIVE

Shirley Chisholm's Place

Winning New York's 12th Congressional District (1968)

O NE YEAR AFTER ED BROOKE TOOK THE OATH OF OFFICE, SHIRLEY Chisholm opened up another set of political possibilities on an entirely different terrain.

African Americans flocked to Brooklyn from near and far. They came from the rural South, fired by visions of freedom. Many thousands emigrated from the Caribbean, opening stores and eateries amid the brownstones and the projects. Others embarked on shorter treks, boarding the A train that whisked them from Harlem to Brooklyn, hoping they would find the air of *this* New York City just a little less constraining. With the influx of these groups, Bedford-Stuyvesant became, in the words of the *New York Times*, the "country's largest Negro area." This populace found its political champion in Shirley Chisholm.[1]

She is known to history as the first black woman to serve in the United States Congress, and as both the first woman and the first African American to mount a nationwide campaign for president. Chisholm and her Bedford-Stuyvesant home can seem like perfect foils for Ed Brooke and his "color-blind commonwealth." Chisholm represented a single urban area with a black majority; Brooke traversed a mostly white state that contained only one large city. And while Brooke approached his own racial identity as a political problem to manage (or elude) on the campaign trail, Chisholm explicitly embraced her blackness as well as her womanhood.

At the level of national politics, Bedford-Stuyvesant voters had been powerless. In 1961, the New York state legislature enacted a law that broke the sprawling black neighborhood into so many jagged fragments. The 10th Congressional District took in a slice of Bedford-Stuyvesant along with East Flatbush, Park Slope, and Brownsville. Emanuel Celler represented this area in the United States Congress. John Rooney's 14th district wound along the waterfront neighborhoods of Williamsburg, Greenpoint, Brooklyn Heights, Carroll Gardens, Cobble Hill, Red Hook, and Bay Ridge. It also included a sliver of Bedford-Stuyvesant. Edna Kelly's 12th district encompassed Crown Heights, Flatbush, and Kensington, and swooped through the heart of Bedford-Stuyvesant. The 15th district, represented by Hugh Carey, began near the Brooklyn Navy Yard and snaked slightly inland for some twelve miles, down to the Verrazano Bridge. These four white politicians—Celler, Rooney, Kelly, and Carey—represented one community of African Americans.[2]

Although Brooklyn possessed one of America's largest black areas, all of the borough's congressional districts held white majorities. This began to change under the weight of federal legislation and a series of court rulings. The Supreme Court's 1964 decision in *Reynolds v. Sims*, known as the "One Man, One Vote" ruling, outlawed systems of gerrymandering that diluted the voting power of racial minorities. While this was aimed at enfranchising black voters in the Deep South, blacks in Brooklyn glimpsed its potential to transform New York City politics. In 1967, a Federal Statutory Court directed the New York state legislature to redraw Brooklyn's congressional districts.

The new 12th Congressional District, created in 1968, would envelop all of Bedford-Stuyvesant. But not only that. It also included much of Bushwick and parts of Crown Heights, Williamsburg, and Greenpoint. African American residents were at its heart and in its majority. Yet they alone would not determine the identity of the new representative. The successful politician would have to build a multiracial coalition, winning over blacks in Bedford-Stuyvesant—who were themselves a diverse lot in terms of origin and culture—as well as the Italians of Bushwick, the Jews of Crown Heights, the Polish Catholics of Greenpoint, and the Hasidim and Puerto Ricans of Williamsburg. Shirley Chisholm would later be portrayed as a black politician who enlisted in the black struggle, and as a champion of women's causes. Indeed, she would portray herself this way. But the key to her electoral success lay elsewhere. She built multiracial alliances and spoke many languages—both literally and metaphorically. The pitch of Chisholm's campaign revealed her not so much as Ed Brooke's opposite, but as a kindred spirit.

The story of Chisholm's election holds within it a profound irony. In order to win a seat in the United States Congress, and thus to become a symbol for African Americans and for women across the land, she first had to win the Democratic primary in one slice of Brooklyn. And to emerge victorious in that primary, she had to reach above and beyond her base of African American voters in Bedford-Stuyvesant. She carried parts of the 12th Congressional District where white voters held political clout.

And she stands as a transitional figure in the larger history of the northern mystique. She still represented the interracial promise of the early- and mid-1960s, yet she won office at a time when the racial divide in Brooklyn—as in the Northeast—grew ever wider.

To understand Chisholm's ceiling-shattering victory, the local context is everything.

Joe's Restaurant, a diner on Court Street in Carroll Gardens, loomed large in Brooklyn politics. Stanley Steingut and his lieutenants plotted over breakfast each morning in Joe's back room. Steingut headed the Kings County Democratic Party. From Joe's he dispensed favors, collected on debts, devised electoral strategies, crafted policies, and pulled the levers of Brooklyn's Democratic machine.[3]

The Kings County Democratic Party was the largest Democratic organization in America. The *New Yorker* noted the Brooklyn machine's ability to "turn its vote on like a faucet." When Brooklyn Democratic politics stand in for Northeastern politics, the notion of a northern mystique becomes easier to dismiss. From the vantage point of Joe's back room, the

Northeast looked not like a bastion of progressivism but a world rough and raw.[4]

If Joe's Restaurant was the unofficial locus of Democratic power in Brooklyn, the headquarters of the Madison Club often acted as the official one. Located at 739 Eastern Parkway in Crown Heights, the "chocolate-colored" three-story brownstone displayed a sign that read: "Democratic Club 18th A.D." This was Stanley Steingut's clubhouse. New York City contained hundreds of Democratic clubhouses with names such as the Tally-ho Democratic Club and the Tilden Club. Voters in each assembly district elected a district leader, a coleader, and an assemblyman. The reigning club's leaders picked who would run for those offices and who would reap their spoils. District captains walked the streets, rang doorbells, and returned phone calls. They helped with welfare claims and spots in public housing, and even distributed Thanksgiving turkeys. While the idea of a political machine suggests images of rigid hierarchy, this world of the Brooklyn clubhouses was in fact quite decentralized. All politics were local. Within the Democratic Party itself, clubs and districts competed for leverage and power.[5]

The 1960s were trying years for the Brooklyn Democratic machine. "Participatory democracy" was more than just a catchphrase. Americans craved an active role in the political decisions that affected their lives. It was an era of big ideas, grand visions, political rebellion, and cultural creativity. The regular political organizations offered no such novelty. They prided themselves on a kind of "workaday responsiveness" to the needs of their constituents. In the 1960s, Americans searched for answers to issues on a much larger scale: issues of racial injustice, war overseas, and personal and collective liberation. Party machines fit poorly within this emergent political culture. And new technology added another wrinkle. With the advent of television, political candidates could bypass the regular party organizations and take their message directly to the voters. Furthermore, in large northern cities like Brooklyn, the swelling black migration changed the calculus of local politics. The machines had to adapt to these sweeping transformations in demography, technology, and political culture. They would either adjust or perish.[6]

The Democratic organizations in New York City had already met one of their foes: reform. In 1949, a group of World War Two veterans on Manhattan's Upper East Side formed the Lexington Democratic Club.

They were idealistic liberals from the middle class, and they soon took control of the 9th Assembly District. Eleanor Roosevelt and Herbert Lehman helped to found an organization called the Committee for Democratic Voters. It endorsed reformers across the city. District by district, reformers challenged the old Democrats—setting up rival clubhouses, dispatching their own captains to the streets, and running candidates for office. This was a fight for the soul of the Democratic Party in New York City: a civil war. As of 1966, some 25,000 New Yorkers belonged to reform clubs—among them ten assemblymen, five state senators, and one borough president. Twenty-four reform clubs had established themselves in Manhattan; the Bronx boasted nine reform clubs, and Queens possessed six. But in Brooklyn, the most populous borough, only four reform clubs had emerged. While the wheels of the old machines were slowing all across New York City, Stanley Steingut kept his apparatus in motion.[7]

SHIRLEY CHISHOLM TESTED THE WATERS OF BOTH POLITICAL WORLDS. First, she dipped her toes into the pools of the old clubhouses. In the late 1940s, Chisholm attended weekly meetings at Vincent Carney's Democratic Club in the 17th Assembly District. Carney's organization was comprised mostly of Irish Americans, though the district included a wide swath of Bedford-Stuyvesant. Chisholm participated in these meetings week after week, year after year, alternately trying to gain a foothold in the organization and challenging the local leadership.

In 1953, Chisholm joined with other black leaders in an effort to elect Lewis Flagg (an African American) as a civil court judge. The movement for Flagg grew into the Bedford-Stuyvesant Political League. In 1954, the League ran a slate of candidates against the machine Democrats. Yet African Americans split their votes among multiple black candidates, and Vincent Carney's regulars prevailed. Chisholm continued to attend meetings at the regular Democratic club even as she worked in the League. She held on to the hope of reforming politics from within.

Chisholm soon butted heads with Wesley "Mac" Holder, founder of the Bedford-Stuyvesant Political League. She left the organization in 1958. Two years later, Chisholm joined the Unity Democratic Club (UDC). Attorney Thomas Jones, a "golden-tongued orator," had constructed the UDC through his contacts with Jewish radicals and politically active African Americans. The UDC's goal, as Chisholm explained, was to "take over the entire Seventeenth Assembly District political organization and to boot out the failing but still potent white machine." The UDC made common cause with a group of local white reformers. Though their candidates were defeated in the 1960 campaign, they had lit the spark of the reform movement in Bedford-Stuyvesant. Neither Vincent Carney nor Stanley Steingut would extinguish it.[8]

Chisholm was a fitting symbol of this unique urban area. In a black neighborhood comprised of immigrants from the Caribbean, native New Yorkers, and migrants from the South, Chisholm had both Brooklyn and Barbados in her blood. With the triple consciousness of being black, female, and American to boot, she knew what it was like to navigate multiple worlds. Chisholm's background had prepared her to become the consummate outsider-insider.

Shirley St. Hill was born in Brooklyn in 1924, the child of Caribbean immigrants. At the age of three, she sailed with her mother, Ruby, and her sisters to Barbados. Shirley attended elementary school in the British-based educational system, acquiring a distinctive manner of speech that would stay with her through the decades. In 1934, the St. Hill family reunited in Brooklyn. They settled at first in Brownsville. Chisholm retained vivid memories of Brownsville's Saturday morning rituals: "We would sneak out and sit on the fire escape and watch Jewish people pray at the synagogue." She attended Public School 84, which was mostly Jewish and about 80 percent white. Ruby St. Hill worked as a domestic in Jewish homes, and also counted some Jewish women as close friends. This upbringing invested Shirley with "a certain affinity for the Jewish people. . . . Jewish people seem to understand me." Chisholm's earliest American memories came as a black girl in a poor Jewish neighborhood. It was an experience that would serve her well in the 1960s.[9]

The St. Hill family lived in four different Brooklyn homes over the course of a decade, including those on Ralph Avenue and Patchen Avenue in Bedford-Stuyvesant. Shirley's parents had both been backers of Marcus Garvey. Charles St. Hill was a proud union man and a major influence on his eldest daughter. In college, Shirley cemented her own interest in political affairs. She attended Brooklyn College, thrived in the classroom, and joined the local branch of the NAACP.[10]

Chisholm graduated in 1946, when few career paths beckoned to black women. The teaching profession was one of them. She was turned down for numerous teaching jobs, but finally found employment as a nursery school teacher. She also decided to enroll at Columbia University's Teachers College. Chisholm worked by day, attended classes at night, and participated regularly in the local political clubs. She married Conrad Chisholm, a private investigator born in Jamaica. In 1959, she took a position with the City Division of Day Care. Chisholm had moved, finally and ineluctably, into government.[11]

In 1962, the Unity Democratic Club ran its own candidates in the local elections. Thomas Jones won a seat in the New York State Assembly, and Ruth Goring was elected district leader. Chisholm exulted: "The white organization was dead at last in Bedford-Stuyvesant." The truth was more complicated. Many white leaders entered into interracial alliances, and tried to absorb African Americans within the existing party structure.[12]

Chisholm's opening appeared in 1964, when a spot was vacated on the civil court. Steingut, seeking to appease the growing number of black voters on the Democratic rolls, looked for a black judge to fill the vacancy. Thomas Jones made known his interest in the court. As Jones prepared to leave the New York State Assembly, Chisholm announced her candidacy for that assembly seat.

Chisholm eventually gained the UDC's endorsement, but only after she won over several skeptical men. In an assembly district that was more than 80 percent black, the regular machine mounted merely "token opposition." Chisholm won the Democratic primary with ease. In the general election, she garnered almost 90 percent of the vote. She was off to Albany—the only black woman in the New York State Assembly.[13]

Meanwhile, changes had coursed through the UDC in 1963 and 1964. Jones worried that his ties to white leftists would endanger his chances for the judgeship. He initiated a red-baiting campaign to push the radicals out of the organization. According to some former members of the UDC, Jones used Shirley Chisholm as his "hatchet-person." In this saga, Chisholm's actions were at odds with the images of principled radicalism and righteous independence that she would later project. Chisholm dirtied her hands in order to advance politically.[14]

Once in Albany, Chisholm defied Stanley Steingut. The Democrats had swept into the majority in 1964, and Steingut mounted a bid for Speaker of the Assembly. His opponent was Anthony Travia, the longtime Democratic minority leader in the assembly. Travia led a rival faction of Brooklyn Democrats who were allied with New York City mayor Robert Wagner. Thomas Jones had grown close to Steingut; thus Steingut assumed he could count on Shirley Chisholm's support. But Chisholm decided to back Travia. She explained that she thought Travia's work as minority leader had earned him a chance at the speakership. She was already flashing her sharp political skills. She played two machine politicians against each other, and served notice that her vote could not be taken for granted.[15]

In her first term, Chisholm helped to pass legislation that established the Search for Education, Elevation, and Knowledge (SEEK) program, which provided college funds to disadvantaged students; she also cosponsored a state law that would grant unemployment insurance for domestic workers. Another of Chisholm's bills ensured that female schoolteachers could not have their tenure rights imperiled by pregnancy.[16]

Shirley Chisholm crunched the voting numbers on November 2, 1965. Chisholm, an assemblywoman at the time, was running for reelection. In 1968, she would win a seat in the United States Congress—becoming the first black woman on Capitol Hill. ROGER HIGGINS, STAFF PHOTO, *NEW YORK WORLD-TELEGRAM AND THE SUN* NEWSPAPER PHOTOGRAPH COLLECTION, LIBRARY OF CONGRESS.

Chisholm endured what she called the "unfortunate experience of having had to run for office three times in three years." She won in 1965 and again in 1966. All over Brooklyn, district lines were in flux. Politicians could count on nothing.[17]

FOR EDNA KELLY, THESE CHANGES SPELLED DOOM. KELLY GOT HER start in politics in 1942, when Irwin Steingut (Stanley's father, who was himself the Speaker of the New York State Assembly) hired her as a research director in Albany. She rose through the Democratic ranks, and in 1949 won election to the United States Congress from Brooklyn's 12th Congressional District. This district contained Stanley Steingut's assembly district as well as his home. Although Kelly was reelected nine times, Steingut would ultimately hasten her demise.[18]

Kelly served on the House Foreign Relations subcommittee and gained a reputation as an arch anticommunist. She was no leftist. Yet her congressional district encompassed the liberal Jewish neighborhoods of Flatbush and Crown Heights as well as a large chunk of Bedford-Stuyvesant. Kelly held on to her seat in Congress only "by virtue of the machine," asserted Marshall Dubin, a local labor organizer and a white member of the UDC. "She wasn't representative of the people in the district in any manner, shape, or form—racially or ideologically." While Kelly continued to receive the support of party leaders, she drifted further away from the residents of her district.[19]

In the summer of 1967, violence erupted in Bedford-Stuyvesant. At the local police precinct, Kelly reportedly encouraged officers to "shoot to kill." She disputed that account, but it fit with her image in the neighborhood: as a congresswoman terribly out of touch with her African American constituents. She had already fended off election challenges from reformers in 1964 and 1966. Even if Kelly's congressional district had stayed intact in 1968, there was no guarantee that she could hold on to her seat.[20]

The courts never gave her that chance. In June 1966, a black activist and journalist named Andrew Cooper filed a lawsuit. He asked a United States District Court to prevent congressional elections in Brooklyn until the district lines were redrawn. He described how Bedford-Stuyvesant's African Americans had been partitioned "in so tortuous, artificial and labyrinthine a manner" as to strip them of political power. Shirley Chisholm agreed. "You have minimized whatever potential power we had," she said in a later interview. "You have come into Bedford-Stuyvesant, you've taken a ruler and a pencil and you have chopped us up in about four or five different ways so as to be sure that each of these little areas are attached to a white congressman." If the term "gerrymander" had not existed, Chisholm wrote, "it would have been necessary to invent it." In May 1967, the court ruled unanimously that the 1961 reapportionment had been unconstitutional. Legislators would have to draw a new map. In December 1967, the United States Supreme Court upheld that decision.[21]

So Stanley Steingut added one more item to his breakfast docket. He helped to supervise the drawing of district lines. The new 12th Congressional District would encompass almost all of Bedford-Stuyvesant along with parts of Bushwick, Williamsburg, Greenpoint, and Crown Heights. The rest of Edna Kelly's district—Flatbush, Kensington, and Borough Park—was folded in with much of Emanuel Celler's old district. In February 1968, the New York state legislature voted to enact these changes. As the plan awaited final approval from the courts, Celler and Kelly both lashed out in anger. Said Celler, "I don't believe in carving out a new district for the Negro. It's segregation in reverse." Edna Kelly's resentment was more personal. She felt betrayed. According to Kelly, Stanley Steingut and his cronies had conspired to end her career. Kelly accused Steingut of "bossism" and "discrimination." If she wished to remain in the United States Congress, she would either have to challenge Celler in his own backyard or campaign in a district with a black majority. The elder Steingut had started Kelly's political career; the younger, acceding to changes in race and demography, now tried to end it.[22]

Steingut altered the color of the 12th Congressional District. By the beginning of the twenty-first century, many parts of that district— namely, Williamsburg and Greenpoint—would represent America's cultural frontier. Today, hipsters rule the streets; cold-brewed coffee fills the cafés; locally raised pork sits on every restaurant table. In the late-1960s, these neighborhoods—at least in the eyes of their boosters—had embodied urban America's last best hope.

During a time of urban riots and the hollowing of the inner cities nationwide, local leaders touted Williamsburg and Greenpoint for the happy diversity that they fostered. In Williamsburg, Yiddish and Spanish could be heard frequently. Greenpoint added large numbers of Polish Americans, Italian Americans, and Irish Americans to the ethnic mix. These neighborhoods had formed the heart of the 14th Congressional District, John Rooney's terrain.

As the "urban crisis" wore on, neighborhood leaders hoped for increased resources from the city. Writing in support of the proposed Kent Village Urban Renewal Project at the end of 1967, the editors of the *Greenpoint Weekly Star* hailed District 14 as "composite urban America. It would be wrong to say (as WNYC does) that these people live in peace and harmony. But so far they have channeled their rivalries without major violence, without major dislocation." The editors urged city officials to invest in job-creation programs and urban renewal. In so doing, New York City's leaders would "help us make diversity work." But without such funds, the neighborhoods might fall victim to the forces that were fracturing cities across America. "The alternative is to prove that the only way that works today is Black Power or Jewish Power or Spanish Power or White Power." The Greenpoint weekly championed a version of multiracial democracy. On February 23, 1968, the *Star* insisted: "If the city is to succeed . . . in the inner city struggle, it is either in Greenpoint and Williamsburg or no place." If urban interracialism could work anywhere, it was there.[23]

One week later, Greenpoint's leaders sang a different tune. The state legislature had just announced the altered congressional district lines. It sliced off large pieces of John Rooney's district, and thrust several sections of Greenpoint and Williamsburg into the new 12th district. Politicians and voters immediately understood the racial implications of this move. James Amelia, the leader of the 35th Assembly District, complained that his "political home base" had been placed within the "new 'Bedford-Stuyvesant Congressional District.'" Others shared his disgust. Anthony DeRosa, who was an officer in the Peoples Regular Democratic Club of the 35th Assembly District, said the new lines "now connect about a dozen election districts in the Greenpoint vicinity to the Bedford-Stuyvesant community." DeRosa lashed out at Greenpoint's state senator, Edward Lentol, who had voted in favor of this plan. "I will fight Mr. Lentol for playing political games for which we citizens of this community must pay . . . in spades."[24]

The phrase was no idle cliché. Whites in Greenpoint felt they would be ripped from their "natural" political home and moved forcibly into an African American district. A black politician would represent them. "I have nothing against Bedford-Stuyvesant having a congressman," said Joseph Savino, leader of the Knickerbocker Democrat Club, "but I call cutting up the 35th A.D. in this way as unnecessary to achieve that aim. The lines are unfair." Anthony DeRosa further faulted Lentol for "voting away the southern part of the assembly district." This portion of the neighborhood would be lost forever.[25]

In the doomsday vision, Greenpoint would be subordinated to Bedford-Stuyvesant, homeowners to tenants, the working and middle classes to the destitute, the upstanding to the criminal, and the needs of a majority-white community would be subsumed by those of the black ghetto. The *Greenpoint Weekly Star* editorialized: "The newly enacted congressional district lines hurt Greenpoint." Leaders of Williamsburg and Greenpoint touted the racial diversity of their neighborhoods just as they insisted that their political district should maintain a white voting majority.[26]

Residents of Greenpoint and Williamsburg were not the only white Brooklynites who confronted a new political plight. In Crown Heights, Judith Berek actually appreciated the integrated character of the redrawn 12th Congressional District. "I think it's very good that the district doesn't end on Eastern Parkway. It comes over into an area which is probably predominantly white, although I would say completely integrated." The legislature's "objectives were not to make a black district, but a fair district." She believed the legislature had succeeded.[27]

While Berek lauded the new district's multiracial character, and while Greenpoint leaders feared this composition, many observers had not even recognized that such a racial mix existed. They still asserted that the new district would be an African American district. As Shirley Chisholm herself declared, the legislators "created a district which would now ensure the election of a black person to Congress."[28]

There was nothing inevitable about such a result. On March 5, 1968, the group that had originally filed the lawsuit over gerrymandering now updated its complaint. Paul Kerrigan, a coplaintiff and a reformer, sounded a note of alarm. For all of the griping in Greenpoint and Williamsburg, the legislature had only "*appeared* to create a black district in the new 12th CD," Kerrigan noted. That appearance could deceive:

> By including heavily white areas in Bushwick and Crown Heights, the Legislature created a district in which the ethnic ratio of registered voters—as opposed to gross population—is about 50–50. The apparent attainment of long-awaited representation for the people of Bedford-Stuyvesant can turn out to be a vicious delusion.

Kerrigan charged that the legislature had strengthened the position of white incumbents. It increased the percentage of white voters in John Rooney's 14th district. It carved up the Puerto Rican areas of Williamsburg, pushing some of them into the 12th Congressional District. At the same time, the 12th district included enough whites from Bushwick and Crown Heights to dilute the votes of those racial minorities. "The new districts . . . are still clearly drawn to benefit the clubhouse politicians. They are designed to curb Reform movements and to keep Negro and Puerto Rican representation to a minimum." According to Kerrigan, the legislature had created the impression of empowering racial minorities just as it bolstered the reelection prospects of many white incumbents.[29]

Leaders of the Pioneer Democratic Club considered running an Italian American candidate in the congressional primary. They believed that several African American candidates might split the black vote, and that Bushwick and Greenpoint housed enough Italians to elect the Pioneer candidate. For the same reason that Italian Americans saw opportunity in the new district, Felix Cosme was moved to outrage. Cosme, a Puerto Rican and a candidate for the state senate, argued that Williamsburg's Puerto Rican population had been split down the middle. Puerto Ricans would have clout neither in the 12th district nor in the 14th. The election of a racial minority was far from fated.[30]

The *New York Times* overstated the power of white voters—but only by a little. "Although the white population makes up only half the district," Martin Tolchin reported, "they vote in much greater numbers than the Negroes." In reality, white residents constituted about one-third of the population in the 12th Congressional District. Blacks accounted for slightly less than 60 percent of the population, and Puerto Ricans for almost 10 percent. But Tolchin was right about the fact that whites registered, and voted, in much higher numbers. Among registered voters, whites made up at least 45 percent of the district.[31]

Stanley Steingut understood this. He knew that the right white candidate might have been able to win the Democratic primary. But Steingut was not opposed to an African American congressman in the 12th district. This could help to make Bedford-Stuyvesant and its black voters loyal parts of the Brooklyn Democratic machine. Heeding Steingut's wishes, the Democratic clubhouses put forth no white nominees. Furthermore, the Kings County Democratic organization decided not to back any particular black candidate. The voters would decide.[32]

So was born a "black district," containing one of America's largest black areas, primed to send an African American to Congress, in which nearly half of the registered voters were white.

SHIRLEY CHISHOLM LAUNCHED HER CANDIDACY IN DECEMBER 1967, two months before the legislature released its final redistricting plan. The Committee for a Negro Congressman from Brooklyn (CNC) had worked for several years to try to end the gerrymander, and it had run African Americans for Congress within the existing district lines. Late in December, after the Supreme Court's ruling, the CNC moved fast to choose a candidate. The committee was composed of community leaders—not only African Americans but also white Brooklynites and Puerto Ricans. Committee members interviewed about a dozen potential candidates; Chisholm was the only woman. The CNC then reached out to Chisholm. "It was about three days before Christmas," Chisholm remembered. "About a quarter to twelve that night . . . I got a call. . . . I'll never forget this, I don't know where they got all the phones from, but it was a Jewish man on one wire, a Puerto Rican man, and a black man. All wanted to break the news to me." The committee had agreed unanimously to endorse Chisholm. "That was my Christmas present, 1967."[33]

Calculation more than sentiment drove the CNC's decision. Knowing neither the precise shape of the new district nor whether Steingut would run his own candidate, the CNC wanted an individual with a proven record of turning out votes. The CNC also cited Chisholm's "political independence." It released a statement on December 28, 1967: "The

Bedford-Stuyvesant community is resolved to see to it that the white machine bosses no longer call the tune for black people." Chisholm formally announced her candidacy in January. She emphasized many programs for the working class: low-cost housing, quality education, and federal support for day care and hospital facilities.[34]

As the contours of the congressional district hardened at the end of February, Chisholm's opponents came into focus. Two other African Americans jockeyed for position. In early March, state senator William C. Thompson declared his intention to run for the Democratic nomination. So did Dollie Robinson, former Secretary of the New York Department of Labor. On March 20, 1968, the federal court approved the state legislature's new congressional map. As Chisholm recalled, "And here is where the big fight starts."[35]

Thompson and Robinson gathered important political endorsements. On Easter Sunday, Reverend Gardner C. Taylor endorsed Dollie Robinson in front of his four-thousand-member congregation at Concord Baptist Church. Robinson also won the support of Bertram Baker. Of the nine assemblymen whose districts fell within the new 12th Congressional District, Baker was the only one (aside from Chisholm herself) to openly back a congressional candidate. The seven other assemblymen, as the *Amsterdam News* reported, "have shown an unwillingness to take sides or to name a candidate at the risk of being accused of 'White bossism.'" This was central to Stanley Steingut's thinking. He wanted to avoid the perception of meddling in the political affairs of the black community. In Bedford-Stuyvesant, the white machine's official endorsement might have acted as the kiss of death.[36]

Shirley Chisholm told a different version of this story. She felt that Steingut opposed her, but that he wanted to avoid publicizing this. In Chisholm's eyes, the CNC's endorsement—combined with her general popularity in Bedford-Stuyvesant—had established her as the clear choice of the people. If any other candidate had possessed this kind of backing, the Kings County Democratic Committee would have announced its support for that person. It was unthinkable for the organization not to choose a candidate at all. This was one of the organization's raisons d'être. The new congressional district "embraces a vast area," Chisholm explained, "and unless you have the political leadership in back of you in each of these areas, it's hell on wheels." But "they couldn't agree on anybody. . . . Never before had the organization left the decision to the people." This was not a gesture of largesse toward the voters. "The reason it was done . . . is because they knew that the sentiment of this community was for Shirley Chisholm." She concluded, "The whole thing that bothered so many of these professional politicians is that I cannot be disciplined." In the end, the leaders did not remain neutral. They settled on someone else.[37]

The Kings County Democratic Party's support of William C. Thompson became the worst-kept secret of the campaign. The *Amsterdam News* explained that Thompson had been "tabbed" as "Brooklyn's first nonwhite congressman." According to the *New York Times*, this fact was "widely reported." As Chisholm recalled, "Everyone knew that silently they were backing the senator. . . . Thompson was the kind of person that they felt they could work with. . . . But you see they didn't want to come out openly for Senator Thompson because it would be thwarting the will of the people." Chisholm seized on this. She could paint Thompson as the candidate of the Democratic organization, and Dollie Robinson as the lackey of Brooklyn's black power brokers. Chisholm thus presented herself as the only candidate of the people. It was a brilliant bit of political marketing. She alone, as her campaign pins would declare and as her volunteers would blare through so many megaphones, stood "Unbought and Unbossed."[38]

This slogan had the potential to cut across racial and geographic lines. It could appeal to any individual who felt that the men in power had overlooked his or her interests. It might resonate as deeply with a young black mother in Bedford-Stuyvesant as with an elderly Jew in Crown Heights. And the "unbossed" part of Chisholm's slogan contained an obvious double meaning. She was a strong woman who portrayed herself as apart from the political machine.

In effect, two Democratic primaries would take place: one in the majority-black neighborhood of Bedford-Stuyvesant, and the other in the four neighborhoods that had large numbers of white voters. The new congressional district held 73,000 registered Democrats. Among the white voters, 16,000 were concentrated in Bushwick, with another 17,000 scattered through Greenpoint, Williamsburg, and Crown

Heights. Chisholm realized that African Americans' votes were "going to be divided in the Black Belt" among three different black candidates. And she was concerned that African Americans might not make it to the polls in significant numbers. Thus, white voters "could be the balance of power." As Chisholm put it: "I knew that if I had to beat William Thompson . . . I would have to garnish the votes in the Bushwick area." Each candidate had to develop one message that would play in Bedford-Stuyvesant, and another to win over neighborhoods with more white voters. Yet the two messages had to cohere.[39]

In a vast and diverse urban area, Chisholm wished to present herself personally to all of the different groups. "All I was doing was marching, night after night after night in the ten [assembly] areas. Jewish people's homes, black people's homes, Puerto Rican people's homes, churches, every place I could go. Anybody who wanted me, I was running." She was not above the time-honored practice of culinary pandering. "In the black neighborhood I ate chitlins, in the Jewish neighborhood bagels and lox, in the Puerto Rican neighborhood arroz con pollo." She also relied on the deft strategies of Wesley "Mac" Holder. Chisholm and Holder had long since resolved their differences, and Holder signed on as Chisholm's campaign chief. Chisholm allowed, "I didn't know what was going on in terms of finances, committees to raise money for me. I didn't know what was going on in terms of papers being put out." Holder handled all of those details.[40]

Before his career in politics, Holder had worked as a statistician—first for the War Production Board and then for the district attorney's office in Brooklyn. Holder informed Chisholm that in the 12th district women outnumbered men on the voting rolls by about 2.5 to 1. The difference was 3 to 1 in Bedford-Stuyvesant. This gave Chisholm all the more reason to concentrate on black women. As their assemblywoman, she was already their champion. As the first black woman in Congress, she could become their hero. "The women are fierce about Shirley," Conrad Chisholm remarked. "She can pick up the phone and call 200 women and they'll be here in an hour." Chisholm's campaign truck would roll up to a public housing project like the Breevort Houses, announce the candidate's arrival, and watch the women pour out onto the sidewalks. The black women of Bedford-Stuyvesant formed the heart and soul of her campaign.[41]

Thompson was perceived as the front-runner, and Chisholm the underdog. Thompson believed that he would win big in the white areas where Steingut's network could deliver the votes. "Willie felt the white boys would get the vote out for him," Chisholm recalled. Bushwick "was strong for Senator Thompson." In response, Chisholm waged a grassroots campaign. "I knew that if I had to make inroads to beat the senator in these areas, that I would have to really go out and develop my own organization, my own contacts." She mapped "a tremendous campaign that went all the way to the Kings County line."[42]

The road to Washington traveled through Bushwick. "I told my husband, 'I'm leaving you for three days, honey. Come and visit me. . . . Check on me every night, see what I'm doing, but I have to live for three days in Bushwick. . . . I have to organize." She reached out to women's organizations. "I have to go into the three big housing projects in that area and take my story to the women in those buildings." She contended that Thompson and Steingut were playing the gender card. The *Amsterdam News* referred to this as "'male image' propaganda." And some male voters were responding. "Although I did not want to interject the sex angle in the campaign, I was forced to bring it into the open. Because the undercurrent of, 'we don't want a woman, we don't want a woman,' was really beginning to get in my way." Chisholm pursued a three-pronged strategy in Bushwick: she made a pitch to the women, against sexism; she touted her own political independence, in contrast to the Democratic machine; and she focused on grassroots organizing.[43]

In neighborhoods accustomed to supporting white men, Shirley Chisholm cut a striking figure. "You are going to have a black representative," she told the voters. But "if you want a representative who truly represents your hopes . . . in terms of principles, et cetera, there is not one who can match me." She emphasized what they had in common. "I said, 'you don't know me, I'm fighting Shirley Chisholm from the neighboring district. . . . And if you want your own in Congress, you've got to help me.'" She was one of their "own," for she shared their principles. "I told them about my record, I told them about what I stood for." To the women especially, Chisholm stressed that they all stood on a historic threshold. "I told them I was about to make history in this country." Furthermore, she claimed that Stanley Steingut wanted nothing to do with her. "The structure doesn't want me, and you must ask yourselves, 'why doesn't the structure want this woman in Washington?'" Chisholm in-fused her campaign with a streetwise populism. "I went out on the trucks, told the people we could all be liberated from the machine." This formed the essence of Chisholm's appeal. "This is the way I preached to them . . . and it caught on. . . . The Italian people said they'd never seen this kind of campaigning." Her primary campaign felt fresh and novel.[44]

The white neighborhoods exhibited important differences. Crown Heights was historically more liberal, and more Jewish, than Greenpoint or Bushwick. Williamsburg also possessed a large Jewish population, more of it made up of Hasidim. While many Williamsburg residents coped with poverty, Crown Heights retained a middle-class ethos. But this was changing in the late-1960s. Many whites had left Crown Heights for outlying neighborhoods. For Judith Berek, Crown Heights residents all needed the same sorts of things: more economic security and increased government services. "Shirley Chisholm could just as easily represent the whites in the community as the blacks," Berek said. "It's significant that she'll be the first black woman in Congress, but it's more significant that she'd be replacing Edna Kelly—who didn't do a thing for anyone who lived in that neighborhood for a very long time. [Chisholm] cares about the neighborhood. She lives in it." In the assembly, Chisholm had pursued policies that benefited working and poor people. "These are the kinds of things she can do for the whole community. Everyone there needs this kind of help." Black, white, or brown, Chisholm could repre-sent them all.[45]

Chisholm always looked for messages that worked as well at spaghetti socials as they did over jerk chicken. She hammered away at "the ma-chine" as forcefully in Bushwick as she did outside the Breevort Houses. And when she emphasized her gender, Chisholm found that this won women's support across racial and neighborhood lines.

If there had been both a white primary and a black primary in the 12th Congressional District, they would not have sufficed. This was because Puerto Ricans made up half of Williamsburg's population and num-bered 50,000 in Bedford-Stuyvesant. Chisholm held a decided advantage among those voters. If she spoke two slightly different political languages in Bushwick and in Bedford-Stuyvesant, then in the Puerto Rican neigh-borhoods she spoke—quite literally—a third. There she conducted much of her campaign in Spanish. "None of my opponents have ever been able to do this, and so this in itself is a common bond between myself and the Puerto Rican people." Puerto Rican voters warmed instantly to her.[46]

On Primary Day, June 18, Chisholm captured 46 percent of the votes compared to 39 percent for William Thompson. Chisholm eked out victories in Williamsburg, Greenpoint, and Crown Heights. Thompson carried Bushwick, but by only fifty votes. As Chisholm would reflect several years later, "the leader of that district—he looks at me, he doesn't understand what happened." She carried Bedford-Stuyvesant more convincingly. Yet while the percentage of registered voters had increased in Bedford-Stuyvesant, and while happy anticipation greeted the prospect of a black representative, few turned out for the primary. In the new 12th district, only 12,000 voters went to the polls. In the adjacent district, by comparison, 43,000 turned out to vote in the primary between Emanuel Celler and Edna Kelly. Celler won. In John Rooney's district, 21,000 voters went to the polls. Many would forget the 12th district's disappointing turnout. They would remember only the result.[47]

The campaign barely finished, a certain narrative about Chisholm's victory began to take hold. She helped to author that story. "From the beginning of this campaign, I was aware of the barriers . . . that stood in my path," Chisholm said in her hour of triumph. She drew her strength from African Americans in Bedford-Stuyvesant. "The reason for continuing in the race was the faith that the people of Bedford-Stuyvesant had in me." The media—local and national, black and white—spun the same tale. Here the black voters, long oppressed and finally empowered, had selected a black woman to lead them. The *Amsterdam News* declared that Chisholm showed "her extraordinary ability to sweep up the black and the Puerto Rican vote." If white voters had proved crucial during the primary campaign, they became tangential to the victory narrative. The story was that Bedford-Stuyvesant had picked Chisholm up on its broad shoulders and carried her ever closer to Capitol Hill.[48]

THE GENERAL ELECTION CAMPAIGN PITTED TWO CIVIL RIGHTS TITANS against each other. And they came from two different worlds. Chisholm had spent decades navigating the Brooklyn clubhouses. She belonged to the realm of black politics much more than black protest. By contrast, James Farmer was a renowned civil rights leader who had helped to organize the 1963 March on Washington. While the 1968 campaign promised a black congressman for black Brooklyn, it also featured a battle over the issue of gender in politics, and it showed the strength of Shirley Chisholm's multiracial coalition.

Chisholm enjoyed one distinct advantage. She was now the Democratic Party's nominee. In the new 12th district, Democrats comprised 80 percent of registered voters. The irony was that her primary victory had exposed the weakness of the party's apparatus in Bedford-Stuyvesant. She would have to turn the party's endorsement back into a strength.

Farmer secured the Republican and Liberal Party nominations. He knew he stood little chance with those who had voted Democratic all their lives. So he fixed his sights on those for whom voting was novel rather than routine, among whom party affiliation might not count for so much. This meant that the battle would be joined in Bedford-Stuyvesant. The candidates would concentrate on migrants from the South and the islands, and on all those gerrymandered New Yorkers who thought their vote would never matter.

James Farmer grew up in Holly Springs, Mississippi, and in Austin, Texas—a far cry from Chisholm's Brooklyn-and-Barbados roots. He was the son of a preacher and a child of the Jim Crow South. When the civil rights struggle rose in the years after World War Two, James Farmer ascended with it. He became national chairman of CORE, but eventually left CORE when the organization moved toward militancy and away from interracialism. Farmer was living in Manhattan in 1968, and he watched with interest the political events that unfolded across the East River. When the new congressional districts took shape, Farmer moved to Brooklyn and declared his candidacy. The preacher's son from Holly Springs soon found himself pounding the pavement on Lewis Avenue.

Shirley Chisholm and James Farmer both knew how to command an audience. Chisholm had a lilting voice that recalled her years in Barbados. She often played the part of the folksy campaigner, but she could be strong and stern. She did not suffer fools. James Farmer was resonant at the podium if not downright stentorian. His orations possessed within them the cadence of the black church. In 1968, he labored to meld that with the language of the Black Power movement and, together again, with the mandates of a modern political campaign. He learned as he went.

Farmer referred to himself as the underdog, and to Chisholm as the chosen candidate of Brooklyn's power brokers. He called for "the end of the old plantation politics of the past." On July 25, he appeared before a crowd in Bedford-Stuyvesant and declared, "We must prove there is such a thing as people's power." He charged that Democrats "thought they had us in their pockets." Farmer argued that Brooklyn blacks had failed to exercise their political power. "We must be in a position to use our power as a swing vote." Here were familiar themes: an end to "plantation politics"; a plea for African Americans to wield their votes as weapons; an appeal to "people's power" and frequent jabs at Brooklyn's Democratic machine. But it was not Shirley Chisholm who articulated such points. It was her opponent.[49]

Chisholm was not ready to cede this ground. Her motorcades rolled through the neighborhoods, declaring that Chisholm still stood "Unbought and Unbossed." She remained adamant that "the party leaders do not like me," and that "I cannot be controlled." She claimed that she would finance her campaign through only small donations, "because the moment I take money from any special interest groups or any big groups, I do not belong to you." Chisholm staked her campaign on this concept—that the politician would actually "belong" to the people of the district. She alleged that Farmer's campaign "had money dripping all over it." He was endorsed by Governor Nelson Rockefeller and bankrolled by the Republican Party. In addition, Farmer was an outsider—a Manhattan resident and a native southerner. In Chisholm's parlance, Farmer could never *belong* to the people of Bedford-Stuyvesant.[50]

Chisholm promised that if citizens organized for her, she could lead them out of this urban wilderness. The women of Bedford-Stuyvesant responded in kind. "A group of welfare people in this community . . . decided that in their own little way, they're going to have parties in their kitchens and their apartments and their homes, and whatever they were able to raise at the end of each week when they got together, they were going to give it to me. . . . That moves me." Chisholm tied herself to the poor black women of Bedford-Stuyvesant.[51]

Unwittingly, James Farmer helped to strengthen that bond. On policy matters, Chisholm and Farmer rarely disagreed. They both pledged themselves to expanded social services and funding for impoverished urban areas. In the escalating fight over the public schools in Ocean

Hill-Brownsville, both candidates supported local black parents' efforts for "community control." Both also opposed the Vietnam War. So Farmer chose to accent two points: his national civil rights experience and his identity as a black man. "The racists and bigots are going to be in a strong position in Congress next year, and we will need strong, experienced people who can command national attention to stand up to them." According to Farmer, a lifetime in the civil rights movement outweighed two decades in Brooklyn's Democratic clubhouses and two terms in the New York State Assembly. "I don't intend to be a freshman Congressman. I graduated a long time ago." Farmer posed as the strong black male, and tried to portray Chisholm as the fragile woman. His flyers emphasized the need for a "strong male image" and a "man's voice" in Washington. He was suggesting that a woman's place was in the home, not the House.[52]

Farmer also inserted himself in the arc of the rising Black Power movement. From the back seat of a convertible that whisked him through the district, he often clenched his fist in a Black Power salute. When Farmer walked the streets of Bedford-Stuyvesant, he brought along a group of men who sported Afros and beat bongo drums. Across the nation, Black Power advocates were encouraging black men—who white Americans had long tried to press into straitjackets of deference—to embrace their masculinity and to seize their manhood. Crown Heights resident Marshall Dubin acknowledged that such points were "difficult for white people to understand. There is a feeling among the militants that a black *man* must come to the fore. Shirley Chisholm . . . is keenly aware of it." If Farmer ever targeted the votes of women, it did not show. Neither did he commit much time to white voters in Crown Heights, Bushwick, or Greenpoint.[53]

Scholars have many ways of tracking voters' preferences: polling data, letters to newspaper editors, politicians' correspondence with constituents, oral history caches, and voting results. For this campaign between Shirley Chisholm and James Farmer, a rather unique resource exists. It is unscientific, inexact, and difficult to interpret—but one would be hard-pressed to find a source that better evokes the time and the place, or that presents the historian with a more direct line to the appeals of the candidates. In audio recordings of Shirley Chisholm's street rallies, one can hear her motorcade, her volunteers, and Chisholm herself; one is also treated to informal interviews with bystanders in Bedford-Stuyvesant.

Clearly, Farmer's appeals resonated with a part of the electorate. While watching a Chisholm rally on October 29, 1968, one Haitian American man predicted that Farmer would win the election: "I think the American public is more interested in having a man." Another black male confessed his preference for Farmer. "I'd like Farmer in Congress. I don't like to see a woman in that seat. Because it's more of a man's seat. It's a hard job, you see . . . it's a little too rough for a woman. I think a man will listen to a man quicker than they will listen to a woman. . . . [Farmer] did an awful lot for civil rights, yes, that's why I would consider him over this lady for Congress." Still another man volunteered that he would vote for Farmer, and all his friends would do the same. All of these men offered their pro-Farmer statements while watching a rally for Chisholm.[54]

The *New York Times* reinforced Farmer's description of the race as a man-versus-woman struggle. It placed Farmer at the center of the story, with Chisholm on the periphery. An October article was headlined, "Farmer and Woman in Lively Bedford-Stuyvesant Race." This nudged Chisholm further toward a gendered pitch for votes. She explained, "It was not my original strategy to organize womanpower to elect me. . . . But when someone tries to use my sex against me, I delight in being able to turn the tables on him."[55]

Chisholm told the women of the 12th Congressional District to make good on their numerical advantage. "You've got to elect one of your own to dramatize the problems that are focusing on us as black women. There's 13,000 more of you . . . in the assembly districts that are registered." She always insisted that she had been forced to play up the gender issue. "I hate to do this, but the men are carrying on in this campaign. So they forced me into this position." Her claim contained strands of truth as well as pieces of political strategy. On the one hand, Farmer really did make political hay out of Chisholm's sex. On the other, Chisholm and Mac Holder had long realized that women outnumbered men on the voter rolls—and that in this statistical fact existed a potential political treasure.[56]

Whether a defensive maneuver or an attack, this line of campaigning proved potent. Marshall Dubin was an organizer for Local 1199, a hospital workers' union. Local 1199 contained hundreds of women who worked as nurses and orderlies—many of them in the Downstate Medical Center. In Bedford-Stuyvesant, Dubin noted, often "the woman's the sole supporter for the family. And I tell you this is very common in the hospital." In Shirley Chisholm these women saw themselves. Yet they also saw a leader who climbed to heights that they would never contemplate. Dubin observed how Chisholm had inspired the women in his union—how she had drawn them into electoral politics, a realm heretofore meaningless to so many. "She has captured the imagination of our people . . . people in Bedford-Stuyvesant, working people. . . . Women do identify with her." Chisholm "was born and raised in the midst of this mess," managing "to come up out of the bottom, and make something of herself, and still relate to them. And that means something." Dubin noted that Chisholm's critics had leveled only one charge. They maintained, "you really can't have a woman in a job like this." It was a sexist claim, and it overlooked an obvious fact: the current representative, Edna Kelly, was a woman. "To then object to a black woman doing this, who is of the people . . . is I think the height of unfairness."[57]

Chisholm crafted a message that men could also rally around. On October 29, she brought her campaign to one of the newer housing projects in the area. These were the Ebbets Field Apartments, a 1,300-unit complex that started accepting tenants in 1963. It stood on hallowed ground. "You know I have worked in the legislature. You know what I have stood for. You know I'm unbought and unbossed." At large rallies, Chisholm often used such generalities. Campaign workers picked up the megaphone to communicate the details of her platform: "Adequate pay for the thousands of unemployed, quality education in all the schools, adequate housing for both low- and middle-income families, better support for daycare centers, unemployment insurance for the domestic workers." Chisholm continued, "Vote for a congressman that belongs to this community." And she attacked James Farmer. "Send me to be your voice. Do not let anybody from Manhattan, or any place else, come over here and be an opportunist and try to be your voice." Voters appreciated her Brooklyn roots. A man of Jamaican descent predicted victory for Chisholm. "I think Chisholm will win—based on the fact of her popularity and the work she has done in the community." A Jewish man expressed his approval. "I'd just as soon vote for her." He was a longtime constituent of Emanuel Celler who found himself in the new 12th Congressional District. Celler had "been in [Congress] about forty years," he reflected. "Maybe she'll stay in that long. If she's as good as Celler was, let her stay in." That a

Brooklyn Jew would announce such support for a black candidate during the fall of 1968 was no small feat.[58]

TENSIONS BETWEEN JEWS AND AFRICAN AMERICANS HAD RISEN TO historic heights. The crisis revolved around public schools in the Ocean Hill-Brownsville district, where African Americans composed a vast majority of the student population. The teaching force was mostly white, with a large number of Jews. Black parents began to seek more power over the conditions in local schools. They gained support from the New York City Board of Education, the Ford Foundation, and Republican mayor John Lindsay. In 1967, community control became a reality. Neighborhood residents elected fellow parents to serve on the Ocean Hill-Brownsville Governing Board, which exercised authority over the curriculum and personnel in local schools.[59]

African Americans' thirst for community control collided with the prerogatives of the teachers and their union. The union resisted many reforms that the Ocean Hill-Brownsville Governing Board attempted to implement. In May 1968, the Governing Board resolved to terminate the contracts of those teachers who proved most hostile. The United Federation of Teachers (UFT) organized a series of strikes, paralyzing schools across the city. Black leaders charged the UFT with racism. UFT head Albert Shanker hurled allegations of anti-Semitism. The protests and the strikes grew increasingly hate-filled.[60]

In 1968, Americans had witnessed the assassinations of Martin Luther King Jr. and Robert F. Kennedy as well as the "siege of Chicago" during the Democratic National Convention. The nation tore along so many different axes: liberal versus conservative, young versus old, counterculture versus establishment, hawk versus dove, black versus white. And Brooklyn seemed to teeter on the precipice of a race war.

In the middle of it all, Chisholm and Farmer fought for a seat in the United States Congress. The candidates held a debate in October before a packed crowd at the Pratt Institute. When it came to the subject of Ocean Hill-Brownsville, Farmer delivered a diatribe about white racism and paternalism. Chisholm had attacked Albert Shanker many times before, and had pledged her support to the Governing Board.

But during this debate, she deplored the venom on both sides. "The solution must come from black as well as white. . . . I think that there should be a denunciation of both groups coming from all segments of the community." She attempted to rise above the controversy. While Brooklyn seemed a cauldron of racial tension, Chisholm held on to an inclusive message.[61]

Both candidates expected victory. Chisholm displayed supreme confidence in her grassroots network and in the power of her popularity. She had also picked up the endorsements of several labor unions as well as the *Amsterdam News*. Farmer boasted that his own polling numbers promised a triumph. "On the evening before the election, my staff of volunteers believed the election was in the bag," Farmer wrote in his autobiography. "I took a walking tour through the streets of the twelfth district in Brooklyn. . . . The response was overwhelmingly favorable." Farmer thought he had his finger on the political pulse.[62]

On the night of the election, November 5, Farmer conceded defeat two hours after the polls closed. In a conversation with Chisholm, Farmer promised his assistance. Farmer grew more confrontational when he spoke to his supporters. He vowed to run again. But his margin of defeat was enormous. Chisholm won two-thirds of the total votes to Farmer's 26 percent. This was Shirley Chisholm's place.[63]

The woman whom the *Amsterdam News* dubbed the "first lady of black politics" took the podium at her headquarters on Bergen Street. Buoyed by a feisty crowd, Chisholm placed the United States Congress on notice. "I have no intention of being . . . a quiet freshman Congressman. My voice will be heard." To the members of Brooklyn's Democratic hierarchy, Chisholm delivered a mixed message. "I have nothing to say about Mr. Steingut tonight. He has been very lovely to me since the primary. In fact, all of the Brooklyn clubs have been supporting me beautifully since I won the primary." She was indeed backed by the machine in the general election. The candidate who advertised that she was "unbossed" then faulted the Democratic Party for not backing her before that. "I needed their support in the primary, not now." In the end, this victory was one for Chisholm and her constituents to savor. "Once again the people of this community have spoken." She basked in her moment. "I'm deeply grateful and deliriously happy."[64]

In an evening, Shirley Chisholm had become an icon. The national media focused on the fact that Chisholm had become the first black congresswoman. This alone would ensure for her a special place in American political history.

Many of her constituents emphasized Chisholm's Brooklyn identity more than her womanhood. As one volunteer said on Election Night, Chisholm "played in these streets and knows what we need." The precise place of her triumph—the heart of black Brooklyn, an area of meat pies and soul food, graceful old brownstones that stood alongside the travesties of the slumlords, crime-besotted corners and rat-filled groceries, the racial smorgasbord that was Crown Heights, the Old World fabric of Greenpoint, the Williamsburg where Hasidic Jews shared the avenues with migrants from San Juan, the housing complex that inherited the legacy of Jackie Robinson's mad dashes, and all the places in between—remained meaningful to those who had elected her. "It's also significant that people are sending one of their own," reflected Judith Berek. "Not just because she's black and most of them are black. But because she lives there. And I imagine it would be a really kind of spectacular feeling to send your next-door neighbor to Congress." If the women of Bedford-Stuyvesant could send Chisholm to Congress, "maybe the great Horatio Alger really works. You really can go from being a neighborhood schoolteacher to being a Congresswoman. The kind of thing where when your mother hits you over the head to do your homework and say . . . you can go to Congress like Shirley Chisholm, it really happens." Suddenly, Bedford-Stuyvesant possessed hundreds of future Shirley Chisholms.[65]

In a time of Black Power, urban riots, and the Ocean Hill-Brownsville crisis, Chisholm fashioned a campaign that was multiracial and multilingual. Roy Wilkins, head of the NAACP, wrote in the *Amsterdam News*, "Here in New York City they turned a deaf ear to those who preach a psychological and physical separation." Wilkins titled his article, "The Black Vote Was For Inclusion." A member of James Farmer's campaign staff reinforced this line of thinking, though in a totally different sense. To Fred Beauford, Chisholm's victory was a catastrophe. "I think it was a tremendous setback for the whole black power movement. I don't think the message got to the people." The message certainly did reach the people. Chisholm showed the viability of a multiracial politics.[66]

IN WASHINGTON, CHISHOLM DISPLAYED HER TRADEMARK INDEPENDENCE. She refused an assignment to the House Agriculture Committee, defying Democratic leaders, and ultimately secured a position on the Veterans' Affairs Committee. Chisholm delivered her maiden speech on March 26, 1969, a vigorous attack on the Vietnam War. She vowed to oppose every bill on defense spending "until the time comes when our values and priorities have been turned right side up again." Chisholm beseeched "every mother, wife and widow in this land who ever asked herself why the generals can play with billions while families crumble under the weight of sickness, hunger and unemployment" to raise their voices in opposition to the war. In this first speech, Chisholm decided not to address racial equality, women's issues, or the problems of the cities. She would proceed to champion many policies for working-class Americans.[67]

Still, Chisholm was frank about her goals: "My first priority is the liberation of Blacks from second-class status in America." She had strong ideas about how to achieve that end. Chisholm scoffed at black separatism. She counseled integration and negotiation, building coalitions across lines of race, sex, and party. She worked within the system.[68]

Chisholm garnered the most publicity in 1972, when she ran for president. She rolled out the rhetoric of multiracialism. "I want to be the candidate for those who see beyond my blackness and femaleness and see a candidate who has ability, guts, leadership, talent, honesty, sincerity and who refuses to indulge in sham and hypocrisy." When Chisholm formally announced her candidacy for the Democratic nomination, she looked especially for those who looked beyond. "I am not the candidate of Black America, although I am Black and proud," she said on January 25, 1972. "I am not the candidate of the Women's Movement of this country, although I am a woman, and I am equally proud of that. I am not the candidate of any political bosses or special interests . . . I am the candidate of the people and my presence before you now symbolizes a new era in American political history." This occurred at a crucial moment in the history of black politics. Chisholm had recently helped to form the Congressional Black Caucus. African American militants and integrationists were beginning to come together in the electoral arena. Chisholm also forged a coalition between black radicals and white feminists. She earned the support of the Black Panther Party. But many other black males kept their distance from her 1972 campaign, as did the national Democratic Party. Her presidential campaign ultimately withered "in the face of a broad constellation of outside pressures and internal fissures," as historian Joshua Guild explained. Still, it left a significant legacy.[69]

On Capitol Hill, Chisholm continued to stand strong for progressive causes. But when it came to New York politics, the "unbought and unbossed" slogan seemed like an empty mantra. She pledged allegiance to political boss Meade Esposito. She allied herself with the preferred candidates of the Democratic Party, often siding with moderate and conservative whites over black reformers. In 1977, she refused to endorse the African American Percy Sutton in his bid for mayor of New York. Sutton had supported Chisholm in her own bid for the presidency. Instead, Chisholm favored Mayor Abe Beame and then Ed Koch. She also involved herself in a mayoral race in Buffalo, campaigning against a state assemblyman who chaired the Black and Puerto Rican Caucus. In addition, she opposed several feminist candidates for office. In 1978, the *Amsterdam News* published an editorial regarding "The Shirley Chisholm issue." The editors hoped either to "make her accountable to a higher standard of political wisdom and loyalty, or to mount a serious effort to remove her."[70]

An article in the *Village Voice* was more scathing. Andrew Cooper noted that black New Yorkers remained "sentimentally attached" to Chisholm, "still charged by the image of a spunky black woman with a fiery tongue and unpredictable spirit. But we have become—in some ways—a victim of our own imagination. We want that kind of indomitable hero so deeply that we create them . . . and we go on stubbornly believing in them through decades of contrary realities." Cooper detailed Chisholm's history of campaigning against reform candidates. He also acknowledged Chisholm's prodigious abilities: "She has the capacity to make poor people, women and blacks believe in themselves." But Cooper could not understand why Chisholm had traded her independence for security, why she believed "that the only force that can guarantee her political security at home is the organization, not the people." Her fealty to the machine was tragic and unnecessary. "Shirley Chisholm has underestimated herself. The organization could never beat her. . . . If she believed in her own rhetoric, the people would have taken care of her. They still will." For all of this, Chisholm was still able to burnish the image that she preferred.[71]

She lived on in lore as the "Fighting Shirley Chisholm" of the 1972 presidential campaign, and the "Unbought and Unbossed" leader of her own writings. In 2010, New York assemblyman Hakeem Jeffries said this: "Shirley Chisholm blazed a trail from the streets of Brooklyn in 1972 to the White House in 2008." Yet to understand Barack Obama's epic multiracial triumphs in 2008 and 2012, Chisholm's 1968 congressional victory is more instructive than her presidential campaign. In 1968, Chisholm displayed her facility with so many different languages; she painstakingly built coalitions and successfully straddled different political worlds.[72]

The 1968 campaign also provides a way of understanding race and politics in the Northeast. By that year, Brooklyn was a place with entrenched spatial segregation, black poverty, urban blight, and racial tension. And yet, at this seemingly bleak moment, it still demonstrated a capacity for multiracial democracy. To place Chisholm within the Northeast's history of interracialism is to wedge her into an area where she fits—but not with complete comfort. Brooklyn's future portended even more polarization. The dispute over Ocean Hill-Brownsville tore blacks and whites in New York City apart much more than Chisholm's victories ever unified them.

Chisholm shattered sexual and racial barriers, and carried with her the hopes of many different peoples. But the anger of Ocean Hill-Brownsville brought one ugly truth into focus: the Northeast of interracial politics was giving way to the Northeast of racial enmity. The region had long held both traditions within it. In the 1970s, the hatred would bubble furiously to the surface. Shirley Chisholm, symbolizing all that she did, stood on the precipice of that transition.

PART III

MIRRORS

SIX

"The North Is Guilty"

Abraham Ribicoff's Crusade (1970)

W HILE SHIRLEY CHISHOLM JOINED A NEW WAVE OF AFRICAN Americans in Congress, making Capitol Hill more integrated than at any time since Reconstruction, Washington greeted the 1970s with a great debate over race and region. Six weeks into the new decade, the junior senator from Connecticut stood on the Senate floor and issued a withering indictment. "The North is guilty," he declared—guilty of "monumental hypocrisy in its treatment of the black man." Abraham Ribicoff focused national attention on the North's open secret. The ensuing days and weeks featured fiery speeches about the plight of African Americans in northern cities, the racism of white northerners, and the issue of de facto segregation. These rhetorical jousts led to no new legislation. But they underscored a crucial shift in Americans' understanding of race in the North.[1]

Over the course of the 1970s, the Northeast would show itself to be no archetype of racial progress. Instead, it became a mirror for America's troubles—reflecting, rather than surmounting, the nation's deep divisions over race, class, and politics. By the end of the decade, this region would become the center of the white backlash while segregation in housing and schools grew ever more entrenched.

Abraham Ribicoff was born in New Britain, Connecticut, in 1910. The son of immigrant Jews from Poland, he was raised in a tenement on Star Street. The New Britain of his youth was a polyglot place. As Ribicoff recalled, "You were intermixed with people of every race, color, creed, and religion." In this regard, New Britain looked something like Springfield, Massachusetts—or even a miniature Brooklyn. "The New Britains of America gave birth to the melting-pot theory," Ribicoff wrote, "and the theory was valid." Before World War Two, in the small cities of the Northeast, Ribicoff believed that the melting-pot notion actually worked. As the years passed, he would watch that vision disintegrate.[2]

Ribicoff described his own life as "a typical Horatio Alger story." During high school, he worked odd hours for a zipper-and-buckle company. The company eventually hired him to head its operations in Chicago, and he ended up earning a law degree from the University of Chicago. In 1933, he returned to Connecticut and settled in Hartford. Ribicoff worked as a lawyer before beginning his ascent in state politics.[3]

In 1948, he won election to the United States Congress. He served two terms before running for governor in 1954. Ribicoff squared off against John Davis Lodge, the Republican incumbent. One of Lodge's supporters engaged in an anti-Semitic whispering campaign. Ribicoff delivered his response in a televised address, with Lodge scheduled to go on the air after him. Speaking off the cuff, Ribicoff tried to summon an idea of America at its aspirational best. He later recalled the speech:

I had no script, nothing. And I said, what is America all about? I said, remember as a kid going out in the fields and lying under an apple tree and dreaming the dreams of what America was and that anybody could be anything in this great country of ours. And here I am, a man of the Jewish faith, the first time that anyone of the Jewish faith has ever been nominated for high public office in Connecticut, and the important thing isn't that I be elected. The important thing for America was that everybody could aspire and that everybody should have an opportunity.

Ribicoff said in the speech, "Any boy, regardless of race, creed, or color, has the right to aspire to public office. . . . I know that the American Dream can come true." As Ribicoff walked offstage, Lodge and his wife walked on—the two of them "stricken," Ribicoff remembered, "deeply touched themselves." In Ribicoff's telling, "there wasn't a dry eye in the state of Connecticut." That speech clinched his victory. "I am sure that without the American Dream speech I would have never won." Ribicoff became the nation's second Jewish governor. His victory helped to reinforce the Northeast's reputation as a land of breakthroughs.[4]

While Ribicoff was serving in the House of Representatives, he had befriended a young Democrat from neighboring Massachusetts. John F. Kennedy ran for president in 1960. Ribicoff provided early and instrumental support. Kennedy eventually offered the position of attorney general to Ribicoff, but Ribicoff opted instead to become the secretary of Health, Education, and Welfare (HEW). In 1962, he won election to the United States Senate.[5]

Abraham Ribicoff was savvy and calculating. He did what it took to climb the political ladder in Hartford and in Washington. He talked often about the "integrity of compromise." He saw the wisdom of political deals. Yet his liberal credentials remained impeccable. Lowell Weicker, another senator from Connecticut, described Ribicoff as a man who "did what he thought was right, the devil take the consequences." Ribicoff was unafraid to say what he believed.[6]

That side of Ribicoff gained him fame at the 1968 Democratic Convention in Chicago. The Vietnam War threatened to explode the Democratic Party. Inside the convention hall, the major candidates competed for delegates. Outside, antiwar protesters staged massive demonstrations. The Chicago police savagely beat the protesters. Tear gas wafted through the streets as Ribicoff took the podium at the convention. He denounced the "Gestapo-like tactics" of the police. From the front row, Chicago mayor Richard Daley barked anti-Semitic epithets. Ribicoff absorbed the vitriol and pressed on. A year and a half later, his name resurfaced in banner headlines.[7]

The crusader in Ribicoff remained on full public display. His 1970 speech came as a response to the machinations of John Stennis, a Mississippi senator and longtime segregationist. Stennis had occupied his winter days by entering into the *Congressional Record* school segregation statistics for northern cities. Stennis proposed a series of amendments to the Elementary and Secondary Education Act. (This was a bill to fund schools that came up in Congress on a regular basis.) One of Stennis's proposals would make school integration measures uniform across the nation. If southern counties had to enact widespread transfer policies in order to integrate their schools, Stennis asserted, then northern cities should have to do the same. But Stennis was not interested in speeding up the desegregation process, in either the North or the South. His amendment was a tool to lambast the North and to relieve the pressure from the South. "If you have to integrate in your area," Stennis said to northerners, "you will see what it means to us." By forcing political leaders to take the same actions everywhere, Stennis hoped they would be paralyzed into taking action nowhere.[8]

Ribicoff did not much care about John Stennis's motivations. In the Stennis Amendment he glimpsed an opening. He could draw attention to the racial inequalities in the North and revolutionize perceptions of racism, segregation, and region. He could confront the northern mystique head-on.

It wasn't every Sunday that John Koskinen got called into work. But for Abraham Ribicoff's top aide, the first weekend in February proved to be unusual. Ribicoff phoned him on Saturday, February 7. "He said that he was going to support the Stennis Amendment." Koskinen remembered the moment vividly because it sent him into a small panic. "I must admit, I wasn't totally sure what the Stennis Amendment was. . . . Everyone else had paid no attention to it including yours truly." Ribicoff scheduled a Sunday meeting with Koskinen and another staffer, Paul Danaceau. They spent all day drafting the senator's speech. "It was probably the most eventful of the four years I was there," Koskinen recalled.

The speech came as a shock to many in Washington. "There was consternation. The southerners were stunned."[9]

Ribicoff had been thinking about the problem of segregation in northern cities and suburbs. In the first week of February, he traveled to the University of Texas and spoke about this very issue. When Ribicoff returned to Washington, debate over the Stennis Amendment had begun.[10]

On Monday, February 9, Ribicoff rose to support Stennis's proposal. "The North is guilty," he declared. "Northern communities have been as systematic and as consistent as southern communities in denying the black man and his children the opportunities that exist for white people." Racism "knows no geographical boundary and has known none since the great migration of rural blacks after World War Two." He wanted white northerners to acknowledge racism's pernicious existence. "Perhaps we in the North needed the mirror held up to us by the Senator from Mississippi, in order to see the truth." This was Ribicoff's primary aim—to peel away the layers of illusion, to deaden any sense of self-congratulation, to disabuse white northerners of their assumptions that things were better up above the Mason-Dixon line. More specifically, Ribicoff was thinking about cities and suburbs. A vast gulf separated "the black society of the central city and the white society of the suburb." Here was the root of the problem. By 1970, the urban-suburban divide supplied the fundamental source of racial inequality.[11]

Ribicoff was at once a fitting and a surprising spokesman for this cause. His home state had become a land of glistening bedroom communities and struggling cities. Connecticut was riddled with income inequality. The state boasted the highest per capita wealth in America. The poverty rate in its urban areas was also the nation's highest. Vast chasms separated the poor cities with racial minorities, such as Bridgeport and Hartford, from the affluent white towns nearby. Ribicoff's speech was not designed to score points with his suburban constituents. He took some of Connecticut's more tried-and-true traditions—from neglect of urban minorities to righteous rectitude and hypocrisy—and decried them, on the Senate floor, in one fell swoop.[12]

In his speech, Ribicoff noted that northern leaders were quick to attack segregation in the South, "yet we turn away—our faces, our minds, our hearts, and our heads—from problems that are six blocks from where we live." He had in mind those New York City denizens who lived in opulence on the Upper West Side, and in such proximity to Harlem. "We look down our noses at the people in the South . . . without having the guts to face up to our own problems." He thanked Stennis again for holding "the mirror up to northern hypocrisy." Ribicoff grabbed that mirror and forced every senator to gaze into it.[13]

Southern senators hailed Ribicoff's speech as the best they had ever heard—from a Yankee, at least. It lifted J. William Fulbright's spirits, gave Howard Baker hope that the Civil War had finally ended, and made Richard Russell's "heart feel good."[14]

Jacob Javits of New York leaped into the fray. He agreed with Ribicoff that northern leaders were "decades behind what we ought to be doing as far as our minorities are concerned." But he thought Ribicoff had focused on spectacle more than substance. What exactly did Ribicoff want the Senate to do about it? Javits worried that with the adoption of the Stennis Amendment, "we are going to compromise . . . the effort to deal with de jure segregation" in the South. Javits and Ribicoff, two Jewish liberals from neighboring states, had been longtime allies—especially on civil rights issues. Ribicoff later described their friendship as "close," though "not intimate." The Stennis Amendment brought them to loggerheads. They would spar for days and weeks, even into the following year.[15]

If Javits was Ribicoff's foil, Walter Mondale became Ribicoff's principal critic. The liberal Minnesotan pointed out that the Senate had already moved against de facto segregation. The 1968 Fair Housing Act struck at Jim Crow housing throughout the country. Ribicoff responded that the Fair Housing Act was a "fakery."* Still, Mondale offered this law as evidence that the Senate had already accepted segregation as a national condition. And he noted that the Senate had passed this legislation over a filibuster of southern senators, including Stennis. The Stennis Amendment "satisfies our feelings of guilt about hypocrisy," said Mondale. Other than that, it would accomplish little. "We have the sanctimonious proposition against de facto segregation and we do nothing about it." This was grandstanding, not legislating.[16]

---

*The bill that Congress passed was a compromise measure. The next chapter provides more details.

Then Mondale raised the issue that other senators would bury. It already dripped of political poison. Four years later, this issue would bring a virulent white racism to the surface of northern life. It was school busing. In Mondale's mind, busing was "the best known way to overcome de facto segregation." Yet no senator would rise in its defense. John Stennis was vehemently opposed to busing, and his amendment retained previous prohibitions on busing. Ribicoff himself asserted, "We are not going to solve the problem of the schools by busing. Who are we, whose faces are white, to think that the blacks ought to be bused?" Ribicoff criticized one policy that might actually deliver integration to the North.[17]

FOR A MOMENT, AMERICANS ENGAGED IN PRECISELY THE KIND OF conversation that Ribicoff hoped to provoke. Every publication in the country seemed eager to probe the contours of northern segregation. The North's dirty secret was out.

And white southerners had a new hero. Leaf through the newspapers of the South during the second week of February 1970, and behold the headlines, editorials, and cartoons. For the *Richmond Times-Dispatch*, Ribicoff's speech was "as welcome as a sparkling sunrise after a stormy troubled night. Dawn comes at last." A Richmond resident, J. Luther Glass, clipped the editorial and mailed it to Ribicoff. He scribbled a personal note: "Nice going, Senator." A cartoon in the *Times-Dispatch* showed just how venerated Ribicoff had become. In the drawing, a statue of Ribicoff was being erected on Richmond's Monument Avenue. (A Lincoln-like figure was on his knees with a chisel, working to build the statue.) A Connecticut Jew took his place betwixt two Confederate war heroes: J. E. B. Stuart and Robert E. Lee.[18]

Ribicoff's speech inspired many cartoons, each of them flaying northern liberals. Most of the cartoons traded in the same essential caricature. They all agreed that the prototypical northern liberal was a white man with glasses, a coat and tie, and often with Semitic features. A *Denver Post* cartoon depicted an obese white southerner (identified by the rebel flag on his T-shirt), with his foot upon the neck of a helpless African American. A "northern liberal" stood facing him. Well-dressed, with reading

'He's Going Between Lee and Stuart on Monument Ave.'

In February 1970, Connecticut's Abraham Ribicoff stood on the Senate floor and charged that the North was guilty of racial hypocrisy. White southerners hailed Ribicoff as a hero. In this cartoon from the *Richmond Times-Dispatch*, a statue of Ribicoff was erected in Richmond—next to the monument to Robert E. Lee. A Lincoln-like character built the statue. CHICK LARSEN, *RICHMOND TIMES-DISPATCH*, FEBRUARY 11, 1970, SPECIAL COLLECTIONS AND ARCHIVES, JAMES BRANCH CABELL LIBRARY, VCU LIBRARIES.

glasses perched at the end of his long nose, this white northerner held a black man in a headlock. A tiny figure at the bottom of the cartoon explained: "But we segregate (blush) gently!" The southerner chided the northerner, "Tsk! Tsk! Tsk!" This was, of course, an indictment of northern liberals. It also hinted at a subtle but significant difference between the North and the South. African Americans found themselves defeated in the South, the white man's foot on their necks. In the North they were stuck in headlocks. But they were not yet lying on the ground. They still had a fighting chance.[19]

The *Daily News* of Washington, DC, portrayed the white northerner with a glowing halo above his head, so high was his opinion of himself. Ribicoff held up a mirror so that this northerner could see his true reflection. It revealed the man wearing a Klan hood. In this reading of the situation, Ribicoff had exposed the evil that resided in the soul of the white northerner. The North was full of segregation, so it was also full of Klansmen.[20]

This equation did not quite add up. In Ribicoff's original metaphor, the South held the mirror up for northerners to look into. But this was less than apt. For the metaphor to be precise, John Stennis would have already admitted that he wore a Klan hood himself. And he would then have shown white northerners that they were the same. The problem was that neither Stennis nor any of his southern brethren were interested in addressing the racial evil that defined their own careers. Stennis had spent many hours obstructing and defeating civil rights bills. "It is not a matter of record," Richard Rovere pointed out in *The New Yorker*, "that the Senator from Mississippi has ever acknowledged the wickedness of any kind of segregation or accepted any accusation of guilt or hypocrisy on the part of his region for *its* treatment of Negroes." Stennis did not admit that he had wronged anyone. Thus the mirror metaphor was misplaced in a crucial respect. Yet this imprecision did not make the metaphor any less powerful. It got Ribicoff on the front page everywhere from Stamford, Connecticut, to Jackson, Mississippi.[21]

White southerners flooded Ribicoff's Senate office with their congratulations. One Dallas resident wrote, "This is a true mark of a statesman. We need more like you in Washington." This man couldn't resist sharing an anecdote with Ribicoff. "On our visit with relatives in Dierian [Darien], Conn. they were bragging about being integrated—they had one eighty-one-year-old colored man live in a garage." Ribicoff received hundreds of letters like this. Unwittingly, Ribicoff had transformed himself into one big receptacle. The South contained its share of grievance-compilers. Now they had a depository for all of those resentments.[22]

Almost as one, white southerners celebrated Ribicoff's stand. A lone voice of dissent rang out from Little Rock. The *Arkansas Gazette* issued a scathing critique of Ribicoff. The editors saw his speech as a sham. "Abe Ribicoff has displayed astonishing naivete." For the Stennis Amendment would delay desegregation in the South, or even expedite resegregation. Ribicoff had truly mismeasured his man. "When John Stennis of Mississippi starts playing the role of Abraham Lincoln, everybody in the country, North and South, had better watch out!" Ribicoff's political antennae had failed him. "Senator Ribicoff has been taken in, duped, had." The *Gazette* hoped that the United States Senate would tackle the problem of de facto segregation. But John Stennis was not the man to follow. The Mississippi segregationist had waved his wand, entrancing the liberal Jew from New England. And America was worse for it.[23]

The *Gazette*'s response stood as the exception that proved the southern rule. In the North, reaction was more divided. The *Boston Globe* hoped that "suburbia" would hear Ribicoff—and that it might come to prioritize the welfare of a distraught nation over the "sweep of its own lawns." But the editors of the *New York Times* criticized Ribicoff: "School desegregation faces lynching by amendment." The Stennis Amendment represented a "most sophisticated assault" on racial integration. "The whole effort is to convert liberal guilt into segregationist glee."[24]

Observers debated whether Ribicoff's actions would help to speed up, or slow down, efforts for integration. Ribicoff's own Connecticut constituents offered a host of different responses. Some of them were unsettled. Others heartily applauded their senator. The controversy pushed many to pinpoint exactly what was different about race in the North and the South, what was the same, and what it all meant.

In the beginning, Ribicoff's mail ran well in favor. One Hartford resident wrote that "the suburbs might just as well be in the South." A Stamford man assured Ribicoff that "there are many people in Connecticut who stand behind you." A dentist from New London was downright effusive: "Your stripping away the veil of hypocrisy may prove a milestone on the road toward an America that fulfills its promise. I have seldom felt the pride as a constituent as I did in reading your speech." These three residents, all urban dwellers, offered enthusiastic support.[25]

The most heartening response came from a black man in Ansonia, a small town in Connecticut's Naugatuck River Valley. He was infuriated by a previous letter that the *Ansonia Sentinel* had published. One local white woman had written a letter titled "Integrated Valley," in which she contended that conditions for African Americans in Ansonia remained "better than they were down South." Now this African American responded with a letter titled "Discrimination in the Valley." He criticized all of those whites who believed that things were better for blacks up north. "That is a myth that must be realized and accepted as untrue." African Americans suffered from discrimination in employment, and from inferior housing and schools. "Equal opportunity—not 'integration'—in education, housing, and working conditions is what we want and have not attained in the Valley." Ribicoff's speech had finally exposed those conditions, and had encouraged one man in Ansonia to articulate the reality of life for local blacks.[26]

Others in the Nutmeg State were less impressed. The editors of the *Hartford Courant* accepted Ribicoff's assertion that racial segregation was entrenched in the North. But this was all the *Courant* would grant. Ribicoff had spoken only in the "merest generalities," and had offered no way to solve the problem. Worse, he had provided fuel for John Stennis's "vengeful plan to hamper desegregation." In the same vein, New Haven's *Journal-Courier* called the senator's speech "true—but redundant." For two years had passed since the Kerner Commission issued its famous finding about America's cities and suburbs.* In addition, Middletown's newspaper worried that the Stennis Amendment would derail the effort to desegregate southern schools. Ribicoff's stance had about it a maddening inconsistency: "It is impossible to be against busing and at the same time to insist on integration." It was not that the Middletown editors longed for a school busing plan. But they recognized busing as one way to strike at segregation in northern schools, and they were puzzled by Ribicoff's objections to such plans.[27]

Ironically, many constituents denounced Ribicoff's speech because they heard it as a call for school busing. In West Hartford, a suburb bordering the capital city, one resident wondered just how far Ribicoff would go. With all the sarcasm he could muster, D. J. Doudera asked Ribicoff to introduce a bill that would "make it illegal for white families to move to the suburbs and black families to move to the cities until the proper population mix is established." If Ribicoff could mandate integration in

---

*President Lyndon Johnson had formed the Kerner Commission after the urban riots of 1967. The commission issued a report, in 1968, in which it warned of the increasing segregation—and the widening racial gulf—in the nation. It concluded that urban riots resulted from such conditions. It laid the responsibility for this at the foot of American leaders, and indicted white society more generally.

northern schools, Doudera mused, he could also tell citizens where to live. Doudera added a rider to his hypothetical proposal. It would compel the children of elected officials to attend public schools, subjecting politicians' families to "the same pressures as the rest of us poor, beleaguered citizens." As Doudera sized up the situation, this would be the real way to stamp out hypocrisy.[28]

Some Connecticut citizens insisted that de facto segregation could not be equated with the de jure version. To the editors of the *Meriden Record*, the actions of political leaders showed a crucial distinction between the regions. Northern governors did not look to evade the Supreme Court, nor did they whip their constituents into frenzies of resistance. Northern leaders wanted to end inequalities rather than preserve them. It was unfortunate, though not hypocritical, that the results failed to match the intentions. According to the Meriden editors, white northerners may have been troubled and conflicted—but not guilty of the sins that Ribicoff had charged.[29]

The most prophetic response came from the *Hartford Times*, the city's afternoon newspaper. These editors applauded their senator and reveled in his speech. Still, they thought Ribicoff had wasted his energy and his eloquence on John Stennis's behalf. They didn't see why one needed to insist that de facto segregation was "indistinguishable" from de jure segregation. The differences were legion, and they were important. One could acknowledge the horror of de facto segregation in its own right, without equating it to the de jure version. The *Hartford Times* pushed Ribicoff to put forth his own positive plan in place of the "dubious" Stennis Amendment. "Wouldn't it be a great deal better if Senator Ribicoff offered his own amendment—one that deals with the central cities and the suburbs, with industry and housing and employment, and offered new incentives to cure the problems of our segregated society?" Ten months later, Ribicoff would do precisely that.[30]

As the Senate neared a vote on the Stennis Amendment, the chamber erupted again in debate. On February 17, eight days after Ribicoff's landmark speech, Jacob Javits broached the issue of school busing. Javits expressed frustration with the 1964 Civil Rights Act, for it permitted busing only to combat de jure segregation. Likewise, he regretted that the Stennis Amendment included antibusing language. The antibusing view "is the overwhelming sentiment in this Chamber, and no bill could be passed unless it contained that prohibition." But if senators were serious about moving against de facto segregation, Javits noted, they would have to consider busing. Javits aimed most of his barbs at southerners. As he saw it, the real hypocrites were those southern senators who for decades opposed school integration. Now they had the gall to indict the North. Javits demanded: "Who is charging monumental hypocrisy to whom?"[31]

Ribicoff rose to respond. He had no interest in the motivations of the southern senators or in their history of duplicity. "The great issue facing the United States today is the intentions and the bona fides of those of us in the North." Ribicoff and Javits were speaking past each other. Ribicoff wanted to effect a change in attitudes. He asserted that "the public opinion that has been brought to focus on this problem during the past week is what is right with the Stennis proposal." He only wished America would see northern segregation; the solutions for it would come later. Many Americans associated the very term "segregation" with images of specific places: Birmingham; Little Rock; Albany, Georgia; Philadelphia; Mississippi. "Segregation" meant the South. Ribicoff wanted to change that perception.[32]

Javits was less interested in public opinion. Whether or not ordinary Americans thought much about northern segregation, Javits believed that the senator from Connecticut was unlikely to overhaul their views. Besides, Ribicoff had come late to his discovery. Javits declared, "I do not think we are bedazzled by generalizations which are beautiful and which we can agree on." To Javits, Abraham Ribicoff was all bluster. John Koskinen, Ribicoff's aide, phrased the point more generously. "Basically Ribicoff's instincts were right, that we could no longer sweep the problem in the North under the rug. . . . But you could give the speech, and then the question is: What next?"[33]

The debate continued for eight hours, spilling into the night. On Wednesday, February 18, the Stennis Amendment passed with surprising ease. Fully 56 senators supported it, with 36 opposed. Southern senators stood strongly for the bill; senators from the border states and the West joined them. So did Winston Prouty and George Aiken of Vermont, along with Maine's Margaret Chase Smith. Javits and Mondale led the opposition. Ed Brooke also voted "No." But Ted Kennedy did not vote at all. Neither did liberals like Oregon's Mark Hatfield or Indiana's Birch Bayh and Vance Hartke. On the subject of segregation in the South, it was clear where these senators stood. But when Ribicoff muddied the waters, they could not find their way to one side or the other. The generous scribe would note that Kennedy was battling pneumonia at the time. The pessimist would argue that Kennedy understood how thorny an issue this had become.[34]

John Stennis interpreted the amendment's passage as a major victory. The vote signaled a "change in direction" on integration policy, Stennis declared. It was "a new gateway, a turning point," and a "landmark."[35]

If a liberal's best stance was no stance, the cause of racial integration in America found itself in serious trouble. In 1964 and 1965, the United States Senate had passed civil rights legislation only when liberals and moderates from non-southern states presented a united front. Now the wall was breached. Ribicoff long maintained a reputation as a steadfast ally of civil rights causes. Unwittingly, in 1970, he provided cover for other politicians who never had the civil rights credentials that he possessed. Other senators could simply claim that they were following Ribicoff, even if their ultimate intention was to halt integration or to do away with it. Moderates and border state Democrats could more justifiably join John Stennis—and they could do so in good conscience. To so many politicians, "forced integration" was at best a change to accommodate—not a policy to champion. Now they could more easily stand against it.

It would become ever harder to cobble together a majority of politicians who would support robust desegregation measures. To columnist David Broder, the cause of integration had thus moved from its deathbed into its coffin: "Desegregation is probably finished. No politicians—and few judges—will work very hard at propping up a corpse." Without a strong and clear mandate for integration, he thought, there would be no integration at all. The enactment of Stennis's proposal could create a situation in which every integration measure had to be a sweeping plan for the entire country. Leaders could no longer concentrate on eliminating Jim Crow schools in the South. As such, the movement to integrate southern schools would lose all of its momentum. One Connecticut senator, with one speech, had broken its back.[36]

By 1970, schools in the South had become more integrated than those in other regions of the country. The Supreme Court's *Alexander v. Holmes County* decision, announced in October 1969, brought desegregation to many corners of Dixie. At the end of 1970, almost 45 percent of southern black children would attend majority-white schools. The South surged past other parts of the nation while the North lagged behind. As Ribicoff later wrote, "What an unlikely turnabout that the model for *segregation* should come from the North."[37]

Ribicoff embarked upon a speaking tour, eager to publicize and explain his views. He traveled to Philadelphia on March 2. "If segregation is bad in Mississippi," he said to a crowd of 700 at the University of Pennsylvania, "it is bad in Pennsylvania." He asserted that the working and middle classes shouldered too much of the blame for racial bigotry. "The only difference between them and us—the affluent and suburban Americans—is that we have zoning boards to legalize our prejudices. Or we send our children to private schools." Before this audience of Ivy Leaguers, Ribicoff played the role of truth-teller.[38]

Ribicoff wanted to open up American society—North and South, city and suburb—to racial minorities. Yet throughout this political battle, his basic problem remained the same: the company he kept. John Stennis viewed integration as a burden. For Stennis, desegregation was a nightmare that the North should have to share. Ribicoff, in baring the North's racial soul on the floor of the Senate, had provided a great boost to Stennis's cause.

Prominent black northerners took Ribicoff to task. One was Carl Rowan, a syndicated national columnist. To him, Abraham Ribicoff had become John Stennis's pawn. Stennis shanghaied Ribicoff into helping him forge "a nationwide alliance of segregationists." Thus, "the bright hopes of racial justice and racial harmony that lighted the horizon 14 years ago have given way to ominous clouds of repression." For this shift in the national mood, Rowan blamed Richard Nixon and Spiro Agnew as much as Abraham Ribicoff. Rowan also faulted the violent "black firebrands" who handed moderate and liberal whites an excuse to give up on racial integration. Now Ribicoff had encouraged those moderates to ally themselves with Stennis. Carl Rowan could barely imagine a grimmer political picture.[39]

Ribicoff's stance also tormented many veterans of the civil rights struggle. In a letter to Ribicoff, the NAACP's assistant executive director expressed his anguish. "No one here questions your essential commitment to the objectives we are all seeking," John Morsell assured Ribicoff. Morsell mentioned the NAACP's bona fides in the struggle against de facto segregation. Indeed, the NAACP had carried that crusade from New Rochelle and Springfield to Gary, Indiana, and Denver, Colorado. But Morsell registered "sharp disagreement" with Ribicoff's position. The Stennis Amendment would have "pernicious effects." Moreover, Ribicoff had misunderstood the different American regions. "The fundamental and inescapable fact is that the South *is not* the North. The North may well be hypocritical; but the *South* has been blind, vicious, hateful, and despotic," a congeries of attitudes and behaviors all buttressed by "a massive and intricate framework of jim crow law." Hypocrisy was not barbarity.[40]

Nobody understood this better than white southern liberals. Tom Wicker, Robert Sherrill, and Pat Watters, all journalists as well as native southerners, denounced Ribicoff in the pages of national publications. Tom Wicker titled his *New York Times* op-ed "The Death of Integration." If pressures against school segregation must be applied evenly everywhere, Wicker ventured, they would not be applied at all. To call *Brown v. Board of Education* outmoded, as Ribicoff essentially had done, was to "denigrate" the actions of thousands of southerners—black and white—who worked for the better part of two decades to achieve equal and integrated education. In Greenville, South Carolina, in Yazoo City, Mississippi, and in many southern hamlets affected by the recent *Alexander v. Holmes County* decision, the hope of *Brown* had finally been realized. At that exact moment, Wicker noted, the Senate eased the pressure on the South.[41]

For South Carolina native Pat Watters, the Stennis Amendment looked like an obvious ruse. Stennis tried "to perpetuate a hoary article of Southern racist faith: that the nation ought to get the mote of racism out of its own eye before messing with the beam in that of the South." Nothing lifted white southerners' spirits like the sight of racial violence in Chicago or in Brooklyn—or of a New England liberal denouncing northern hypocrisy. For the majority of white southerners, this suggested that America had finally come around to their way of seeing things. But for Watters, Ribicoff's support of the Stennis Amendment demonstrated "the naivete of Northern liberalism." Watters still clung to a fundamental optimism. He thought that white northerners were more capable than either southern congressmen or black radicals would have America believe. Watters thought that integrationists possessed within them one more great fight. He hoped the North would rise again. The fate of the nation depended on it.[42]

Ribicoff, in battering away at the northern mystique, had threatened to crush something that the country desperately needed. Even if the mystique was mainly aspirational, it still operated as an important force. Without the mystique there as an ideal, the national reality of segregation would become that much easier to stomach.

The anti-Ribicoff forces laughed last. The House had also passed a school aid bill, but without the Stennis Amendment. So the House-Senate conference committee hashed out the differences and watered down the Stennis Amendment. On March 19, 1970, the committee added two provisos to the amendment. One proviso stated that federal obligations to enforce desegregation, as spelled out in the 1964 Civil Rights Act, still applied in full force. This required cutting off funds to those southern counties that failed to integrate their public schools. Stennis and Ribicoff both opposed the altered amendment, but to no avail. In the end, the Stennis Amendment amounted to so much sound and fury.[43]

Yet Abraham Ribicoff's impact endured. He helped to transform the politics of race in America. He opened a fault line among the traditional supporters of civil rights legislation, a crack that over the course of the 1970s would widen into a chasm. He got northerners yelling at each other about race. At the very same moment, northern senators were banding together to block Supreme Court nominees who were racial conservatives. But when it came to integration policy, northern regional unity was in decline.

Ribicoff refused to go quietly. Though the House-Senate committee weakened the bill, Ribicoff resolved to carry his message far and wide. Ribicoff's trips around the country acquired the feel of a crusade. He stopped in the Midwest in April, and in May he traveled to San Francisco. "We're all too willing to commiserate about the evils in the South, or the need to integrate our central cities, while we live serenely in our lily-white suburbs," he told the American Society of Newspaper Editors.

"We've refined the art of making sure blacks can ride at the front of buses we never ride, can attend schools we avoid, can live in someone else's neighborhood, and can work somewhere in the lower reaches of our own organization." Having shredded the hypocritical lifestyle of the liberal northerner, he launched his assault on de facto segregation. Discrimination had the "same smell" in northern cities as it did on southern plantations. "And those who clasp the artificial distinction between de jure and de facto close to their hearts will soon find the stench rubs off." He pointed out that as the South urbanized, and as the legal doctrine of "separate but equal" receded further into the past, de facto segregation would reign throughout the nation. Then he unveiled his own plan.[44]

It turned out that Ribicoff wasn't all talk. He and his staff worked for the rest of the year on a proposal for school integration in metropolitan areas. At the end of 1970, he submitted a grand plan. It took the form of an amendment to an education bill, and it applied uniformly across the country. In each metropolitan area, cities and suburbs would merge into one school system. Each school within a given system would have to contain a percentage of racial minorities that amounted to at least half the percentage of minorities in that metropolitan area. Ribicoff pledged more than $20 million in federal assistance. His plan allowed each locale the flexibility to decide exactly how it would achieve integration. He envisioned a combination of educational parks, magnet schools, redistricting, and perhaps even busing. A companion bill would increase funding for the construction of low-income housing in affluent suburbs. Ed Brooke agreed to cosponsor this companion bill, the Government Facilities Location Act. It would also halt the expansion of government offices in suburbs until those towns took steps to provide more integrated and low-cost housing. "Our problem is that time is running out," Ribicoff declared on the Senate floor. "This country is on its way to total apartheid." That did not mean Ribicoff believed his goal could be achieved anytime soon. His proposal allowed for two years of planning and ten years of implementation. It was enormous and expensive, and it promised integration by the year 1983.[45]

Looking back on Ribicoff's proposal, it boggles the twenty-first-century mind. Try to imagine the integration of every school system within a twelve-year span. It sounds fantastical, too good to be true. But at the time, many civil rights advocates opposed it. Twelve years seemed too long to wait. A lot could happen in that span of time. For civil rights leaders, memories of massive resistance in the South were still fresh. The NAACP's Clarence Mitchell feared "another 12 years in which footdraggers and obstructionists could think of new schemes" to block desegregation. Mitchell noted that Ribicoff's plan would not address segregation in rural schools. Moreover, Mitchell believed that it was too risky to entrust Congress with such a plan. What Congress passed one year, it could undo the next. John Koskinen, during an interview in 1980, reflected back on the proposal: "My prediction was in 1970, to Clarence Mitchell, and others of the civil rights people was, that I would bet them that ten years later, had they adopted the Ribicoff proposals, the country would be more integrated . . . I can look back over the ten years and say that we won the bet." In retrospect, the Ribicoff plan represented an opportunity that was never seized.[46]

Ribicoff converted many former opponents. Walter Mondale volunteered to cosponsor Ribicoff's education amendment. David Broder published a favorable column. Ribicoff's plan might "convince fleeing whites that they literally cannot leave the city's problems behind," Broder wrote. In the *New York Times*, Tom Wicker had hammered Ribicoff's original speech on the Stennis Amendment. Now, Wicker's March 1971 piece was headlined, "Mr. Ribicoff Comes Through." Wicker applauded Ribicoff for "boldly following the position he took last year." Ribicoff's plan was truly national in scope, and it came with a bill that placed the suburbs within reach of the lower class. The *Hartford Courant* called these "the most sweeping desegregation measures ever introduced." Abraham Ribicoff showed that he had in him one more good fight.[47]

As Ribicoff won back progressive northerners, he enraged the white South. Their Yankee hero revealed himself as just another meddling northern liberal. Back in February 1970, Richmond's two leading newspapers had both saluted Ribicoff. In December, they withdrew the compliments. J. Luther Glass clipped the latest editorial and mailed it to Ribicoff, just as he had done with the cartoon of the Ribicoff statue next to Robert E. Lee. On December 3, 1970, the *Richmond News-Leader* wrote, "We take back everything nice we said about Connecticut Senator Abraham Ribicoff." J. Luther Glass added: "And so do I." White southerners had no interest in a large-scale integration plan. They wanted to stop integration in the South and to eviscerate northern liberals. Ribicoff received a letter from Jackson, Mississippi, courtesy of the owner of the Sun-n-Sand Motor Motel: "Sir—Surely you do not *really* believe you can *force* integration. Let's be honest and admit it." Once Ribicoff provided a policy to match his rhetoric, white southerners recoiled and retreated.[48]

The world had tilted 180 degrees. Many New Englanders supported Ribicoff's new plan. The *Providence Journal* remarked, "The Connecticut lawmaker has done better this time." For residents of West Hartford, the proposal hit close to home. As a heavily white suburb ringing a mixed-race city, West Hartford would stand to welcome an influx of racial minorities under the Ribicoff program. "In his mind's eye," the editors of the *West Hartford News* imagined, "Senator Abraham Ribicoff must have gingerly run down the litany of Hartford suburbs, with which he is so intimately familiar, as he put forth his proposal." Perhaps he thought of West Hartford and Farmington, Bloomfield and Windsor. Given that Ribicoff relied on the votes of so many white suburbanites, his plan was especially bold. It did not promise any obvious political payoff. Walter Mondale called Ribicoff's plan "the most courageous" to come before Mondale's Senate committee.* The West Hartford editors agreed. In this Connecticut suburb, Ribicoff won plaudits for his stand.[49]

The legislation came up for debate in April 1971. Abraham Ribicoff and Jacob Javits jabbed at each other again. Ribicoff denounced northern senators in general, and Javits in particular, on the Senate floor: "I don't think you have the guts to face your liberal constituents." Javits, with head in hands, denied Ribicoff's charges. On April 21, Javits declared, "We in the North are not guilty of the same thing which the people in the South have been guilty of for so long." Javits opposed the bill. The majority of senators ultimately sided with him.[50]

Southern senators helped Ribicoff bring his education amendment to the floor. This was because they wished to place northern liberals in an uncomfortable spot. Northerners would have to either support Ribicoff's massive proposal or stand against a school integration bill. When Ribicoff's legislation came up for a vote, it was defeated by a margin of 51 to 35. Senators from the North and West divided again. Ed Brooke and Ted Kennedy voted with Ribicoff. Connecticut's freshman senator, Lowell Weicker, voted against. The four senators from Vermont and Rhode

---

*Mondale was chairman of the Senate Select Committee on Equal Educational Opportunity.

Island were opposed as well. Ribicoff thus fractured northern liberals. But he also split southern segregationists. John Stennis and Alabama's James Allen voted in Ribicoff's favor; Harry Byrd of Virginia and Herman Talmadge of Georgia voted against. A look at the roll-call vote on the Urban Education Improvement Act of 1971 produces no small measure of cognitive dissonance. Just by glancing at the yeas and nays, it would be difficult to determine whether this was a bill to speed up integration or to slow it down. Voting in favor, James Eastland of Mississippi joined Walter Mondale; Louisiana's Allen Ellender joined George McGovern of South Dakota. The list of nay votes produced the oddest of pairings. In voting against this school desegregation bill, Jacob Javits allied himself with the longtime segregationist from South Carolina: Strom Thurmond.[51]

Ribicoff's Connecticut constituents showed the racial split in the Northeastern soul. Thomas Kelley, a Farmington resident, commended Ribicoff for his "political courage" and his "responsibility to his individual conscience." But in nearby Newington, a rage was building. Joseph Nieman was an attorney, a veteran Democrat, a father of five, and the chairman of the Kellogg School Building Committee. He issued a warning to the senator, even after Ribicoff's proposals went down to defeat. Nieman argued that parents possessed the "absolute right" to send their children to "good schools in areas where their children face no threat of bodily harm." He was looking out for "those persons who invested their life's savings in homes located near schools offering a first-rate academic program." And if Ribicoff continued to support plans that allowed for the busing of schoolchildren to achieve integration, Ribicoff would live to regret it.* "Feeling runs high on this point," Nieman cautioned. "So high that, if your proposal were to receive serious consideration, the 'long hot summers' would be duplicated in our nation's suburbs—but the violence would last far into the fall and winter. I myself would be inclined to 'man the barricades.'" Nieman did not question Ribicoff's motivations. To the contrary, "I feel that your social conscience has far outrun mine." Across the Northeast, many liberal senators would outrun their constituents.[52]

In the end, it was not Abraham Ribicoff who pierced the heart of the northern mystique. It was all those white northerners who foamed at the mouth at the very mention of school busing. Mrs. Corrado Puglisi

---

*Ribicoff offered his metropolitan integration bill again in February 1972, but it met defeat.

was one of them. Puglisi, an Italian American from Hartford, wrote a letter to the *Hartford Courant* after Ribicoff's initial speech in 1970. She wanted Ribicoff to know that Connecticut did not stand with him. Ribicoff's whole thrust struck her as that of a probusing social engineer. "I'm burned up enough concerning the bussing issue," Puglisi wrote on March 2, 1970. If the Senate was bent on "passing laws to please a minority," then she would withdraw her children from "this so-called education-by-integration system." Of course, Puglisi was not opposed to busing in itself. She dreamed about busing her child into leafy West Hartford. But she knew the Board of Education would never go for that. "They say it's de facto segregation because of economic reasons. I claim the same reason. I can't afford to live in West Hartford. So bus my children for economic reasons." Puglisi identified herself as a member of the "silent majority," and she expressed its fury. "I want nothing I can't work for, but will go down fighting if forced to. After all, I have rights too."[53]

In Hartford, nobody went down fighting over busing—nor anywhere else in Abraham Ribicoff's Connecticut. The same could not be said for Massachusetts. There, the violence over busing would form the ugliest racial saga in the twentieth-century Northeast.

SEVEN

"This Bedeviling Busing Business"

The Long 1970s, the Trials of Edward Brooke, and the Fall of the North (1968–1979)

A S ABRAHAM RIBICOFF WAS BREAKING APART THE COALITION of northern liberals in the Senate, Ed Brooke tried to hold it together.

When Brooke first entered the Senate in 1967, two issues overshadowed all others: the war in Vietnam and America's unfulfilled promises to its black citizens. On Vietnam, Brooke tested out a host of different positions. He moved from dove to hawk to "owl." On matters of black equality in America, however, Brooke stood strong and firm. In 1970, when a battle broke out for the soul of the Supreme Court, Brooke led the fight against the nominations of three racial conservatives. "Black issues have sought him out rather than the other way around," the columnist Mary McGrory wrote. "He has become . . . an ad hoc spokesman for the rights of his race." Brooke was most comfortable when charting a quiet middle ground. "I am a man of caution," he told a television audience shortly before he took office. "I try to think before I act." But the events of the 1970s would chip away at Brooke's reserve.[1]

The issue of school desegregation burst onto the national scene with a kind of divisive power that it had not possessed since the days of *Brown v. Board of Education*. It morphed into a war over school busing. Nowhere was the fight bloodier than in Boston. Most politicians ducked the issue of school busing, either offering equivocations or pillorying federal judges. To defend busing was to plunge the political dagger in one's own chest. But Brooke viewed integration as a necessary end, and busing as the instrument of the hour. He stood on the Senate floor and railed against one antibusing bill after the next. At a time when racial hatred poisoned the cities of America, Ed Brooke took his lonesome stand.

Brooke held fast to his vision of a multiracial America, and he followed that vision wherever it led. In the end, it forced him onto perilous political ground. Brooke's political demise in the late 1970s ultimately paralleled the fall of the North and its mystique.

ED BROOKE WAS NO TYPICAL SENATE FRESHMAN. AS A *BOSTON GLOBE* reporter wrote, "If the first Negro senator since Reconstruction sneezes, it's news."[2]

The "long hot summer" of 1967 provided the new senator with a chance to define himself. During the first days of June, riots flared in the heart of Boston's Roxbury neighborhood while violence rippled through several other American cities. Brooke denounced the violence, but he gave voice to the grievances that lay at its root. On July 11, the NAACP bestowed upon Brooke the organization's highest honor: the Spingarn Medal. Accepting the award, Brooke asserted that rioting resulted from the awful conditions in American cities. "If Congress, out of fear or anger, continues to choose the path of inaction, racial violence in the United States will not only continue, it will recur with ever-increasing intensity." He explained why Roxbury's leaders had become increasingly militant: "They argued with validity that years of moderation had achieved few substantive gains." At this NAACP dinner, Ed Brooke acknowledged the appeal of Black Power and open rebellion: "Black Power is a response to white irresponsibility." For a onetime critic of Stokely Carmichael, so much had changed in a year.[3]

The following night, Newark, New Jersey, erupted in riots. National Guard tanks patrolled the streets; city blocks were reduced to bricks and ash. Then nearby Plainfield burned, as did New Brunswick. In Hartford, Connecticut, African Americans and Puerto Ricans rioted in the city's North End. Brooke tried to get out in front of the issue. He helped to propose a special commission that would investigate the causes of the riots and suggest some solutions.

On the night of July 23, Detroit blew. The Motor City burned for two weeks, establishing a new standard for destruction. And on July 28, President Lyndon Johnson formed a commission to study the riots. The eleven-person commission had two African Americans: Ed Brooke and Roy Wilkins. It excluded militant voices. In the end, the Kerner Commission's moderate makeup was part of its genius. For it reached conclusions so damning, they would please any radical. "What white Americans have never fully understood—but what the Negro can never forget—is that white society is deeply implicated in the ghetto. White institutions created it, white institutions maintain it, and white society condones it." Brooke's work on the Kerner Commission began to establish him as a leader on racial issues.[4]

Although Brooke wanted to be remembered as something more than a "black senator," his compass tracked the truest when it came to the problem of racial inequality. He recognized that housing segregation undergirded many of the other problems facing African Americans. They could now vote everywhere. They could patronize any business in America, and technically they could attend integrated schools (though that right was often breached). Housing segregation stood as a last frontier. Brooke worked on conquering it. In February 1968, he cosponsored a fair housing amendment with Walter Mondale. Lyndon Johnson eventually signed the Fair Housing Act into law on April 11. Brooke would go on to propose additional housing bills. The Brooke Amendment, passed in 1969, provided subsidized public housing for the poor. Over the years, open housing would become one of Brooke's signature causes.[5]

The 1968 presidential election ended up as a three-way race between Richard Nixon, Vice President Hubert Humphrey, and George Wallace. Brooke had initially favored liberal Republicans for president, but when Nixon emerged as the Republican nominee, Brooke supported him. Quickly, Nixon tested Brooke's loyalty. Nixon hurled the phrase "law and order" on the campaign trail. It was heard universally as an appeal to white racial fears. Still, Brooke agreed to travel with Nixon in September. The

Nixon campaign positioned Brooke front and center at major events from San Francisco to Chicago. Nixon's running mate, Governor Spiro Agnew of Maryland, continued to perform the dirty work. Brooke asked Agnew to refrain from using the phrase "law and order." Agnew declined the request. In South Carolina, Nixon called it a "dangerous doctrine" for the federal government to withhold funds from school districts that had failed to integrate. Brooke wondered whether Nixon knew of a more effective way to promote integration. The truth was that Nixon had no integration plan at all. Brooke could not see this as clearly as others. Jackie Robinson supported Humphrey, though Robinson had been a longtime Republican. Robinson insisted that "any black man who has any concern for the future of the United States" would back Humphrey. Robinson called Nixon "anti-black." Nixon was "in bed with [Strom] Thurmond . . . and the rest of the old South." Brooke admitted that he based his support of the Nixon-Agnew ticket more on faith than anything else. "Agnew is not a racist," he asserted. "I hope I'm right. I hope for the good of the country I'm right." In time, the Nixon administration would prove Ed Brooke wrong.[6]

Brooke remained popular in the Bay State. A 1969 poll found that 78 percent of Massachusetts residents approved of Brooke's actions; only 8 percent disapproved. But Brooke fared the worst among African Americans. Twenty percent of blacks in Massachusetts disapproved of how Brooke handled his job; 64 percent approved. Many Bay State blacks questioned why Brooke had allied himself with a president who soared to power on the wings of the "silent majority."[7]

When Brooke had first joined the Senate, early in 1967, it was embroiled in a debate over whether to weaken the filibuster—a weapon of southern whites. Liberals asked Brooke to speak out on the matter. He was quiet in the weeks leading up to that vote, although he eventually voted to curb the filibuster. Brooke's silence enraged Clarence Mitchell, the NAACP's top lobbyist. In a fit of fury, Mitchell demanded, "What the hell kind of a Negro is he?!" In 1969, many African Americans in Massachusetts were wondering the same thing.[8]

OVER THE COURSE OF THE NEXT DECADE, ED BROOKE ANSWERED THIS question. For those who had sized him up as an African American who spoke too softly for civil rights, Brooke would prove his mettle.

Once in the White House, Richard Nixon demonstrated that the "southern strategy" was more than an electoral device. It was also a way of governing. Nixon dragged his feet on school desegregation in the South. When the Supreme Court considered the case of *Alexander v. Holmes County*, the Nixon administration asked the Court to delay. As the drift of Nixon's policies became clearer, Ed Brooke's disappointment mounted. Unease soon turned into alarm.

In May 1969, Supreme Court justice Abe Fortas announced his resignation amid charges of ethical misconduct. Nixon declared that he would fill the vacancy with a "strict constructionist." He also preferred a southerner. In August, he settled on a federal judge from South Carolina named Clement F. Haynsworth Jr.—whose record on the bench revealed a history of opposition to integration. Most damning, Haynsworth sided with white officials in Prince Edward County, Virginia, who closed their public schools rather than integrate them. The United States Supreme Court unanimously reversed his decision. Brooke had the sinking feeling that Haynsworth was "chosen because of, not despite, this sorry record."[9]

If a president could get his nominee to the floor, he could often persuade a majority of senators to vote for confirmation. It was 1930 when the Senate had last voted down a nominee to the Supreme Court. Initially, Brooke believed Haynsworth's nomination would never make it out of the Senate Judiciary Committee. But the committee ultimately did send Haynsworth's name to the Senate floor.

Black members of the House, Shirley Chisholm included, had been railing against Haynsworth's rulings on school desegregation. Brooke coordinated his efforts with these congressmen, and with the NAACP's Clarence Mitchell, as he moved into striking distance. At the beginning of October, Brooke asked Nixon to withdraw the nomination. He was the first Republican to make this request.

Brooke was concerned primarily with civil rights. In addition, it came to light that Haynsworth had engaged in questionable business dealings. Given the firestorm surrounding Abe Fortas's conduct, Brooke argued that Haynsworth was hardly the man to restore America's faith in the integrity of the Court.[10]

Nixon dug in deeper. He increased the pressure on the Senate's forty-three Republicans, contending that he should have whatever judge he pleased. In turn, the Senate sharpened its scrutiny of Haynsworth.

Senators asked Haynsworth if he had changed since the time of the Prince Edward County decision. His answer was cryptic: "Haven't we all?" Brooke continued to rally votes in opposition. On November 17, he stood on the Senate floor and spoke against Haynsworth. He also placed some final phone calls to moderate Republicans, urging them to reject the nomination.[11]

On November 21, 1969, fifty-five senators voted against Haynsworth. The rejection of a Supreme Court nominee was improbable enough; the ten-vote margin had no modern precedent. Senators lined up more by region than by party. All of the senators from Massachusetts, Connecticut, and New York voted against Haynsworth. So did those from Rhode Island and Maine. Northeastern senators voted as a regional bloc. They tried to protect the Supreme Court from a southern judge who had a troubling record on issues of desegregation. And as the battle over Supreme Court nominees escalated, Brooke became a champion of civil rights.

NIXON TREATED THE SENATE'S REJECTION OF HAYNSWORTH AS A BLUFF. With his next nominee, he did not pick a judge who was more likely to gain confirmation—but one who was likely to raise the stakes. He directed aide Harry Dent to "find a judge further to the South and further to the right." In G. Harrold Carswell, Dent got his man. As Ed Brooke reflected, Carswell was "an even less qualified judge" than Haynsworth. With temerity and bluster, Nixon challenged the Senate to vote down not one but two of his nominees. It was a dare.[12]

G. Harrold Carswell had not only buttressed white supremacy with his judicial rulings. He also lived it and believed it. When Carswell ran for the Georgia legislature in 1948, he said as much in a speech before the American Legion:

> I believe that segregation of the races is proper and the only practical and correct way of life in our states. I have always so believed, and I shall always so act. I shall be the last to submit to any attempt on the part of anyone to break down and to weaken this firmly established policy of our people.
>
> If my own brother were to advocate such a program, I would be compelled to take issue with and to oppose him to the limits of my ability.

I yield to no man as a fellow candidate, or as a fellow citizen, in the firm, vigorous belief in the principles of white supremacy, and I shall always be so governed.

In the ensuing years, Carswell made good on his promises.[13]

Once Carswell was nominated, he repudiated this 1948 speech, calling it "obnoxious and abhorrent to my personal philosophy." But Carswell's actions suggested that it was quite consistent with his philosophy. In 1953, he had become a member of the Seminoles Booster Club in Tallahassee, Florida. The club's charter excluded African Americans. Carswell drafted the charter himself. Three years later, Carswell played a leading role in converting Tallahassee's only public golf course into a private club. It was a ruse to evade the desegregation of the course. The Capital City Country Club promptly banned racial minorities. Carswell served on the United States District Court in Tallahassee from 1958 to 1969, where he compiled a dreadful record. On civil rights cases, fifteen times the appellate court voted unanimously to reverse Carswell. In every instance, Carswell had ruled to delay or obstruct desegregation. All of this led Clarence Mitchell to issue a warning: "A vote for the nominee would be a vote to place an advocate of racial segregation on the highest court of the land." Mitchell did not exaggerate.[14]

Ed Brooke hardly relished the thought of crusading against another of Nixon's nominees. Nixon had first announced the nomination on January 18, 1970, and for five weeks Brooke remained silent. His delay angered many liberals. Brooke wanted to be sure that the evidence against Carswell was strong, and that a significant number of senators might actually oppose the nomination. In those five weeks, only one Republican senator had made public his opposition: Charles Goodell of New York. Liberals in the House worried that Brooke might never come around. Activists, ministers, and labor leaders from Massachusetts began to bombard Brooke with mail and telephone calls. Meanwhile, Brooke pored over Carswell's decisions. He was appalled by what he found.[15]

Brooke had hoped otherwise. "I was eager to discover such evidence" that attested to Carswell's change of heart, Brooke told his colleagues in a speech on February 25, 1970. "I searched the record for convincing proof that Judge Carswell's later actions revealed a true dedication to the principles of equal rights under [the] law. I searched in vain." Carswell had developed a reputation for hostility toward civil rights lawyers. In the field of school desegregation, "Judge Carswell appears to have consistently moved at the slowest possible pace . . . effectively delaying relief for those seeking reasonable compliance with the . . . 1954 *Brown* decision." To confirm Carswell, Brooke declared, would be "a great mistake." The country "cannot afford G. Harrold Carswell on the Supreme Court."[16]

Ted Kennedy rushed to the dais after Brooke's speech, seconding his assertions. According to Mary McGrory, the *Washington Star* columnist and Boston native, "Few Republicans wanted to hear the Senate's only black member eloquently laying out the case against Carswell and removing, one by one, the props they are leaning on to justify a vote for a Southern judge whose partisans have admitted is mediocre." A March 15 poll indicated that Carswell would win confirmation nonetheless. Three days later, Brooke received a glum memo. "People ran out of things to say about Carswell 3 weeks ago," Richard Seymour lamented. Seymour was an assistant to Marian Wright Edelman at a leading civil rights organization that was working to derail the nomination. Seymour noted that most senators seemed resigned to Carswell's confirmation. "This nomination is the most blatant kind of symbolic gesture to the South (and to the nation) that if we really want to, we can roll back the clock of racial progress in this country to at least 1948." He urged Brooke to increase the pressure.[17]

Brooke took to the Senate floor again on March 19. He spoke for some 75 minutes without notes. Brooke framed his speech around one question: "What kind of man is he?" Brooke had read Carswell's 1948 address over and over, and compared it with his actions during the 1950s and 1960s. "It seemed to me that Mr. Carswell . . . was talking his innermost, heartfelt, in-depth feelings." Brooke also reprised a theme from his 1966 campaign. "I do not believe in white superiority, and I do not believe in black superiority." If senators wished to deplore Black Power and black separatism, as many did, they would also have to oppose this longtime white supremacist. Brooke invoked the venerated role of the Senate. The whole purpose of the confirmation process was for senators to scrutinize each nominee. In the case of Carswell, any senator who was serious and fair could reach but one conclusion.[18]

Mary McGrory lauded Brooke's oration as "the most powerful speech against the Carswell nomination." It was also the least attended. Only four senators witnessed Brooke's extemporaneous peroration. But one of them held a crucial vote. Alaska's Mike Gravel was the sole Democrat from a non-southern state who had voted for Clement Haynsworth. Now Gravel sat through Brooke's entire speech, and announced that he would oppose Carswell. He concluded that since 1948, Carswell's racial beliefs had grown "into something more subtle" and even "more diabolical." Carswell was no longer a vocal defender of white supremacy; he had become its sly advocate. For Gravel, this nominee had to be stopped. The black Republican from the Northeast thus won over the white Democrat from The North.[19]

Richard Nixon protested too much. He charged that the Senate had overstepped its bounds. "The traditional constitutional balance is in jeopardy," the president claimed. Nixon further inflamed the controversy.[20]

The anti-Carswell forces moved to send the nomination back to the Senate Judiciary Committee. This would have effectively killed Carswell's candidacy. Three New Englanders remained undecided on this motion: the Vermont Republican Winston Prouty, the Connecticut Democrat Thomas Dodd, and Republican Margaret Chase Smith of Maine. On April 1, a *Boston Globe* editorial summed up the stakes: "New England Can Save the Court." The *Globe* noted that Oliver Wendell Holmes had once occupied this Supreme Court seat. A white supremacist from the Deep South threatened to sully it. The *Globe* hoped the New England senators would overlook political calculations and party allegiance, and vote their conscience. "They can save the day—and the Court."[21]

On Monday, April 6, Margaret Chase Smith and Winston Prouty both opposed the motion to recommit the nomination—thereby supporting Carswell. The measure was defeated by a 52 to 44 margin. So the vote for confirmation would occur on April 8. Brooke and his allies had two days to persuade several more senators. New England had not saved the Court. At least, not yet.

In the hours leading up to the final vote, both sides targeted Margaret Chase Smith. She was the Senate's only woman and its third-ranking Republican. She wore a fresh red rose in her lapel each day. *Time* called her "formidably taciturn." Smith had gained fame in 1950 when she denounced the tactics of Senator Joseph McCarthy—a fellow Republican. Smith cherished her reputation for political independence. Ed Brooke described her as "a classic Mainer, honest and unadorned, blessed with a steely intelligence, and famous for her rock-ribbed aversion to all personal lobbying before a Senate vote." Brooke knew she had her doubts about G. Harrold Carswell. She asked Brooke to prepare a memo about the segregated golf club. By the time Brooke delivered this material, he learned that Nixon had already summoned Smith to the White House and presented the case for Carswell. Her intentions remained a mystery.[22]

Smith told Brooke that she would not make a final decision until the time of the vote. On the morning of April 8, however, one of Brooke's aides discovered that Smith had promised the White House her support. Moreover, Nixon's staffers were using this piece of information to try to sway undecided senators. Brooke interrupted Margaret Chase Smith during lunch in the Senate Dining Room. He asked her about the swirling rumors. Smith was furious. She called Bryce Harlow, a top Nixon advisor, demanding to know how widely he had publicized her decision. In Smith's eyes, the Nixon administration was "impugning her independence." She cursed Harlow, slammed down the telephone, and headed to the Senate chamber.[23]

Senators gathered at one o'clock in the afternoon while spectators in the gallery grew increasingly raucous. Vice President Spiro Agnew, presiding over the chamber, asked for silence. The roll call began. Ed Brooke was the second senator to vote against confirmation. Carswell led by a margin of 9 to 4 before the clerked called the name of Kentucky's Marlow Cook. Cook was a southerner, a Republican, and a freshman senator. He had been a strong supporter of Clement Haynsworth. But now he answered, "No." The spectators gasped. Cook, a lawyer by training, would explain that the Supreme Court had always inspired awe in him. Judge Carswell did not measure up to that high standard. Two other southerners, J. William Fulbright and Albert Gore, also opposed Carswell. The votes against Carswell began to pile up. Mike Gravel voted against confirmation. So did the liberal stalwarts Jacob Javits, Ted Kennedy, and Walter Mondale. The outcome still hinged on two Republicans from New England: Winston Prouty and Margaret Chase Smith. Prouty felt deep party loyalty, but his Yankee constituents stood strongly against Carswell. Prouty voted "No," and a burst of applause rang out from the gallery. Now Nixon needed help to save his nominee. He needed Margaret Chase Smith's vote as well as those of two southern Democrats—Virginia's William Spong and Texas's Ralph Yarborough.[24]

When Smith's name was called, she answered with a "No" that was barely audible. The spectators erupted in cheers. Spong and Yarborough both voted to reject, bringing the tally to 46 to 44. Carswell was finished. Six holdouts then decided to cast their votes, making the final count 51 to 45. Whistles and applause rained down from the gallery. Spiro Agnew pounded his gavel, calling for order. Senator Richard Russell asked the Sergeant at Arms to clear the galleries. The crowd streamed outside and onto the Capitol steps. Brooke recalled, "I will never forget walking into that throng to cheers and shouts of Bravo! They felt, as I did, that it was a great day for America."[25]

This was the thinking throughout the Northeast. The *New York Times* called it an "astonishing vote." The *Boston Globe* reveled in an "intoxicating triumph." To Brooke's African American constituents, it was a victory indeed. For the *Bay State Banner*, Brooke "has rapidly become a powerful defender of this community's interests." And if Nixon nominated yet another judge with segregationist leanings, "we hope that Senator Brooke will rise from his Senate seat once more to do battle." Brooke had become their pugilist.[26]

The occasion brought Brooke a letter from Shirley Chisholm. "I just want to say thanks for your work on the Carswell case," she wrote on April 17. "Your brand of quiet persuasion is very much needed."[27]

Less than a week after Carswell's defeat, Nixon nominated Harry Blackmun to the Supreme Court. Blackmun was from Minnesota, and he was known as a conservative. The Senate confirmed him in a unanimous vote. In 1973, Blackmun would write the majority opinion in the case of *Roe v. Wade*.

Nixon eventually got a southerner as well as a racial conservative. Two more vacancies appeared on the Court in the fall of 1971. Nixon nominated Virginia's Lewis Powell, a racial moderate and a corporate lawyer with close ties to the tobacco industry. He won confirmation by a huge margin. For the other seat, Nixon nominated William Rehnquist—a lawyer with a soft spot for the "separate but equal" doctrine of *Plessy v. Ferguson*. Ed Brooke voted against Rehnquist's nomination, but he could not stop it. Brooke was one of only twenty-six senators who opposed William Rehnquist.

In the end, Brooke had helped to keep Haynsworth—and more importantly Carswell—off the Supreme Court. Northeastern senators banded together to protect the Court from the stain of segregation. They showed how powerful a force northern regionalism could be.

If they could save the Supreme Court, they could not save Boston.

FOR RUTH BATSON, THE 1960S AND 1970S WERE "A HORRIBLE TIME TO live in Boston." From an early age, this Boston native realized "there were flaws in the cradle of liberty. . . . Racism abounded here in Boston." Batson devoted much of her life to the cause of school integration. In the early 1960s, she headed the NAACP's Education Committee. Again and again, black leaders had to point out that schools with a majority of white children possessed the majority of resources. "That's where the care went," Batson recalled. "That's where the books went. That's where the money went." While the NAACP increased the pace of its activism, Louise Day Hicks became the face of white intransigence. Hicks and her followers met demands for school integration with fear and rage and force.[28]

All of this seemed incongruous. The state of Massachusetts had passed the Racial Imbalance Act in 1965. It outlawed the very conditions that Ruth Batson was protesting. And because racial minorities accounted for less than 20 percent of Boston's population, the desegregation of its schools seemed feasible. Ed Brooke remarked, "If integration can work anywhere, it can work in Boston." Moreover, the state of Massachusetts stood as a citadel of political liberalism. The Bay State's voters were alone in their choice of George McGovern over Richard Nixon in the 1972 presidential election. That year, they reelected the nation's only black senator.[29]

Governors John Volpe and Frank Sargent were both liberal Republicans and champions of the Racial Imbalance Act. Volpe passed the bill; Sargent led a long struggle to enforce it. When Sargent became governor in 1969, he inherited an explosive situation. Leaders in Boston and Springfield were still defying the law. And state legislators were trying to strike it down. Springfield faced a cutoff from state funds on April 1, 1971, if it failed to present an integration plan. Springfield representatives filed a bill to prevent the funding cutoff; this bill passed the state senate as well as the House. Sargent vetoed it. Then in 1972, Sargent opposed eleven different bills aimed at the Racial Imbalance Act. Against rising opposition, the governor dug in his heels.[30]

As Sargent upheld the Racial Imbalance Act, he invoked a mystique about the Bay State—a belief that it led the nation and looked ever forward. In a May 1973 speech, Sargent narrated a celebratory history of the state. He cited John Winthrop, the Puritan leader who proclaimed, "the eyes of all people are upon us." Sargent portrayed Massachusetts as a beacon: "When this nation cried out for leadership during the uneasy period of the civil rights struggle, Massachusetts, in its great tradition, stepped forward and provided that leadership. We adopted the historic Racial Imbalance Act that guaranteed equal and integrated education for *all* our citizens." He wanted Massachusetts to act as a model. "Leaders all over the country are watching to see if Massachusetts has the true commitment to equality for which it is so widely known and admired, or whether it has, for over 100 years, simply paid lip service to this doctrine." By 1973, Boston's schools were even more segregated than when the Racial Imbalance Act was passed. Those who took the "lip service" side of the argument gathered steady support.[31]

The campaign for "racial balance" had become synonymous with busing. In 1971, the United States Supreme Court ruled that busing could be used to achieve integration. In cities riddled by neighborhood segregation, busing seemed the most effective way to integrate schools. The Massachusetts Board of Education then concluded that it was insufficient to close down majority-black schools and bus only black students. The Board urged Springfield and Boston to explore cross-busing plans, in which students would be bused not only from majority-black schools but also from majority-white ones.

Boston became a center of antibusing ferment. Resistance to school integration had been germinating there for years, especially in the working-class neighborhoods of South Boston, East Boston, and Charlestown. The antibusing movement also gained support from middle-class parents in areas like West Roxbury. On April 3, 1974, the antibusing movement enlisted a citywide army when some 20,000 demonstrators gathered on Boston Common. Bolstered by this outpouring at the grass roots, the state legislature offered its boldest gesture. It passed a repeal of the Racial Imbalance Act. On May 1, 1974, the repeal landed on Frank Sargent's desk.[32]

Sargent delivered a televised address. He considered what "caused one of the most progressive legislatures in America to vote repeal of one of the nation's most historic efforts to further social justice." He distinguished between southern resistance to integration in the 1950s and 1960s, and northern resistance to "racial balance" in the 1970s. In Massachusetts, "those who resist have not made their life's work blocking a good education for *other* children. Rather, they seek to insure a better education for their own." Sargent ultimately agreed to repeal the Racial Imbalance Act. He offered in its place a voluntary integration plan that stripped the state's Board of Education of the authority to redistrict or bus students. At long last, Sargent had caved.[33]

Black leaders were outraged. State Representative Mel King perceived Sargent's proposals as "reactions to a hostile white majority." Indeed, Sargent was mistaken in his assessment. He claimed that those northerners who opposed busing "have not made their life's work blocking a good education for *other* children." But by 1974, to oppose busing in Boston was akin to opposing integration. White Bostonians had resisted all attempts to integrate schools in the nine years since the Racial Imbalance Act was passed. They would not willfully opt for integration. The range of practical choices had been narrowed down to two: busing or segregation.[34]

African Americans had no other recourse but to file a lawsuit, which the NAACP did in March 1972. Black parents "tried everything," Ruth Batson remembered. "They tried the appeals. They tried going to the school committee. They tried going to everyone to get help." Tom Atkins, president of Boston's NAACP branch, called the lawsuit a "last resort." Atkins had repeatedly met with the Boston School Committee and the superintendent, and never gained an inch. Out of desperation, the NAACP turned to the courts. The NAACP filed a class-action lawsuit on behalf of fifteen black parents and forty-three children. The case became known as *Morgan v. Hennigan*. The lead plaintiff was Tallulah Morgan, a mother of three; James Hennigan was the chair of the Boston School Committee.[35]

On June 21, 1974, U.S. District Court judge W. Arthur Garrity ruled in favor of the African American parents. Garrity found that Boston's leaders had engaged in a series of practices designed to keep the schools racially segregated. He ruled that Boston must desegregate its schools at once. Garrity drew up a busing plan. In a fateful decision, he paired Roxbury with South Boston. African American students would attend South Boston High School, and Irish Americans from Southie would board buses to Roxbury. Boston soon exploded in racial violence.

HISTORY HAS NOT BEEN KIND TO THE DEFENDERS OF MANDATORY SCHOOL busing. Into the twenty-first century, busing remains one of the few issues on which the Right and the Left can agree. To conservatives, "forced busing" is the exemplar of big government run amok. Most liberals will also argue that busing was a failure—a wrongheaded policy that affluent suburbanites foisted upon the white working class. But such views too often ignore the perspective of African Americans. Ed Brooke took up their cause, and he argued eloquently for the necessity of school busing.

Boston's ordeal with busing thrust the nation's only black senator into a wretched predicament. Brooke represented Boston while he defended busing on the Senate floor. Exploring how Brooke navigated the busing crisis, from Washington to Boston, one views it in a new light.

Each year from 1966 to 1977, the United States House of Representatives passed at least one law designed to restrain school integration—often in the guise of antibusing bills. The Senate turned back each of those bills until 1974. As busing beset Boston, and as white resistance escalated around the country, the House's antibusing majority pulled more and more senators to their side. Brooke never crossed over.

Decades later, Brooke would play down his stance. "I was no *great* supporter of busing," he said in 2009. "I wasn't an advocate of busing; I was an advocate of desegregation of the schools." Busing "was an inconvenience to the parents, inconvenience for the children. . . . You can strongly make the case against busing." Yet Brooke never made that case. The historical record reveals the opposite.[36]

For Brooke, integration was an absolute imperative. "We had all-black schools and all-white schools." Busing "was the best thing that we had to at least desegregate the schools at that time in our history. And I thought we didn't have anything better." The goal was a desegregated society. "Busing was one of the tools." Many white Americans thought they could support integration in the abstract while opposing the vehicle that would deliver it. Brooke labored to keep alive the connection between them. Up against vicious resistance in the streets of Boston as well as a rising backlash on the floor of the United States Senate, Brooke became a champion for busing.[37]

In March 1974, Nixon's Watergate impeachment hearings dominated Washington. The House took time out to consider the Elementary and Secondary Education Act. Michigan's Marvin Esch proposed an amendment to the bill, stating that a child could not be bused beyond the nearest school. Esch's amendment passed easily, with more than 70 percent of House members in support.[38]

The Senate received the bill in May, days before the twentieth anniversary of the *Brown v. Board of Education* decision. This irony was lost on many senators. The Senate version of the bill stipulated that no child could be bused past the two closest schools. On May 15, Brooke delivered an emotional address on the Senate floor. Such an amendment would "put us back decades," he angrily declared. Blacks who lived in ghettoes would be trapped in ghetto schools. The amendment could even cause the resegregation of many schools—mainly in the South—where integration had only recently begun to operate with success. To restrict busing so severely would be to sanction a return to separate and equal schools. "For two decades, the course has been sure but slow. And now we ask to hastily and drastically alter it. Why? Because many Americans have become confused by the rhetoric on busing." Brooke boiled it down for them. "The issue is simple. Shall we or shall we not permit necessary remedies to a constitutional violation? . . . The fact is that in many cases, busing is necessary to uphold the law." Brooke called the amendment "unconscionable and unconstitutional." For him, this was not an antibusing amendment. It was an antidesegregation bill.[39]

One senator matched Brooke's passion: Ted Kennedy. He followed Brooke's speech with a rousing one of his own. Kennedy said the amendment would "precipitate a constitutional crisis," for it struck at equal protection rights. Listening to Kennedy's words, one could hear echoes of Robert Carter's closing argument in the Springfield courtroom a decade prior. "Any demand to return to the neighborhood school," said Kennedy, "is a call for a return to segregated schools." The Senate tabled the amendment by a vote of 47 to 46. The *Bay State Banner* saluted Brooke for his work against this "insidious" amendment: "Right on, Senator!"[40]

The Senate vote broke down along geographical lines. Southerners supported the antibusing amendment. From the thirteen states of the Old Confederacy, twenty-five senators voted for the amendment; Arkansas's Fulbright abstained. Southern leaders may have boasted that their schools were now more integrated than those of the North. But they unanimously opposed busing. Eleven of twelve New England senators voted to table the amendment. So did New York's Jacob Javits. Northern cities were most threatened by the prospect of busing. Yet it was northern senators, together with those from the West Coast and the Midwest, who preserved busing as an option.[41]

The amendment defeated, Brooke turned his attention back to the Bay State. He examined Frank Sargent's voluntary integration plan and pronounced it "dead wrong." Brooke said on June 1, "I cannot support any plan that eliminates busing as a tool to achieve school integration." In a city so shaped by spatial segregation, and up against a white population opposed to anything but "neighborhood schools," no voluntary plan could work.[42]

UNDER JUDGE GARRITY'S RULING, BUSING WAS TO BEGIN IN BOSTON ON September 12, 1974. Through the summer, members of the antibusing movement swamped Judge Garrity with letters and telephone calls. They transformed the sidewalk outside his Wellesley home into a convention for the white backlash. As the first day of school approached, antibusers set their sights on Ted Kennedy and Ed Brooke. They planned to take over City Hall Plaza on Monday, September 9, to protest the senators' repeated votes in favor of busing.

At 9:30 that morning, 8,000 demonstrators gathered on Boston Common. They marched toward Government Center, lifting their voices in a rally cry: "Here we come, Teddy, Here we come, Ed!" Two people dressed in chicken outfits. One, identified as "Kennedy," donned a white mask; the other wore a brown mask and bore the label "Brooke." Ed Brooke stayed in Washington, as he did through much of September and October. The marchers, a cross section of Boston's white working and middle classes, had never really supported Brooke. He felt little need to confront them. But they formed part of Ted Kennedy's core constituency.[43]

Without warning, Kennedy appeared at City Hall Plaza. He strained to make himself heard above the din. Signs read, "Impeach Kennedy." A woman punched Kennedy on the shoulder. One man yelled, "Shoot him!" Another hollered, "You're a disgrace to the Irish!" The crowd screamed taunts about Kennedy's slain brothers and his crippled son. The senator was jeered off the stage, his blue pin-striped suit stained red with bits of tomato. He retreated into the John F. Kennedy Federal Building. The crowd surged to the door and pressed upon the glass. Protesters beat on the windows, shattering the huge panes into a thousand pieces.[44]

An elevator whisked Kennedy to the safety of his office, high up on the twenty-fourth floor. He needed a cup of coffee before speaking with reporters. He poured milk into the paper cup, unable to keep his hand from trembling. After righting himself, he met with the media. "I am hopeful that this will dissipate. The constitution . . . has come to Boston." In desperation, Kennedy invoked Boston's lofty heritage and its progressive reputation. "I just hope Boston will make it through this and continue to set an example for the rest of the country." Indeed, Boston would set an example. It would display the fury that was mounting against "forced integration."[45]

Blood began to flow in Boston. White mobs attacked African Americans, hurling bricks at yellow buses that carried black children. In turn, Boston's Tactical Police Force brutalized a group of whites at a bar in South Boston. Race riots engulfed South Boston as well as Roslindale, West Roxbury, and Hyde Park. On October 7, a Haitian immigrant had the misfortune to stop his car at a traffic light in South Boston. As a mob surrounded him, André Jean-Louis got out of the car and ran for his life. He bounded onto the porch of a nearby house, but the mob ripped him back down to the sidewalk and savagely beat him. Over the coming months, the list of casualties would grow.[46]

The violence in Boston fascinated the American public. Due to the media coverage at the time, as well as to a spate of books written in the decades since, Americans have long viewed the busing crisis through the eyes of working-class whites in Charlestown and South Boston. But to focus on their grievances is to miss a significant part of the story. While Garrity's busing order sparked violence and accelerated white flight to the suburbs, it also brought desegregation to many schools. So concluded the United States Commission on Civil Rights in its 1975 report: "Throughout the Nation the prevailing view is that court-ordered desegregation of the public schools in Boston proved to be a disaster. . . . We take issue with this conclusion." Overall, "substantial progress was made in Boston in 1974–75 in the direction of upholding and implementing the constitutional rights of children and young people." Because of busing, several schools experienced peaceful integration. This did not make the headlines.[47]

Still, the busing plan horrified the black community as well as white Bostonians. It was not easy for black parents to send their children on buses to South Boston. They knew the racism that enveloped the neighborhood, and they realized that South Boston High School was no educational promised land. Many black parents nevertheless saw busing as a first step.

In an excruciating way, Tom Atkins found evidence to support his probusing convictions. Under his direction, the Boston branch of the NAACP had conducted a survey in 1974 among black students who were bused to South Boston High School. The completed surveys sat in the bottom of Atkins's briefcase for a week. In his office one night, Atkins pulled out the pile of papers. "I began, sort of absently, to read through them." It was "like being hit with a sledge hammer. It was an experience I'll never forget as long as I live. . . . What I saw was that these kids couldn't spell. They could not write a single, declaratory sentence. They couldn't spell the name of their street. . . . They couldn't spell Boston. They couldn't spell high as in high school. They couldn't spell negro, they couldn't spell *black*." Atkins was unable to contain himself. "I just started to cry." Yet he felt more than sadness. "It was impossible to explain the feeling of pain, on the one hand, but on the other hand, I knew we were right." He was emboldened, armed with devastating proof. "We had to get those kids out of those schools and this proved it."[48]

Atkins had become well acquainted with the venom of the antibusing movement. For one year, beginning in August 1974, he received an average of forty death threats per week. To him, the message of the antibusing movement was clear: "Keep the niggers in their place." As much as antibusers insisted they were not racist, their actions during 1974 and 1975 told a different story. There were truths they could not explain away: the most vocal supporters of busing in Boston were all black people. And African Americans were also the most frequent victims of the violence that broke out.[49]

The furor in Boston inverted popular conceptions about region and race. "The rest of the republic, believing all the clichés it had ever read about the city," journalist Alan Lupo wrote, "was confused or shocked or, in the case of the South, delighted." Virginia Beach resident Elizabeth

Neal broadcast her euphoria in a letter to the *Boston Globe*: "My eyes and ears must be deceiving me! Is it really true that Boston, the cradle of liberty, freedom and democracy, is experiencing integration difficulties?" She articulated John Stennis's longtime hope. "Methinks the . . . pious Northerners . . . would do better to solve their own problems . . . before pointing their fingers at the South." The *Globe* printed many such entreaties. One woman from Shreveport, Louisiana, penned an open letter to the people of Boston. "Where were you in the 50s and 60s," Barbara Hodges asked, when "integration and busing were forced on the South? Where were your voices, where was your indignation, where were your protests?" Hodges implored Bostonians to vote their liberal senators out of office. Jimmy Howle of Quincy, South Carolina, used the occasion to play upon stereotypes. "Us poor, ignorant, racist, redneck Southerners sure do admire the brotherly, civilized and orderly manner in which you enlightened, cultured, dignified Bostonians are handling your school integration problems." The idea of Boston as a place of civility and enlightenment was a joke.[50]

While these individuals greeted Boston's racial woes with an intense schadenfreude, they did not speak for all white southerners. Jim Evans had lived in Little Rock in 1957, when that city pronounced itself the center of American bigotry. He was bewildered by the hate that coursed through the streets of Boston. "Why you? How could the city which gave us the Kennedys, and the state which had the good fortune to vote for McGovern in 1972 be guilty of this?" Evans reported that Little Rock had successfully implemented a school integration plan, replete with busing, in subsequent years. "Why can't you Northerners accept integration as well as we Southerners have?"[51]

Boston residents had no answer. "Boston has acquired the reputation of being a progressive, open-minded city where anyone can live in peace." So wrote Peter DiBartolo, who had recently moved to the area. He was saddened that his new home had become "a nightmare for children who happen to be black." Mark Brightman was a Boston native and a senior at Purdue University. "When confronted with the question, 'Where are you from?' I have always been proud to respond, 'Boston, Mass.'" Brightman noted that he opposed "forced busing." But he was disgusted "to see the insults and injuries inflicted upon the black students who were guilty of no offense except that of obeying a Supreme Court decision." A core part of Brightman's identity had been challenged. "The pride that I once knew has been severely damaged." He would now have to confess his hometown with an offer of apology and a shrug of embarrassment.[52]

To see busing succeed, Americans could look to the South. In Charlotte, North Carolina, sixteen-year-old Tina Gouge was one of many busing pioneers. At West Charlotte High School, Gouge's student government committee started a campaign to write letters to Boston's students and citizens. Gouge, an African American, acknowledged her initial trepidation at the prospect of a twelve-mile bus ride. But she eventually found integration to be "a fantastic experience." She counseled Boston students to exercise patience and openness. Don Turbyhill, a white student, wrote, "You can't expect to adjust overnight—but please give it a chance." The Charlotte students then extended an invitation to their Boston brethren. In the last week of October, four students from Hyde Park High School traveled to North Carolina. As Linda Lawrence, a seventeen-year-old Bostonian, admitted, "I never thought I'd be going South for a lesson in racial relations." The world turned upside down.[53]

Charlotte was an anomaly. In the vast majority of southern cities, whites resisted attempts at integration—especially two-way busing. Private white "segregation academies" sprouted across the South. But while Charlotte was exceptional in the way that it embraced busing, Boston was exceptional in its level of violence.

Boston remained a cauldron of racial hatred through October, punctuated by stabbings in the schools. As the city careened toward the brink, Governor Frank Sargent mobilized the National Guard.[54]

The northern mystique seemed dead and gone. In its place stood hatred and blood, lies and hypocrisy.

LETTERS POURED INTO ED BROOKE'S OFFICE. CAROL MURPHY, A HYDE Park resident, spoke for many whites. "We are heading for a revolution—a 'Race War,' for we the people of Boston will not accept forced busing." As a way of legitimizing her antibusing views, Murphy highlighted her ancestry: "Member #A 473, Descendants of Governor William Bradford of Plymouth Colony . . . Direct Mayflower Descendant of: Francis Cooke, Henry Samson, George Soule and others." In Murphy's eyes, her "race war" kept with the long tradition of freedom seeking on these shores. Six

South Boston parents wrote together to remind Brooke that he could still win them over. "Not anti-Brooke—just opposed to busing—change your views." Six other Bostonians took a more fixed position: "Will not vote for Brooke because of his stand on school busing."[55]

Brooke continued to stand on principle. He insisted that integration was right. Not only that: the Constitution required it. Buses could bring desegregation; thus they were necessary.

Brooke instructed his staff about how to reply to the deluge of antibusing correspondence. He scrawled his notes on Senate stationery. "Begin busing letter to those who phoned with following: Many thanks for your deeply felt telephone call to our Boston office. I respect your honesty, your caring, your sincere conviction though we come down on opposite sides." Brooke's torment showed on the second page of the document. He recognized that in defending busing he was walking treacherous political ground. Atop page two, Brooke used big blue letters to spell out his dilemma: "This Bedeviling Busing Business."[56]

Brooke knew he could not persuade these parents; neither could he stop himself from trying. To mount his strongest argument in response to his constituents' mail, he narrated the recent history of school integration. Ever since the 1954 *Brown* decision, "the Boston School Committee has been on notice." Boston officials understood that "action/leadership were required." In 1965, the Massachusetts legislature demanded action against segregation. But Boston officials shirked their duties. "Instead of compliance, imaginative action, preparation for the inevitable day of legal reckoning, I ask you to look long and hard at what has happened in Boston in the last ten years. And more." The members of the Boston School Committee, a body on which no black person had ever served, attempted to thwart the law. "Judge Garrity entered [the] picture only because the duly elected public officials of Boston did not/could not act." Brooke acknowledged the flaws in Garrity's busing plan. But Boston's leaders had placed the city in a hole, and Garrity was trying to dig out of it. "There is a less than perfect busing plan, by order of a federal judge, *only* because *yesterday* the Boston men and women who should have led, planned, organized, educated chose to lull you to sleep about the harsh realities of what the law meant and mandated." The Boston School Committee had compounded the problem.[57]

Late in 1974, there was no time to draw up a perfect solution. That hour had passed. "Busing isn't the perfect/or even a very good/answer to the problem of desegregating the public schools. But it's *an* answer which—in its final analysis—federal judges will make if local officials all abdicate their responsibilities." When one considered the history of resistance to integration, busing looked like a reasonable response. "That— in my judgment—is why we are where we are in Boston."[58]

The intransigence in Boston fed the beast in Washington, and vice versa. On October 12, Brooke explained that antibusing politicians had created "a Frankenstein monster." They unleashed a fearsome entity and it began to mutate. A Maryland congresswoman took the antibusing cause to its logical conclusion. That October, Marjorie Holt attached an amendment to a Health, Education, and Welfare (HEW) appropriations bill. It required the federal government to continue funding school systems that had disobeyed integration orders. It also prohibited collecting data on race and sex from students and teachers. If there were no statistics, there could be no more laws aimed at "racial balance." True to form, the House adopted the Holt Amendment.[59]

In the Senate, Brooke continued to act as the last line of defense for busing—and for school integration measures more generally. He successfully led a move to table the Holt Amendment. In mid-December, the Senate took up the amendment again. Liberals added language that would essentially nullify it. Before that weakened bill could come up for a vote, Senator James Allen of Alabama orchestrated a filibuster. Brooke urged his colleagues to cut off the filibuster. In a rare show of rage, Brooke pounded upon his desk. "If we have to stay here until the next Congress comes here on January 14, we will not accept the Holt amendment!" In this battle, Brooke bested his colleague from Alabama. With a vote of 56 to 27, the Senate invoked cloture. The Holt Amendment was defeated.[60]

All of this went a long way toward establishing "what kind of Negro" Ed Brooke had become. He would stand up for the cause of school integration. The *Chicago Defender* singled out Brooke for the "stellar role" he played in this saga. In the season of "forced busing," Ed Brooke remained in the progressive vanguard.[61]

Brooke waged a two-pronged struggle. He rose on the Senate floor, and pounded on his desk when necessary, to turn back the most repellent of the anti-integration bills. He also kept an eye on the situation in Boston. The two busing battles had little legal connection, for no bill passed in the Senate (short of an amendment to the United States Constitution) could interfere with Judge Garrity's order. Yet Brooke was enmeshed in both ordeals, his plight tied to the legislation on the Senate floor as surely as it was to the horrors that unfolded on the streets of Boston.

As the Christmas holiday approached, Brooke gazed toward home. On December 23, 1974, he wrote an open letter to Boston's citizens. The *Boston Herald-American* published the letter on Christmas Day; it appeared in the *Boston Globe* the morning after. Into the letter Brooke poured his deepest convictions about race, integration, and the city upon a hill. This Christmas, Boston was besmirched. "This holiday season finds our proud city imbued with anguish, bitterness, and divisiveness. It finds our children scared and abused. It finds our neighborhoods seared with fear and hate." Brooke appealed to Bostonians' better angels by invoking their sense of history. "All of us should be ashamed. Boston is the cradle of liberty. It was here in the 18th Century that the very rights being denied our children today were so eloquently articulated." He kindled the memory of the abolitionists, and pointed out that Bay State residents had lent great support to the southern civil rights movement. "This is our heritage, and we have asked others to accept it. Yet sadly we seem unable to commit it to our own benefit in our own city." Bostonians possessed a lofty history, but they refused to use it to their advantage.[62]

This was not the Boston that Brooke had come to love. This was not the city that provided cultural, social, and professional refuge for a son of black Washington. "I cannot accept, nor can I believe, that Bostonians want a segregated school system." Left to their own devices, Brooke asserted, Boston's citizens would have accepted integration. But local politicians whipped them into a frenzy. He noted that the vicious reaction had a lot to do with the presumed place of the school within American society. For the working class, education was the ticket up and out. It formed the first rung on the ladder that led to the "American Dream." "Our nation has always held education to be our hope for the future." Many political leaders, like Ted Kennedy, tried to shift the focus from "forced integration" to "quality education." Brooke exposed this as a false dichotomy. Integrated schools were crucial parts of a quality education. Brooke revived ideas about democratic pluralism. Education was not simply math, reading, and science. "Rather, education is preparation for living in our diverse society." The purpose of the school "is to ready our children for the very serious duties of citizenship. Its goal is to ensure an enlightened citizenry, without which our democratic experiment would fail."[63]

Brooke put forth an expansive conception of democracy. In contrast, the antibusing movement was concerned with a narrow understanding of individual rights. This was why the antibusing struggle struck Brooke as so foul. To "consciously shield" children from those of another race was to "consciously retard their education." This would "leave them critically ill prepared to deal with and relate to the great pluralism that is our society." If Ed Brooke's life experiences had taught him anything, it was the invaluable worth of interactions with other races and creeds. He was a pioneer of interracial politics in America. And Brooke still believed that multiracial democracy was essential to America's greatness. The "neighborhood school" would leave American children unfulfilled and strip the country of its promise. Brooke's vision anticipated future arguments for affirmative action just as it looked back to the professed pluralism of the Springfield Plan.[64]

Brooke ended his letter in sadness more than indignation. "The strife in our city reveals how far we have to go." That strife also showed something about the North. "It reveals that the fear, the hate, the suspicion that is racism, looms darkly not only in the 'Heart of Dixie' but in the 'Cradle of Liberty.'" This was not a novel insight—not in 1974. But the violence in the streets of Boston brought this truth home like nothing else did. When Christmas morning came, hatred still blanketed Boston as melancholy enveloped Ed Brooke.[65]

In 1975, the youngest member of the Senate became Brooke's chief antagonist. Joseph Biden was a thirty-two-year-old Democrat from Delaware who owned a liberal voting record. Biden had previously stressed his commitment to school desegregation, and for that he earned the ire of his constituents. So Biden quickly moved against school busing. He pressed his finger to the nation's pulse. He saw busing as a "domestic Vietnam." The analogy applied not to the bloodshed in Boston but to the emotional and psychic toll that busing had exacted—the way it tore America apart. Biden railed against those "federal bureaucrats" who had jettisoned "good old common sense." He viewed busing as most Americans did: It was a senseless struggle, a quagmire in which overzealous policy makers had en-snared innocent parents and students.[66]

George McGovern, a liberal Democrat, went along with the busing-as-Vietnam analogy. But he placed a different spin on it. The Demo-cratic Party had lost its soul on Vietnam, thought McGovern. Now he feared the party would "sell its soul on the issue of busing." He worried that liberals might troll for the votes of the antibusers and leave African American children confined to ghetto schools. McGovern's fears came to life. When Joe Biden offered antibusing amendments, many liberals joined him. Their discomfort with racial integration, in evidence for several years, at once became a full-scale retreat.[67]

Brooke was left by himself to plead and cajole. He could count on the votes of liberals like Javits, Kennedy, and Mondale, but they no longer summoned any passion. Brooke still believed busing was worth a fight. In that conviction he stood increasingly alone.

On September 17, 1975, Senator Jesse Helms went on the attack. Helms, a racial conservative from North Carolina, offered a forceful anti-integration amendment. It would prevent HEW from collecting any data needed to identify segregated school systems. Brooke sprung to action, and the Senate tabled Helms's amendment. When a southern segrega-tionist led the antibusing charge, Brooke could rally his troops.

Joe Biden proved a more formidable adversary. When this young lib-eral from a border state delivered the antibusing message, it was more difficult to discredit as a segregationist ploy. Biden attached a rider to a $36 billion education bill, prohibiting the use of federal funds "to assign teachers or students by race." In proposing his amendment, Biden an-nounced: "This chamber should declare busing does not work, and leave it." A majority of senators were happy to oblige. The Senate quickly adopted Biden's amendment. Jesse Helms was delighted. He welcomed Biden "to the ranks of the enlightened." A number of former busing supporters followed him there: Warren Magnuson and Scoop Jack-son of Washington, where Seattle faced likely integration orders; and Thomas Eagleton and Stuart Symington of Missouri, where Kansas City confronted a similar fate. Mike Mansfield, the majority leader from Montana, jumped on board, along with Wisconsin's Gaylord Nelson. Watching his liberal colleagues defect, Jacob Javits declared, "They're scared to death on busing."[68]

Brooke was livid. He had guided the larger education bill to the Senate floor. Now this bill possessed a tail—in the form of a noxious rider—that threatened to wag the dog. Brooke called the vote on Biden's amendment "the greatest symbolic defeat for civil rights since 1964"—when Congress passed the Civil Rights Act. He pointed out that Biden's amendment would eliminate virtually every remedy for segregation. It was an assault on the very idea of integrating schools.[69]

On September 24, another border-state Democrat moved against busing. Robert Byrd, the West Virginian who had since repudiated his Klan past, offered an amendment to prohibit busing beyond a student's nearest school. This kind of amendment had met defeat in May 1974. Now it passed the Senate by a vote of 51 to 45.[70]

If northern regional unity reached a sort of apogee on the Haynsworth and Carswell nominations, and if the Ribicoff controversy began to divide northern senators, then the issue of school busing finally splintered Capitol Hill's old civil rights coalition.

In the end, Biden drew up a compromise measure that the progressive northern bloc was forced to accept. It barred HEW from ordering busing, though it left other integration measures intact. This amendment, known as "Biden II," sailed through the Senate on September 26. Brooke lamented, "It is just a matter of time before we wipe out the civil rights progress of the last decade." The clock was turning back.[71]

At first, Brooke and his staff believed that their defeat was more symbolic than substantive. Ralph Neas, Brooke's top legislative assistant, drafted a memo that recapped the floor fight over busing. "The practical effect of the Biden Amendment is not too severe," Neas asserted. Busing was most often the result of court orders, and the courts were unaffected by the amendment. Furthermore, Biden's amendment could have an unintended effect. To restrict HEW's power would be to push more cases into the legal system, potentially inducing even more court-ordered busing. In tangible terms, Biden II posed little direct threat. "The symbolic effect of the Biden Amendment and the other antidesegregation amendments is far greater," Neas cautioned. "For the first time the Senate has retreated on its commitments to the desegregation of our public schools." Brooke and his aides could sense—but not yet fully see—that when it came to policies on race, the line between symbol and substance was fluid.[72]

A certain set of circumstances had to exist in order for America's white majority to stomach strong integration policies. Public support depended upon the idea of a battle between good and evil. White Americans had to see desegregation as a moral imperative. The situation could not seem ambiguous. Once those stakes became clouded, the fight was lost.

African Americans in the North felt no such conflict. As Tom Atkins said, "An anti-busing amendment is an anti-desegregation amendment, and an anti-desegregation amendment is an anti-black amendment." Atkins had little trouble sifting right from wrong.[73]

Most white northerners saw it differently. They had viewed racial inequality in the South as a struggle between right and wrong. But in the North, the villains and the heroes did not seem so obvious. The city of Springfield, in rejecting the idea that it needed to integrate, had used the line: "If we were segregationists." For white northerners, the moral waters were already murky. The busing issue turned that muck into a thick sludge.

The original purpose of Ralph Neas's memo, drafted on October 1, 1975, was to prepare Brooke for a string of interviews with the press. In one resulting article, *U.S. News & World Report* presented "both sides of the busing issue." Ed Brooke was the face of the probusing side. Joe Biden represented the antibusing position.[74]

The article read like a tale of the tape. A photo of a youthful Biden, sporting sideburns and a full head of hair, topped the left column. When asked whether busing caused more harm than good, Biden answered: "Absolutely." Biden argued that the concepts used to justify busing "now seem to me to be profoundly racist." By Biden's logic, busing reinforced the idea of black inferiority. Busing implied that African Americans could "cut it educationally" only if they sat next to white students. "It implies that blacks have no reason to be proud of their inheritance and their own culture." In Biden's act of rhetorical jujitsu, the antibusing position was the one that respected African American culture. Biden also insisted that the vast majority of white Americans had no objection "to their child sitting with a black child, eating lunch with a black child—all the things that were the basis for the racist movement in the past." White Americans simply wanted to send their children to nearby schools. Biden divorced the antibusing position from the racial hatred that encircled it. He expressed pride in the fact that many Senate liberals had supported his amendments. The antibusing position was "becoming more respectable." Biden happily took credit for that development.[75]

Brooke presented a nuanced defense of busing. "It is not necessarily the best way, but in certain instances busing is the *only* way to achieve desegregation." Brooke favored the building of new schools and the consolidation of old ones, for example, if such measures could bring integration. "But when these fail or are inappropriate, busing is a constitutional tool that should be used, and is being used, but *only* as a last resort." Brooke called the busing issue a "red herring." Thousands of American students had been bused for many years. In the South, busing helped to bring desegregation. "I don't think the positive story about busing has been told." School buses were helping to bring about the integrated society of Brooke's dreams. "It's not popular—certainly among my constituents. I know that. But, you know, I've always believed that those of us who serve in public life have a responsibility to inform and provide leadership for our constituents." It seemed like a revolutionary concept. Brooke knew that voters disagreed with him. But the rights of a minority were on the line. Brooke could not bend. He had to lead.[76]

As more liberals voiced doubts about busing, the Senate's civil rights bloc fractured completely. Meanwhile, the antibusing movement grew further emboldened. It proposed a constitutional amendment to ban busing. In December 1975, Brooke met with Boston's leading antibusing group—Restore Our Alienated Rights (ROAR)—about this amendment. A member of ROAR reported on the meeting: "We did not receive any hope for our cause." There was no confusion about where Brooke stood.[77]

Brooke still flew below the radar. Columnist Carl Rowan termed Brooke "the most underrated . . . of all the prominent black politicians." At least Rowan himself was on notice. "The truth is that no black politician has talked more sense more forcefully about the highly emotional issue of school busing than Brooke. And it has taken a measure of courage for him to do so, since busing in Boston may be the most dangerous political issue in his state." Brooke realized this, but only to a point. He did not grasp the full depth of that political danger.[78]

To his antibusing constituents, Brooke remained a source of outrage and of mystery. Did he not know he was committing political suicide? Mrs. John E. Naoum, a white mother in Dorchester, wrote to Brooke in July 1975. She enclosed a letter that Brooke had sent to her in October 1974.

She demanded: "I would like to know if you still feel the same way in July of 1975? . . . Please help us. We are not against integration in our society. We are against the forceable [forcible] abduction of our children." Naoum could not have been pleased when Brooke's response arrived in the mail a week later. As Brooke explained, "My feelings are indeed the same as I expressed to you last October." Busing was "by no means the cure-all," but it "must be available as a remedy." Brooke continued to stand firm. In July 1976, he replied to Irena Greatorex of Marblehead. She was another constituent with whom Brooke had an ongoing exchange. Brooke wrote, "I am sorry that we must continue to disagree about the issue of busing. I am afraid I cannot change my position, because I believe strongly in upholding the Constitution." In choosing to uphold the Constitution, however, Brooke was loosening his grip on his high office.[79]

IT WAS NOT THAT BROOKE LOST THE SUPPORT OF SO MANY MASSACHUSETTS citizens who joined the antibusing movement. He had not depended upon their votes to begin with.

The crucial dynamic was more subtle. Because of Brooke's stance on busing, the Bay State's moderate and liberal white voters came to perceive their black senator in a different light. Previously, voters had convinced themselves that Brooke transcended race. But Brooke's position on busing gave the lie to that myth. In the 1966 and 1972 elections, whites could believe that voting for Brooke had nothing to do with school or housing integration. If race was a factor in their voting behavior at all, it was that many were pleased to elect and to reelect the nation's only black senator. But when Brooke acted that part too well, he placed himself in political peril.

It is impossible to know whether that alone would have been enough to doom Ed Brooke. In the end, many issues converged to seal his fate. Boston was not only the center of the antibusing movement; it was also a hotbed of antiabortion activity. After the Supreme Court's *Roe v. Wade* decision, Catholics in Massachusetts mobilized against abortion. In 1975, a doctor named Kenneth Edelin was convicted of manslaughter in a Boston courtroom. Edelin's crime was that he had aborted a fetus. He was also an African American. Edelin decried the racial and religious prejudice in Boston, and declared that such an atmosphere made a fair trial impossible.[80]

Brooke fashioned himself as a strong defender of abortion rights. On the Senate floor, he upheld a woman's right to choose with the same intensity that he backed the authority of government officials to bus children. One Catholic constituent warned Brooke: "Our convictions in this matter will certainly be reflected in our voting." While resentment over race and integration swirled around Ed Brooke, he also crossed the Massachusetts electorate on issues of sexuality and religion. The two struggles over busing and abortion helped to spotlight what Ed Brooke thought he had buried long ago: he was still an African American and a Protestant in a state that remained heavily white and Catholic.[81]

Ted Kennedy agreed with Brooke on abortion and on busing. But Kennedy's situation differed from Brooke's in that he was an Irish Catholic, a Democrat, and a member of political royalty. In addition, Kennedy seemed to be made of Teflon. Kennedy drove a woman to her death on Chappaquiddick Island in 1969. One year later, the voters returned him to the Senate. In 1976, Kennedy campaigned again for reelection. He faced a leader of ROAR in the Democratic primary. Kennedy's challenger was perceived as a one-note politician who offered nothing but the antibusing message. Kennedy cruised to reelection. The age of busing was not an easy time for Ted Kennedy, but neither did it spell political death.

Nothing damaged the image of Boston's antibusing movement, or of Boston itself, more than one infamous photograph. It appeared shortly before Kennedy's victory in the Democratic primary. The photograph was titled "The Soiling of Old Glory." On April 5, 1976, an African American lawyer named Ted Landsmark found himself rushing across City Hall Plaza while late for a meeting. At that moment, an antibusing march rounded the corner. In the resulting frenzy, white youths attacked Landsmark with the only weapon at their disposal: an American flag. The image appeared on front pages of newspapers. The photographer, Stanley Forman of the *Boston Herald-American*, won a Pulitzer Prize.[82]

Despite the ongoing busing crisis and the abortion controversy, Brooke was able to find some calm amid the storm. In many moments, he still appeared to be the old Ed Brooke: the dapper dinner-party guest, polished and unflappable. But the political tempest of 1978 would shake that smooth demeanor.

Brooke's marriage had been failing for several years. Rumors swirled when he was photographed with Barbara Walters or with Elizabeth Taylor.

He had filed for divorce in 1976. The *Boston Globe* detailed the drawn-out divorce proceedings. In May 1978, the *Globe* reported that Brooke had given a false statement about the source of a personal loan. A "stricken" Brooke admitted the "mistake." But he insisted that the loan had no material impact on his divorce settlement, and that he had broken no law. The Senate Ethics Committee would eventually absolve Brooke of wrongdoing on this specific matter, but not before long and withering scrutiny.[83]

Avi Nelson had already declared that he would challenge Brooke for the Republican nomination in 1978. Nelson, the son of a Brookline rabbi, was known as a fiery conservative. He hosted a nightly radio show and a television program. Through the spring of 1978, he hammered Brooke on busing and abortion, and denounced Brooke's vote in favor of the Panama Canal Treaty. Nelson reflected the rightward tilt of the national Republican Party. Leading conservatives organized direct-mail campaigns on his behalf. The New Right had arrived in the Bay State.

Back in Washington, Brooke tried not to notice Avi Nelson. Joe Biden sponsored another antibusing amendment, one the *Globe* described as "particularly bad." It sought to bar federal judges from ordering busing in all but the most blatant instances of segregation. Brooke led the charge to table the amendment. He prevailed by a two-vote margin. This saga highlighted the "overriding question in Massachusetts politics," according to the *Globe*'s editors. "Will Brooke be there next year?"[84]

Attention focused on the Bay State's small Republican electorate. Brooke and Nelson both encouraged Democrats to switch their affiliation to Independent, and to cast votes in the Republican primary. Brooke's staff concentrated on black Democrats in Roxbury. "Do not for a moment underestimate what is at stake," the *Bay State Banner* cautioned. The *Banner* noted Brooke's work on public housing and the battle against Carswell. "Brooke's absence in the Senate would be an obvious disaster to minorities."[85]

On Primary Day, September 19, state senator Bill Owens made the rounds through Roxbury. He repeated one message: "Don't forget about Brooke, now." A middle-aged black man responded: "How could I forget about Brooke? I'm breathing, ain't I?" It was hyperbole, but it made the point. Brooke's African American constituents still believed in him. Overall, Brooke garnered 53 percent of the vote to Nelson's 47 percent.

Before a packed crowd at the Parker House Hotel, Brooke declared that his triumph sent a message to the Republican Party: "If the Republican Party is to become the majority party, there must be room for liberals and moderates as well as conservatives." Brooke was no prophet. But on the evening of the primary, he was a winner.[86]

In 1966, Brooke had hailed the "color-blind commonwealth." That phrase resurfaced in 1978. And it assumed a new meaning. Congressman Paul Tsongas, the Democratic nominee, used the language of color blindness to frame the general election campaign. Tsongas asserted that "it is the other side of racism" to reelect Brooke *because of* his race. "After twelve years, that's enough for a symbol." National columnists Jack Germond and Jules Witcover agreed. The question of the Senate campaign was "whether the liberals in this capital of liberalism can display the political maturity to be color blind." In this twist, it was the height of "political maturity" to disregard Brooke's standing as America's only black senator—and then to defeat him.[87]

Brooke picked up an array of endorsements. Gloria Steinem and Barney Frank (a state legislator at the time) stood strongly for Brooke. So did Ronald Reagan and Henry Kissinger. Brooke also won the backing of the NAACP's Clarence Mitchell. Brooke had amassed an appeal that crossed partisan and ideological lines.[88]

Paul Tsongas was a second-term congressman from Lowell. He had a liberal voting record and kept a low profile. Tsongas, like Brooke, defended school busing as well as abortion rights. On policy alone, they had few differences.

Brooke's record was strongest on issues of racial equality. He could have emphasized his campaigns against Haynsworth and Carswell, his work on fair housing, and his crusades for school integration and school busing. But Brooke rarely played up that part of his senatorial career. The sword had two edges. If he ran on the strength of his civil rights record, he would have forsaken the strategy that won him all four of his statewide elections: the appeal to color blindness. Yet if Brooke did not highlight racial issues, he would leave in his pocket a trump card.

Brooke's advisors urged him to play that card, in a subtle way if possible. An internal memo spelled out what Brooke needed to do. "Appeal to this state's pride, her sense of being unique. There are still a lot of romantic liberals out there, waiting to be moved. . . . You have to convince them that the whole world is watching, that the ultimate issue at stake is not only who can do more for Massachusetts, but who means more for America." Brooke had to remind the Bay State voters, ever so gently, that he was the nation's only black senator.[89]

Brooke's financial and personal issues refused to die. The Senate Ethics Committee continued to investigate the actions of Brooke's attorneys. And his divorce produced a fallout: Brooke's daughter, Remi, denounced her father in bitter language. Brooke endured "months of almost Shakespearean nightmare," as the *Washington Post* put it. Into late October, polls gave Tsongas a decisive lead.[90]

In a sign of Brooke's desperation, he considered raising the issue that held the greatest potential for risk as well as for reward. On October 26, Brooke and Tsongas engaged in a televised debate. The moderator asked Brooke about his personal and financial problems. Brooke said he felt targeted and victimized. The experience was like "running through the woods. The hounds were yelping and the posse was behind me and I didn't know why." Brooke conjured up an image of the black man's terror in the South, a lynch mob at his heels. Brooke proceeded: "I am sure that every little black child looks up and says, 'If Ed Brooke can make it, I can make it.'" He added, with a chuckle, "And I think every little white child looks up and says, 'By God, if Ed Brooke can make it, I'm sure I can make it.'" Brooke focused on the symbolism that he had carried—so uncomfortably—throughout his political career. "Obviously, I am the only black that's ever been popularly elected to the United States Senate." This "only meant to me that Massachusetts was colorblind." In response, Tsongas urged voters to look exclusively at the candidates' records. Both candidates sang the praises of a color-blind electorate.[91]

Brooke's staffers felt he had fallen short in that debate. As the second debate approached, one aide wanted Brooke to offer as selling points his positions on integration as well as abortion. "Bite the bullet: who had the guts to stand up for the rights of poor women and demand equal rights for them in the abortion controversy?" Brooke's aides urged the senator to pull at voters' heartstrings. "Do the people of this state wish to reject a man who has . . . led a virtual crusade in the Senate . . . for all those ideals of equality and justice that we like to think of as uniquely American?" And he needed to connect more with the voters on the basis of the racial issue. "Get them to say, 'well . . . I don't want to be responsible, even in my own mind, for depriving 20 million Americans of representation.'" Brooke had to transform the election into a matter of conscience.[92]

To Mary McGrory, Brooke's "greatest asset now is his race." Brooke had to hope that Bay State voters would prove "reluctant to retire the Senate's only black member, the living proof of its advanced liberalism." Brooke was pushed toward a position he had always tried to avoid. But Brooke seemed to sense, better than Mary McGrory had, and more keenly than his own staff had, that he could never truly sell himself as *the black politician*—not if he wished to win.[93]

As Election Day drew near, Brooke summoned the northern mystique. On November 2, the *Globe* offered front-page space to each candidate. Tsongas focused on policy details while Brooke unveiled the rhetoric. Brooke noted that a senator had to work on subcommittees, craft legislation, and tend to his constituents. But one also needed a broader understanding of what it all meant, "a vision of life in Massachusetts as it should be." Brooke touted himself as a voice for the voiceless. "The rich and the powerful have spokespersons. The underprivileged do not. I believe they have come to rely upon me to give voice to their frustrations and ambitions." Brooke played up the Bay State's regal history. "I stand in the proud tradition of Massachusetts senators who, from the days of Webster to Kennedy have spoken to a national and international audience, while never forgetting the real needs of the people at home." Massachusetts needed not just a representative for its interests, but a senator worthy of its historic greatness.[94]

This pitch had lost some of its luster. Boston stood guilty before the nation and the world, disgraced by the recent racial violence. The turbulence of the 1970s altered the stakes. Voters had been buffeted by school busing and the oil crisis, neck-deep in malaise. In this circumstance, they craved more than the grandiose rhetoric of prior years. The aspiration that Brooke offered had become but a flimsy reed.

Brooke was also caught in a difficult political spot. Liberals were content to support Tsongas. Antibusers detested Brooke. Conservative Republicans remained suspicious of him. This left few votes for the taking.

Brooke's campaign literature declared, "Ed Brooke Means a Lot To Us." To reinforce that message, civil rights icons like Coretta Scott King and Jesse Jackson came to Boston during the first weekend of November. Brooke also meant a lot to liberal Democrats. Barney Frank, Joe Rauh (a well-known civil liberties lawyer), and Elizabeth Dunn (the head of the National Organization for Women in Massachusetts) coauthored a letter to the *Globe*. "His civil rights record is unsurpassed. He has been our most effective advocate in the quest for equality of opportunity for all Americans. . . . We need Ed Brooke in the US Senate. The loss of Ed Brooke would be a tragedy for the Commonwealth and for the nation."[95]

On Election Day, November 7, the voters spoke clearly. The early returns showed Tsongas with a double-digit lead. Brooke was as gracious as ever in his concession speech. He thanked Tsongas for "the honorable manner he has conducted his campaign." To those who voted against him, Brooke held "no bitterness in my heart." To the end, Brooke floated above the fray.[96]

An irony marked the end of Ed Brooke's political career. The state that had elected Brooke four times, wrote *Globe* reporter Norman Lockman, "had also been colorblind enough apparently, to replace him with a more liberal white opponent." Such reasoning appealed to many white progressives, for it allowed them to champion their own enlightened bona fides all over again. African Americans in Massachusetts disagreed. They believed Brooke had lost because of his race. According to black Bostonian Alvin Holland, "the *Globe* never went after anyone . . . like they went after Brooke." Brooke refused to see his own defeat as racially motivated. But among African Americans, his sentiment was not the prevailing one. "Blacks don't have a prayer," said Doraleena Summons, a graduate student at Harvard. "Who is on our side in Congress now? We just lost 200 years of progress." The Senate was losing its old liberal lions. Hubert Humphrey had passed away early in 1978, as had Philip Hart of Michigan a year prior. Increasingly, Brooke stood for the political, social, and racial progress of the 1960s. That era seemed more and more like a distant memory.[97]

Over the course of two decades, blacks in Massachusetts had assured themselves that Brooke's appeals to color blindness were merely a crafty electoral strategy—not something that the senator actually believed. For Bay State blacks, Brooke had sealed his campaign slogans with a wink and a smile. They all knew that Massachusetts was never a color-blind haven. Citing Ted Kennedy's rebound after Chappaquiddick, Needham resident Robert Robinson charged, "There is a double standard among liberal voters when it comes to judging the conduct of political candidates with different skin colors." In 1978, Brooke's skin color stood out. As many black voters saw it, this determined his fate.[98]

Brooke struggled with his defeat. He was fifty-nine years old and newly divorced. "I was hurt, embarrassed, and depressed." Politics had occupied Brooke for years. Now the action was gone. "The winter of 1978–79 marked the lowest point in my life."[99]

This also marked a low point in the life of the North. It was not that Ed Brooke's defeat caused the fall of the North. The Boston busing crisis had already achieved that. But Brooke's loss at the polls paralleled the larger regional demise, reflected it, and crystallized it. In 1967, he had integrated the Senate with such a flourish. Now the resegregation of that body was complete.

As the 1970s ended, even the pretense of progress seemed gone. The last pieces of the Northeast's once-proud industrial cities would finally crumble. Tax revolts loomed. The suburbs continued to swell, leaving ever more impoverished cities in their wake. As racial minorities in the region—from Boston to Hartford to New York City—looked toward the final decades of the twentieth century, many of them arrived at the same conclusion that had settled upon Ed Brooke: the future did not look promising.

Backlash from seg.
complete w/ busing
crisis - turning point
optamism → defeat Brooke/
busing

PART IV

THE DEATH AND LIFE OF THE NORTH

EIGHT

A Tale of Two Hartfords

Politics and Poverty in a Land of Plenty
(1980–1987)

FROM THE VANTAGE POINT OF INTERSTATE 91, THE DEPTHS OF Hartford's problems were easy to miss. In that way, the capital city symbolized Connecticut as a whole. To those in cars and commuter trains, the state offered so many facades. This was true for investment bankers hurtling into New York City from New Canaan and Darien, for Manhattanites fleeing to country homes in Old Lyme or Sharon, and for travelers heading from Boston to New York. The parkways of Connecticut could impart the impression that it was a place of wealthy suburbs and precious small towns, of trees and greenery, of oceans and rivers. At the end of the twentieth century, Connecticut had the highest per capita income in the nation. But Connecticut's cities existed in an entirely different reality. In 1980, Hartford was the fourth-poorest city in the nation; New Haven and Bridgeport also ranked among the most destitute. By 2010, Hartford was America's poorest city. Connecticut's cities were clusters of poverty in a land of plenty.[1]

Hartford itself contained two separate cities. Downtown, insurance buildings reached toward the sky and the top of the Old State House sparkled. Hartford also had temples of high culture: the Wadsworth Athenaeum, the Bushnell Theater, the historic homes of Mark Twain and Harriet Beecher Stowe. But the places that bustled by daylight were shuttered and abandoned at night. Hartford's African American population huddled in the North End, along with many of the city's Puerto Ricans. This neighborhood featured boarded-up buildings, grinding poverty, and a bevy of unemployed residents. Here, the northern mystique landed on its rear. Hartford epitomized the failures of the urban North during the 1980s.

At the same time, Hartford became a center of black politics. As more white residents moved to nearby suburbs, Hartford's racial minorities flexed their political muscles. In 1981, Hartford voters elected the first black mayor in New England. Thirman Milner assumed power just as his city hemorrhaged jobs, capital, and residents. He inherited a host of problems too debilitating for any political leader to solve. His career set an example, by turns inspiring and cautionary, for those black mayors who would follow.

The ordeal of Hartford during the 1980s showed that even as African Americans claimed historic advances in politics, their economic plight could worsen. Hartford's story posed questions about the very meaning of racial progress.

THE LAND OF STEADY HABITS WAS ONCE TOBACCO COUNTRY. Connecticut's tobacco farms lured laborers from far and wide. When World War Two broke out, many workers shipped off to Europe and the Pacific. The tobacco companies, eyeing new sources of labor, helped to fuel the Second Great Migration. About 18,000 southern blacks, along with several thousand Puerto Ricans, migrated to Hartford during the war. Some of them landed jobs in the state's booming defense industries. Others ended up in the tobacco fields of the Connecticut River Valley, exchanging one kind of agricultural existence for another.[2]

As the wartime labor shortage grew more acute, tobacco companies started to contract with black colleges in the South. In June 1944, a group of students from Morehouse College set off for the farms of Simsbury,

Connecticut. One student, a fifteen-year-old Atlanta native, was ready to enroll at Morehouse in September. For Martin Luther King Jr., the journey to the North left an indelible imprint. On June 15, 1944, King wrote a letter to his father: "On our way here we saw some things I had never anticipated to see . . . all the white people here are very nice. We go to any place we want to and sit any where we want to." In a separate letter to his mother, a disbelieving King reported, "Negroes and whites go [to] the same church." King and his friends used a weekend afternoon to explore Hartford. "We really had a nice time there. I never [thought] that a person of my race could eat anywhere but we ate in one of the finest restaurants in Hartford. And we went to the largest shows there. It is really a large city." He felt an "exhilarating sense of freedom." For the young King, the North delivered on its promises.[3]

At the end of the summer, King returned to the South with a "bitter feeling." As his train rumbled through Virginia, he ventured into the dining car. A waiter ushered him to a table in the rear and pulled a curtain down, sparing white passengers the misery of watching a black boy eat. King recalled, "I felt as though a curtain had dropped on my selfhood." In King's memory, the contrast between Connecticut and Virginia was stark.[4]

In part, King succumbed to adolescent naïveté. Hartford was no racial paradise. On the other hand, African Americans could indeed dine in many of the city's restaurants. They could even attend small-town white churches like the one in Simsbury. His observations reflected something important about the racial flexibility of wartime Hartford.

King went home after the work was done, but many other southern blacks stayed in Connecticut for good. African Americans increased their voting strength as they expanded their numbers. They pushed political leaders toward racial progressivism. In 1947, the state assembly passed an FEPC law. By that point, African Americans represented 7 percent of Hartford's population. During the 1950s, the suburbs boomed. As 95,000 people left the city, Hartford welcomed 56,000 new denizens. Almost one-third of them were racial minorities. Politicians tried to keep pace with this transformation. Connecticut banned housing discrimination in residences with five or more units. And in 1955, Hartford voters elected John Clark, an African American, to the City Council. By 1960, African Americans accounted for 16 percent of Hartford's population. More and more, they would help to define the city's character.[5]

Urban renewal greeted Hartford with bulldozers. Highways carved up poor neighborhoods and displaced black people. This solidified patterns of spatial segregation while encouraging the suburban boom.[6]

The summer of 1967 was long and hot. Many of Connecticut's cities erupted in violence: New Haven, Bridgeport, Waterbury, Middletown, New Britain, Stamford, Norwalk, and New London. The riots hit Hartford the hardest. Then in 1968, after the assassination of Martin Luther King Jr., African Americans surged through Hartford's streets, hurling bricks and stones at the police. Violence again gripped the city in 1969: on Labor Day, crowds of blacks and Puerto Ricans set a public library ablaze, battled with police officers, and laid waste to almost one hundred buildings. State police patrolled the city with shotguns. The summer of 1970 saw more unrest. Hartford's political leaders stood by helplessly as flames licked the sky for the fourth summer in a row.[7]

And they watched with chagrin as businesses picked up and left. Between 1960 and 1980, Hartford lost more than half of its manufacturing jobs while Connecticut's tobacco industry shed fifteen thousand jobs. The southern blacks and Puerto Ricans who had come to work in the fields and the factories now grappled with a bleak economic landscape.[8]

Hartford seemed to escape the worst of it. The insurance industry helped to blunt the economic devastation. Out of a mix of self-interest and goodwill, corporate executives "kept Hartford going," as Thirman Milner remembered. "Had they not been there, it would have been a ghost city." No company embraced the spirit of noblesse oblige with more gusto than Aetna. It reserved entry-level positions and maintenance jobs for Hartford residents. The heads of four companies formed the Greater Hartford Corporation in 1969. They devised a fifteen-year, $800 million plan to renovate the city. In this vision, the business community would help to erect vast housing complexes and design new parks. What was good for Hartford was good for the insurance titans.[9]

In the wake of the riots, politicians and businessmen agreed: Hartford needed to change, and to change fast, or the anger that raged in the North End would engulf the entire city.

Hartford was looking for a strong hand, and Nicholas Carbone provided it. As chairman of the Democratic Town Committee, Carbone ran Hartford's Democratic machine from 1969 to 1979. He also served on the City Council. In many northern cities, white leaders responded to black violence with cries of "law and order." Not in Hartford. Carbone pumped money into poor neighborhoods through Community Development Block Grants. He inaugurated a neighborhood-policing program and funded the Hartford Food System. He also developed a close relationship with the head of Aetna. Carbone helped to build the Hartford Civic Center and lured a professional hockey team to the city. Eventually, Carbone overreached. In 1979, he ran for mayor. He lost badly to the incumbent, George Athanson.[10]

For all of Carbone's policies, and all of the corporations' financial resources, Hartford residents grew more destitute. Factories fled the city, as did white residents.* Most new job openings involved clerical or service work. There was little for an unskilled laborer to do. By 1979, the city had a total of 134,000 jobs. Fully 100,000 of them were held by people who lived in the suburbs. Hartford became the first majority-minority city in the Northeast. Forty-six percent of its population was white. African Americans counted for 34 percent, and another 18 percent were Puerto Rican. It was a city with abundant poverty, and a large and growing number of racial minorities.[11]

It also provided the setting for New England's first black mayor. Late on the night of Thirman Milner's election (in 1981), members of his staff whisked him across the Connecticut River to a twenty-four-hour diner in East Hartford. It afforded Milner a view of the Hartford skyline. He looked at his staffers and asked: "What did you get me into? What have I done?" Milner gazed at the city where he was born and raised, and marveled at his journey.[12]

Milner was born in 1933, the sixth of seven children. His mother's family had roots in Connecticut. During the eighteenth century, they lived in bondage near Middletown. In the 1930s and 1940s, Milner's mother worked as a domestic in West Hartford, "scrubbing floors on her hands and knees in kitchens where she was not allowed to eat." He never bought into the region's racial mystique.[13]

---

*Middle-class blacks also left the city for the suburbs—with mixed results. In Manchester, two African American homes were firebombed. In 1981, an all-white jury acquitted the suspect.

His boyhood summers were divided in two. Each half of the season represented one of the Northeast's warring strands. He spent his best weeks at Camp Bennett, an interracial haven in nearby South Glastonbury. (The camp was founded at a time when the Hartford YMCA refused membership to black youths.) But the dog days of summer found Milner in the tobacco fields. He awoke early and boarded a school bus that ferried black youths from Hartford out to the fields. He remembered the labor as miserable. After his freshman year of high school, he transferred to Glastonbury High—the only black student amid a sea of white.[14]

Milner did not attend college. Instead, he served a stint in the Air Force during the early 1950s. He enlisted along with a white friend from Glastonbury. They were stationed in Mobile, Alabama, where Milner encountered a new kind of misery. One weekend, Milner and his friend headed off of the base and into downtown Mobile. The pair of Yankees boarded the bus together, then immediately realized their mistake. The bus driver jumped out of his seat, grabbed a monkey wrench, and hollered at Milner to get out and go around the back. He continued into town on the back of the bus.[15]

Milner was more familiar with Hartford's version of racial discrimination, the kind that consigned black people to certain neighborhoods and specific jobs. He helped to found the local CORE chapter. Hartford CORE organized demonstrations against G. Fox & Co., a large department store that hired African Americans only as elevator operators and janitors. Milner went south again in 1962, joining civil rights protests in Albany, Georgia. He cut his teeth on direct-action campaigns.

Through the 1960s, he toiled variously as a drug store clerk and a hospital orderly. At the end of the decade, Milner moved to New York City and worked in the Parks Department. He returned to Hartford early in the 1970s and took a position with the Community Renewal Team. Milner forged a relationship with the leader of Hartford's civil rights struggle: state senator Wilber Smith. In 1976, Smith pushed Milner into electoral politics. Early on a Saturday morning, Smith dragged Milner to an apartment in the Bowles Park public housing complex. Ruby Law, a resident of the housing complex and a friend of Wilber Smith's, sat the men down and filled them up with coffee, grits, eggs, and sausage. "She looked at me and said, 'You're going to run for state representative,'" Milner recalled. It was more of a demand than an inquiry. The incumbent in the 7th Assembly District was an African American, Clyde Billington, but many activists perceived him as in the pocket of the Democratic machine. Wilber Smith saw in Milner a man who was committed to civil rights activism but who could also succeed in the larger electoral arena. Milner ran for the assembly seat and lost to Billington by a grand total of five votes. He ran again in 1978, and coasted to victory.[16]

It was Milner's boss in the private sector who steered him toward City Hall. Jim Monroe headed a small oil company for which Milner worked part-time. Monroe urged Milner to run for mayor. In the beginning, Milner was skeptical. "I had no inkling, no ambitions. . . . I said, 'Look, Jim, we've never had an African American mayor not only in Hartford but in New England.'" But he allowed the idea to work on him. Milner talked with his family, then sought the advice of the state's Democratic Party. Democratic leaders had a simple message for him: "Stay where you are." Throughout the city and state, leaders belittled Milner's aspirations. When Mayor George Athanson heard that Milner was considering a run for mayor, he dismissed it as a joke. The head of Hartford's NAACP told Milner that he would be "wasting the black vote." Out of this aching experience came Milner's almost sarcastic—and soon ubiquitous—campaign slogan: "Why Not? Milner for Mayor."[17]

Milner ran on neither bitterness nor blind faith. His political team crunched the numbers. If Milner could win a large majority of black votes, and if he could split the Latino vote, he would need about 20 percent of the white votes. This provided a plausible path to victory. The journey up from poverty just might lead to City Hall.[18]

MOST OBSERVERS THOUGHT THAT A MAYORAL BID WAS NAÏVE AT BEST and suicidal at worst. Milner had just begun his second term in the state assembly, where he was an assistant majority leader. George Athanson had won five straight mayoral elections.

One *Hartford Courant* article suggested that if Milner pitted black and Puerto Rican voters against whites, he could effectively split Hartford in two. Then the campaign would get interesting. Milner rejected this notion. "I would not want to become mayor of a multiethnic city by just winning the votes of any one ethnic group," he wrote in a letter to the *Courant*. He hoped voters would choose their mayor based upon ability and commitment, without regard to race. He might have sounded like Ed Brooke fifteen years earlier, but Milner's terrain was quite different. He needed to run a campaign that was race-based in one crucial respect. He had to rustle the sleeping giant of Hartford's body politic: the black voters of the North End.[19]

On June 14, 1981, Milner formally announced his candidacy. Standing before a crowd at the Old State House, Milner took care to characterize himself as a candidate "who happens to have been born this color." He was eager to bring white voters into his coalition while simultaneously galvanizing the North End. It was not at all clear whether the two desires could coexist.[20]

Milner drove a yellow Cadillac and favored three-piece suits, facts that the *Courant* never let the public forget. The newspaper was taken with Milner's "impeccable" appearance; it described his speech as "articulate."[21]

In the final week of July, Hartford's Democratic Town Committee met to select its slate of candidates for the upcoming primary. George Athanson emerged with the party's mayoral endorsement. A Latino member of the selection committee informed Milner that Hartford was not ready for a black mayor. This was the explanation that Milner's campaign slogan alternately begged and rued. The slogan itself—"Why Not?"—mixed laziness with insight. It failed to define the candidate in any positive way. It even invited negative characterizations. But if voters thought about the slogan, there was one obvious reason to oppose Milner: his race. That realization pained New Englanders. It would be unseemly to deny Milner the office because he was black. And yet, in back rooms and quiet corners, observers insisted that the racial barrier was impregnable. For Milner to win 20 percent of the white vote seemed impossible.[22]

The morning of August 27 brought stunning news. The *Hartford Courant* endorsed Milner. The *Courant*'s editors saw in Milner an individual who could plant one foot in the corporate boardrooms and another in the struggling neighborhoods. The *Courant* urged citizens to disregard Milner's race when they stepped into the voting booth. At the same time, the election of an African American played into a basic argument about progress. The *Courant* asserted that a vote for Athanson was a vote for the desolate status quo. Hartford could "take a step forward by voting for Thirman Milner, whose victory would signify a new adventure for the city." A new frontier was within reach.[23]

Over the course of the 1980s, a pattern would come into focus. In the sagging cities of the Northeast, citizens craved change. Nothing was fresher than an African American candidate who offered a hopeful way out of the morass of the hour. Voters seemed to be thinking that if they were ready to elect a black leader, then their cities might stand on the cusp of a more general transformation.

For Milner, the *Courant*'s endorsement came as a shock. He had always regarded the *Courant* as a newspaper that catered to insurance executives and suburbanites, and that neglected the city's racial minorities. "We had, in the civil rights days, called the *Hartford Courant* the un-Hartford Courant!" The paper's endorsement reshaped the contours of the campaign. Suddenly, Thirman Milner had become a serious candidate.[24]

It was a four-way race. Johanna Murphy, a progressive from the city's West End, also vied for the nomination; so did Deputy Mayor Robert Ludgin. In two debates, the challengers ganged up on Athanson. They charged that during Athanson's decade at City Hall, the mayor had looked askance as housing and unemployment problems intensified. Milner promised increased spending on government services, and a more visible presence at the State Capitol.[25]

As the day of the primary approached, Athanson coasted on confidence. The latest poll gave him a comfortable lead: fully 36 percent of voters supported Athanson; Milner placed third, with 21 percent. Milner charged that the poll was flawed in its methodology. Because it targeted *likely* Democratic voters, the poll underestimated the African American turnout. Overlooked by polls and pundits, Hartford's African Americans still loomed as invisible men and women.[26]

On Primary Day, September 8, these voters stepped into the political light. Wilber Smith attached a loudspeaker to the top of his car and drove through the North End. "Wake up, North Hartford," he implored. "Wake up!" To several women gathered at a bus stop, he blared, "Don't cook your husbands one crumb of food until they come home and say they voted for Thirman Milner." Throngs of young volunteers knocked on doors for Milner and handed out campaign literature at housing projects. State Representative Carrie Saxon Perry canvassed the 30th Assembly District. "Vote righteously," she told her constituents. "I knew there was a time [for a black mayor]. This is the time." Milner amassed huge vote totals throughout the North End. According to Rudolph Arnold, a black city councilman, the vote for Milner was prompted by "a sense of magic and racial pride."[27]

Milner spent the evening at his campaign headquarters at Unity Plaza in the North End. As the voting results trickled in, it was hard to tell whether they were building slowly toward a triumph or winding down to a defeat. As each new number went up on the wall, hundreds of volunteers and well-wishers strained to view the tally. The mood was "a mixture of elation and doubt," as the *Courant* reported. George Athanson's headquarters exhibited a perfect contrast—gloom mingled with shock. At nine o'clock, Democratic leader James Crowley finally admitted the obvious: "It's not going to be a landslide." Athanson withdrew behind closed doors and puffed nervously on a cigar.[28]

At the end of the night, both headquarters showed the same result: Thirman Milner led by forty votes. Unity Plaza was a picture of pandemonium. People danced and jumped with joy. Milner was mobbed as he smiled wide. Early editions of the *Hartford Courant* congratulated Milner on his "magnificent victory."[29]

Late at night, the absentee votes came in. They propelled Athanson into first place with a 94-vote cushion. This constituted an important margin of victory. A differential of anything less than eighty votes would have triggered an automatic recount. Athanson ultimately tallied 5,229 votes to Milner's 5,135. (That worked out to 32.9 percent against 32.3 percent.) In the end, Democratic Party leaders dusted themselves off and declared victory. At Unity Plaza, euphoria turned quickly into confusion and anger.[30]

The voting returns revealed a tale of three cities. In Hartford's largest voting district, the North End area of Blue Hills, Milner won 67 percent of the vote. He replicated that kind of strength across North Hartford. In the white ethnic neighborhoods of the South End, Milner fared poorly. The vote in the 6th district was particularly grim: there he won only 6 percent of the vote. In the West End, Milner ran a close second behind Johanna Murphy. Milner polled well enough among these white liberals, and inspired a large enough turnout in North Hartford, to force the virtual tie.[31]

The morning after the primary, Milner's staff began to comb through the absentee ballots. One young campaign worker recognized her grandmother's name on an absentee ballot. She insisted that her grandmother lived in a convalescent home and was incapable of voting. Thirty years later, Milner did not mince words. When asked whether Athanson and his supporters stole the primary election, Milner was unequivocal: "They did."[32]

Milner's volunteers swung into action; each one paired up with a notary public. The teams tried to track down every senior citizen whose name appeared on an absentee ballot. Within two days, Milner's staff had collected signed statements from sixty individuals. They all swore that they had not actually cast ballots. According to Milner, such foul play was standard practice among Hartford's Democratic leaders. "We did find out that every election, they'd hold these ballots off that they'd get from these senior centers, that are signed by staff. And if they need them, they'll rush them in."[33]

As if the absentees were not enough to cast doubt on the election, more than 100 mayoral votes had gone missing at one polling place. Five hundred and fifty-nine people voted at the Martin Luther King Jr. School in the North End. Mysteriously, 118 of those ballots registered no vote for mayor. The reason for the missing votes remained unclear. Was it machine error? Human error? Random coincidence? Or fraud? For the time being, the voting machines at the King School remained locked and sealed.[34]

If Milner wished to challenge the election results, the law allowed him only three days to file an appeal. The judges at Hartford Superior Court were all Democrats. To a man, they owed their positions to party leaders. At first, none would review Milner's motion. Minutes before the Superior Court closed its doors for the weekend, however, a "godsend" appeared. Judge William Bieluch agreed to certify Milner's appeal. Bieluch was about to retire, and thus felt little political pressure. He ordered a hearing to begin the following Wednesday. The challenge was on.[35]

City officials offered to settle the lawsuit with a recount. Milner declined. He believed that fraud had plagued the primary. He wanted the court to investigate the possible instances of fraud, and to either declare him the victor or order a new election.[36]

George Athanson acknowledged the "imagined cloud" that enveloped City Hall. But he insisted that he had won the primary election fairly. Athanson exuded the cockiness of a five-time incumbent. He believed that he would rout Milner in any potential rematch. On September 22, without waiting for the legal challenge to run its course, Athanson acceded to Milner's request. Surprisingly, he agreed to a new primary election. As Milner put it, Athanson only consented to a new election "because he automatically thought that he'd win." As Athanson himself said, he endorsed this settlement because he "wanted to expose Milner for what he is." He took Milner for an easy mark. He relished a second showdown.[37]

The court settlement gave Milner new life. When Milner returned to his campaign headquarters that evening, he found that hundreds of supporters had beaten him there. They celebrated all over again.

The following morning, Hartford officials disposed of their most pressing task. On Wednesday, September 23, four city officials drove to the Martin Luther King Jr. School. Under the terms of the court settlement, Judge Douglass Wright had nullified the results of the September 8 primary. He ordered the city to prepare for a new election. So Nicholas Bonadies, the Registrar of Voters, beat a path to the King School—where 118 ballots had registered no preference for a mayoral candidate. Bonadies entered the school and promptly reset the voting machines, erasing every last trace of the September 8 primary. Later that morning, an attorney for the state of Connecticut, John M. Bailey, called Bonadies and asked when the voting machines would be reset. Bailey was preparing an investigation into voter fraud, and he wanted to send a representative from his office to the King School. Bonadies informed him that the deed had already been done. The slate, quite literally, was wiped clean.[38]

THE COURT AGREEMENT CALLED FOR A NEW PRIMARY ELECTION ON Tuesday, October 13; all four candidates would partake.

Milner's racial identity quickly became a subject of discussion. In a radio debate on October 5, Robert Ludgin charged that Athanson was mounting a "whisper campaign" in the white ethnic neighborhoods. It centered on one basic message: "We don't need a black mayor." The debate concluded with a plea from Milner: "We don't need that kind of hatred in the city of Hartford."[39]

Milner pursued a two-pronged strategy. On the one hand, he stepped up his efforts to gain the endorsements of African American leaders. On the other, he insisted that his campaign had nothing to do with race. For the African American politician, it was the classic balancing act. Many leaders have practiced this "syncretic" kind of black politics, including Edward Brooke, Los Angeles mayor Tom Bradley, Virginia governor Douglas Wilder, and Shirley Chisholm. Of course, not every black politician sought such a balance. For instance, Coleman Young—the mayor of Detroit—identified himself as "a black first and a Democrat second." On paper, Hartford looked a lot like Detroit. But Milner did not adopt Coleman Young's strategy. In terms of rhetoric, temperament, and how he ultimately governed, Milner emphasized interracial unity.[40]

Milner went hunting for votes in the black churches. At Union Baptist Church, Reverend A. Roger Williams told 250 worshipers, "I trust no one will be bashful in voting for Brother Thirman Milner. We would like to see a face that has never been on the Hartford scene before. One that looks like us." Other religious leaders had declined to lower themselves into the profane world of city politics. More than once, Milner reached out to Rev. Alfred White, whose A.M.E. Zion Church boasted the largest congregation in the North End. More than once, White rebuffed him. But on Sunday, October 4, the message seeped through. White encouraged his congregants to vote on Primary Day. He concluded: "What more can I say except, 'Why not?'"[41]

On October 5, Jesse Jackson came to town. He packed 600 people into the Horace Bushnell Congregational Church. In a speech that mixed politics and sermonizing, Jackson situated Milner's campaign within the national context. It was the beginning of the Reagan era. The new president had slashed social services for the poor and cut federal funding for cities. Such policies pushed struggling cities like Hartford ever closer to economic catastrophe, and blacks bore a disproportionate share of the burdens. But Jackson counseled the audience not to despair. "Don't stand around here looking pitiful. Use what you got. You got votes, use them." As grim as the economic situation had become, urban black voters held more political power than ever.[42]

With Jackson's seal of approval, Thirman Milner's transformation seemed complete. In the space of a month, the little-known state representative had become a significant figure in the black political world.

Milner continued to tell Hartford voters that his campaign had nothing to do with race. During the October 5 radio debate, Milner had declared, "No one should vote for me based on color." Certainly, he knew that thousands of voters in the North End would do just that. But he also emphasized economic policies that would help Puerto Ricans and working-class whites as well as African Americans. He called for the creation of a city housing policy and maintained that the city had to breathe new life into its poverty programs. He insisted that "there is no such thing as black legislation or black problems." Milner's focus on economics gained him the support of the Greater Hartford Labor Council. This organization, headed by a Puerto Rican named Edwin Vargas, represented about thirty thousand workers. Milner's dual strategy seemed to be succeeding: he was galvanizing North End voters just as he broadened his citywide appeal.[43]

In all the controversy over black and white, it was easy for Hartford's Puerto Ricans to feel overlooked. They comprised 18 percent of the city's population. Many of them endured the same poverty and sub-standard housing as African Americans. Milner sought to highlight that shared experience. United States congressman Robert Garcia, the only Puerto Rican on Capitol Hill, visited Hartford on Milner's behalf. The Bronx representative spoke at Sacred Heart Church in the North End. "The time to put aside differences in color is now," Garcia said. He connected the Puerto Rican struggle with the African American one. "You have a chance to demonstrate here what no one else can in 1981. You can elect a mayor who comes from within our ranks." Strikingly, Garcia spoke of Milner as one who hailed from "our ranks."[44]

Up until October 1981, the northern mystique played little role in Thirman Milner's campaign. In this majority-minority city, few white voters felt inspired by the prospect of a black mayor. More often, they viewed him as a threat. In October, however, something was awakened in the body politic. The botched first primary election had unleashed a new spirit in the city. It was one thing for Hartford to wallow in a high poverty rate—middle-class citizens could feel insulated from those hardships. But the primary election made a mockery of democracy in Hartford. Moreover, the second primary campaign had become mired in mudslinging; Athanson appeared to be rousing a racism in the South End. This atmosphere pushed voters to consider more seriously how they wanted to see their city, and how they hoped Hartford would be perceived.

On October 9, the *Hartford Courant* endorsed Milner for a second time. The editors asked: "Who has been most impressive by showing moderation, by not indulging in divisive rhetoric and by expressing genuine concern for all areas of the city?" Their final question was the most telling: "Who is more likely to bolster the national image of Hartford as an enlightened, a tolerant city?" It had come down to this. Would Hartford prove it was enlightened and tolerant? Or would it succumb to hatred and division?[45]

THE COFFEE WAS ALREADY BREWING AT FIVE O'CLOCK IN THE MORNING, the tables piled high with doughnuts. Unity Plaza was awash in caffeine and sugar, energy and excitement. Volunteers poured in by the busload from Boston and Bridgeport, New Haven and Albany. As the polling places opened on October 13, the North End pulsed with a kind of community spirit.[46]

This election held few surprises. "It was over early today," admitted James Crowley, the chairman of the Democratic Town Committee. Indeed, it was over when North End voters surged to the polls. Well over 60 percent of registered voters turned out in the North End. At eight o'clock in the evening, Milner was sequestered in a small room at the West Indian Social Club. The election seemed well in hand, but Milner, scarred by the late-night shenanigans of the first primary, delayed as long as he could. He appeared in the ballroom at 9:30. Amid "shrieks and cheers," Milner declared that he had won a "citywide victory." He promised, "We are going to have a citywide love-in." In Milner's triumphant narrative, he had proven that he could win over all the people.[47]

The numbers told a somewhat different story. Out of thirty-two voting districts in the city, Milner and Athanson won sixteen apiece. Overall, Milner won 48 percent of the vote; Athanson corralled 35 percent. Milner won more than 80 percent of the votes in the North End, and also carried the West End. But Athanson won every district in the South End.[48]

Once assured of the Democratic nomination, Milner had a clear path to City Hall. Seventy-one percent of registered voters were Democrats, and 12 percent were Republicans. The Republicans nominated Michael McGarry. In addition, Robert Ludgin announced he would run as an Independent. McGarry tried to present the campaign as a battle between big-government and small-government visions. McGarry offered himself as a Reaganesque figure of the 1980s, and portrayed Milner as a man still stuck in the 1960s. But the 1980s were not only a decade of political conservatism. They were also the heyday of black mayors.[49]

By November 3, Election Day had taken on the humdrum feel of a routine. Yet in the North End, the mundane act of voting turned into a neighborhood-wide celebration. Milner compiled enormous margins in the North End. And he performed well throughout the city. All told, he won 57 percent of the votes. In the South End he surpassed all expectations, losing to Ludgin by 42 percent to 36 percent.[50]

At the West Indian Social Club, an audience of more than one thousand watched Milner's victory speech. He could have reveled in his pathbreaking achievement. But he chose the opposite strategy. He looked forward to the day when he was "simply Hartford's mayor"—not its black mayor. Though Milner spoke to a crowd teeming with African Americans, he reached out to the citizens beyond that ballroom. "I've said before there's no such thing as 'black legislation.' When we pass a law on housing, for example, it's housing for everyone." Milner offered himself as a coalition builder, a conciliator, and a unifier. Though black voters had lifted Milner to City Hall, he spoke in a tongue that whites could easily understand.[51]

When the victory party died down, Milner's staffers asked him if he needed a bite to eat. They packed into a car and sped across the bridge to East Hartford. It was not until Milner crossed over the river, and looked back at the city, that the impact of the election hit him with full force. He had risen to become the mayor of his native Hartford. He fought three bruising campaigns to get there, dislodging a powerful incumbent and toppling a racial barrier along the way.

Soon, the North's mystique surfaced in Hartford. The *Courant*'s political cartoonist brought it to the fore. The morning after Milner's victory, a drawing by Bob Englehart appeared on the editorial page. It featured Thomas Hooker, the founder of Connecticut, a figure known to all of the state's schoolchildren. Bob Englehart situated his cartoon in front of Hartford's Old State House, where a statue of Hooker stood sentinel. Thirman Milner walked toward the Hooker statue; the mayor-elect was resplendent in a three-piece suit with a "Why Not?" button on his vest. Hooker, facing away from Milner, allowed his arm to dangle behind his back. Hooker extended an open palm and declared: "Gimme Five!" Hartford had long revered its father of representative democracy; now it had a new symbol of multiracial democracy. The *Courant*'s readers could picture one sweet low-five.[52]

On November 3, 1981, Hartford voters elected as their mayor Thirman Milner. He became the first black mayor of any New England city. This cartoon was published on the morning after his election. Milner exchanged a low-five with Thomas Hooker, the founder of democracy in Connecticut. BOB ENGLEHART, NOVEMBER 4, 1981, *HARTFORD COURANT*.

On Inauguration Day, December 1, that sense of history was everywhere. But when Milner took the dais, he had another homage to pay. "Today has been called a historic day in the City of Hartford and indeed it is. This date is also one of special significance. On December 1st, 1955, Rosa Lee Parks, a tired domestic in Montgomery, Alabama, refused to . . . stand at the back of the bus." New England's first black mayor transported his audience to the cradle of the Confederacy. "Today I stand before you as a product of those struggles." He drew a line from the iconic struggles of the southern civil rights movement to Hartford's City Hall.[53]

Then he turned to Hartford's history. "I also stand as a symbol of the history of this city for since the time Thomas Hooker founded our great city of Hartford in 1636 each group that migrated here has had to struggle to overcome barriers." Milner's rhetoric about the past mixed with a sobering assessment of the future. He confessed that he had "no magic solutions" for Hartford. He made only a general promise to "wage an attack upon our housing crisis, crime, high and unfair taxes, high unemployment and poverty." He inherited huge problems. Manufacturing continued to decline, suburbs continued to grow, and the Reagan administration reduced its funding to cities. In such an environment, even the most skilled political leader would be hard-pressed to create jobs, lower crime, and improve the quality and availability of low-income housing.[54]

It was a job fit for Sisyphus. And black mayors across the country would find themselves in predicaments like Milner's. They were characters worthy of Camus, men and women who had battled to enter the political arena, who had pushed the boulder up the hill and won "historic" elections only to find their cities back at the bottom.

In the days after the election, many black citizens harbored high hopes. As Albert Grant told a reporter for *Northend Agents*, the city's black newspaper, "We need better housing . . . and get some jobs. That's what I think he can do. I think this is great and, I think Milner is what we need to get these things done." Milner rode into City Hall with an electoral mandate, and with the weight of history on his own shoulders. He quickly realized that Hartford in 1981 was no place for honeymoons.[55]

ONCE IN OFFICE, MILNER BEGAN TO IDENTIFY EVEN MORE OPENLY WITH Hartford's minority population. "Although I'm mayor, I still live in what some people call the ghetto. . . . Whatever hurts the minority community hurts me." He took home a paltry salary of $17,500 per year and continued to reside in the North End.[56]

Milner reoriented the way the city conducted business, especially with regard to minority workers. While many Hartford residents struggled through the late-1970s and early-1980s, the downtown enjoyed a development boom. When Milner took office, eight projects worth over $300 million were at or nearing completion. The developers received major tax breaks; they also fell short of affirmative-action goals. The Greater Hartford Affirmative Action Plan had previously required only a "good faith effort" to hire more minorities. Milner put some teeth in it. After he intervened, the developer of a thirty-three-acre housing complex committed to hiring minorities as 15 percent of its workforce and to use minority firms in 20 percent of subcontracts. Milner also challenged the developer of the city's largest building project, the thirty-eight-story

CityPlace office tower. CityPlace ultimately agreed to hire minorities as 10 percent of its workers. Milner provided black-owned companies with more access to municipal dollars. He was willing to spend his political capital on this issue, and to persuade members of the City Council. During his second term in office, some 26 percent of municipal contracts would go to minorities. As both cause and effect of the city's success, Hartford secured a major federal grant to aid minority businesses in 1985.[57]

Such an outcome was more the exception than the rule. Milner often seemed hesitant to exercise his influence. He could have developed a more assertive style. As Robert Ludgin later observed, "He had the bully pulpit." Milner had won the general election by a landslide, and generated excitement when he took office. "He could have done what Nick [Carbone] did for four or five years," Ludgin explained, "which is if you control five council votes, you control the city." This meant building political power and deciding how to use it. "You've got to be on the phone all day, cajoling [the city councilors], convincing them." Instead of brawling in the world of city politics, Milner increasingly directed his energies outward—toward Washington and the nation.[58]

Milner likened the Reagan administration's "New Federalism" to a new form of Jim Crow. Reagan cut funding for food stamps, Community Development Block Grants, and unemployment assistance. As Milner said to the Willimantic NAACP, "We are being told to tell our poor . . . our disadvantaged . . . to pull themselves up by the bootstraps—while at the same time Reagan is taking away their boots." Early in 1983, Milner called upon the president to declare a state of emergency in the nation's ten most impoverished cities—which included Hartford. Then the federal government could open its stockpiles of surplus food and distribute it to the urban poor. To deal with the growing number of homeless people on Hartford's streets, Milner proposed transforming federal and state armories into homeless shelters. Ernest "Dutch" Morial, mayor of New Orleans, helped to formulate these suggestions. Such ideas fell on deaf ears in Washington, but they raised Milner's national profile.[59]

In Hartford, Milner was gaining enemies. He stopped granting interviews to the *Courant*. He also alienated members of the Democratic Town Committee when he endorsed his own slate of candidates for the City Council. In addition, after Wilber Smith uttered racially inflammatory remarks, Milner defended his colleague. Despite these missteps, Milner remained popular with the voters.

In February 1983, Milner let it slip that he was planning to run for reelection when his two-year term expired. This led to the next firestorm. The controversy revolved around a Bob Englehart cartoon. Englehart's drawing pictured Milner in a janitor's closet, surrounded by buckets and brooms. A cleaning lady approached, mop in hand, as Milner declared: "Yes, I will run again."[60]

The black community voiced shock and outrage, and mounted a defense of the maligned mayor. In response, the *Courant*'s editors explained the cartoon. Bob Englehart had situated Milner in a janitor's closet only to highlight "the weakness of the incumbent mayor under the present system of city government."* The editors admitted that the cartoon "missed the mark." But they were unwilling to concede that it carried any racial undertones. "We had hoped that the idiotic notion of blacks as janitors would be long discarded in a city where the mayor, the deputy mayor, the fire chief and the city manager are black." Given blacks' obvious electoral power, the *Courant* insisted, it was silly to think that crude old racial stereotypes could cling to Mayor Milner.[61]

That was the rub. To many African Americans, it was no coincidence that the cartoon played upon well-worn racial myths at the precise moment when blacks were rising so high. *Ebony* had recently featured Hartford as a budding site of black political power. It seemed that the *Courant* was trying to bring African Americans back down a notch.[62]

The *Courant*'s explanation came off as defensive and condescending. Milner's mother had toiled as a domestic worker. The mayor himself had worked as a hospital orderly. The images of African Americans as janitors and maids may have struck the *Courant*'s editors as "idiotic." But to blacks themselves, these images were all too real.

The editors had evaded a substantive issue—the fact that black political power coexisted with black economic weakness. One African American suggested that Milner's link with poor people was neither something to mock nor to discard—but to celebrate. In the cartoon, "the implicit statement is that power and workers don't mix," Hartford resident Thomas Hoyt Jr. observed. "Brooms and buckets, mops and maids are contrasted

---

*Hartford's municipal government had a weak-mayor/strong–City Council setup.

with mayors and degrees in places of power." But for Hoyt, this missed the whole point. "What could be more powerful than a man in an office of power who identifies with the poor, the weak, the helpless, the needy?" Martin Luther King Jr. himself had been cut down at a moment when he was championing downtrodden garbage workers. Hoyt wrote, "Our mayor similarly relates, and to that extent is powerful." Milner's identification with poor black people only increased his power in that community.[63]

Another local black leader probed the relationship between poverty and progress. Thomas Wright, former president of the Greater Hartford NAACP, was incensed by the *Courant*'s blasé response. "Can the *Courant* be so naïve as to believe racism is long gone, just because Hartford now has a few black city officials?" He cited the high unemployment rate as well as the North End's severe housing crisis. Milner's election had yet to solve much of anything.[64]

In these responses to the cartoon, there was rage and disbelief. But there was also pride. For many African Americans, Milner's presence in City Hall was personally important; an injury to him was an injury to them.

Milner himself bristled at the cartoon. He called it "an insult to every black mayor." He also pointed out that the date of the cartoon's publication was a crucial one in the history of African American politics. On February 23, 1983, in Chicago, Harold Washington won his city's Democratic nomination for mayor. Washington would go on to victory in November. And he was aware of Milner's victory less than two years prior. "I benefited from Milner's election," said Harold Washington. He called the victories in Chicago and in Hartford "part of a continuum."[65]

That same November, Milner's strength at the grass roots helped propel him to reelection. The *Courant* had endorsed him again. Despite the frayed relationship between the newspaper and the mayor, the editors agreed with Milner on important issues: job creation and job training, police-community relations, affirmative action, and tax reform. Milner also brought "new dignity to the office of mayor. He still has a rare opportunity to lead. He can . . . help bridge the gaps that exist between rich and poor, neighborhoods and big business, city and suburbs." He could keep one foot in the North End housing projects, and the other in the downtown office buildings. Or so the *Courant* hoped. Milner had indeed proven himself a reliable ally of developers during downtown's building boom. But what was good for the corporations was not always good for city residents. At certain moments, leaders had to choose sides.[66]

On December 2, 1983, the City Council passed the Downtown Development Plan. This zoning measure would increase the number of retail businesses in downtown Hartford, including construction of a shopping mall and a parking garage. It would also grant businesses unprecedented autonomy over the use of downtown land. Local groups had asked developers to commit 5 percent of each project's cost toward job training and neighborhood development. That provision was not included in the final plan. The City Council passed the final bill, 7 to 2.[67]

Milner had a weapon: the veto. Ordinarily, the City Council could override a veto with a two-thirds majority. But this was a special circumstance. These councilors were set to leave office, and they would not be able to reconvene. On December 6, Milner vetoed the bill. He explained that "development must take place with, as well as for, our residents." To the glee of community leaders, Milner insisted that the ordinance should have included proposals for affordable housing and job training.[68]

His veto outraged local power brokers. The *Courant* clung to the fiction that the mayor could stand equally for the plunderers and the plundered. On December 8, Bob Englehart unfurled his brush in a cartoon titled "Milner's Downtown Plan." It pictured the mayor with a pair of scissors, standing over a map of the city. The map had a gaping hole in place of the downtown area; the mayor flicked a square of paper into the air. He had ripped the corporate heart out of the city.[69]

Neighborhood groups gathered at City Hall to show their support for Milner. While the *Courant* insisted that the debate over the zoning plan "should not be seen as a test of corporate power compared to neighborhood clout," most city residents viewed it in precisely those terms.[70]

The new City Council revisited the zoning plan when the councilors took office in January 1984. This time, two councilors introduced an ordinance that gave preference in hiring to Hartford residents. On February 14, the City Council adopted the new plan by an 8-to-1 vote. Yet Milner remained dissatisfied. He wanted the City Council to postpone its vote until neighborhood groups had time to examine the details. He decided not to veto this piece of legislation. Neither did he sign it. The Downtown Development Plan became law without Milner's signature. It showed the mayor's weakness and the corporations' strength.[71]

In the spring of 1985, Hartford hosted the National Conference of Black Mayors. This was Milner's shining moment. By 1985, 290 different towns and cities across America had black mayors. The majority hailed from the South. Alabama, that old fiefdom of George Wallace and Bull Connor, boasted 31 black mayors. Milner had mounted an intense lobbying effort to bring the conference to Hartford. It was not an easy sell. Many of the mayors held a common stereotype about the North, as Milner observed: "that we have no soul." The North seemed impersonal and antiseptic. "Most southerners feel that New Englanders are cold, indifferent, and unfriendly." Once Milner persuaded the mayors to convene in Hartford, he had to disprove their preconceptions.[72]

On April 17, 150 mayors arrived in Hartford. Milner marked the occasion with an op-ed in the *Courant*. He recounted his own barrier-breaking experience. After his election, Milner recalled, he felt himself in a fishbowl. "It seemed as if the world was waiting to see my first blunder." White constituents subjected black leaders to unforgiving scrutiny. At the same time, African American voters expected the world. Black mayors struggled with these lofty standards—judged by whether they could deliver not only jobs and housing, but also unity and healing.[73]

The mayors drafted a set of resolutions that centered on jobs, housing, and how to approach the cuts in federal funding. At best, they could only chip away at these issues. But for African Americans living in Hartford, the assemblage of visiting black leaders—from Harold Washington to Shirley Chisholm—had a real impact. The mayors' conference made blacks in Hartford beam. John Wardlaw, the executive director of the Hartford Housing Authority, found himself influenced by the conference. "I have attended some of the events and have been made to feel much more comfortable in terms of the country I live in." The sight of these 150 mayors was a striking one. For a moment, blacks in Hartford could allow themselves to think that the "American Dream" was not a ruse—that some tiny sliver of it might still be claimed by people in dark skins.[74]

The conference was most important for its symbolism. Milner's career in City Hall was similar; its significance was mainly symbolic. He failed to lessen poverty, solve the housing crisis, or prevent jobs and residents from leaving the city. Yet the symbols still mattered. On the night of May 5, Milner visited an Albany Avenue storefront to meet with Puerto Rican leaders. When the meeting ended, a young boy approached Milner. He asked, "Are you *really* the mayor?" Milner admitted that he was. The subject turned to Milner's attire. He assured the boy that one did not have to be wealthy to wear a suit or to attain high office. The boy was skeptical: "I can't get to be a mayor from here." Milner explained that he had grown up close to Albany Avenue himself, and had lived on welfare. "You *can* be mayor," Milner insisted. The boy watched Milner intently for the rest of the evening until the mayor climbed back into his car and departed.[75]

The tale held both hope and heartbreak. For the truth was that this boy would likely toe the poverty line for much of his life. Hartford had become more inclusive in terms of racial democracy, yet more oppressive in terms of economic inequality.

Downtown became a boomtown. Between 1980 and 1987, the amount of office space more than doubled. In 1986, neighborhood groups lobbied City Hall to establish a policy of linkage. Such a plan would levy additional taxes on downtown development and use the funds for housing and jobs. The City Council voted it down. Neighborhood leaders were incensed. "Downtown has to look out their back door," charged Jacqueline Fongemie, president of Hartford Areas Rally Together. It was as if the downtown skyline had "blocked the neighborhoods from sight."[76]

The economic indicators remained grim. In 1980, one-quarter of Hartford residents lived in poverty. By 1990, 27.5 percent were impoverished. Fully 39 percent of Hartford's children lived in poverty—the second-highest percentage in the nation. And more whites continued to leave the city. In the public schools, only 8 percent of students were white; 92 percent were racial minorities. Although the state of Connecticut maintained one of the lowest unemployment rates in the nation, Hartford's rate increased from 7.7 percent in 1980 to 10.4 percent in 1991. When Milner stepped down at the end of 1987, after three terms in office, the city was more impoverished and more segregated than it had been on the day of his inauguration.[77]

Flora Hogg was one of the thousands without a job. Hogg, a mother of two, had worked at a diesel engine factory for nearly a decade before she was laid off. "Being in the factory the last nine years, I never learned any other skills." The labor market was so tight that she could not find another job. Few refugees from the factories or the tobacco fields had skills fitted for the service economy. "I can't find a job, even washing dishes,"

Hogg said in 1983. "It makes you teary-eyed. . . . There's so much money in Hartford. Office buildings are going up. The town is flourishing." She never shared in that prosperity.[78]

In old manufacturing cities like Cleveland and Detroit, this was a familiar story. Hartford exhibited the duality better than most. The destitution coexisted with the abundance. A soup kitchen stood across the street from Aetna's headquarters.

John Robinson understood the two sides of Hartford. He was a high school graduate and an Army veteran. Robinson had worked as a security guard at the Hartford Civic Center until 1982. After losing his job, he bounced from one soup kitchen to the next. "My basic skills are security and cooking, and there's nothing in them. I just figure in Hartford there are the fortunate and the unfortunate. And I am one of the unfortunate." Thirman Milner's Hartford was also John Robinson's, and Flora Hogg's too.[79]

MILNER DID NOT PURSUE A FOURTH TERM. HE THREW HIS SUPPORT TO A state representative and longtime community activist from the North End: Carrie Saxon Perry. Perry went on to serve as mayor for three terms. She was more forceful than Milner in attacking racial and economic inequality, and in taking on the corporations. But the poverty continued to worsen.

African American mayors led Hartford from 1981 to 1993, establishing it as a center of black political power. Yet both Thirman Milner and Carrie Saxon Perry have been overlooked by their contemporaries as well as by historians. Hartford's geographical location is partially responsible for this. It is sandwiched halfway between Boston and New York, two metropolises that soak up the spotlight. In addition, Boston and New York exhibited more dramatic racial problems. The poverty in Hartford remained a quiet scourge. In Boston and New York, extraordinary episodes of racial violence seized headlines and gripped the imagination of the American public.

Memories of the Boston busing crisis remained raw, and racial violence continued into the 1980s. Mel King tried to build a progressive black politics atop the embers. King lost two Boston mayoral campaigns, in 1979 and 1983, in which he crafted a multiracial political coalition. African Americans joined with Latinos, Asians, and white liberals. In 1983, King polled well enough in the Democratic primary to win a place in the run-off election. As Deval Patrick—the future governor of Massachusetts—remembered, this result "blew people's minds." While King ultimately lost, he garnered about 20 percent of white votes—a higher percentage than Harold Washington received that same year in Chicago. King gained significant white support even as he referred constantly to the "incredibly high level of racism in Boston."[80]

It did not soon abate. On October 23, 1989, Charles Stuart—a white man—called 911 to say that he and his pregnant wife had been shot by a black man. Police swooped into Boston's black neighborhoods, harassed residents, and arrested an African American. It gradually became evident that Stuart had murdered his own wife. But for those awful days in the fall of 1989, every black man was a target. The lesson for blacks in Boston seemed clear: racism was always lurking just around the corner, and often it was much closer than that.[81]

In New York City, the portrait was just as grim.

NINE

The Ghost of Willie Turks

Racial Violence and Black Politics in New York City (1982–1993)

ONE NIGHT IN JUNE 1982, WILLIE TURKS FOUND HIMSELF ON the southern tip of Brooklyn. The thirty-four-year-old Turks worked for the New York Transit Authority. He was a subway maintenance man at the sprawling Coney Island Rail Yard. For many trains, Coney Island marked the end of the line.

This part of Brooklyn was for African Americans a forbidding place. Since the 1950s, working-class and middle-class whites had been leaving Central Brooklyn for neighborhoods like Bay Ridge, Bensonhurst, and Gravesend. There they could buy small homes and, many hoped, re-create homogeneous communities. By the middle of the 1980s, whites no longer comprised a majority of New York City's population. But in these neighborhoods near the water's edge, they tried to shelter themselves from the demographic changes that engulfed the city.

Shortly after midnight on June 22, 1982, having just finished his shift, Turks piled into a car with two coworkers. They drove to a bagel shop in Gravesend, bought beer and bagels, then began driving away. A group of young whites noticed the car and its three African American passengers. They threw bottles and trash at the car, and hurled racial epithets at the black men. The car stalled at the corner of Avenue X and East 1st Street. A crowd of whites encircled it, fifteen or twenty in all. Donald Cooper was in the car with Turks. "They were shaking the car," Cooper recalled, "throwing garbage at it and breaking the windows." Cooper fled on foot, as did Dennis Dixon. Members of the mob pulled Willie Turks out of the car and tackled him when he tried to run away. One youth engaged Turks in a fight. Then Gino Bova picked up a stick and beat Turks over the head. Turks fell to the ground. The white youths stomped upon the defenseless black man and left him unconscious in the gutter. At Coney Island Hospital, doctors pronounced him dead.[1]

Four Gravesend youths were convicted variously of manslaughter, assault, and civil rights violations. A judge summed up the attack: "There was a lynch mob that night. . . . The only thing missing was a rope and a tree." African American demonstrators marched through Gravesend. The story flitted in and out of the newspapers. But Willie Turks's death caused only a minor stir in New York. His name did not become a battle cry; the crime did not fuel any significant civil rights activism. He was just a black man who had been stomped to death, and who faded from the city's collective memory.[2]

New York City had flirted with bankruptcy during the 1970s. Poverty increased as blue-collar jobs grew scarce. Income inequality deepened through the 1980s, pushing many New Yorkers toward one economic extreme or the other. As reporter Jim Dwyer recalled, there was "a social moat that divided these two New Yorks." Streets were awash in crack cocaine and homelessness. The crime rate soared. The AIDS epidemic ravaged the city. New York was no longer the nation's urban gem.[3]

Many African Americans and progressive whites blamed Mayor Ed Koch. In 1982, when Koch attended Willie Turks's funeral, he was serving the second of his three terms. Liberals charged that Koch, a Democrat, had played to the white backlash—and that he smoothed the journey for all those Jews in the outer boroughs who became Reagan Democrats.

During his first term, Koch had ordered the closing of Harlem's Sydenham Hospital. The hospital was losing money amid allegations of poor performance. But it stood as a refuge for black doctors who had trouble practicing at other city hospitals, and it remained an important institution for Harlem residents. Koch came off as unconcerned with the needs of African Americans. "I see him as an instigator of the climate of racial fear in this city," said Reverend Calvin Butts, the minister of Harlem's Abyssinian Baptist Church. A Brooklyn-born filmmaker arrived at a similar conclusion. "Black and Puerto Rican life here is very cheap," Spike Lee lamented. "It's sad, and it's no mistake that all the incidents like this have occurred under Ed Koch." Irving Howe was less direct in faulting Koch, but no less caustic. "Once Ed Koch became mayor of New York," wrote the founder of *Dissent* magazine, "human nature" started "to display its shabbier sides. The mood of the city seemed to grow sullen." If Koch was not the architect of this change, he encouraged and amplified it. New Yorkers "now revealed a weariness with the language of idealism," Howe wrote, "a coarsening of social sentiments, a resignation before inequities that had once troubled consciences." Koch both shaped and reflected this psychic transformation.[4]

And yet there was another side to Ed Koch. He had begun his political career as a liberal and a reformer. A leader of the Village Independent Democrats in the 1960s, he helped to unseat the political boss Carmine De Sapio. He had also traveled to Mississippi in 1964 to work for civil rights. This background helped to explain why many white liberals and moderates continued to vote for Koch, despite his troubling stances on racial issues. New Yorkers credited Koch with bringing the city back from the verge of bankruptcy. Koch cozied up to developers as real estate prices soared. To his proponents, Koch was the one who restored New York City's glitz. In addition, he funded a subsidized housing program that helped to revive several black and Latino neighborhoods. He eventually built or rehabilitated some two hundred thousand housing units, many of them in low-income neighborhoods. He was a powerful and complicated leader with a messy legacy.[5]

If one could generalize about a city with seven million souls, then emotions were raw and fear was palpable. Through the 1980s, waves of racial violence washed across the city. The episodes only grew more spectacular and more gruesome. New York looked like a backwater of racial hatred, not a colossus of cosmopolitanism. Claims to a mystique about equality and progress seemed empty. And yet at the very end of the 1980s, black politics crested. The decade illuminated two dueling forces. It exposed African Americans as both victors and victims.

THE GHOST OF WILLIE TURKS HAUNTED NEW YORK. FOUR YEARS AFTER Turks's death, his specter hovered over Howard Beach. This white enclave in southern Queens was bounded by Brooklyn to the West, Jamaica Bay to the South, the Belt Parkway to the North, and Kennedy Airport to the East. Physically as well as racially and psychologically, it was a closed community.

By 1987, whites made up 46 percent of New York City's population. In Howard Beach, they accounted for 94 percent. Yet neighborhood residents could not stave off all the signs of racial change. Howard Beach's congressman was Floyd Flake, an African American who had patched together a multiracial coalition en route to victory in November 1986. One month after Flake's election, Howard Beach became the new face of northern racism.[6]

This saga began at night on December 19, 1986, when four blacks from Brooklyn were traveling on the Belt Parkway. Curtis Sylvester, the driver, was a newcomer from Tampa, Florida. His cousin, Michael Griffith, sat in the front passenger seat. Griffith had been raised in Bedford-Stuyvesant; Griffith's mother was engaged to thirty-six-year-old Cedric Sandiford, who sat in the backseat that night. Timothy Grimes, a convicted felon, rounded out the foursome. As the car neared its exit, smoke started seeping from the hood. Sylvester accidentally took the wrong exit, easing his car down the ramp and onto Cross Bay Boulevard. He drove along the boulevard for several minutes before the car sputtered to a halt. The men decided they would walk to the nearest subway station and head back to Brooklyn. Sylvester stayed with his car; the others promised to come back for him later. So Sandiford, Griffith, and Grimes trudged four miles in the cold, walking right past a poorly marked subway entrance, and into the heart of Howard Beach. They spotted the New Park Pizzeria and stopped in for a slice. As they sat with their pizza, a car of local whites drove by. The two groups exchanged looks. The white boys continued on to a house party. Jon Lester had a message for his friends: "There are some niggers on the boulevard—let's go and kill them!" This information circulated rapidly around the party. Robert Riley shouted, "There's niggers on Cross Bay!" The word was out.[7]

During the 1980s, New Yorkers found themselves uttering one phrase over and over: "He was just in the wrong place at the wrong time." For random crimes like mugging and burglary, the aphorism rang true. But on this night, a group of whites from Queens was determined to make Howard Beach the wrong place for three black men. Thirteen boys headed to the pizzeria. Some ran there; others jumped into cars. They brought along aluminum baseball bats and tree limbs. Jason Ladone yelled, "Niggers, get out of the neighborhood! You don't belong here!" One boy struck Sandiford in the legs with a bat as Sandiford cried, "God, don't kill us!" The three black men sprinted away. Grimes escaped, but the mob pursued Sandiford and Griffith. A group of white boys cornered Sandiford against a fence and bludgeoned him with a baseball bat. Another group in a car pursued Michael Griffith. He ran down 90th Street to where it met the Belt Parkway. Robert Riley remembered, "We were screaming, 'Nigger, you ain't getting away. We're gonna fuckin' kill you.'" Griffith sized up his options and ran onto the Belt Parkway. He made it out to the center divider, hopped the barrier, and was struck by an oncoming car. As Riley testified in court, "I saw his body go up a couple feet in the air." The boys watched Michael Griffith die, then they headed back toward Cedric Sandiford.[8]

When the police finally arrived, Sandiford was bloody and shivering. Yet the cops treated him more as a criminal than a victim. They questioned him about another crime in the area. They ordered him to assume a spread-eagle position and frisked him. Twenty years earlier, James Baldwin had written about relations between black New Yorkers and the police. He called the city "occupied territory." On that score, New York had made little progress.[9]

New Yorkers digested the news about Howard Beach just as the trial of Bernhard Goetz began. In December 1984, Goetz, a white man, was approached on the subway by four African American youths. Thinking he was about to be mugged, Goetz shot all four of them. Two of them he shot in the back. Many white New Yorkers hailed Goetz as a vigilante hero. In the spring of 1987, Goetz would be acquitted of all charges except for gun possession. For African Americans, this only added to the outrage.

Michael Griffith's death rocked the city in a way that the murder of Willie Turks had not. In black neighborhoods, a simmering rage advanced to a boil. The Howard Beach incident demonstrated the depths of racism that existed in the nation's supposed capital of enlightenment. As white Brooklynite Jeffrey Trachtman wrote in a letter to the *New York Times*, "Let no one say, 'It can't happen here.'" To many white New Yorkers, the idea of mobs beating defenseless black men was something that made sense only in the South. A string of notorious events would explode that myth.[10]

The residents of Howard Beach, horrified by the violence, grew more vexed each time the media described their neighborhood as racist. Roger Wilkins understood this reaction. Wilkins, a former United States assistant attorney general, asked, "Why shouldn't the people of Howard Beach feel aggrieved to be singled out?" It was the moment of political conservatism, the witching hour for the Reagan Democrats. "Had President Reagan and his Administration not signaled in hundreds of different ways that some level of racism was not only permissible but could be officially sanctioned—as with providing tax breaks to schools that segregate—then the white Howard Beach youngsters might not have acted as they did." The boys took their cues from the nation's leaders, Wilkins argued. Given the broader atmosphere in America, "youngsters are emboldened to chase blacks at midnight." Their behavior was not anomalous. They had "acted out the national mood."[11]

This pointed up an irony about the Northeast and the nation in the 1980s. Just as white youths from Boston to Brooklyn were expressing the national mood of racial backlash, many Americans portrayed the Northeast as a liberal outcast. Far from a pacesetter or a prototype, the Northeast was perceived as the "other"—the stronghold of liberalism during the rise of the New Right. Regional images rested uneasily alongside stubborn facts. In reality, Ronald Reagan swept New York, Massachusetts, and Connecticut in the 1980 presidential election, as well as in 1984. Moreover, the Northeast was no stranger to the conservative tax revolt. In 1980, Massachusetts voters approved a far-reaching anti-tax measure known as Proposition 2½. Yet just as Massachusetts residents were cutting taxes and backing Reagan, their reputation as foot soldiers for liberalism grew even stronger. While Americans at large bought into a progressive mythology about the Northeastern states, the land from Boston to Brooklyn had become a center of the white backlash. And in national politics, these states marched in lockstep with the rest of the country.[12]

In New York City, the Howard Beach killing caused an uproar. The African American community was ready for action. "Things well up," said Basil Paterson, a black political leader and the former deputy mayor of New York City. "This was the tipping point."[13]

The day after Michael Griffith's death, Mayor Ed Koch weighed in. "They were chased like animals through the streets. . . . The attack rivals the kind of lynching party that existed in the Deep South." The media kept the story on the front pages as African Americans waged a series of protests. The state's Democratic governor, Mario Cuomo, appointed a special prosecutor to investigate the case. In December 1987, three young whites were convicted of manslaughter. The verdict warmed the hearts of New York liberals. According to the editors of the *New York Times*, "The trial ended by showing the city at its best, upholding civilized values." But those "civilized values" were in short supply.[14]

Willie Turks's ghost flew over Staten Island in October 1988. In the Rosebank neighborhood, a group of whites shouted racial epithets from their car as they ran over an African American named Derek Tyrus. Tyrus died at the scene. One more black man met a grisly death.[15]

Forty years earlier, E. B. White penned his homage to the city: *Here Is New York*. New York City had long accounted for its "hazards and deficiencies" by "supplying its citizens with massive doses of a supplementary vitamin—the sense of belonging to something unique, cosmopolitan, mighty, and unparalleled." This was what made New York great: not the tall buildings, the famous newspapers, the fine restaurants and museums, but the broad-minded spirit they helped to generate among the people. By the 1980s, however, the city had exhausted its stockpile of supplements.[16]

For E. B. White, the intense intermingling of so many cultures and creeds made New York City unique. Yet these close quarters also provided explosive tinder. "The city has to be tolerant," White counseled in 1949. He was writing in the heyday of Jackie Robinson. If New Yorkers failed to practice tolerance, their city "would explode in a radioactive cloud of hate and rancor and bigotry. If the people were to depart even briefly from the peace of cosmopolitan intercourse, the town would blow up higher than a kite. In New York smolders every race problem there is, but the noticeable thing is not the problem but the inviolate truce."[17]

No truce was permanent. At the end of the 1980s, New Yorkers tore up the last shreds of their implicit pact.

New York City was rocked by racial violence in 1989. The first major event occurred on April 19. At nine o'clock that night, about thirty black and Latino youths gathered in East Harlem and entered Central Park at 110th Street. They embarked on a spree of violence. They bloodied a Latino man and poured beer on him. The boys proceeded to the Central Park Reservoir and set upon several white joggers. One runner was beaten unconscious. At the same time, Trisha Meili had been jogging in another part of the park—along the 102nd Street Transverse. She was twenty-eight years old and worked as an investment banker. Meili was smashed on the back of the head with a large branch and dragged off the road. She was raped, beaten in the face with a rock, and left for dead. Meili spent the next twelve days in a coma.[18]

The New York Police Department extracted confessions from five of the Harlem youths. The police pieced together a narrative that gripped the city's imagination. As a news story, it had everything: race, sex, violence, and terror. Every major newspaper and magazine bought this version of the story and then resold it. The "wolf pack" of black and Latino youths had gone "wilding" that night in Central Park. According to this story, they gang-raped Meili and beat her within inches of her life. Eight teenagers were indicted. Ed Koch called them "monsters." Donald Trump paid for full-page advertisements in all four of New York's major newspapers, demanding a return of the death penalty. Governor Mario Cuomo added, "This is the ultimate shriek of alarm. This is the ultimate siren that says: 'None of us are safe.'"[19]

The crime stunned even the most hardened city dwellers. It became the symbol of a city that had spiraled out of control. The Central Park attack altered the rhythms of everyday life for many New Yorkers. And it changed the city's racial calculus.

Five boys were convicted variously of rape, sexual assault, and attempted murder. They served between seven and thirteen years in jail, ranging from juvenile detention centers to Riker's Island. In 2002, a serial rapist named Matias Reyes confessed to the crime. Reyes was the real culprit; the youths had been wrongly convicted. In the spring and summer of 1989, while New Yorkers traded sociological theories about the indicted youths, Reyes had gone on to rape five more women. But at the time, nobody had heard of Matias Reyes. The story of the "wilding" youths was the one that transfixed and transformed New Yorkers.[20]

The city was at its least forgiving in the summertime. The streets were sultry; the humid buildings rendered apartment life unbearable. The tension rose with the temperature. In June 1989, a new film captured it all: Spike Lee's *Do the Right Thing*. The film is set on one block in Bedford-Stuyvesant during the hottest day of the year. "The film has to look hot, too," Lee wrote in his journal. "The audience should feel like it's suffocating." Much of the action takes place at Sal's Famous Pizzeria, a white-owned business in the heart of the black neighborhood. Near the end of the film, a scuffle breaks out at the pizza parlor. Police officers arrive and kill a black youth. In response, African Americans riot and ravage Sal's Famous. Lee's own character starts the riot, hurling a garbage can through the window of the pizzeria. According to Lee, originally he had planned to send his character toward the pizza parlor yelling, "An eye for an eye, Howard Beach." In the final cut, he performs the deed in silence. Lee came up with the idea for *Do the Right Thing* after reading about the Howard Beach incident. Sal's Famous Pizzeria was a nod to the New Park Pizzeria in Howard Beach. In the credits, Lee dedicated the film to the family of Michael Griffith—and to the families of four other deceased African Americans. *Do the Right Thing* articulated black grievances and forced New Yorkers to keep talking about racism.[21]

THERE WAS LITTLE DANGER OF THE ISSUE FADING AWAY. ANOTHER transformative event of 1989 occurred in Bensonhurst, Brooklyn. Bensonhurst was an insular neighborhood, home to rows of small brick houses. More than 60 percent of its residents were Italian American, making it the largest Italian community in the city.[22]

On August 23, Troy Banner—a black teenager from the East New York neighborhood—noticed an advertisement for a used car. He asked three friends to accompany him to look at the car. Yusuf Hawkins agreed to go along. That night, the group of African Americans boarded the N train, bound for Bensonhurst.

The teenagers emerged from a subway station at about nine o'clock. They asked for directions and walked south along 20th Avenue. They stopped at a newsstand, where Hawkins bought a candy bar, then turned onto Bay Ridge Avenue.

Trouble was brewing in Bensonhurst. Thirty local whites had gathered at a nearby schoolyard. One of them was Keith Mondello, whose ex-girlfriend had begun to date an African American. She told Mondello that a group of blacks and Puerto Ricans would soon seek him out. The white boys in the schoolyard stood ready for a confrontation.

Meanwhile, Yusuf Hawkins and his friends had been conspicuous as they strolled down 20th Avenue. One white youth spotted them, hurried to the schoolyard, and yelled, "They're here! The niggers are here!" A large group of white boys ran down the street. At least seven of them wielded baseball bats; one carried a gun. On Bay Ridge Avenue, they surrounded the four black boys. Hawkins and his friends stood unarmed and alarmed.[23]

One white youth yelled frantically, "Is this them?!" He motioned toward sixteen-year-old Yusuf Hawkins: "Is he the one?" Joseph Fama pointed his gun at Yusuf Hawkins and fired four shots. Hawkins fell to the ground. An ambulance whisked Hawkins to Maimonides Medical Center. He was pronounced dead on arrival.[24]

New Yorkers struggled to absorb the facts of another racial killing. Television reporters flocked to the Hawkins home. Yusuf's father, Moses Stewart, spoke out. He declared that his son had been "tried, convicted, and executed" solely "because of the color of his skin. I just want to ask New York and America as well: When will it stop?"[25]

City officials suggested a somewhat different interpretation of the murder. They argued that this was a crime of passion as much as an act of racism. Police Commissioner Benjamin Ward noted that "at least one witness heard the word 'nigger' used." But "in this case, it's a spurned lover who is jealous and is looking for the new boyfriend." Ed Koch agreed. "This is a case involving bias, but it's more than that. It's a spurned lover." Koch allowed, "This says that in the U.S., there is still racism." In New York, he claimed, "racial relations are far better than in many other cities, but they are not good enough." It was a bad time to accent New York's "far better" race relations.[26]

Moses Stewart wanted the world to know what happened to his son. So he called in Reverend Al Sharpton for assistance. Sharpton, a polarizing figure, organized a protest march through the heart of Bensonhurst. He explained his reasoning: "I knew that Bensonhurst would clarify whether it was a racial attack or not." If this was the goal of the march, it surpassed all expectations. On August 26, hundreds of African Americans trooped into Bensonhurst, marching three and four abreast, protected by a throng of police officers. The marchers chanted, "Whose streets? Our streets." The marchers condemned the murder of an innocent youth. In response, the white citizens of Bensonhurst turned out in force. They taunted the demonstrators, shouting: "Niggers go home! Niggers go home!" A small white boy spat in the face of a black adult. As the marchers wound through major thoroughfares and small residential streets, they took up a new chant: "Yusuf, Yusuf." White spectators replied: "Central Park! Central Park!" The black marchers shouted back: "Howard Beach!" These were the names for the city's ongoing racial crisis: Howard Beach, Central Park, and now Bensonhurst.[27]

Whites in Bensonhurst showed New York at its most vicious. Bob Herbert, a *New York Times* columnist and an African American, described the epithets and the anger. "It was the most vivid exhibition of racial hatred that I had ever seen." The crowd grew most excited at the sight of Sharpton himself. Sharpton admitted, "I was never so scared at any march I've ever been part of in my life." That march in Bensonhurst produced many remarkable images. A photo showed whites simultaneously embracing racism and denying it. One person in the crowd held up a sign that declared, "We are not racists." The man next to him hoisted a watermelon into the air. African Americans marched through Bensonhurst seven more times in the weeks that followed. Each time the tension rose higher.[28]

Robert Carter felt ill-prepared for the events of 1989. Carter had been based in New York for decades, and after his career at the NAACP he became a federal judge. He knew the many varieties of northern racism. But the hatred displayed in 1989 still stunned him. Carter had to transport himself backward in time, and southward in space, to make sense of it all. "I feel as vulnerable and as exposed to physical danger because of the color of my skin as I felt in rural Mississippi, South Carolina, Louisiana, or Georgia in the 1940s, 1950s, and 1960s." Carter lamented, "The climate is bleaker than I can ever recall."[29]

If Jackie Robinson's Brooklyn had been an interracial prototype, it was now an unrecognizable borough. But the old Brooklyn was also a place where the ghettoes had metastasized and where neighborhoods had congealed by race. The racial tension of the 1980s can seem like a climax to a long tale of discord.

Ed Koch did nothing to improve the atmosphere. His comments were more tone-deaf than bigoted. On August 28, Koch called a news conference. He deplored the murder of Hawkins and denounced the racial slurs that the people of Bensonhurst lobbed at the protesters. But Koch also criticized the black demonstrators. "Communities ought not to be condemned. Bensonhurst ought not to be condemned, Howard Beach, or any other part of town. . . . It's just as wrong to march into Bensonhurst as it would be to march into Harlem after that young woman in the jogging case." Koch offered no sympathy—except, perhaps, for the benighted residents of Bensonhurst and Howard Beach.[30]

Yusuf Hawkins's body lay in wake at the Lawrence H. Woodward Funeral Home in Bedford-Stuyvesant. On August 29, Ed Koch traveled there to pay his respects. Sharpton was inside the funeral home when Koch arrived. Sharpton recalled, "All I heard was what sounded like a million voices booing outside." The crowd hurled projectiles at the mayor and his entourage. "All [Koch] saw was black faces," remembered Dominic Brown of WLIB Radio, "and he didn't know what to do." Koch hurried back into his limousine. The driver put the car in reverse, stepped on the gas, and sped down the street—backward. New York's racial terrain had shifted profoundly in the wake of Hawkins's death. There were places where the mayor was not welcome.[31]

The murder of Yusuf Hawkins created a new sense of community among New York's African Americans. That feeling was palpable at the funeral. On August 30, East New York attracted political royalty from across the nation. More than a thousand people squeezed into Glover Memorial Baptist Church, which sat on a slumping block of boarded-up buildings. Jesse Jackson attended, as well as the Nation of Islam's Louis Farrakhan. So did Mario Cuomo and Spike Lee. Reverend Curtis Wells delivered a thunderous speech. "Let freedom ring from Howard Beach. Let freedom ring, yes, from Bensonhurst. We want to walk where we want to walk!" Then the mass of humanity processed to Evergreen Cemetery to bury the boy. For African Americans in New York, it was a moment of political baptism. "You knew that there was a bond that brought everybody together," remarked journalist Pamela Newkirk. "It was something that united all African Americans that day. . . . It was a loss for all of us."[32]

In 1989, Yusuf Hawkins was killed in Bensonhurst, Brooklyn. The murder capped a year—and a decade—of racial violence in New York City. Hawkins's funeral was held on August 30, 1989. Two men mourned outside of Glover Memorial Baptist Church in the Brooklyn neighborhood of East New York. ANDREW LICHTENSTEIN/CORBIS.

For years, African Americans in New York City had divided along many different fault lines. There were splits between Manhattan and Brooklyn, between Harlem and Bedford-Stuyvesant, between Caribbean immigrants and native blacks, militants and moderates, protest leaders and machine politicians. The horrors of the 1980s, punctuated by the murder of Yusuf Hawkins, obliterated many of these differences.

THIS BLOODY LANDSCAPE GAVE RISE TO AN EXTRAORDINARY POLITICAL moment. As it united black New Yorkers, it also deepened white voters' doubts about Ed Koch. This set the stage for New York's first black mayor.

The city had produced its share of black political titans—Shirley Chisholm, Adam Clayton Powell, Charles Rangel, Percy Sutton, and Basil Paterson among them. But no African American had served as mayor of New York City; none had even come close. By 1989, New York was the only one of America's ten largest cities never to have elected as its mayor an African American or a Latino. Percy Sutton, Manhattan's longtime borough president, had seemed the most likely contender. Sutton prided himself on his multiracial coalition. But when he ran for mayor in 1977, he was portrayed as *the black candidate*. "It was the most disheartening, deprecating, disabling experience," Sutton lamented. "I was rather unprepared for the isolation of me as a candidate on the grounds of race." Assemblyman Denny Farrell mounted an unsuccessful bid in 1985. "If you work to unify the black votes you're a racist," Farrell observed, "and if you don't do that you're in trouble because you don't have a base." No black politician could solve the basic riddle: how to excite the city's diverse African American community while also winning the support of white voters.[33]

David Dinkins surprised even himself. When asked who among his generation was most likely to become the first black mayor, Dinkins admitted, "I wouldn't have thought of me first." He would have picked one of his Harlem colleagues, Sutton or Basil Paterson. But in a decade when so many New Yorkers found themselves in the wrong place at the wrong time, David Dinkins ran for mayor at precisely the right moment. It was a moment in which Dinkins could offer himself as everyone's instrument. For African Americans, he could deliver pride and power. To whites, he promised peace and healing.[34]

Dinkins grew up in Trenton, New Jersey, with a brief stint in Harlem. He attended Howard University and Brooklyn Law School. Then he started his ascent in New York politics, beginning as a lackey in Harlem's Democratic machine. He served in the New York state assembly for one year, and later became City Clerk. In 1977 as well as in 1981, he ran for Manhattan borough president. He was beaten both times. Ever the grinder, he ran again in 1985—and won.

He was avuncular, decent, and unfailingly proper. He was old school. Rarely did a newspaper article appear without a reporter waxing about Dinkins's "courtly" demeanor. On February 15, 1989, Dinkins announced that he would challenge Ed Koch in the Democratic primary. "I am running because our city has become sharply polarized," he declared. "We need a mayor who can transcend differences so we can work together to solve our problems." As the columnist Earl Caldwell wrote in the *New York Daily News*, Dinkins promised "a city not as mean or as violent as the New York of now." Dinkins said then what he would repeat hundreds of times over the next nine months: "This city is not a melting pot but a gorgeous mosaic." Each ethnicity, each race, and each religion contributed to New York's greatness. From the beginning, Dinkins celebrated the city's diversity.[35]

To win the mayor's office, Dinkins had to appeal to three very different constituencies. He needed unprecedented black turnout, together with a percentage of white votes that no African American candidate had previously approached, together again with a majority of Latino votes. In March 1989, Dinkins's political consultant sent him an exhaustive report. John Marttila outlined the obstacles that Dinkins confronted: "Frankly, it will be an extraordinary accomplishment if you receive 25 percent of the white vote in November." Pundits and politicians had a good idea about how blacks and whites would vote. As one African American leader put it, "Blacks vote Democratic. Whites vote white."[36]

The racial violence of 1989 altered the terrain. It was not at all obvious that this atmosphere would fit David Dinkins so well. The violence could have produced the opposite effect. It could have built an impermeable wall between whites and African Americans, thwarting any black candidate's attempts to reach white voters. But Dinkins stumbled into a situation that suited his temperament. He also worked to fashion a language that would resonate during this moment in the city's history.

Two decades earlier, Ed Brooke had divorced racial tension on the ground from the realm of electoral politics. Dinkins tried something different. He conjoined the social with the political. He focused voters' attention on the racial hatred that pervaded the city, and offered himself as the candidate best equipped to tame that tension. The mayoral campaign was not above the racial enmity in the city, but about it. Dinkins defined himself as a healer and a conciliator, a vessel to transport New Yorkers away from the toxic times.

In the city as a whole, whites were becoming further outnumbered. The 1990 census would count whites as 43 percent of the overall population. African Americans would account for 25 percent, and Latinos for 24 percent. Yet whites comprised 56 percent of New York's registered voters and 52 percent of registered Democrats. White voters still held the key to City Hall.[37]

So the Dinkins campaign targeted white liberals. In New York City, winning liberal votes meant winning Jewish votes. This was a tricky proposition for Dinkins. The three other Democratic candidates were all Jews. (City Comptroller Harrison Goldin and businessman Richard Ravitch also vied for the nomination, along with Koch.) Moreover, relations between African Americans and Jews had been deteriorating ever since the Ocean

Hill-Brownsville school crisis of 1968. Dinkins appeared before many Jewish groups. He reminded Jews that he had spoken out repeatedly against anti-Semitism, and he pledged to be "mayor of all the people."

Dinkins also put voters in touch with their hopes for the city—their sense of what it had been and their wishes for what it still might be. In May, he secured the endorsement of Robert Abrams, the longtime attorney general for the state of New York. Abrams articulated Dinkins's core message, telling New Yorkers what they already knew: that their city was the center of the universe. "What happens in New York, what we think and do here, what we accomplish in our town, has a tremendous impact on all Americans. We can and should lead the nation." Given the current tumult, achieving that aim did not look easy. "In 1989 our city is beset by ills, our people in pain. Before it can lead the nation, New York City will have to heal itself." This situation called for the unifying powers of David Dinkins, said Abrams. In mass mailings, Dinkins stressed these same themes. The message seemed to be getting through. On May 16, an Orthodox Jew in the East Village penned a letter to Dinkins. "Wouldn't it be wonderful, if we could find a person, who could be a mayor to all races, religions, and colors?" Leonard Wacholder continued: "The mixture of so many different cultures in our city is what makes us great. In closing, let me wish you the best of luck." Wacholder was convinced that Dinkins could return New York to greatness.[38]

An April poll showed Dinkins with a 14-point lead over Ed Koch. In July, Koch unleashed a multimillion-dollar advertising campaign. He raised questions about Dinkins's past financial imbroglios and about his leadership ability.* By mid-August, the race seemed too close to call.[39]

Dinkins remained true to his base. On August 22, he held a fundraiser at Sylvia's Restaurant in Harlem. Dinkins reminded the audience, "I could not possibly succeed unless it was understood that I have to be mayor of all the people of the city of New York." But this was not the sentiment that had drawn the crowd to Sylvia's. He concluded with a more stirring refrain: "I am your instrument. I really am."[40]

The following night, Yusuf Hawkins and his friends walked out of a subway station and into the Bensonhurst air. Hawkins's murder trans-

---

*In 1973, Dinkins was tapped as deputy mayor. An investigation of Dinkins's finances revealed that he had failed to file tax returns for four years. He bowed out of consideration for the job.

formed the mayoral campaign. African Americans needed an instrument now more than ever.

At the same time, white voters looked for a way to stop the racial violence. Out of pure self-interest, they hoped to avert a race war. But more conceptually, they wished to live in a city whose public image was not dominated by thugs in Bensonhurst brandishing watermelons and baseball bats. They longed for a new symbol for New York.

As the September 12 primary approached, Dinkins talked more and more about Yusuf Hawkins. In appearances from Chinatown to the Bronx, he vowed to bind up the wounds that the boy's murder had inflicted. On Labor Day, Governor Cuomo framed the campaign this way: the key question was which candidate could bring the city together. One Brooklyn doctor wrote to Dinkins: "There is too much antagonism between the races in Mayor Koch's N.Y. Heal the wounds." If the election hinged on racial healing, Ed Koch was doomed.[41]

On September 5, Ted Kennedy traveled to New York. He was the keeper of the mystique of liberal Massachusetts as well as the Kennedy family's own mystique. In a speech at a Latino community center, Kennedy called New York "a city that has always been a national beacon of opportunity and progress." Now it was "pained by division and fear." Kennedy concluded that Dinkins offered "the only real chance for New York to become again the greatest city in the world—in spirit as well as wealth."[42]

The following day, a dozen Jewish leaders called a news conference to endorse Dinkins. The most profound comments belonged to Rabbi Gilbert Klaperman, who admitted that he had initially opposed Dinkins. "I had a niggling reserve in my mind about supporting Dave Dinkins. . . . When I thought it through I discovered that the reason for it, and I must say it publicly, was because he is black. And when that realization came to me I discovered in my own soul that I had done something wrong." Dinkins could hope that thousands of other white voters embarked upon similar mental journeys.[43]

On September 12, more than one million Democratic voters went to the polls. By nine o'clock that evening, the media was projecting Dinkins as the winner. Before Dinkins appeared at the Penta Hotel's ballroom, Jesse Jackson commandeered the stage. Jackson declared that the voters "turned pain into power." Out of the ashes of an excruciating decade, black New Yorkers scored a grand triumph.[44]

Dinkins won by a margin wider than any observer had dared to predict. He finished with 51 percent of the vote, compared to 42 percent for Ed Koch. Among African Americans, he won 94 percent of the votes. In Harlem and in Crown Heights, voter turnout had doubled since 1985. And Dinkins captured 56 percent of Latino votes. Racial minorities thus formed Dinkins's base of support. But it was not enough. As the editors of the *New York Times* pointed out, Dinkins's victory "could only have happened because a stream of white voters joined with black voters in supporting Mr. Dinkins—a hopeful portent that many New Yorkers yearn for racial peace and harmony." Dinkins won almost one in three white votes. In a sign that many did turn to Dinkins because of a yearning for racial peace, 38 percent of voters said that the events in Bensonhurst had made them more certain of their choice. Dinkins stitched together a coalition that looked like a gorgeous mosaic.[45]

Minutes after midnight, Dinkins took the stage at the Penta Hotel. He thanked the voters and reveled in the unique strengths of New York City. "You voted our hopes and not your fears and in so doing you said something profound today about the soul and character of this town. . . . You the people of New York stood up in this election for what is best in our heritage." They made good on New York's great history.[46]

For years, New Yorkers had seemed collectively frightened and deflated. On this night, they could celebrate their city anew. As Columbia professor Herbert Gans reflected, New York "is the most liberal city in the country. We get blamed for it all the time. So we might as well get some credit." The proof existed in the person of David Dinkins. A Japanese American sent Dinkins a letter of congratulations. "You have done what most people thought impossible," wrote Katsuya Abe. "*You* are the fulfillment of my hopes and aspirations for New York City."[47]

THE CITY HAD FIVE REGISTERED DEMOCRATS FOR EVERY REPUBLICAN. In order for Dinkins to lose the general election, a powerful force would have to be present—something more elemental than party or principles. It had to be something visceral and divisive, like race.[48]

The Republican nominee was Rudy Giuliani, a United States attorney and a Brooklyn native. His mayoral hopes rested upon his ability to convince roughly half a million Democrats to pull the Republican lever.

Both the Dinkins and the Giuliani campaigns acknowledged that Giuliani would perform well among white Catholics. There was no question that African Americans would support Dinkins in large numbers. Dinkins also maintained an advantage when it came to Latinos. That left one major group of voters: Jewish Democrats. As recently as 1988, Jews had cast 28 percent of the votes in New York City's Democratic presidential primary. This was why in the fall of 1989, a veteran politician from Harlem and an upstart Italian American prosecutor raced from borough to borough, and from temple to temple, with yarmulkes fixed to their heads.[49]

Giuliani played on the fears of Jewish voters. He claimed that a vote for Dinkins was a vote for Jesse Jackson. Among New York Jews, Jackson was reviled. In 1984, Jackson had referred to New York as "Hymietown." He apologized to the Jewish community, but the epithet still rang in their ears. Jackson had campaigned with Dinkins during the Democratic primary. In addition, millions of New Yorkers had watched the television coverage on the night of the primary election. They saw Jackson preside over Dinkins's victory party. Many Jews were outraged. On September 13, Hugh Rubin—an East Village resident—sent a letter to Dinkins:

> I voted for you in the hope, that . . . you can bring us together. . . . However, I was deeply disappointed seeing Jesse Jackson taking over your campaign headquarters while we were waiting for your arrival. Jesse Jackson is anathema to me. . . . I can never forgive him . . . for using a pejorative term toward [Jews]. . . . If you truly want to bring the city together and if you want the vote of people like me in the general election, please dissociate yourself from Jesse Jackson.

Dinkins heeded Hugh Rubin's advice. He would keep Jackson far away from New York City.[50]

Giuliani continued to press the issue. He labeled Dinkins a "Jesse Jackson Democrat," and ran an ad in a Yiddish newspaper that featured a photo of Dinkins with Jackson. In the short term, these attacks backfired. Giuliani came off as a "moral midget," in the words of journalist Joe Klein. On October 6, the *Jewish Daily Forward* endorsed David Dinkins.[51]

At the Jewish Leadership Breakfast the following week, Dinkins was at his aspirational best. As if his very belief could create the fact, Dinkins proclaimed, "There is something in the character of New York that is prouder and nobler and more decent than the cynics ever imagined." He deplored negative campaigning, the "politics of slam and slash and anger." He referenced a teaching from the Talmud, that all humans were descended from a single source. "This is the glue that binds the glorious mosaic of our city—which has been before—and can be again—an example to the world of how men and women who are different in many ways can live together and strive together and advance together." Then Dinkins pivoted. The self-professed racial healer admitted, "I believe there are more important issues in this election than race and religion." He was thinking about crime. Dinkins proposed a cop on every subway train. He promised to double the number of police officers on foot patrol. He put forth an "anti-wilding law" that applied to "urban terrorists" of every stripe. With some tough talk added to his uplifting vision, he won over the breakfast crowd. Three of New York's four daily newspapers endorsed Dinkins. By the end of October, he had a commanding lead in the polls.[52]

But Dinkins handed Giuliani a gift in the form of his ever-evolving financial blunders. It came to light that Dinkins had sold some stock holdings to his son at a drastically undervalued price. When Dinkins gave conflicting explanations for this, the story mushroomed into a scandal. In addition, Dinkins's campaign finances were in disarray. As a penalty, the Campaign Finance Board withheld public matching funds.

Giuliani linked Dinkins with black radicalism and anti-Semitism. Giuliani focused on Jitu Weusi, an unpaid adviser to Dinkins's campaign staff. In 1968, during the height of the Ocean Hill-Brownsville school crisis, Weusi had written a grossly anti-Semitic poem and read it over the radio. Worse, reporters discovered a connection between the Dinkins campaign and Sonny Carson. Carson was a black activist from Brooklyn and an acknowledged anti-Semite. Dinkins was forced into damage control. He condemned Sonny Carson and met with Jewish leaders to explain his actions. Giuliani brought up Jesse Jackson again: "The naked truth is that David Dinkins will be the trusted servant of Jesse in City Hall." Giuliani painted Dinkins as dishonest, incompetent, and guilty by association.[53]

In Crown Heights, local Jewish leaders endorsed Dinkins nonetheless. Dinkins sang the praises of that unique neighborhood. "Crown Heights is an historic community—the archetype of the pride and diversity that makes our city so rich and so vibrant." Orthodox Jews shared the streets with Caribbean immigrants. "It's a community in the heart of Brooklyn that has not been without its share of problems—crime and housing, to name two. But it's a community that can symbolize as well the ability and desire of all New Yorkers of all races and religions to live together and work together to overcome those problems and to build a true community of safety, security, tolerance, and understanding." To Dinkins, Crown Heights was a model for his gorgeous mosaic. The coming years would expose this as aspirational rhetoric at its flimsiest. In 1991, Crown Heights would become an archetype of racial hatred—not harmony.[54]

For every question about Jesse Jackson or Sonny Carson, about Dinkins's taxes or his stocks or his campaign funds, a white Democrat swung to Rudy Giuliani. But Dinkins's base of support never shook. African American voters prepared to descend upon the polling places. The hip-hop group A Tribe Called Quest paid tribute to Dinkins. In "Can I Kick It?," the group articulated the enthusiasm and the anticipation that coursed through New York's black population: "Mr. Dinkins, would you please be my mayor? You'll be doing us a really big favor."[55]

On Election Day, November 7, almost two million New Yorkers went to the polls. African Americans turned out in record numbers, comprising 28 percent of all voters. (Whites comprised 56 percent of voters, and Latinos 13 percent.) Dinkins won 91 percent of black votes, and 70 percent of Latino votes. Even with the long lines at polling places in Harlem and Bedford-Stuyvesant, however, victory still was not assured. In the end, Dinkins defeated Giuliani by all of 47,000 votes: 50 percent to 48 percent.[56]

The city's white voters either carried Dinkins to a historic victory or attempted to derail him. The observer could take his choice. Dinkins won 30 percent of all white votes. It was a level of white support that no other big-city black mayor had attained, except for Tom Bradley in Los Angeles. After Dinkins's victory, Jesse Jackson hailed "the maturing of white America." One white Dinkins supporter spoke for the thousands. Dan Longiaru voted in Co-op City. The thirty-five-year-old admitted, "I voted for him because he's black and it's an important symbolic gesture. . . . I was upset about the taxes and all. I expect he'll be a little sloppy in office, but the most important problem in the city is the racial division that we're seeing now. . . . It scares me." Longiaru concluded: "He's the best hope to stop the racial confrontations. . . . Things are getting out of hand."[57]

Other white Democrats rejected this logic. A stunning number of them defected to the Republican Party. Dinkins would explain why: "They used to ask me" why the 1989 election was so close, he recalled more than a decade later. "And I'd say, 'Why do you ask?' They ask me now and I say, 'Racism. Pure and simple.'"[58]

On the night of his triumph, however, everything was rosy. Dinkins bounded into the Sheraton Centre Hotel ballroom after midnight. With his eighty-five-year-old father at his side, Dinkins placed his victory within the arc of the African American struggle. "My father remembers when he was young, talking with neighbors who themselves remembered the days of slavery. Tonight, we've forged a new link in that chain of memory." The crowd burst into applause. African Americans wept. If the beginning of Dinkins's speech belonged to black New Yorkers, the end belonged to Jewish voters. He concluded, "I want to say a special word about the Jewish community, because tonight . . . that community again is a light unto the nation." Dinkins won almost 40 percent of Jewish votes. The chosen people had helped to choose a black man as the next mayor of New York.[59]

There was dancing in the streets of Harlem that night, and this spirit swept across the city's black neighborhoods. Said Boris Cadrow, a young African American from Flatbush: "I'm going to be walking on air for the next two weeks because we finally showed we can do something as one." For many of the individuals gathered at a senior center in Jamaica, Queens, Dinkins's victory marked the most profound political event of their lives. Henry Smith, an elderly black man, was "elated beyond words." He elaborated, "New York City is one of the most racist cities, job-wise and in housing and in education. . . . I couldn't imagine a black man being voted mayor in New York in my lifetime." Many African Americans experienced New York as a city of poverty, police brutality, and segregation. Now it was something else as well: a political beacon.[60]

One Italian American hoped that Dinkins's election signaled a new era. "I truly believe that New Yorkers now have another reason to be proud of themselves and their city," this Brooklynite wrote in a letter to Dinkins. This writer noted the pain of the 1980s: "Many of my family live in the Avenue X/Bensonhurst area of Brooklyn. In fact, some live around the corner from the bagel store where Willie Turk[s], the transit worker, was killed." He proposed a novel idea. "What I would like to suggest is that you and Mrs. Dinkins partake in a traditional Italian meal with a traditional Italian-American family. What a great way for the healing process to begin!" Over lasagna, Dinkins could start to exorcise the demons of the decade.[61]

Congratulations poured in from all quarters. David Wells was associate director of the International Ladies' Garment Workers' Union. "I'm sure that as a New Yorker you know what 'mazel tov' means," Wells wrote to Dinkins on November 8. "So as one of the 40 percent of Jewish voters who contributed to your victory, let me add mine." There was no question: David Dinkins knew what "mazel tov" meant.[62]

THE MOST MONUMENTAL EVENT OF THE YEAR (AND OF THE DECADE) occurred on November 9, 1989. The Berlin Wall fell. Europe's burgeoning revolution swept everything else into the background.

Yet for anyone equipped with a cursory understanding of race and American history, the elections of November 7 still possessed the power to startle and stun. Dinkins's victory was not the only racial breakthrough of that day.

Before the Berlin Wall crumbled, German television reporters had camped out in Virginia. They traveled to the Old Dominion to witness an epic moment in America's racial history. Douglas Wilder ran for governor. Wilder became the first African American ever elected to that office, in any state. Because this occurred in the former stronghold of the Old Confederacy, Wilder's election shocked Americans.

During the campaign, Wilder highlighted his pro-choice views. This placed him in a progressive "new mainstream," as Wilder declared. His ads proclaimed, "Keep Virginia moving forward. Don't let [Republican] Marshall Coleman take us back." As R. W. Apple wrote in the *New York Times*, the ad "reminded the state's voters of the days of massive resistance to integration, when schools were closed and the proud old commonwealth's reputation was corroded." Wilder navigated the specifics of Virginia's past—the blemishes of slavery and segregation on the one hand, as well as the celebrated tradition of the Founding Fathers on the other. His presence in the Richmond statehouse could help Virginia overcome the pain and reassert the pride. Wilder triumphed on Election Day. The *Washington Post* columnist Jonathan Yardley marveled that Wilder's victory "borders on the miraculous." It suggested "that somehow, that history has been overcome."[63]

In Seattle, where only one in ten residents was an African American, Norm Rice performed a similar magic act. While his opponent in the mayoral election exploited white fears about school busing, Rice won a 16-point victory.[64]

In the Northeast, another black mayor won election. New Haven was the setting. John Daniels, a child of New Haven's public housing projects, had risen to become a state senator. During the Democratic primary, Daniels styled himself as a reformer at odds with the powerful Democratic Town Committee. The racial issue was also essential. Daniels asked: "How can a black man who has worked within the party, who has the credentials, be elected in a city which is working class and predominantly white? Can the city overcome racism?" Whites formed about half of New Haven's population; African Americans accounted for 36 percent of city-dwellers; and Latinos made up another 13 percent. In the nation's fourth-poorest city, Daniels ran on an avowedly progressive platform. He won the primary handily, and in the general election he garnered 68 percent of the overall vote. Daniels proclaimed, "People are busting with pride and joy.... My victory indicates that a black can run for major office and be elected with white support." New Haven saw no widespread defection of white Democrats.[65]

The nation had some experience with black mayors who led majority-black cities, and with members of Congress—such as Shirley Chisholm—who represented districts with large black populations. But the elections of 1989 signaled something different. They represented "*trans*-racial triumphs," gushed the editors of the New York Times, "once as unimaginable as the end of the wall." They spoke for a nation in transition, moving "messily, unevenly, toward a standard of racial equality probably unknown in history." It was a time for superlatives. Yet to trade in such hyperbole also required an exercise in forgetting. In Massachusetts, Ed Brooke had made a career out of "trans-racial triumphs."[66]

In all four of the 1989 campaigns, some white voters embraced black candidates *because* they were black. In New York and Seattle, Dinkins and Rice promoted themselves as instruments of unity and racial healing. In Virginia, Wilder offered a way to move beyond the region's heritage of racism. And in New Haven, a city struggling with poverty and crime while in the grip of a political machine, Daniels's racial identity was an integral part of his novelty.

A comparison of David Dinkins and Douglas Wilder reveals something more about the northern mystique at the end of the twentieth century. On the surface, Dinkins and Wilder ran similar campaigns. Both individuals distanced themselves from Jesse Jackson in an attempt to appeal to white voters. In both cases, the polls underestimated how many white Democrats would ultimately vote Republican. Both were forced to eke out victories.

Yet regional distinctions loomed large. History itself operated very differently in the two campaigns. Wilder's rhetoric was all about overcoming the past. By voting for Wilder, white Virginians could bury a long history of racial oppression. He would put the past to rest.

For Dinkins it was the just the opposite. The present looked frightful. Dinkins wanted to light a path that led back toward the past—to rediscover the proud city of cosmopolitanism and pluralism. New Yorkers did not need to overcome their history. They needed to affirm it.

DINKINS TOOK OFFICE IN JANUARY 1990, WITH NEW YORK IN DIRE straits. Its economy had not recovered from the October 1987 stock market crash. Under the Reagan and Bush administrations, federal funds to New York decreased by $2 billion per year. The AIDS and crack crises both worsened. To compound the new mayor's problems, the media highlighted his Cadillac and the black-tie dinners he frequented. Playing into the stereotype, Dinkins—an avid tennis fan—took a helicopter from Manhattan to Flushing Meadows, Queens, to attend the U.S. Open. Dinkins had an image problem. That would not have mattered had he soothed the city's racial tensions.

Trouble began early in the year. At a Red Apple grocery in Flatbush, Brooklyn, the Korean proprietors became involved in an altercation with a black woman. She accused them of racism. Black activists organized a boycott of two Korean groceries. Dinkins dithered for several weeks as conflict escalated between African Americans and Asian Americans. A judge admonished Dinkins for failing to mediate the dispute. Meanwhile, juries neared their verdicts in the trials of Joseph Fama and Keith Mondello—the Bensonhurst youths who were accused of killing Yusuf Hawkins.[*] If they were acquitted, African Americans might take their anger into the

---

[*]Eight Bensonhurst youths faced charges in the killing of Hawkins. Attention focused on Fama and Mondello, the alleged leaders of the mob. On May 17, 1990, Fama would be convicted of second-degree murder. The following day, a jury would acquit Mondello of murder and manslaughter charges—though it convicted him of several lesser offenses.

After Hawkins's death, black protesters marched several times through Bensonhurst. White residents taunted the demonstrators and slung racial epithets. In 1990, Keith Mondello was acquitted of murder charges. After Mondello's acquittal, black marchers returned to Bensonhurst. White residents turned out in full force. RICKY FLORES.

streets. *Newsday* showed on its front page a lighted match with the headline: "City on the Edge."[67]

Dinkins had to face uncomfortable questions: What if more blood was spilled during his first term? What if the gorgeous mosaic fell to pieces?

On May 11, 1990, Dinkins delivered a speech at City Hall. He asked for calm from all corners of the city and urged citizens to rise above the charged emotions of the moment. A new forcefulness crept into his voice. He deplored the black boycott, calling it inappropriate and intimidating. For the first time, he was leading the city. At one point, Dinkins criticized the news media for its part in heightening the tensions and he uttered platitudes about fighting bigotry and teaching tolerance. To Dinkins and his staff, this was a throwaway line. Yet the packed crowd erupted in applause. The sustained ovation had about it a "surging, visceral quality," Joe Klein wrote in *New York* magazine. "It seemed to last forever." The city was desperate for inspiration.[68]

That weekend brought more violence. Several blocks from the Korean fruit markets in Flatbush, a gang of young African Americans set upon three Vietnamese boys. Tuan Ana Cao was beaten senseless. Dinkins called the attack what it was: "Tuan Ana Cao is Yusuf Hawkins in

Bensonhurst. He is Michael Griffith in Howard Beach. . . . Where did you learn to hate people of a different color?" Dinkins connected this act of anti-Asian violence to the anti-black violence that preceded it. The following week, a black teacher named Fred McCray led his students into a Korean grocery on Church Avenue, ending the four-month boycott. The mayor had spoken, finally, and the city moved with him.[69]

Dinkins tried to tackle the problem of crime. By 1990, the city's murder rate had reached an all-time high. He inaugurated a program that would become one of his hallmarks: Safe Streets, Safe City. It moved thousands of police officers from desk jobs to the streets and implemented a community-policing strategy. Later in Dinkins's term, the city hired another 5,000 police officers. The crime rate dropped during his last three years in office. But the general perception did not match the statistics. For many residents, the city felt ever meaner.[70]

Safe Streets, Safe City landed in the dustbin of history, alongside many of Dinkins's other programs. Because one event came to overshadow everything else. As Dinkins told an interviewer, "I'm confident that in my obituary, high up in the first 'graph somewhere, will be mention of Crown Heights. I guarantee you."[71]

If Willie Turks's ghost tormented New York through the 1980s, the new decade brought new apparitions. The deaths of Gavin Cato and Yankel Rosenbaum, horribly intertwined, would poison the city.

On the evening of August 19, 1991, Gavin Cato stood on the sidewalk outside his apartment building on President Street in Crown Heights. He tended to his bike and played with his cousin Angela. He was seven years old, the son of immigrants from Guyana. Shortly after eight o'clock that night, Cato crossed paths with a prominent neighborhood resident.

Grand Rabbi Menachem Schneerson was the head of the Chabad-Lubavitcher Hasidim. On August 19, Schneerson traveled to a cemetery in Queens to visit the gravesite of family members. A police-led caravan whisked Schneerson to the graveyard and back. As the procession headed west on President Street, the police car continued through a traffic light at Utica Avenue. Schneerson's car followed. The third car lagged further behind. Yosef Lifsh sailed through the intersection; some eyewitnesses claimed that the traffic light had already turned red. Lifsh's car collided with another car that was coming down Utica Avenue. His station wagon sped out of control and careened onto the sidewalk. It smothered Gavin and Angela Cato, pinning the children beneath the car.[72]

Spectators gathered as two ambulances arrived at the scene. One was a city ambulance, the other a Hatzoloh ambulance operated by Orthodox Jews. As E.M.S. paramedics attended to the Cato children, police officers instructed the Hatzoloh paramedics to treat the Jewish victims. The police ferried Yosef Lifsh away from the angry crowd.[73]

Angela Cato survived. Gavin Cato did not. When word of the boy's death reached the masses in Crown Heights, rumors swirled. One rumor posited that the Hatzoloh ambulance had treated the Jews and left the black child to die in the street. The crowds grew larger and more unruly. Accident, tragedy, and confusion turned to riot.

Later that evening, Yankel Rosenbaum walked north on Brooklyn Avenue toward his home. Rosenbaum was an Orthodox Jew and a visiting scholar from Australia. At the corner of Brooklyn Avenue and President Street, a group of African Americans beat Rosenbaum and stabbed him several times. Mayor Dinkins visited him at Kings County Hospital. Doctors assured Rosenbaum as well as Dinkins that Rosenbaum would survive. He was not so fortunate. Yankel Rosenbaum died at 2:25 in the morning.[74]

For three nights, mobs ruled Crown Heights. African Americans burned cars and assaulted firefighters, police officers, and photographers. Jews were also the aggressors in more than one incident. Dinkins tried to reach out to both sides. He appeared at a public school in Crown Heights on August 21. A hostile black crowd booed him and chased him away. African Americans charged that Dinkins favored the Orthodox Jews. In turn, Jews blamed the mayor for the murder of Yankel Rosenbaum. They called him an anti-Semite, and alleged that he had condoned a "pogrom." For Dinkins it was the perfect storm.

Police officers finally restored order to Crown Heights on the morning of August 23. By that time the damage was done. Dinkins had campaigned as a uniter and a peacemaker. But as the flames engulfed Crown Heights, Dinkins had to admit: "I alone cannot do it." In 1989, he had called upon the city's spirit of multiracialism. Now that spirit seemed dead and gone, another phantom in an era of ghosts.[75]

LEMRICK NELSON, A BLACK TEENAGER, WAS CHARGED IN THE SLAYING of Yankel Rosenbaum. On October 29, 1992, a jury voted to acquit Nelson. The verdict reopened year-old wounds. Orthodox Jews held Dinkins responsible for the acquittal. The man who wouldn't be caught without a yarmulke in 1989 had now been labeled a "Jew-hater." One poster featured Dinkins's face with the caption: "Wanted: For the Murder of Yankel Rosenbaum." In turn, some African Americans celebrated Nelson's acquittal.[76]

As tensions rose again, Dinkins scheduled a speech for the day before Thanksgiving. He asked for racial harmony and defended his actions during the days of rioting in Crown Heights. He detailed his visit to Yankel Rosenbaum's deathbed and his personal brushes with angry mobs. Dinkins criticized those individuals who would use the Nelson verdict to whip up racial resentment. And he championed the New York way of life. The "rabble-rousers do not understand our lives. . . . Because every day and every night, on subways and buses . . . in our parks and in our movie houses, New Yorkers live and work and learn and play, side by side and shoulder to shoulder." This was the everyday tolerance, the intermingling, that E. B. White had lauded decades earlier. Dinkins summoned that feeling. Still reeling from one of the worst moments in New York's racial history, he needed it more than ever.[77]

Dinkins chided his antagonists. To the "race-baiters" he said, "We don't need any more finger-pointing." And to a chorus of critics among New York's civil rights organizations he advised, "We don't need any more study groups." His answer was simpler: "We need each other." The *New York Times* called Dinkins's speech "timely and masterful." But Dinkins's solution was far too simple. He still seemed to believe that his words could heal the city.[78]

This kind of naïveté had appeared in the months following the 1991 riots. To those who wrote him letters about Crown Heights, the mayor responded: "Local residents, both Jewish and African- and Caribbean-Americans, have continued to live together in harmony." But this was not the case. Tensions enveloped Crown Heights. Moreover, Dinkins struggled to outline any sorts of policies that might improve the situation. Said Michael Meyers, executive director of the New York Civil Rights Coalition, "Denouncing bigotry is not doing enough."[79]

In Dinkins's 1992 Thanksgiving Eve speech, he offered a five-point plan of government and community initiatives. For instance, he would work with leaders of the school system to create a policy against hate and bias. These were vague initiatives designed to realize his vision of harmony. But many New Yorkers felt that the fires of Crown Heights had finally killed that dream. The goal of a multiracial society seemed unattainable and the payoff uncertain. During those nights of violence in Crown Heights, Dinkins lost many Jewish votes. He also lost something less tangible and more crucial. His vision for the city no longer carried the day.[80]

As Dinkins began to run for reelection in 1993, his opponent articulated a different vision. It was a message rooted deeply in an alternate reading of New York City's history. It aspired to make New York a city of safe ethnic neighborhoods. In such a place, residents might be isolated from individuals of other cultures; perhaps they would even become more tribalistic. But at least they would be safe. This was Rudy Giuliani's New York City.

In racial polarization, Giuliani glimpsed electoral treasures. One of Dinkins's Jewish supporters said this about Giuliani's campaign team: "I don't think they have to do a lot of strategizing on this. There are a lot of angry people out there, and all they have to do is turn 'em loose and hope a polarized city will help them." Giuliani's lowest moment occurred in September 1992, when he spoke before a rally of off-duty police officers. They had gathered to oppose Dinkins's proposal for a Civilian Complaint Review Board. One officer waved a sign that read, "Dump the Washroom Attendant." Blocks from City Hall, Giuliani delivered a volatile speech. He referred to Dinkins's proposal as "bullshit." The officers were whipped into a frenzy, and later swarmed the Brooklyn Bridge. It showed that Giuliani had an army behind him.[81]

Giuliani encouraged white nostalgia for an imagined past just as he profited from a bubbling racial discontent. He marched in the St. Patrick's Day parade on Staten Island amid signs proclaiming: "Dinkins Sucks," "Save us, Rudy," and "No Queers Here." He also played to conservative fears over sex education in the schools. All of this led reporter Todd Purdum to wonder whether a "hopscotch candidate" could "win and govern a hip-hop city." Queens College professor Andrew Hacker explained Giuliani's supporters this way: "It's not a hate vote, it's a fear vote. I was brought up in a city that was a white city. We ran it. . . . [Whites] want their city back and that's what Rudy Giuliani represents to them." In this hip-hop city, Giuliani danced to the polka and klezmer tunes of the white population.[82]

Giuliani did more than just exploit racial resentment. Since his initial defeat in 1989, he had educated himself on New York and on urban policy. He met with one expert after another. Andrew Cuomo, who had founded a non-profit organization to help the homeless, tutored him on homeless policy. And the president of Yale counseled Giuliani on education. Harvard's George Kelling offered a refresher course on the "broken windows" theory of fighting crime. Giuliani read up on workfare programs and garbage collection. He demonstrated an increasingly sophisticated grasp of the issues. Now the brusque prosecutor was also a policy wonk. He brought all of this to the table in the 1993 campaign.[83]

Race relations swirled at the center of the rematch. All of the main issues in the campaign possessed a racial tint: crime, welfare, the police, Crown Heights, and even Giuliani's promise to rid the city of the windshield squeegee men. Dinkins emphasized "community policing." His ads hailed New York's parks and public spaces as so many "fields of dreams." Giuliani's ads tapped into a deeper rage about job losses, taxes, and crime. And the candidates peddled two very different versions of New York's history. Giuliani would return the city to a placid past of white ethnic neighborhoods. Dinkins trumpeted a multiracial mosaic that once had been and could still be.[84]

President Bill Clinton appeared on Dinkins's behalf. Clinton wondered why Dinkins was ensnared in a close contest in such a Democratic city—especially given that Dinkins had balanced the budget in a weak economy and overseen a decrease in crime. Clinton concluded, "Too many of us are still too unwilling to vote for people who are different than we are." Clinton lamented voters' inability to transcend race. *Times* columnist Bob Herbert observed that in New York, this was asking the impossible. "Race is the one issue guaranteed to get New Yorkers crazy. It's the one issue this city can't handle. We can handle almost anything else. The [February 1993] bombing of the World Trade Center. Blackouts. The Mets. But not race."[85]

It became apparent that the "gorgeous mosaic" had never entranced many white New Yorkers in the first place. More likely, whites supported Dinkins in 1989 because of the self-interested hope that he could make racial violence disappear. In 1993, these whites would vote not for the person who embodied racial harmony, but for the one who fought on their side. They admitted this was no mosaic. They acceded to the metaphor of a battleground.[86]

Giuliani surged to victory on November 3, 1993. African Americans certainly viewed the election as a referendum on race. "A lot us were fooling ourselves about race in this city," reflected Geoffrey Canada, the executive director of the Rheedlen Centers for Children and Families. "We had a taste of inclusion, many of us for the first time in our lives . . . really felt part of this city. . . . We feel that's over."[87]

And if Dinkins had won? Would his victory have brought inclusion and progress? That is highly unlikely, though ultimately unanswerable. Yet it is possible to know what Dinkins would have said in the event of a victory. Of course, he had prepared a victory speech as well as a concession speech. Standing in the Sheraton's Imperial Ballroom, he would have declared, "Tonight, we proved the pundits wrong. . . . We've learned that . . . New Yorkers speak with truth and with tolerance—and not with polarized prejudice." And in the victory speech, he would have appealed to New Yorkers' sense of aspiration—asking for their commitment "to ensure that the promise of New York is not the privilege of generations past, but the birthright of generations to come." He would have reflected on his own unlikely journey. "When I was a boy, selling shopping bags on the streets of Harlem, I never dreamed I would come this far . . . I never dreamed we would make history—not once, but twice." He would have criticized those New Yorkers who pined for "the good old days that never were." Giuliani had traded in nostalgia for a New York City that never actually existed. Even Jackie Robinson's Brooklyn was a tangled place. The old New York was a city of segregation, fierce racism, and poverty as much as interracial daydreams.[88]

By the end of the twentieth century, it had become a tricky business to mobilize northern history as an aspiration. In New York, the recent past was filled with names like Willie Turks, Michael Griffith, and Yusuf Hawkins. In Massachusetts, the horrors of the Boston busing crisis had become a part of the collective consciousness. The question of northern history had become more perplexing. Which history to reference? Was it something to realize, or to overcome?

TEN

The North Rises Again

Deval Patrick, Barack Obama, and the Twenty-First Century (2006–2012)

I N THE TWENTY-FIRST CENTURY, IT COULD BE BOTH. THE NORTHERN past could operate as a source of inspiration as well as a burden.

In the hands of a new generation of black leaders, northern history—like American history—functioned as an aspirational force. For Deval Patrick, the American Dream was neither a myth nor a ruse. It was a living and breathing thing. "The 'rags to riches' story is distinctly American," Patrick wrote, "and though it is not told often enough, it is still told more often in this country than anywhere else on earth." And the man who would become America's first black president struck a similar note. Barack Obama summarized his own "American story" in his famous speech of March 2008. "I have brothers, sisters, nieces, nephews, uncles and cousins, of every race and every hue . . . and for as long as I live, I will never forget that in no other country on earth is my story even possible." On the night that Obama won the 2008 presidential election, he affirmed that America was an exceptional place "where all things are possible." Obama and Patrick were the living proof.[1]

The aspirational dynamic in American politics, and in American history, has long stood at the heart of the northern mystique. At the turn of a new century, Patrick and Obama both mobilized such forces as they forged racial breakthroughs.

Patrick's political ascent showed something additional about the North's recent history. By the end of the twentieth century, Boston still suffered from a reputation as a racist and hostile place. Patrick's victory raised the prospect that this history could be overcome. He promised to transform the state's civic life. The North could rise again.

DEVAL PATRICK'S INAUGURATION WAS SUFFUSED WITH SYMBOLISM. In 2007, Patrick held the first outdoor inaugural in the Bay State's history. The idea was that more citizens would be able to attend, and that this open-air ceremony would exemplify the inclusiveness of Patrick's administration.

The weather cooperated. For a January day in New England, it was unseasonably warm. Patrick's predecessors sat in chairs at the base of the statehouse steps, Republican William Weld and Democrat Michael Dukakis among them. Mel King, the Boston activist and former mayoral candidate, was also there to witness Massachusetts's first black governor take the oath of office. Douglas Wilder traveled from Virginia for the occasion.

Shortly after noon, Patrick placed his hand upon the Mendi Bible. A group of African slaves had presented this Bible to John Quincy Adams in 1841. The kidnapped Africans had risen in revolt aboard the *Amistad* slave ship. Adams had argued their case before the United States Supreme Court. Now, on January 4, 2007, the spirit of the African American struggle permeated Boston Common. "My journey here has been an improbable one," Patrick declared. "To this kid from the South Side of Chicago, Massachusetts is my shining city on a hill. Let's . . . make it shine again."[2]

Patrick's story began in an apartment on Chicago's South Side. Born in 1956, Patrick shared a bedroom with his mother and sister. There was just one bunk bed for the three of them. Every third night he slept on the floor. Racial segregation defined Chicago's neighborhoods, and racial strife tore the city apart. Martin Luther King Jr. led a march for open housing there in 1966 and was stoned by local whites. King remarked, "I think the people from Mississippi ought to come to Chicago to learn how to hate." The South Side burned in 1968, after King's assassination. Through it all, Patrick attended what he called "big, crowded, broken public schools." But his memories were not altogether desolate. He had some great teachers in those "broken" schools. One teacher guided him toward a program called A Better Chance. It took high-achieving youths from impoverished urban areas and shipped them into the nation's best prep schools.[3]

So it was that Patrick arrived at Milton Academy in September 1970. As he recalled, "Coming to Massachusetts was like landing on a different planet." The school's vast and verdant grounds boggled his mind. "I remember thinking I had never seen so much privately owned lawn in one place before." He made friends and his classes opened his mind, but he did not adjust easily. Others expected Patrick to adopt the culture of the white prep school. "I was welcome in that new world, it seemed, so long as I did not bring too much of my old world along." By the time Patrick served in the United States Department of Justice, sat in Texaco's boardroom, and ran for governor, he had become so adept at bridging cultures that one would think it natural. In reality, it was an excruciating process. "There's something extraordinarily painful about learning to live in more than one culture, to speak in more than one language." It was a skill that he would come to master.[4]

Patrick enrolled at Harvard in September 1974, the same month that buses carried students from Roxbury into South Boston. He later attended Harvard Law School. "I thought of law school as a way to express my commitment to social and economic justice—and also to make a buck." Patrick eventually took a job at the NAACP Legal Defense Fund, and in 1984 he married the former Diane Bemus. All the while, the town of Milton exercised its pull on Patrick. The Patricks ultimately settled in Milton and took jobs at Boston law firms; they even bought a house on Deval's old newspaper route.[5]

In 1994, Bill Clinton appointed Patrick as Assistant Attorney General for Civil Rights. For twelve years, the Reagan and Bush administrations had relaxed enforcement of civil rights laws. The Justice Department's Civil Rights Division was moribund. Patrick helped to resurrect it. His division aggressively enforced housing discrimination laws, challenging homeowners as well as housing lenders. In addition, he negotiated a $54 million settlement of a racial bias suit with Denny's Restaurants. He pushed for the creation of more majority-black congressional districts. He presided over a multiyear investigation into the burning of black churches in the South. In a controversial case, Patrick defended the school board of Piscataway, New Jersey, which had fired a white teacher. This prompted a scathing attack in *The New Republic*. "Deval Patrick has committed the Clinton administration to a vision of racial preference that fulfills the most extravagant fantasies of a conservative attack ad," Jeffrey Rosen wrote. Patrick looked nothing like a "post-racial" leader. He knew that to attack racial inequality was to engage in battles over power, economics, and the law.[6]

His stint in Washington complete, Patrick rose high in the corporate world. He served as general counsel for Texaco and for Coca-Cola, after both companies had settled discrimination lawsuits with black employees. Patrick ultimately resigned from Coca-Cola at the end of 2004.

That was when he set his sights on the statehouse. He first entertained the notion in the wake of President George W. Bush's reelection. Patrick was frustrated by what he saw as Democrats' inability to own their core ideas. He told Diane that he was thinking of running for governor. She was shocked. As she said, "it was a real, real, real long shot." Diane Patrick knew something about electoral politics. She grew up in Bedford-Stuyvesant and was raised by her grandparents; her grandfather was Bertram Baker, the state assemblyman from Brooklyn.[7]

The Boston busing crisis continued to endure in the nation's collective memory. "For too many people around the country," Boston mayor Thomas Menino remarked in 2006, "when they think of Boston the image they remember is of Ted Landsmark getting hit with an American flag." When Patrick began telling friends about his plans for a gubernatorial run, the response was: "Oh, my lord."[8]

Patrick traveled to Washington in search of advice. He scheduled a meeting with the newly elected senator from Illinois. Patrick had first met Barack Obama in 1995. Now, in 2005, he found Obama in a small basement office on Capitol Hill. Patrick told Obama of his idea to run for governor. Obama "leaned back in his chair and rocked on the two back legs, looking first at me and then into the middle distance." Obama said, "I'm in. . . . What do you want me to do?" Patrick flew back to Boston with his first major endorsement in hand.[9]

Boston's political class was skeptical. The Democratic Party already had two potential nominees: Attorney General Thomas Reilly and venture capitalist Chris Gabrieli. Reilly claimed the support of the mayors of Boston, Springfield, and Worcester. And Gabrieli possessed abundant funds. Patrick ran on what he had: idealism and a compelling life story. "I have grown up in poverty and worked my way forward. That is different from a lot of other people," Patrick recognized, "but not different from other people's aspirations." He built an extensive grassroots network, powered by volunteers, that reached into every county. By February 2006, Thomas Reilly had raised $4 million compared with $700,000 for Patrick. But Patrick's precinct-by-precinct organization slowly bore fruit. The early polls showed Patrick and Reilly in a dead heat.[10]

Patrick electrified audiences with his speeches, though he rarely said anything about race. "It is the invisible campaign issue," columnist Adrian Walker wrote in the *Boston Globe*. Walker pressed Patrick on it. "Race is with us," Patrick acknowledged. "It's not all there is, though. . . . I'm asking the people of Massachusetts to see the whole of who I am and how I've done." Walker was not convinced. For alongside the Bay State's claims to color blindness loomed an ugly racial history. Race lurked "at the margins of the campaign," Walker noted, omnipresent yet oddly ignored. "Pretending it doesn't exist is how we mostly deal with race in Massachusetts though, right?" As Patrick leaped over other obstacles—his lack of funds and name recognition—the racial hurdle was one that he always sidestepped but never quite cleared.[11]

In June, the Democratic Party's delegates gathered at the state convention to select their preferred candidate. Before the crowd in Worcester, Patrick delivered a barn burner about hope and idealism. He told stories of sleeping on the floor and of his journey to Massachusetts. He urged the delegates to summon their better angels: "I'm asking you to take a chance on your own aspirations." Patrick referenced the lofty history of Massachusetts. "Those who founded our Commonwealth left their known world, stepped into a wilderness—and built one of the most remarkable societies in human history. That took creativity, imagination, courage and vision—a hope in things unseen. That's the lesson of our founders. That's the lesson of our Commonwealth. That's the lesson of my own life." He wrapped the three stories together as parables of hope. He won the support of 58 percent of the delegates, and the party's official endorsement. The only vote that truly mattered was in the upcoming September primary. But Patrick left Worcester as more than just a viable candidate. He was the favorite.[12]

That warmed Derrick Z. Jackson's heart. Jackson was a columnist for the *Globe*, and an African American. "Forty years after Edward Brooke was elected to represent Massachusetts in the US Senate, the Commonwealth is close to claiming a partial healing of its soul," Jackson wrote. Given a historical backdrop that included Ted Landsmark and Louise Day Hicks, Jackson termed it a "colossal triumph" for Patrick even to have come this far. Moreover, he sensed in Patrick's campaign a new direction for African American politics. Forerunners like Ed Brooke and Douglas Wilder ran as political moderates. Patrick was powered by the grassroots Left. He stood strong for gay marriage, although it earned him the ire of Boston's black ministers. He refused to rule out raising taxes. And he wanted to extend in-state college tuition rates to illegal immigrants. He appealed to voters by defending progressive principles, not by toning down his positions.[13]

On September 19, Patrick won the Democratic primary. He earned 50 percent of the votes in a three-way race. The Republicans nominated Kerry Healey, who was then serving as the lieutenant governor under Governor Mitt Romney.[14]

A Democrat had not occupied the Massachusetts statehouse since Michael Dukakis in 1990. But the early polling figures suggested that Patrick would soon end the streak of Republican governors. Those polls staked Patrick to a 20-point lead. So Kerry Healey descended into the gutter. In a series of vicious ads, she tried to establish a link between Deval Patrick and violent criminals. She hammered Patrick for a death penalty case he had worked on at the NAACP in the 1980s. In addition, it came to light that Patrick had once voiced support for a convicted rapist whose guilt was at that point in dispute. Healey challenged Patrick's credentials and questioned his honesty. By early October, Healey had sliced her deficit to 13 points. The campaign was tightening.[15]

It turned nastier by the hour. The *Boston Herald* revealed that, in 1993, Patrick's sister had been sexually assaulted by her husband. The man served a brief jail term and the couple eventually reconciled. Up until this moment in the 2006 gubernatorial campaign, their children had been unaware of the incident. Now it was newspaper fodder. *USA Today* asked: "How sick is this?"[16]

Patrick was roused into a rage. He called the *Herald* article "pathetic and wrong." He continued, "This is the politics of Kerry Healey. It disgusts me. And it must be stopped. Kerry Healey has never offered a single reason why she should be governor that doesn't depend on tearing me down. She has no vision, no plan, no positive agenda." In a moment of anger and pain, Patrick crystallized his message. He charged that Healey traded in the politics of fear. He offered to replace it with a politics of hope. "That's the change we need. And if anybody in the Healey campaign or in the public thinks I am unwilling to fight for that, you have badly underestimated me." Throughout the campaign, Patrick had been uttering the words "hope" and "change." Now he married these mantras to a new kind of ferocity.[17]

That fire was present on Boston Common, where Patrick held a rally on October 15. Patrick's oratorical gifts had recently become the target of some backhanded compliments from Kerry Healey. At a forum, the candidates were asked what they admired about one another. Healey grudgingly allowed that Patrick could give a good speech. Her staffers took this up as a line of attack. They eagerly painted Patrick as long on rhetoric and short on substance. The argument, as Patrick put it, was that "all I have to offer is words." Patrick's "Rally for Change," where a crowd of five thousand joined him on the Common, became a lesson in the meaning of oratory itself. He reached back into the American past and recalled the country's great rhetorical flourishes. "'We hold these truths to be self-evident.' Just words. 'We have nothing to fear but fear itself.' Just words. 'Ask not what your country can do for you.' . . . Just words. 'I have a dream.' Just words." Patrick quickly admitted that he was no King, no Roosevelt, and no Kennedy. "But I do know that the right words, spoken from the heart and with conviction . . . are a call to action." He talked of a new kind of collective civic life. He mentioned policy specifics, yet none of those ideas would go anywhere "unless we reinvent our politics." It was time "to stop acting like partisans and start acting like citizens again." Patrick said later, "I'm going to stay on that point, because I think it's transcendent." For an afternoon, Deval Patrick achieved that kind of transcendence. And he did it with just words.[18]

Kerry Healey stooped lower. In an apparent attempt to cut into Patrick's advantage among female voters, she aired an unseemly ad. The ad took place in a dark and empty parking garage. A woman walked through the garage, hustling away from an assailant. Then came a clip from an old interview in which Patrick described Benjamin LaGuer as "eloquent." (LaGuer was the convicted rapist whose guilt had seemed in doubt.) The narrator asked: "Have you ever heard a woman compliment a racist? Deval Patrick, he should be ashamed, not governor." The Healey campaign transported the old bugaboo of the white American mind—the interracial rape nightmare—onto Massachusetts television screens. As Michael Dukakis lamented, "It's Willie Horton all over again."[19]

Healey's volunteers followed her lead. They dressed in prison-style jumpsuits and picketed Patrick's home. They pulled the same stunt outside of Boston's Faneuil Hall on October 18, where the candidates were holding a debate. The orange-clad volunteers raised signs that read, "Inmates for Deval Patrick."[20]

These tactics ultimately backfired. After the furor over Patrick's sister, the "Rally for Change," and the parking garage ad, Patrick began to run away with the race. Healey's support from Independents dropped by 12 points. By the end of October, Deval Patrick had soared to a 27-point lead in the polls. The politics of hope was poised to crush the politics of fear.[21]

Patrick rarely addressed the issue of his racial identity in any explicit way. After the election, he explained, "I wasn't campaigning as the black candidate. I understand people saw me that way, but talking across someone's kitchen table, I made it clear that wasn't what was on offer. What was on offer was a range of life experience and a vision of civic life that transcended a lot of differences—race, party, class, philosophical differences." Whenever the campaign's focus might have lurched toward race, Patrick steered it back to his own rags-to-riches tale, to the politics of hope, and the need for a stronger civic life. He never really pretended that the electorate was color-blind. "People saw my race, to be sure," he acknowledged. He just tried not to dwell on it. Kerry Healey's barrage of negative ads failed because Patrick had not given her attacks any space within which they could resonate. As Charles Pierce wrote in the *Boston Globe*, "Nothing about his campaign echoed ominously. It turned out nobody anywhere had much problem sharing a parking garage with Deval Patrick."[22]

At bottom, race was intrinsic to Patrick's appeal. He was indeed an African American from the South Side. And everyone knew it. That was part of what made his message of change so credible. He had an authenticity that was difficult to separate from his blackness.[23]

During the final debate, on November 1, Patrick accented the aspirational dimension of his campaign. "I'm not trying to scare anyone into voting for me," Patrick said in his closing statement. "I'm asking people at home, and all across the commonwealth to vote your aspirations." He knew that voters could base their decision on any number of preferences or policy prescriptions. But elections were also about what world voters wanted to live in, how they wanted to imagine their nation, in what kind of state or city they wished to raise their children. As Patrick later put it, "I feel we are an aspirational nation. And I feel that Massachusetts invented this aspirational nation." When Patrick encouraged people to vote their aspirations, he was urging them to perform a transformative act: to make Massachusetts into a place where a black kid who grew up on food stamps could command the corner office. This kind of aspirational thinking on matters of racial democracy had operated as a critical part of the northern mystique for more than the past half-century. And it proved crucial to Patrick's campaign.[24]

On Election Day, Patrick defeated Healey by a margin of 56 percent to 35 percent. Among whites, Patrick took 51 percent of the vote to Healey's 39 percent. He even carried South Boston.[25]

Patrick's victory speech was no paean to the color-blind commonwealth. He spun stories about some of the voters and paid tribute to the electorate. Then he declared, "You are every black man, woman and child in Massachusetts and America, and every other striver of every race and kind, who is reminded tonight that the American Dream is for you, too." Patrick concluded, "You made a claim on history, and I thank you for letting me be a part of that." His campaign had always been making a claim on history. In this moment, Patrick finally felt free to say so.[26]

Patrick insisted that he did not run for governor so that white voters could overhaul their state's racial reputation. Yet for many whites, his election had this effect. According to Jeff Jacoby, a conservative columnist for the *Boston Globe*, "Patrick's inauguration will finally wash away the shameful stain of that day in 1976" when Ted Landsmark was attacked. The editors of the *Globe* also had Landsmark on their mind. They noted the "powerful symbolism of the giant American flag suspended over Beacon Street" during Patrick's inauguration. Visually, this was the Landsmark assault inverted. "Patrick's elevation is one of many reasons to be optimistic that Massachusetts and especially Boston are overcoming the reputation for aloofness and even hostility that has haunted the region for decades." By voting their aspirations, Massachusetts residents raised themselves up and over that history.[27]

LATE IN 2007, ALMOST A YEAR INTO HIS FIRST TERM, DEVAL PATRICK trooped through Iowa. The nation's only black governor urged whites in the heartland to vote for an African American as president. At rallies beside cornfields and inside high school gymnasiums, Patrick warmed up the crowds. He encouraged Iowans to "take a chance on your own aspirations," and to support Barack Obama. While on the press bus, Patrick explained how he approached his racial identity. He talked about Milton and the South Side, and about the need to maintain a consistent personality across multiple worlds. "For me, and I think the same is true for Barack, what we've learned is to be the bridge. Don't look for some artifice; don't figure out how to be one way in one setting and a different way in some other setting—just be the bridge. You be the one that joins those disparate worlds."[28]

Barack Obama held within him so many different threads, and he merged them so seamlessly. Perched between white and black, between Kansas and Kenya, Obama could hit many different notes all at once. He strove simultaneously to embolden white liberals, link arms with black activists, empathize with white workers, and force conservatives to think twice.

Obama generally avoided speaking about race. Yet he knew that his unique heritage formed a central part of his appeal. It made him a walking embodiment of his own "change" mantra. Obama won the Iowa caucus and opened his victory speech with the words: "They said this day would never come. They said our sights were set too high. . . . But on this January night, at this defining moment in history, you have done what the cynics said we couldn't do." He talked of bridging partisan divides. But no American watching the speech could resist thinking about the racial divide. The day that would never come was the day when a majority-white America elected a black president.[29]

In South Carolina, where African Americans made up half of the Democratic electorate, Obama chose to accent his racial identity. The campaign tried to galvanize black voters. Obama won the primary by a landslide, and he went on to sweep the Deep South. Before African American audiences, Obama would let them know that he was theirs. This was Obama's version of the southern strategy. This strategy could be exported to any state with a large contingent of black voters. In the Germantown neighborhood of Philadelphia, he had an extended back-and-forth with the crowd—joyful, raucous, and none too subtle—about the merits of sweet potato pie. Outside of the South and the big northern cities, however, Obama's racial identity was unspoken.[30]

That changed after incendiary videos of Obama's former pastor began to circulate. Reverend Jeremiah Wright was a black nationalist who had often excoriated America for its legacy of racial injustice. In a clip that was replayed endlessly on television during the 2008 campaign, Wright thundered: "God Damn America!" Because of Wright's comments, more white voters associated Obama with varieties of black radicalism. Obama could no longer tiptoe around the issue of race.

He delivered the most famous speech of his campaign in Philadelphia, on March 18, 2008. In the speech, Obama used American history in several different ways. First, he sang the praises of a nation that could produce a story as improbable as his own. He described how his white grandparents had lived the classic American tale of the twentieth century. Then he explained how he married into a family that had been shaped by America's historic nightmare. His wife possessed "the blood of slaves and slave owners—an inheritance we pass on to our two precious daughters." He had a black wife, a white mother, and a half-sister who was an Asian American. In Obama's own story, America made good on its promise of pluralism. "It is a story that has seared into my genetic makeup the idea that this nation is more than the sum of its parts—that out of many, we are truly one."[31]

Later in the speech, Obama displayed a more complex understanding of America and its racial past. He narrated the long history of discrimination and explained the roots of black rage. Reverend Jeremiah Wright's "profound mistake" was that he remained trapped in this nasty racial past, unable to accept any of the transformations that had shaken

America. Wright "spoke as if our society was static; as if no progress has been made; as if this country—a country that has made it possible for one of his own members to run for the highest office in the land and build a coalition of white and black, Latino and Asian, rich and poor, young and old—is still irrevocably bound to a tragic past." Obama was telling voters, black and white and brown, that America's racial history had in it more than violence and oppression. It also held progress and possibility.[32]

This was a difficult balance to strike. As Deval Patrick reflected, "We as Americans have never quite found a way to talk about [race] that both acknowledges the progress we've made and the progress yet to be made, at the same time." Many Americans "want to either say, 'We're done, and look how well we've done,' or they want to say, 'It's a mess, and we haven't gotten anywhere.' And neither of those statements are true." Obama found a way to toe that fine line.[33]

On the night of the general election, in November 2008, Obama accented the optimistic side of the argument. It was an argument he had won. He told the throngs of well-wishers in Chicago, and across the nation and the world, "If there is anyone out there who still doubts that America is a place where all things are possible, who still wonders if the dream of our founders is alive in our time, who still questions the power of our democracy, tonight is your answer."[34]

FOR POLITICAL CANDIDATES, IT WAS NOTHING NEW TO WAX ABOUT THE wonder of American democracy. But when set within the sweep of the Northeast's racial history, an important dimension comes into view. The history of the Northeast shows that the aspirational aspect has always been critical to the success of interracial politics. When whites voted for black candidates—from Massachusetts with Brooke and Patrick, to Chisholm's Brooklyn and Dinkins's Manhattan—they were acting on a certain vision for their state or city, or for their nation.

Obama's presidency had barely begun before historians and journalists started to jockey over how best to understand his political ascent. The debate revolves around one basic question: Of all the prologues that American history contains, which is the most illuminating? Which best explains the rise of this black president? Scholars have explored Obama's family history, his complex relationship with the civil rights struggle, his debt to the Black Power movement, his place in American intellectual history and in the pantheon of presidents.[35]

Yet an understanding of the man, in whatever context, is only half the equation. The other part is to show how the American people got there with him in 2008. It took a remarkable convergence of the individual and the voters to elect the nation's first black president. It is not enough to sketch several different versions of Obama's own history. One must also write a history of America that can account for the convergence.

On the surface, there were three major reasons that Americans stood prepared to embrace Obama's call for change: the polarizing presidency of George W. Bush, the tragedy of the Iraq War, and the economic crisis of 2008. These developments tipped the electorate over the edge and into the arms of a black president. But the question remains: how and why were the voters ready to seriously consider a black president in the first place?

The long-term picture becomes comprehensible when one studies the history of the Northeast. This was Obama's stronghold, the place where white voters supported him to a far greater degree than anywhere else. In choosing Obama, voters in the Northeast presented themselves once again as leaders in the struggle for interracial democracy. Viewed in this context, Obama looks not like a break with history. He is a continuation of one of its strands.

This history includes experiments in interracialism, from the Springfield Plan to Jackie Robinson's Brooklyn. It also encompasses those moments in which multiracial political coalitions came into being, whether forged by Ed Brooke or Shirley Chisholm, Thirman Milner or Deval Patrick. Obama's messages about hope and change, his mobilization of history itself as an aspirational force, and his ability to speak about race while transcending it—all of this was recognizable to anyone familiar with race and politics in the twentieth-century Northeast.

The appeal of a multiracial politics was particularly fitted to a region where citizens' high conceptions of their own cities and states mingled uncomfortably with a recent history of injustice. Northern history has Ed Brooke and the Boston busing crisis in it, side by side. It has Jackie Robinson's triumph as well as the Crown Heights riots; the Racial Imbalance Act and Ted Landsmark; black political power and widespread black poverty. This tangled history makes the recent advances in black politics both shocking and fitting.

IF THIS IS WHAT THE NORTH CAN TELL US ABOUT OBAMA, THEN WHAT about the reverse? What can Obama's election reveal about the North?

It suggests that a great divide still separates the North and South. In the former states of the Old Confederacy, Obama won just 31 percent of white votes. In the Deep South he encountered particularly fierce resistance, with less than 15 percent of white votes. This cannot be explained just by a general dislike for Democrats, or even for northern liberals. In the Deep South, Obama won a smaller share of white votes than John Kerry had four years earlier. This was striking because Obama's totals outpaced Kerry's nearly everywhere else in the nation. White southerners remained exceptional in their level of opposition. By contrast, Barack Obama won a majority of white votes in every New England state as well as New York. In terms of interracial support for America's first black president, whites in the Northeast led the way.[36]

Yet the duality was forever lurking. The ugly side of northern race relations always seemed ready to rear its head. So it did in Springfield. At three o'clock in the morning, hours after celebrating Obama's election, Bishop Bryant Robinson Jr. was awakened by a phone call. His brother Andrew yelled, "They are burning our church to the ground!" The nightmare followed so closely on the heels of the dream.[37]

Bryant Robinson Jr. was born in Alabama in 1937. When he was a boy, his father moved the family out of the Jim Crow South to a place that beckoned with more promise: Springfield, Massachusetts. Bryant Robinson Sr. started his own congregation there, calling it the Macedonia Church of God. In 1961, the congregation purchased an old Episcopalian church on King Street. The elder Robinson passed away in 2001, and Bryant Robinson Jr. succeeded him.

Robinson had big plans. He proposed a new site for a grand house of worship. He passed many collection plates; he obtained a loan; finally he began to build on a large plot of land in the Sixteen Acres neighborhood. The new church was about three-quarters of the way completed by November 2008. Robinson's congregation had high hopes for the year ahead: a black president as well as a gleaming new sanctuary. As fast as one of those hopes materialized, the other went down in flames.

In the pitch-black darkness, three young white men stole through a wooded area off of Tinkham Road. They carried canisters of gasoline. With accelerant, one of them outlined the words "Hate Nigger" on the edge of the church site. They doused the structure and set it on fire.

Federal investigators quickly found the perpetrators, all residents of Springfield. It was not just the nature of the crime that proved shocking, but also its location. "Not here, we all said," recounted Paul Smyth, an assistant United States attorney. "Not in Massachusetts—a state with a proud abolitionist history." That was what Michael Caron thought when the fire near his home jarred him from his slumber. Said Caron, "This is like Springfield, *Mississippi*, here." Decades after Massachusetts had proven itself quite capable of racial hatred, Springfield leaders and residents continued to display a pronounced regionalism in their reactions to the crime. The editors of the *Springfield Republican* asked the question that so many were wondering: "How could a new dawn in America, tap so much darkness—in Springfield of all places?"[38]

Part of the answer was that Springfield, like the larger Northeast, held the two warring impulses. In certain moments, the region was able to propel itself above and beyond the rest of the nation; its strong support for Obama was one such moment. But even in the hour of the greatest progress, the viciousness could creep in. For Bryant Robinson, the goodness and the hatred of that night were wrapped together so tightly that it was impossible to separate the two. Before America could even begin to launch itself into the future that it had voted for, all the ugly images from yesterday started rushing back.

At first, Robinson despaired. The church site had become "so desolate, so barren, so lifeless." Eventually Robinson secured a government loan guarantee under the Church Arson Prevention Act of 1996. And after Deval Patrick interceded, TD Bank offered a loan of $2 million. Volunteers flocked to Springfield to help rebuild. In September 2011, the church opened to worshippers. It had risen from the ashes.[39]

In another time and another place, there could have been just pain, melancholy, and a bruising struggle. So it often was during the civil rights era, when hundreds of black churches were burned throughout the

South. But Macedonia Church opened its doors to a nation transformed. In 2011, Massachusetts had a black governor and the nation had a black president. Three white men burned down Bryant Robinson's church. But they did so because they knew the world was theirs no longer. That world had passed.

BARACK OBAMA WAS THE MOST POWERFUL SYMBOL OF THE NEW WORLD. Once in office, Obama pursued many policies that helped African Americans. His initiatives expanded access to health care, unemployment benefits, and food stamps, and awarded more education grants to needy public schools. He presented this not as legislation for African Americans, but for Americans from all walks of life. Skeptics have argued that Obama accomplished little for black people *as black people*. The political scientist Fredrick Harris wrote in 2012 that "the Obama presidency has already marked the decline, rather than the pinnacle, of a political vision centered on challenging racial inequality." Cynics like Harris contend that Obama provides an empty symbolism for black Americans, and that this will be the case so long as millions of African Americans remain impoverished, behind bars, in segregated neighborhoods, and in underfunded schools. Furthermore, they argue, the success of the black politician obscures such structural inequities. It tricks white voters into thinking, or allows them to claim, that the day of equality has arrived. Harris argues that too many African Americans "gave Obama a pass" on issues like black poverty and incarceration. They were beguiled by the image of a beautiful black family in the White House. "Sadly, when it comes to the Obama presidency and black America, symbols and substance have too often been assumed to be one and the same." According to Harris, Obama made progress only in the realm of images and perceptions. He achieved nothing real.[40]

For the sake of argument, one might accept that Obama's primary accomplishment has been in the symbolic power of his example. Still, that symbolism has significant meaning. It changes the fabric of the political culture, if not the economic and social structures. Obama has transformed how many Americans view their world. For black children, it is altogether different to be born into a country where the president shares one's skin color. It is possible to overstate the power of this change, yet dangerous to underestimate it.[41]

The problem of symbolic advances versus structural change is central to the history of race and politics in the Northeast. Jackie Robinson broke baseball's color barrier just as ghettoes grew in Brooklyn. Ed Brooke soared into his high office while segregation deepened in Boston's schools and neighborhoods. Thirman Milner, the first black mayor in New England, could only watch as black poverty worsened in Hartford. David Dinkins became mayor of New York City in part because conditions for African Americans were so bad on the ground. Similar conundrums have bedeviled the black leaders of the twenty-first century. These leaders have also suggested some answers to the question of symbol and substance.

Deval Patrick endured criticism for his own policies toward African Americans. In 2009, Reverend Eugene Rivers—a nationally acclaimed black minister in Boston's Dorchester neighborhood—wrote an open letter to Patrick and hand-delivered it to the governor's office. Rivers expressed a "profound sense of disappointment" in Patrick. According to Rivers, Deval Patrick failed to steer federal stimulus money toward African Americans in Massachusetts and focused little on preventing violence among black youths in Boston. Patrick named just two minorities to the state courts out of twenty-nine vacancies. "On the basis of his performance to date," Rivers stated, "there is no rational basis for voting for Deval Patrick for reelection." Patrick eventually rose to meet some of the challenges. He appointed an African American as chief justice of the Supreme Judicial Court, and secured a million-dollar grant to revive Freedom House in Roxbury. Still, much of Patrick's power seemed to rest in his symbolism.[42]

Patrick had visited Dorchester early in his first term. The community was in an uproar over a surge in violence. A young woman had been shot near the Holland Elementary School. Then an eleven-year-old boy found a pistol on the street and brought it into school. Patrick accompanied Mayor Thomas Menino to the Holland School for a meeting with neighborhood residents. Before Patrick spoke, he took a couple of minutes to himself in the principal's office and looked over his notes. He quickly realized that he was not alone. "When I looked up, outside the window were a dozen or more little black boys and girls wearing backpacks, beaming and waving excitedly." Patrick thought back to his own childhood in Chicago. "I'm not sure I would have recognized the governor of my state, beyond perhaps knowing that he did not have my skin color." Patrick looked at the eyes fixed upon him. They were excited not so much for "the history I am making, but the history they have yet to make." His presence in the statehouse allowed them to think bigger. "They see a possibility they might not have seen because I'm in the job." Their range of vision was enlarged.[43]

At the national level, Barack Obama's ascent to the White House altered understandings among black people about what was possible in America. Obama also affected the expectations of white Americans, as the legal scholar Randall Kennedy wrote, "habituating them, like nothing before, to the prospect of people of color exercising power at the highest levels." It was a lesson "daily and pervasively absorbed—the message that a person of color can responsibly govern." Barack Obama was keenly aware of this. Obama embraced his own presidency, as he had embraced his campaign, as an undertaking rife with racial meaning. In 2006, Obama informed his wife and his aides that "he wanted to run for the White House to change children's perception of what was possible." As Jodi Kantor wrote in the *New York Times*, he was "embarking on an experiment in which the Obamas would put themselves and their children on the line to help erase centuries of negative views." By the time Obama ran for reelection in 2012, his wife was the country's most popular political figure; his daughters invited adoration. While Obama stirred up all sorts of racial animosity among fearful whites, many stereotypes faded in the face of his picturesque family.[44]

One photograph hanging in the White House testifies to Obama's transformative power. It centers on a black boy named Jacob Philadelphia. Jacob's father, Carlton, was a Marine who worked on the staff of the National Security Council. When Carlton Philadelphia left that position, his family posed for a photograph with the president. Each of his two sons had prepared a question for Obama. Jacob, five years old at the time, said: "I want to know if my hair is just like yours." Obama responded, "Why don't you touch it and see for yourself?" Obama bent over at the waist, his head within Jacob's reach. Jacob hesitated. The president pressed him: "Touch it, dude!" As the boy felt the president's hair, the White House photographer captured the moment. Obama asked: "So, what do you think?" Jacob answered, "Yes, it does feel the same." While most of the photographs in the West Wing are swapped out frequently, this one stays on the wall. A framed copy also hangs in the Philadelphia family's living room. "It's important for black children to see a black man as president," Carlton Philadelphia said in 2012. "You can believe that any position is possible to achieve if you see a black person in it." By that time, Jacob was eight years old. When Jacob was asked what he wanted to be when he grew up, he offered two possibilities: either a pilot or the president.[45]

The important thing is not whether one places these black leaders in the category of symbol or substance. Either way, their effects are powerful. As Deval Patrick put it, "You don't want to say to people that my election is meaningless from the perspective of the journey we've been on in terms of race relations, because it's just not so. But to say to anybody that we've finished all of our unfinished business because of my election is wrong." In the nation at large, racial inequality persisted. But the fact that a black man actually won election in this majority-white nation, and that he served ably in the White House, has a significance that is real and lasting. That impact might best be measured across the generations.[46]

In 2009, Reverend Joseph Lowery penetrated to the heart of the matter. Lowery was a veteran of the civil rights movement. Barack Obama asked Lowery to deliver the benediction at his inauguration. The day before the ceremony, Lowery appeared on PBS's *NewsHour with Jim Lehrer*. He confessed, "I can't wait for a few years, Barack has been president, to see what happens with the doll experiment, with black kids picking white dolls . . . over black dolls." Lowery tried to foresee the changes. "Well, now that we've got a guy in the presidency who looks like us, I think it's going to impact kids at that level, and I think we'll begin to pick a few black dolls." Seventy years had passed since Kenneth Clark's doll tests in Springfield. In that time, a whole history of interracial democracy was made and unmade, then forged again anew.[47]

OBAMA'S FIRST VICTORY ALMOST INEVITABLY FELT SYMBOLIC. MANY voters pulled the lever for a black candidate in order to prove to themselves—and to the world—that they were capable of a breakthrough. Once achieved, everyone basked in its glow. But when Obama ran for reelection in 2012, something more was at stake. The voters had to pass judgment on the man and his ideas more than on the idea of the man. Ta-Nehisi Coates, a writer for *The Atlantic*, explained the central conundrum of the Obama era: "Barack Obama governs a nation enlightened enough to send an African American to the White House, but not enlightened enough to accept a black man as its president." The prospect of reelection presented the white majority with the ultimate test. Would it *accept* a black man as president and return him to the job?[48]

In 2010, Deval Patrick had confronted the same kind of question. Patrick garnered mixed reviews for his performance during his first term. He had difficulty working with a "mulish legislative leadership," as the *Boston Globe* referred to Beacon Hill Democrats. And whatever the legislature didn't stymie was wrecked by the economic crash of 2008. The state's economy tanked. Still, Patrick reversed many policies of his predecessor, Mitt Romney. He joined the regional greenhouse gas initiative, reinstated some affirmative action measures, repealed regulations on stem cell research, and turned back abstinence-only education requirements. He also fought to keep the question of a gay marriage ban off the ballot. Universal health care coverage, a program passed by Romney, was successfully implemented. Meanwhile, Patrick brought much-needed diversity to Beacon Hill. He chose as his chief of staff an African American lawyer named William "Mo" Cowan. In the governor's office, women held 52 percent of the positions and racial minorities held 27 percent. As the *Globe* noted, "The Beacon Hill power lunch spots just look different." Yet the state continued to suffer from a weak economy and high unemployment rates.[49]

The same could be said for the nation. America staggered through a devastating recession as President Obama's approval ratings plummeted. The Tea Party movement forced the Republicans further to the right. Obama proposed a bill for comprehensive health care reform, modeled on Mitt Romney's legislation in Massachusetts. Fearful Americans blew a collective gasket. As the battle over health care flared, a longtime champion of that cause—Ted Kennedy—passed away. Massachusetts scheduled a special Senate election for January 2010. A little-known state legislator from Wrentham seized the opening. Scott Brown jumped upon a wave of populist anger and rode it to victory. Massachusetts voters picked this thinly credentialed Republican to fill the seat of a liberal legend. The prospects for Democrats looked bleak.

In this atmosphere, Deval Patrick announced that he would run for reelection. For a man who rose through the political ranks so fast, it could all come crashing down at that same high speed.

Patrick entered the campaign as the underdog. His favorability ratings hovered well below 50 percent. But as he began to reintroduce himself to voters across the state, they glimpsed the Patrick of 2006: the magnetic and optimistic leader. He appealed to the voters' ideals while painting Republican Charlie Baker as a cold-hearted businessman. More important was the way that Patrick handled his own record. Patrick had signed a tax increase at a low point in the recession. Baker pilloried him for this, but Patrick defended his actions. The tax increase was necessary, he said, in order to fund public schools, to provide health care, and to maintain clean energy programs. In tough times, Patrick proclaimed, "we must turn to each other, not on each other." He urged sacrifice in the name of the common good. In a nation ravaged by the Tea Party and reeling from a vitriolic fight over health care, Patrick was forthright in his support for higher taxes and for government action.[50]

Patrick pointed to some important distinctions between this campaign and his initial election in 2006. The first election, "I want to believe was an affirmation of those common aspirations. But I hadn't made any decisions yet. And then I made decisions for four years, and some of them were incredibly painful, because they were prompted by a global economic collapse." In 2012, he had a record to run on. He felt it was vital for the voters to evaluate him on that basis. "To win under those circumstances had a different kind of meaning."[51]

This time around, one issue was notably absent from the gubernatorial campaign: race. There were no television ads set in dark parking garages, no potshots about criminal cases from the 1980s, no campaign volunteers in orange jumpsuits. If any white voters needed to search their souls before supporting an African American leader, they had done the searching four years ago.

On November 2, 2010, Bay State voters made Deval Patrick the first black governor ever to win a second term. Just as significant, Massachusetts defied the national political trend. Republicans dominated elections across the country. But in the Bay State, Democrats won every congressional seat and statewide office. In his victory speech, Patrick positioned Massachusetts as a beacon. "We must be, all of us, about lifting the whole commonwealth up, not tearing anyone down, and modeling for a nation hungry for something *positive* to believe in, that we are once again the center, the leader, for this country." While America was mired in economic drudgery and buffeted by political division, Patrick placed Massachusetts back where it was most comfortable: as a leader for the nation.[52]

The rest of the country shook its head in wonder or mockery, or looked on with a yawn. Political analysts dismissed Massachusetts as an outlier. The ghost of George McGovern had returned. This was merely Massachusetts being Massachusetts, which to Red Sox fans was a bit like Manny being Manny: the lunatic exception that proved the rule.

The coming years would suggest that Massachusetts was ahead of the country rather than apart from it. Patrick had actually created a blueprint for Obama. Patrick demonstrated that optimism could still sell, even in tough economic times and for a leader with sagging approval ratings. "Somehow Patrick managed to float above it all," Brian Mooney wrote in the *Boston Globe*. "It was a remarkable levitation act in a toxic political environment." The more Patrick owned his programs of the past four years, the better he fared. He justified the tax increase. He refused to crack down on illegal immigrants. And he articulated, in common sense language, a pro-government philosophy that had been derided for many years.[53]

WHILE BARACK OBAMA SAW PART OF HIS CHARGE AS CHANGING BLACK minds and destroying white stereotypes, he believed that those missions would be incomplete without a second term. As one White House advisor put it, his desire to win reelection was "so implicit it is just like breathing."[54]

His opponent in the 2012 campaign would be Republican Mitt Romney. At the Democratic convention in September, speeches by Michelle Obama and Bill Clinton attracted the most attention. But the finest address belonged to Deval Patrick. He heralded the progress that Massachusetts had made since Romney's departure—including reforms of the education, pension, and transportation systems. Expanding out to the national context, Patrick denounced the kind of conservatism that slashed social services and crushed unions. He lauded Obama's specific achievements: affordable health care, the killing of Osama bin Laden, the repeal of "don't ask, don't tell," the rescue of the auto industry, and the passage of equal pay for equal work. "The list of accomplishments is long, impressive, and barely told." Patrick fairly shouted at the crowd, "With a record and vision like that, I will not stand by and let him be *bullied out of office*—and neither should you!" He hit the sweet spot between passion and anger.[55]

On Election Day, the voters opted decisively for Obama over Romney. For the first time in American history, the percentage turnout of voters was higher among blacks than whites.[56]

Mitt Romney became the latest in a long line of losers from Massachusetts. Like John Kerry and Michael Dukakis before him, Romney could not make the electoral transition from the Bay State to the nation. According to one popular narrative, Romney's failure showed that the Bay State remained a political anomaly. But the opposite was true. Massachusetts voters stepped into the political future with their strong support for Obama. Massachusetts was one of four states in which the president won every county. And Obama won a majority of white votes in all six of the New England states.[57]

As the North leaped ahead, the South fell back. The regions seemed as different in their racial politics in 2012 as they had been fifty years earlier. Among white southerners, Obama's vote totals were stunningly low. In Mississippi, only one in ten white voters pulled the lever for Barack Obama. The South seemed light-years away from overcoming the politics of its past.[58]

In his victory speech, Obama ruminated on the Democratic vision. "We believe in a generous America, in a compassionate America, in a tolerant America open to the dreams of an immigrant's daughter who studies in our schools and pledges to our flag—to the young boy on the South Side of Chicago who sees a life beyond the nearest street corner." The dream would be available to the children of Mexican immigrants as well as black children in poor urban neighborhoods. As Obama summoned a multiracial future, he looked back to the past for inspiration. "I believe we can keep the promise of our founding, the idea that if you are willing to work hard, it doesn't matter who you are or where you come from or what you look like or who you love." In the new America that Obama conjured, race posed no obstacle and sexual preference was no stigma.[59]

In some measure, this America lived in Obama's imagination. By 2012, the United States had less equality of opportunity than most of the advanced industrialized nations. And economics often corresponded with race. Fully 27 percent of African Americans lived in poverty. Latinos experienced a poverty rate of 26 percent. Only one in ten white Americans lived in poverty. Despite all the political progress signified by the "Age of Obama," for a vast number of racial minorities the American Dream remained the stuff of fairy tales.[60]

Perhaps the young boy on the South Side of Chicago could yet see beyond the nearest street corner. Deval Patrick had once been that boy. And he believed that the presence of a black man in the White House amounted to a profound change. "Because it changes that kid's imagination, and that's absolutely critical. Is it enough? No. But you better believe it's meaningful." In the twenty-first century, Americans could dream in a different color.[61]

The history of race in the Northeast is in part a story of those dreams. The region's residents created a mystique about themselves. In some moments that mystique helped to propel them forward as they forged grand experiments on the frontier of interracial democracy: hatching the Springfield Plan, welcoming Jackie Robinson into a democratic Brooklyn, electing Brooke and Chisholm, Milner and Dinkins and Patrick, even providing support for Abraham Ribicoff's audacious plan to integrate every last school. At the same time, white northerners deployed the mystique as a way of obscuring the segregation and racism that shaped their cities. The mystique could operate both ways.

On the matter of race, the Northeast has been a place at war with itself. It has been drawn to its lofty ideals, its dreams of justice, its noble heritage; yet it has also been deeply committed to racial segregation and economic inequality. As such, the Northeast has shaped and mirrored America's adventure with race over the past seventy-five years: able to achieve stunning progress, culminating in the election of a black president, and yet unable to fully turn the page, unable to absorb the new story it has authored, unable to let that future out into the light.

Acknowledgments

I BEGAN WORKING ON THIS BOOK IN 2006, WHEN I LIVED IN BROOKLYN. I carried the project with me for the next eight years while I moved up and down the Northeast—from Brooklyn to Ithaca, then to Philadelphia, Cambridge and Somerville, and finally to Newburyport. The transient life was difficult. Looking back on it, however, I cannot imagine this book coming to fruition in any other way. The transience was essential—not only because it gave me a taste of life in so many different parts of the Northeast, but also because of the wonderful people who fortified me in each place. They nurtured and encouraged me, and helped me to bring this book into the world. *All Eyes Are Upon Us* is the result of their collective generosity and insight.

First, I must thank the two people who have guided me in my historical work since the day I set foot on the Berkeley campus: Leon Litwack and Waldo Martin. They have helped me to make a life as a historian, and they are still my models.

Nick Salvatore and Ann Sullivan eased my transition to Ithaca. Nick also provided thorough comments on my Jackie Robinson chapter; he did so with the passion of one who grew up in postwar Brooklyn, and with the exacting eye of a great historian. In Ithaca, I had the privilege to participate in the Chapter House writing group. When this book was in its early stages, Derek Chang, Jeff Cowie, Aaron Sachs, Michael Smith, Michael Trotti, and Rob Vanderlan offered many helpful suggestions as well as much-needed camaraderie.

I was fortunate to receive a Mellon fellowship from the Penn Humanities Forum. Thanks to Sara Varney and Jennifer Conway at the PHF, and to my cohort of fellows. While at Penn, I had the pleasure to get to know Thomas Sugrue. I thank him for his advice, and for the many discussions that helped me to develop my ideas.

Harvard's W. E. B. Du Bois Institute provided a Sheila Biddle Ford Foundation fellowship in support of this book. Thanks to Henry Louis Gates Jr. for this opportunity—and for his continued support. Thanks also to Abby Wolf and Vera Grant, and to Karen Boutros for her research assistance. In addition, I thank Evelyn Brooks Higginbotham, who appointed me as a Harvard College Fellow in the Department of African and African American Studies. The department afforded me the time and resources to continue writing.

Before taking a position in the History Department at the University of New Hampshire, I could not have known that I would be joining such a warm, collegial, high-achieving, and inspirational group of people. I thank the two most recent chairs of the department: Jan Golinski and Eliga Gould. Many other colleagues offered comments on my book during a faculty seminar: David Bachrach, Jeff Bolster, Jeff Diefendorf, Kurk Dorsey, Molly Girard-Dorsey, Ellen Fitzpatrick, Bill Harris, Jessica Lepler, Julia Rodriguez, Lucy Salyer, and Cynthia Van Zandt. I also thank Sarah Gregg for her research assistance. In addition, the UNH Graduate School awarded a Summer Faculty Fellowship in support of my research. I also thank the UNH College of Liberal Arts for a Liberal Arts Faculty Summer Research Fellowship, and Dean Kenneth Fuld for his support of this project.

I thank everyone who invited me to present various portions of this book, and who gave valuable feedback. They include Michael Ebner and the Chicago Urban History Seminar; Noah Shusterman, who invited me to the Center for the Humanities at Temple University; Jessica Grogan, who brought me to Southwestern University; and Linda Heywood at Boston University. The American Historical Association also provided funding for this project in the form of an Albert J. Beveridge Research Grant.

During my travels, I benefited from the skills of numerous archivists. I thank the staff of the Manuscript Division at the Library of Congress; the Brooklyn Collection at the Brooklyn Public Library; the Hartford History Center at the Hartford Public Library; Columbia University's Rare Books, Special Collections, and Archives; the Columbia Center for Oral History; the Schomburg Center for Research in Black Culture; and Alex Rankin at Boston University's Howard Gotlieb Archival Research Center.

My agent, Brettne Bloom, has been a wonderful advocate. I thank her for pairing me with Lara Heimert at Basic Books. Lara believed in this book from the beginning, and her suggestions have improved it immeasurably. I also thank Leah Stecher for her hard work on this book, as well as Production Editor Rachel King. Thanks to Roger Labrie for his keen line edits, and thanks to John Wilcockson for his helpful copyediting.

I owe a great debt to those individuals who conducted interviews with me. They opened up new ways of seeing my region's past, and of understanding race in America. Edward Brooke was generous with his time, providing forthright recollections about his astounding political career. Charlie Ryan regaled me with stories about a Springfield I had never known. Thirman Milner enlightened me on Hartford's racial history. Deval Patrick graciously sat for an interview and talked far longer than I had any right to expect. Robert Ludgin was extremely helpful with his recollections. Lewis Steel graciously spent an afternoon with me, and provided a window into the NAACP's activities in the North during the 1960s. Without all of these people, I could not have written this book.

I reserve my deepest thanks for those scholars, peers, and friends who agreed to read my work—and who offered invaluable suggestions. To the extent that this book reflects their wisdom, it is so much stronger. Diana Selig read the chapter on the Springfield Plan; Joshua Guild offered thorough comments regarding Shirley Chisholm; Michael Powell took the time to provide suggestions on New York City during the 1980s; Dan Oppenheimer read an early draft of the chapter on the Springfield Plan, as did Tim Rose on the campaigns of Edward Brooke; Joseph Crespino gave helpful comments regarding Abraham Ribicoff. To Steve Estes and Brian Purnell, I am ever grateful. Both of them read through the entire manuscript and offered incisive feedback.

My family has sustained me through these eight years. There were times when none of us knew whether—or where—I would finally land. This book is for my parents, Fred and Betsy Sokol, who give me love when I need it and space when I don't—and unquestioning support either way. It is also for my grandfather, Jim Pirtle, who demonstrates that there is no reason any of us should slow down. And it is for my brother, Scott Sokol, who humors me and who is always there to listen to my gripes. Most of all, this book is for my wife, Nina Morrison. She has lived with this book through its many incarnations. She has steadied me in moments of doubt and celebrated with me in times of triumph. And she has made a life with me in all of these cities: Brooklyn, Ithaca, Philadelphia, Somerville, and Newburyport. Because she has been there with me, each one of those cities is the greatest place I have ever lived.

Notes

ABBREVIATIONS

AN: *Amsterdam News*

AR Papers: Abraham Ribicoff Papers

BE: *Brooklyn Eagle*

BG: *Boston Globe*

BSB: *Bay State Banner*

CCOHC: Columbia Center for Oral History Collection

CD: *Chicago Defender*

CR: *Congressional Record*

DD Papers: David Dinkins Papers

EB Papers: Edward Brooke Papers

HC: *Hartford Courant*

JR Papers: Jackie Robinson Papers

NYT: *New York Times*

SOHC: Schomburg Oral History Collection

SU: *Springfield Union*

INTRODUCTION

1. James Baldwin, *Nobody Knows My Name: More Notes of a Native Son* (New York: Dial Press, 1961), 64.

2. On slavery in the North, see Jill Lepore, *New York Burning: Liberty, Slavery, and Conspiracy in Eighteenth Century Manhattan* (New York: Alfred A. Knopf, 2005); Leslie Harris, *In the Shadow of Slavery: African Americans in New York City, 1626–1863* (Chicago: University of Chicago Press, 2003); Joanne Pope Melish, *Disowning Slavery: Gradual*

Emancipation and "Race" in New England, 1780–1860 (Ithaca, NY: Cornell University Press, 1998); C.S. Manegold, *Ten Hills Farm: The Forgotten History of Slavery in the North* (Princeton, NJ: Princeton University Press, 2010); On the 20th-century North, see Thomas Sugrue, *Sweet Land of Liberty: The Forgotten Struggle for Civil Rights in the North* (New York: Random House, 2008); Thomas Sugrue, *Origins of the Urban Crisis: Race and Inequality in Postwar Detroit* (Princeton, NJ: Princeton University Press, 1996); Arnold Hirsch, *Making the Second Ghetto: Race and Housing in Chicago, 1940–1960* (New York: Cambridge University Press, 1983); Ronald Formisano, *Boston Against Busing: Race, Class, and Ethnicity in the 1960s and 1970s* (Chapel Hill, NC: University of North Carolina Press, 1991); Kevin Boyle, *Arc of Justice: A Saga of Race, Civil Rights, and Murder in the Jazz Age* (New York: Henry Holt, 2004); Martha Biondi, *To Stand and Fight: The Struggle for Civil Rights in Postwar New York City* (Cambridge, MA: Harvard University Press, 2003); J. Anthony Lukas, *Common Ground: A Turbulent Decade in the Lives of Three American Families* (New York: Alfred A. Knopf, 1985); Matthew Countryman, *Up South: Civil Rights and Black Power in Philadelphia* (Philadelphia: University of Pennsylvania Press, 2006); James Ralph, *Northern Protest: Martin Luther King, Jr., Chicago, and the Civil Rights Movement* (Cambridge, MA: Harvard University Press, 1990).

3. Russell Contreras, "NAACP Branch Confronts Hub's Poor Image Among Blacks," *Boston Globe*, January 16, 2011.

4. "Transcript of Wednesday's Gubernatorial Debate," *BG*, November 2, 2006.

5. Margaret Halsey, *Colorblind: A White Woman Looks at the Negro* (New York: Simon & Schuster, 1946), 3, 14, 145, 144. For its frank talk about interracial marriage, the book was banned from schools in Georgia. Dinitia Smith, "Margaret Halsey, 86, a Writer Who Lampooned the English," *NYT*, February 7, 1997.

6. Halsey, *Colorblind*, 85.

7. Baldwin, *Nobody Knows My Name*, 64.

8. Baldwin, *Nobody Knows My Name*, 65.

9. C. Vann Woodward, *The Burden of Southern History* (Baton Rouge, LA: Louisiana State University Press, 1960); Willie Morris, *North Toward Home* (Boston: Houghton Mifflin, 1967), 377.

10. Perry Miller, *Errand into the Wilderness* (Cambridge, MA: Harvard University Press, 1956), 11, 47; Frederick Binder and David Reimers, *All the Nations Under Heaven: An Ethnic and Racial History of New York City* (New York: Columbia University Press, 1995), 32. On important differences between Massachusetts and Virginia in the colonial and antebellum eras, see Robin Einhorn, *American Taxation, American Slavery* (Chicago: University of Chicago Press, 2008).

11. E. B. White, *Here Is New York* (New York: Harper & Brothers, 1949), 23; Eric Foner, *Reconstruction: America's Unfinished Revolution* (New York: Oxford University Press, 1989).

12. Martin Luther King, Jr., *Stride Toward Freedom*, reprinted in James Washington, ed., *A Testament of Hope: The Essential Speeches and Writings of Martin Luther King, Jr.* (New York: Harper Collins, 1986), 468. Also see Gunnar Myrdal, *An American Dilemma: The Negro Problem and Modern Democracy* (New York: Harper, 1944).

13. James Cobb, *Away Down South* (New York: Oxford University Press, 2005), 215.

14. Harry Ashmore, *The Other Side of Jordan* (New York: Norton, 1960), 13. Also see Robert Coles, *Farewell to the South* (Boston: Little, Brown, 1971); Harry Ashmore, *An Ep-*

itaph for Dixie (New York: Norton, 1958); Joseph Cumming, "A Final Farewell," *Georgia* 15 (1972).

15. Leon Litwack, *North of Slavery* (Chicago: University of Chicago Press, 1961), vii; Malcolm X, "With Mrs. Fannie Lou Hamer," in George Breitman, ed., *Malcolm X Speaks* (New York: Grove, 1965), 108–109.

16. Howard Zinn, *The Southern Mystique* (New York: Alfred A. Knopf, 1964), 218.

17. Sugrue, *Sweet Land of Liberty*, xxvii; Richard Current, *Northernizing the South* (Athens: University of Georgia Press, 1983), 12. John Egerton recognized the lack of interest in the North: "Nobody convenes New North conferences, or seminars on the Mind of the East; it is only Southerners who seem to . . . think of themselves as different from other Americans." John Egerton, *The Americanization of Dixie: The Southernization of America* (New York: Harper's Magazine Press, 1974), 14. Jonathan Daniels, a North Carolina newspaper editor, traveled through New England in 1939. He noted the social and ethnic complexity of the North, whereas "our South is a simplicity which contains only the multiple variants of black and white." Jonathan Daniels, *A Southerner Discovers New England* (New York: Macmillan, 1940), 3.

18. Kirkpatrick Sale, *Power Shift: The Rise of the Southern Rim and Its Challenge to the Eastern Establishment* (New York: Random House, 1975), 12–13.

19. Jean Gottmann, *Megalopolis* (New York: Twentieth Century Fund, 1961), ix, 3, 8, 15.

20. Biondi, *To Stand and Fight*, 3. New England's identity as a place apart is long-standing, dating back to the 17th century. New York City's entry into the super-North was a 20th-century phenomenon. New York is technically part of the mid-Atlantic. And it seems a world unto itself. I will show that in matters of racial, political, and cultural history, it belongs with Connecticut and Massachusetts.

21. Kevin Phillips, *The Emerging Republican Majority* (Garden City, NY: Anchor Books, 1970), 54; Nate Silver, 538, www.fivethirtyeight.com/2008/04/electoral-history -charts.html. See Howard Reiter and Jeffrey Stonecash, *Counter Realignment: Political Change in the Northeastern United States* (New York: Cambridge University Press, 2011).

22. John F. Kennedy, "City Upon a Hill," January 9, 1961, millercenter.org/president /speeches/detail/3364.

23. Countryman, *Up South*. For a more complex take, see Matthew Lassiter and Joseph Crespino, eds., *The Myth of Southern Exceptionalism* (New York: Oxford University Press, 2010). Also see Nancy MacLean, "Southern Dominance in Borrowed Language: The Regional Origins of American Neoliberalism," in Jane Collins, Micaela di Leonardo, and Brett Williams, eds., *New Landscapes of Inequality: Neoliberalism and the Erosion of Democracy in America* (Santa Fe, NM: School for Advanced Research, 2008), 24. MacLean allows that it is useful to recognize racial inequality as a national problem. But this "should not rule out attempts to identify powerful regional sources of resistance to change." By the same token, neither should it rule out attempts to identify regional forces of *change* itself.

24. James Baldwin, *Collected Essays* (New York: Library of America, 1998), 622.

25. Interview with Lewis Steel, by Author, New York, NY, June 8, 2010.

26. Ashmore, *The Other Side of Jordan*, 58; Tillman Durdin, "Barriers for Negro Here Still High Despite Gains," *NYT*, April 23, 1956; Baldwin, *Collected Essays*, 198; Claudia Roth Pierpont, "Another Country," *The New Yorker*, February 9 & 16, 2009.

27. Ralph Ellison, "Harlem Is Nowhere," *Harper's*, August 1964.

28. Peggy Lamson, "The White Northerner's Choice: Mrs. Hicks of Boston," *Atlantic Monthly*, June 1966.

29. Myrdal, *An American Dilemma*, 1010, 385, 438.

30. Abraham Ribicoff, *America Can Make It!* (New York: Atheneum, 1972), 23.

31. Robert Sherrill, "Ribicoff Rides the Tide," *The Nation*, March 16, 1970. A strong counterargument would be to point out that the most triumphant struggle in the name of racial democracy—the modern civil rights movement—emerged out of the South. In addition, Patricia Sullivan details movements for interracial democracy in the South during the New Deal and World War Two eras. Patricia Sullivan, *Days of Hope: Race and Democracy in the New Deal Era* (Chapel Hill, NC: University of North Carolina Press, 1996). For an insightful essay on the perils of regional thinking, see Robert D. Johnston, "Beyond 'The West': Regionalism, liberalism, and the evasion of politics in the New Western History," *Rethinking History* 2:2 (1998), 264.

CHAPTER 1: AND TO THINK THAT IT HAPPENED IN SPRINGFIELD

1. Meyer Berger, "At the World's Fair," *New York Times*, July 23, 1939; E. B. White, "A Reporter at Large: They Come With Joyous Song," *The New Yorker*, May 13, 1939.

2. "World's Fair Pays Homage to Its Home State with Lehman the Chief Figure," *NYT*, September 30, 1939.

3. Benjamin Fine, "The Springfield Plan: For Education Against Intolerance and Prejudice," *The Menorah Journal*, Vol. 32, Issue 2 (1944), 162–163; Springfield Council of Social Agencies, *The Social Needs of Negroes in Springfield, Massachusetts* (Springfield, MA, 1942), 3, 5; Clarence Chatto and Alice Halligan, *The Story of the Springfield Plan* (New York: Barnes & Noble, 1945), 5; Helena Huntington Smith, "Your Town Could Do It Too," *Woman's Home Companion*, June 1944, 30; Alexander Alland and James Waterman Wise, *The Springfield Plan* (New York: Viking, 1945), 9.

4. Margaret Ells, "Fair Play in Teacher Selection," *The Journal of Education* (September, 1944), 192–193; Daniel Bresnahan, "The Springfield Plan in Retrospect," Ed.D. Diss., Teachers College, Columbia University, 1971, 65; Smith, "Your Town Could Do It Too," 94, 31.

5. John Granrud, "Education for Democracy in the Springfield Public Schools" (Springfield, MA: January 1943), 2–3.

6. Clyde Miller, "The Control of a Contagious Disease," *Child Study* (Spring 1944), 76.

7. David Hollinger shows the distinction between cosmopolitanism and pluralism. If cosmopolitanism sought "voluntary affiliations of wide compass" and was often "casual about community building and community maintenance," then "pluralism promotes affiliations on the narrower grounds of shared history and is more quick to see reasons for drawing boundaries between communities." Hollinger argues that these ideologies of tolerance and pluralism declined rapidly after World War Two. Daryl Michael Scott argues that the pluralism of the war years was linked to the integrationist ethos of *Brown v. Board of Education*. Scott connects wartime pluralism to later attempts at multiculturalism. David Hollinger, *Postethnic America: Beyond Multiculturalism* (New York: Basic Books, 1995), 84–86; Daryl Michael Scott, "Postwar Pluralism, *Brown v. Board of Education*, and the Origins of Multicultural Education," *Journal of American History*, Vol. 91, No. 1 (June 2004).

8. Chatto and Halligan, *The Story of the Springfield Plan*, 9; Nancy Flagg, "A City Takes the Cure," *Vogue*, February 1, 1946, 169. The Springfield Plan did have precedents. See Diana Selig, *Americans All: The Cultural Gifts Movement* (Cambridge, MA: Harvard University Press, 2008); Zoe Burkholder, *Color in the Classroom: How American Schools Taught Race, 1900–1954* (New York: Oxford University Press, 2011).

9. Scott, "Postwar Pluralism, *Brown v. Board of Education*, and the Origins of Multicultural Education"; Chatto and Halligan, *The Story of the Springfield Plan*, 170, 157.

10. Chatto and Halligan, *The Story of the Springfield Plan*, 175; Fine, "The Springfield Plan," 167.

11. Chatto and Halligan, *The Story of the Springfield Plan*, 62–67.

12. Chatto and Halligan, *The Story of the Springfield Plan*, 157, 78; Granrud, "Education for Democracy," 8.

13. Smith, "Your Town Could Do It Too," 31.

14. Bresnahan, "The Springfield Plan in Retrospect," 143–146.

15. Granrud, "Education for Democracy," 9; Chatto and Halligan, *The Story of the Springfield Plan*, 103; Alice Halligan, "A Community's Total War Against Prejudice," *Journal of Educational Sociology*, Vol. 16, No. 6 (February 1943), 379.

16. Chatto and Halligan, *The Story of the Springfield Plan*, 148.

17. Kenneth Clark, *Prejudice and Your Child* (Boston: Beacon Press, 1963), 31. Clark conducted later tests in several southern towns other than Pine Bluff.

18. Kenneth Clark and Mamie Clark, "Racial Identification and Preference in Negro Children," in Theodore Newcomb and Eugene Hartley, eds., *Readings in Social Psychology* (New York: Holt, 1947), 170. Mamie Clark collaborated closely with her husband Kenneth. Her precise role in the Springfield experiment remains unclear.

19. Clark, *Prejudice and Your Child*, 44–45; Clark and Clark, "Racial Identification and Preference in Negro Children," 170, 174, 178.

20. Clark and Clark, "Racial Identification and Preference in Negro Children," 178; Clark, *Prejudice and Your Child*, 32, 27, 45.

21. Richard Kluger, *Simple Justice: The History of Brown v. Board of Education and Black America's Struggle for Equality* (New York: Alfred A. Knopf, 1977), 356; Clark, *Prejudice and Your Child*, 45; Clark and Clark, "Racial Identification and Preference in Negro Children," 178.

22. Clark, *Prejudice and Your Child*, 45–46; Kluger, *Simple Justice*, 356; Daryl Michael Scott, *Contempt and Pity* (Chapel Hill: University of North Carolina Press, 1997), 122, 124.

23. Kluger, *Simple Justice*, 356.

24. Springfield Council of Social Agencies, *The Social Needs of Negroes in Springfield, Massachusetts*, 5; "Housing Discrimination in the Springfield-Holyoke-Chicopee Metropolitan Area," Massachusetts Committee Against Discrimination (Boston: December 1966), 56–57; William DeBerry, *Sociological Survey of the Negro Population of Springfield, Massachusetts* (Springfield: The Dunbar Community League, 1940), 4.

25. DeBerry, *Sociological Survey of the Negro Population of Springfield, Massachusetts*, 15, 5, 10.

26. Benjamin Fine, "Tolerance Plan Called Success at Springfield," *NYT*, December 7, 1941.

27. Jane Butler, "A Community Demonstrates Democracy," *Parents' Magazine*, December 1942, 20–21, 36, 101.

28. John Granrud, "Schools Training for Citizenship," *NYT*, April 4, 1943; "Pittsburgh Board Okehs Use of Springfield Plan," *Chicago Defender*, December 18, 1943.

29. "Boston Council Rejects Plan for Racial Harmony," *CD*, January 1, 1944.

30. Robert Norton, "Springfield Plan Plants Seeds of Race Tolerance," *CD*, December 18, 1943; "New York Schools Fight Racial Bias," *Pittsburgh Courier*, September 29, 1945; Benjamin Fine, "School Plan Set Up to Aid Community," *NYT*, June 7, 1945.

31. "Delaware School Board Adopts 'Springfield Plan,'" *Philadelphia Tribune*, May 5, 1945.

32. "Springfield Plan Cited as Spreading Across Nation," *Pittsburgh Courier*, February 23, 1946; "Canada Considers Plan for Democratic Education," *CD*, April 27, 1946.

33. Noma Jensen, "The Springfield Plan," *The Crisis*, March 1944, 79, 91; Eugene Zack, "Teacher Awarded High Post in Springfield Plan," *CD*, June 16, 1945; "Interracial Group Protests Abuse of Soldiers at Westover Field, Mass.," *CD*, February 26, 1944; "Stores Willing to Employ Negroes in Springfield," *CD*, May 26, 1945; "Spotlight on Springfield," *Ebony*, November 1945, 28.

34. E. George Payne, "Significant Developments in Education: The Springfield Plan," *Journal of Educational Sociology* (February 1946), 395.

35. "Benjamin Fine Is Dead in Korea," *NYT*, May 17, 1975; Benjamin Fine, "The Springfield Plan: For Education Against Intolerance and Prejudice," *The Menorah Journal*, Vol. 32, Issue 2 (1944), 161, 163, 178–180; Benjamin Fine, "Education in Review," *NYT*, May 20, 1945.

36. Selden Menefee, "America at War," *Washington Post*, February 3, 1945; Anne Stockton Goodwin, Letter to the Editor, *NYT*, May 5, 1944.

37. Smith, "Your Town Could Do It Too," 30, 94.

38. *It Happened in Springfield*: Short Subject Release Sheet, Warner Brothers Pictures (May 1, 1945), Moving Image Section, Library of Congress; Warner Brothers Pictures, "It Happened in Springfield," Promotional brochure, 1945, Moving Image Section, Library of Congress.

39. Thomas Cripps, *Making Movies Black: The Hollywood Message Movie from World War II to the Civil Rights Era* (New York: Oxford University Press, 1993), 202; "Warner Bros. 'Springfield' Short Via NBC Tele Hits Homes With Impact," *Variety*, April 25, 1945; A. H. Weiler, "Varied Notes on the Film Scene," *NYT*, April 22, 1945; L. R. B., "It Happened in Springfield," *School and Society*, Vol. 61, No. 1589 (April 28, 1945), 275–276.

40. *It Happened in Springfield*, Moving Image Section, Library of Congress.

41. *It Happened in Springfield*.

42. *It Happened in Springfield*.

43. Cripps, *Making Movies Black*, 202; "South Bans Negro Teacher in Film," *CD*, June 15, 1946; "Spotlight on Springfield," 29.

44. Eugene Zack, "Real Southern Trick," *CD*, June 23, 1945; "Praise Warner's Film on Teaching Democracy," *CD*, January 20, 1945; Bill Chandler, "Hollywood Dots-Dashes," *Philadelphia Tribune*, March 10, 1945, 13; E. Washington Rhodes, "Under the Microscope," *Philadelphia Tribune*, April 28, 1945.

45. Constance Curtis, "About Books," *Amsterdam News*, August 4, 1945; Alland and Wise, *The Springfield Plan*, 7, 14.

46. Henry McCrary Jr., "Book Review: *The Story of the Springfield Plan*," *Philadelphia Tribune*, September 29, 1945; Ben Burns, "Off the Book Shelf," *CD*, August 18, 1945.

47. Sterling North, "Newest Volumes Range from Pilgrims to Spies—and Springfield Plan," *Washington Post*, August 12, 1945; "Looks at Books," *Pittsburgh Courier*, December 1, 1945; McCrary, "Book Review: *The Story of the Springfield Plan*."

48. "Prejudice: Our Postwar Battle," *Look*, May 1, 1946, 48, 50, 51; Wallace Stegner, *One Nation* (Boston: Houghton Mifflin, 1945), 332–333.

49. Stegner, *One Nation*, 199; "Springfield Plan Set For OWI Broadcast," *CD*, March 17, 1945.

50. "Bilbo Challenged to Debate on Equality," *CD*, September 22, 1945; Theodore Bilbo, *Take Your Choice: Separation or Mongrelization* (Poplarville, MS: Dream House Publishing Company, 1947), 187.

51. Eugene Zack, "'It Happened in Springfield' But Not in Warner's Picture," *CD*, May 5, 1945.

52. Bresnahan, "The Springfield Plan in Retrospect," 134.

53. Bresnahan, "The Springfield Plan in Retrospect," 149, 141, 158; "Says Politics Kill School Race Programs," *CD*, January 26, 1946; "Politics Threaten Springfield Plan for Equality in Schools," *CD*, March 16, 1946.

54. Bresnahan, "The Springfield Plan in Retrospect," 140, 142; James Pitt, *Adventures in Brotherhood* (New York: Farrar, Straus and Company, 1955), 166.

55. Eugene Zack, "War Plant Unionists Rebuff Jamaicans," *CD*, January 13, 1945; Eugene Zack, "Is Famed Springfield Plan Dead? AFL Unions Dig Grave for U.S. Dream," *CD*, March 17, 1945; "Springfield Drops Jim Crow Housing Plan," *CD*, March 17, 1945.

56. Eugene Zack, "Union Flays Bias in Home of Springfield Plan," *CD*, December 22, 1945.

57. "Race Inertia Blocks Springfield 'Miracle,'" *Pittsburgh Courier*, August 10, 1946; "Banning of Negroes in Teaching Cited," *NYT*, February 26, 1956; P. L. Prattis, "Race Relations in Springfield Are Not so Hopeful, Despite Famous 'Plan,'" *Pittsburgh Courier*, September 7, 1946.

58. "Demand Ouster of Solon Who Slurred Negroes," *CD*, March 23, 1946.

59. "Demand Ouster of Solon Who Slurred Negroes."

60. "Demand Ouster of Solon Who Slurred Negroes."

61. "Demand Ouster of Solon Who Slurred Negroes."

62. "Seek Tryout With Boston Red Sox," *AN*, April 21, 1945.

63. Howard Bryant, *Shut Out: A Story of Race and Baseball in Boston* (Boston: Beacon Press, 2002), 24–25.

64. Wendell Smith, "Players Get Try-Outs," *Pittsburgh Courier*, April 21, 1945.

65. Bryant, *Shut Out*, 33.

66. Mabe "Doc" Kountze, *Fifty Sports Years Along Memory Lane* (Medford, MA: Mystic Valley Press, 1979), 47; Bryant, *Shut Out*, 6.

CHAPTER 2: SOMETHING IN THE AIR

1. Myrna Katz Frommer and Harvey Frommer, *It Happened in Brooklyn: An Oral History of Growing Up in the Borough in the 1940s, 1950s, and 1960s* (New York: Harcourt, 1993), 36; Peter Golenbock, *Bums: An Oral History of the Brooklyn Dodgers* (New York: Putnam, 1984), 84.

2. Jonathan Eig, *Opening Day: The Story of Jackie Robinson's First Season* (New York: Simon & Schuster, 2007), 156–157.

3. Ralph Foster Weld, *Brooklyn Is America* (New York: Columbia University Press, 1950), 6–7.

4. Jack Newfield, *Somebody's Gotta Tell It: The Upbeat Memoir of a Working-Class Journalist* (New York: St. Martin's Press, 2002), 4.

5. Kenneth Jackson, *The Neighborhoods of Brooklyn* (New Haven: Yale University Press, 2004); Golenbock, *Bums*, 155; Thomas Oliphant, *Praying for Gil Hodges: A Memoir of the 1955 World Series and One Family's Love of the Brooklyn Dodgers* (New York: Thomas Dunne Books/St. Martin's Press, 2005), 5–6.

6. Oliphant, *Praying for Gil Hodges*, 130, 54; Weld, *Brooklyn Is America*, 188; Wendell Pritchett, *Brownsville, Brooklyn: Blacks, Jews, and the Changing Face of the Ghetto* (Chicago: University of Chicago Press, 2002), 94, 103.

7. Joseph Dorinson and Joram Warmund, eds., *Jackie Robinson: Race, Sports, and the American Dream* (Armonk, NY: M. E. Sharpe, 1998), 67, 43.

8. Craig Wilder, *A Covenant With Color: Race and Social Power in Brooklyn* (New York: Columbia University Press, 2000), 171.

9. "Women Trolley Operators Launch Protest," *Amsterdam News*, June 17, 1944; Wilder, *A Covenant With Color*, 135–136.

10. "'Nigger Haters' Go Wild on Trolley Car," *AN*, January 20, 1945.

11. Golenbock, *Bums*, 156; Frommer, *It Happened in Brooklyn*, 165; Dorinson and Warmund, *Jackie Robinson*, 44.

12. Golenbock, *Bums*, 157.

13. Roger Kahn, *The Boys of Summer* (New York: Harper & Row, 1971), xvii.

14. Dorinson and Warmund, *Jackie Robinson*, 43, 48; Newfield, *Somebody's Gotta Tell It*, 7, 23.

15. Dorinson and Warmund, *Jackie Robinson*, xx; Frommer, *It Happened in Brooklyn*, 15; Oliphant, *Praying for Gil Hodges*, 38; Kahn, *The Boys of Summer*, xvi, xviii.

16. Ira Glasser, "The Baseball Guide to Character and Politics," *NYT*, May 3, 1983; Dorinson and Warmund, *Jackie Robinson*, 88–89.

17. Weld, *Brooklyn Is America*, 13–14.

18. Sugrue, *Sweet Land of Liberty*, 113; Biondi, *To Stand and Fight*, 19, 33.

19. Dan Burley, "To Rickey, Stoneham, and MacPhail: 'Straighten Up and Fly Right!'" *AN*, August 4, 1945.

20. "Bklyn Dodgers Hire Negro Star," *AN*, October 27, 1945; "What They Say About Rickey Act," *AN*, November 3, 1945; Dan Burley, "On Jackie Robinson: An Analysis," *AN*, November 10, 1945.

21. "Writers Lampoon Baseball Bigwigs," *New York Times*, February 4, 1946; Jules Tygiel, *Baseball's Great Experiment: Jackie Robinson and His Legacy* (New York: Oxford University Press, 1983), 92–93.

22. Eig, *Opening Day*, 52; "All Brooklyn Pulling For Him," *AN*, April 19, 1947; Jackie Reemes, "Boro Looms as 'Home' for Robinson," *AN*, April 19, 1947; Tygiel, *Baseball's Great Experiment*, 197.

23. Arthur Daley, "Baseball's Showmen—The Dodgers," *NYT Magazine*, June 18, 1947, SM18; Golenbock, *Bums*, 157; Kahn, *The Boys of Summer*, xviii, xix; Eig, *Opening Day*, 221, 223.

24. Dorinson and Warmund, *Jackie Robinson*, 147.

25. Golenbock, *Bums*, 157.

26. Peter Golenbock, *In the Country of Brooklyn: Inspiration to the World* (New York: William Morrow, 2008), 327–328.

27. "Ex Dodger Rooter" to Arthur Mann, Box 1, Folder 29, JR Papers, Manuscript Division, Library of Congress (Also see Box 2, Arthur Mann Papers, Library of Congress); Eig, *Opening Day*, 41–44; Tygiel, *Baseball's Great Experiment*, 170–172.

28. Dan Burley, "People, World Series and Jackie," *AN*, October 4, 1947; Eig, *Opening Day*, 243, 155; Frommer, *It Happened in Brooklyn*, 169.

29. G. Gilbert Smith to Jackie Robinson (June 1, 1947), Box 1, Folder 29, JR Papers.

30. Jackie Robinson to G. Gilbert Smith (June 10, 1947), Box 1, Folder 29, JR Papers.

31. "There's Nothing to Fear!" *AN*, October 4, 1947; Eig, *Opening Day*, 230–231; Rachel Robinson with Lee Daniels, *Jackie Robinson: An Intimate Portrait* (New York: Harry N. Abrams, 1996), 80.

32. "An Open Letter to Jackie Robinson," *AN*, September 13, 1947; "Fans Supporting Jackie's Day!" *AN*, September 6, 1947; "There's Nothing to Fear!"

33. Dan Burley, "Yankee Razzing Angers Jackie," *AN*, October 4, 1947.

34. "Complaints Still Pour In!" *AN*, October 25, 1947.

35. "Another Job Well Done!" *AN*, October 25, 1947; Dan Burley, "What's Wrong With Jackie? Fans Ask," *AN*, May 1, 1948; "The Brooklyn Dodgers: The Original America's Team" (ESPN Video, 1996).

36. Ron Miller, Rita Seiden Miller, and Steven Karp, "A Sociological History of Brooklyn," in Rita Seiden Miller, ed., *Brooklyn USA: The Fourth Largest City in America* (New York: Brooklyn College Press, 1979), 28; Oliphant, *Praying for Gil Hodges*, 64; Harold Connolly, *A Ghetto Grows in Brooklyn* (New York: NYU Press, 1977), 129–130, 141; Raymond Schroth, "The Eagle," in Miller, ed., *Brooklyn USA*, 113; Jeffrey Gerson, "Building the Brooklyn Machine: Irish, Jewish and Black Political Succession in Central Brooklyn, 1919–1964," Ph.D. Diss., City University of New York, 1990, 162.

37. Jimmy Breslin, "And Proud Of It," *NYT*, August 20, 1975.

38. Joshua Freeman, *Working-Class New York* (New York: The New Press, 2000), 164; Joseph Palisi, "The Brooklyn Navy Yard," in Miller, ed., *Brooklyn USA*, 122; Dorinson and Warmund, *Jackie Robinson*, 89; Wilder, *A Covenant With Color*, 167, 169.

39. Wilder, *A Covenant With Color*, 170; "Brooklyn Navy Yard Cuts Time; To Finish Carriers," *AN*, September 22, 1945; "Washington Order Ineffective As Boro Navy Yard Slashes Payroll," *AN*, September 7, 1946.

40. *Brooklyn Eagle*, August 6, 1954; Connolly, *A Ghetto Grows in Brooklyn*, 130, 141, 135, 134; Pritchett, *Brownsville, Brooklyn*, 67; Ernest Quimby, "Bedford-Stuyvesant," in Miller, ed., *Brooklyn USA*, 233.

41. Jack Newfield, "Bedford-Stuyvesant: Portrait of a Ghetto," *New York Post*, August 2, 1964, Clipping file, Folder: Bedford-Stuyvesant I, Brooklyn Collection, Brooklyn Public Library; Jeffrey Gerson, "Bertram L. Baker, the United Action Democratic Association, and the First Black Democratic Succession in Brooklyn, 1933–1954," *Afro-Americans in New York Life and History*, Vol. 16, Issue 2 (New York: July 31, 1992); David Gelman, "Inside Bedford-Stuyvesant," Folder: Bedford-Stuyvesant I, Brooklyn Collection.

42. Gelman, "Inside Bedford-Stuyvesant," Brooklyn Collection.

43. Oliphant, *Praying for Gil Hodges*, 54.

44. In 1944, Brooklyn's Herbert Miller became the first black American to serve as foreman of a county grand jury. Two years later, Mabel Halstead was selected to serve on a jury for the U.S. Court of the Eastern District. In the fall of 1947, the Brooklyn Football Dodgers signed two African American players. "3 Centuries of Pioneering: Brooklyn's Negroes Have Risen Steadily Ever Since 1633," *BE*, July 25, 1954; "H.T. Miller to Get Award," *NYT*, April 1, 1948; "Brooklyn Woman Named as Juror," *AN*, January 5, 1946; "A Challenge to Borough Negroes," *AN*, June 7, 1947; "Next Year's Assembly Race," *AN*, August 30, 1947; *BE*, August 6, 1954; Chris McNickle, *To Be Mayor of New York: Ethnic Politics in the City* (New York: Columbia University Press, 1993), 101.

45. "Biography—Bertram L. Baker," Folder: Bertram Baker, Brooklyn Collection.

46. Gerson, "Bertram L. Baker."

47. Gerson, "Bertram L. Baker"; "About the 1948 Race in the 17th!!!" *AN*, January 17, 1948.

48. Gerson, "Bertram L. Baker."

49. "Diggs Directs Baker's Drive in 17th A.D.," *AN*, August 21, 1948.

50. "Boro Elects 1st Negro; Wins Assembly Race," *BE*, November 4, 1948; "Negroes Win Strong Voice in Election of Bertram Baker," BE, January 4, 1949.

51. Interview with Rachel Robinson, by Carl Rowan, 1957, p. 4, Box 15, Folder 2, JR Papers; Arnold Rampersad, *Jackie Robinson: A Biography* (New York: Alfred A. Knopf, 1997), 181.

52. Rachel Robinson, *Jackie Robinson: An Intimate Portrait*, 88; Rampersad, *Jackie Robinson*, 195–96; Jackie Robinson, *I Never Had It Made* (New York: Putnam 1972), 85.

53. Interview with Rachel Robinson, by Carl Rowan, p. 5, JR Papers; Robinson, *I Never Had It Made*, 86.

54. Rampersad, *Jackie Robinson*, 221.

55. Roscoe McGowen, "Banta, Dodgers, Blank Dallas, 4–0, as Robinson and Campanella Star," *NYT*, April 6, 1948.

56. Prince, *Brooklyn's Dodgers*, 73–74; "Newcombe Downs Cincinnati, 11 to 5," *NYT*, July 16, 1949.

57. Interview with Rachel Robinson, by Carl Rowan, p. 6, JR Papers; Carl Rowan with Jackie Robinson, *Wait Till Next Year* (New York: Random House, 1960), 306; Rampersad, *Jackie Robinson*, 181.

58. "Cautioned on Bias, Robinson Admits," *NYT*, December 18, 1952; Kahn, *The Boys of Summer*, 164.

59. Golenbock, *Bums*, 433.

60. Milton Gross, "Why They Boo Jackie Robinson," *Sport*, February 1953, 10, 95–97; Jackie Robinson, "Now I Know Why They Boo Me," *Look*, January 25, 1955.

61. Gross, "Why They Boo Jackie Robinson," 96–97.

62. Jackie Robinson, "A Kentucky Colonel Kept Me in Baseball," *Look*, February 8, 1955.

63. Martha Brown to Brooklyn NAACP (April 12, 1955), NAACP Papers, Part 5: Campaign Against Residential Segregation, 1914–1955, Reel 6, II-A-309.

64. Kenneth Jackson, *Crabgrass Frontier: The Suburbanization of the United States* (New York: Oxford University Press, 1985), 219, 225; "1717 Families See Relief in Housing," *AN*, April 5, 1947; "19 New Housing Projects Slated Here," *AN*, August 27, 1949; Charles Grutzner, "Billion Spent in Housing Since '36 Yet One in 5 Here Is Slum

Dweller," *NYT*, March 15, 1954; "Baker Assails Poor Housing in 17th Area," *AN*, October 23, 1948.

65. Earl Brown, "Future Housing Plans," *AN*, January 26, 1952.

66. Frommer, *It Happened in Brooklyn*, 226; Biondi, *To Stand and Fight*, 120; Joseph Plambeck, "Bluesy Home Market With a Jazzy Past," *NYT*, December 7, 2008.

67. Charles Bennett, "Castle Hill Plan Meets City Delay," *NYT*, March 12, 1954; Grutzner, "Billion Spent in Housing Since '36 Yet One in 5 Here Is Slum Dweller"; "Stichman Charges Housing Bias Here," *NYT*, March 15, 1954; Charles Bennett, "Stichman Accused of Slandering City," *NYT*, March 26, 1954.

68. "Statement Issued by Abe Stark, President of the City Council at the Meeting of the Board of Estimate on Thursday, March 25, 1954," NAACP Papers, Reel 6.

69. Walter White to Mayor Robert Wagner et al. (March 18, 1954), NAACP Papers, Reel 6.

70. Sid Frigand, "Brooklyn's Negroes Have Risen Steadily Ever Since 1633," *BE*, July 25, 1954.

71. Sid Frigand, "Negroes in Search of Decent Housing Caught in Squeeze," *BE*, August 1, 1954; Sid Frigand, "Obstacles to Decent Housing for Negroes Begin to Give Way," *BE*, August 2, 1954; Sid Frigand, "Families of Negroes Live Amicably with White Neighbors," *BE*, August 3, 1954.

72. Frigand, "Families of Negroes Live Amicably with White Neighbors"; Gerson, "Building the Brooklyn Machine," 251–253.

73. Letters to the Editor, *BE*, August 15, 1954; "The Eagle's Series on Negroes," *BE*, August 10, 1954.

74. "Legislators Discuss Anti-Discrimination Bills," *Albany Times-Union*, Undated, NAACP Papers, Reel 6; "Bills Target Segregation in Housing," *Albany Times-Union*, Undated, NAACP Papers, Reel 6; "Lawmakers Ask End to Housing Discrimination," *Albany Times-Union*, Undated, NAACP Papers, Reel 6. On federally sponsored housing discrimination under the auspices of the FHA, see Kenneth Jackson, *Crabgrass Frontier*, 204–230; Robert C. Weaver, "The Effect of Anti-Discrimination Legislation Upon the FHA- and VA-Insured Housing Market in New York State," *Land Economics* (November 1955, Vol. XXXI, No. 4), 304, NAACP Papers, Reel 6.

75. "Baker-Metcalf Bill Passes," *AN*, April 2, 1955; "Used in P.R. 4-7-55," Housing Bills, NAACP Papers, Reel 6.

76. "Negro War Hero Owns a Lot But Can't Build," *New York Post*, June 2, 1953.

77. Lemuel Rodney Custis to Walter White (August 16, 1953), NAACP Papers, Reel 6.

78. Rampersad, *Jackie Robinson*, 272; Robinson, "Now I Know Why They Boo Me," 26; Interview with Rachel Robinson, by Carl Rowan, p. 7–8, Box 15, Folder 2, JR Papers; Rowan with Robinson, *Wait Till Next Year*, 309.

79. Interview with Rachel Robinson, by Carl Rowan, p. 8, JR Papers; Rowan with Robinson, *Wait Till Next Year*, 309; Rampersad, *Jackie Robinson*, 272; Interview with Jackie Robinson, by Carl Rowan, p. 15–16, Box 15, Folder 2, JR Papers; Rachel Robinson, *Jackie Robinson: An Intimate Portrait*, 129–130.

80. U.S. Census, Connecticut, 1950; Leslie Chess Fuller, "Breaking Barriers," *New Canaan-Darien Magazine*, December 2006; Interview with Rachel Robinson, by Carl Rowan, p. 8, JR Papers; Rampersad, *Jackie Robinson*, 273; "No. Stamford Nixes Jackie Robinson," *Bridgeport Herald*, October 25, 1953, NAACP Papers, Reel 6.

81. Interview with Rachel Robinson, by Carl Rowan, p. 9, JR Papers.

82. Interview with Jackie Robinson, by Carl Rowan, p. 16, JR Papers; "Robinson Rouses Home-Sale Dispute," *NYT*, December 12, 1953; Arnold De Mille, "Jackie Buys Conn. Home After Fight," *CD*, December 19, 1953; Kahn, *The Boys of Summer*, 405; Rampersad, *Jackie Robinson*, 273, 278; Rowan with Robinson, *Wait Till Next Year*, 313; "Robinsons to Buy Home," *NYT*, December 18, 1953.

83. Interview with Rachel Robinson, by Carl Rowan, p. 12, JR Papers.

84. Interview with Rachel Robinson, by Carl Rowan, p. 13–14, JR Papers; Fuller, "Breaking Barriers"; Robinson, "Now I Know Why They Boo Me," 27; Rachel Robinson, *Jackie Robinson: An Intimate Portrait*, 133.

85. David Anderson, "Darien Puts Curb on Church Camp," *NYT*, June 15, 1955.

86. Golenbock, *Bums*, 430–431.

87. Golenbock, *Bums*, 433; Marc Eliot, *Song of Brooklyn: An Oral History of America's Favorite Borough* (New York: Broadway Books, 2008), 414; Neil Sullivan, *The Dodgers Move West* (New York: Oxford University Press, 1987).

88. Eliot, *Song of Brooklyn*, 92.

CHAPTER 3: "IF WE WERE SEGREGATIONISTS"

1. "Jansen Notes 'Definite Progress' in Integrating the City's Schools," *New York Times*, August 23, 1957; "The Beam in Our Own Eye," *NYT*, January 21, 1957; "Integration Here, Too," *NYT*, March 4, 1957.

2. Waldo Martin, ed., Brown v. Board of Education: *A Brief History With Documents* (Boston: Bedford/St. Martin's, 1998), 84; Washington, ed., *A Testament of Hope*, 219.

3. Irving R. Kaufman, "The New Rochelle Decision: The Facts," *Journal of Educational Sociology*, Vol. 36, No. 6 (February 1963), 263–264, 268; Owen Fiss, "Racial Imbalance: The Constitutional Concepts," *Harvard Law Review*, Vol. 78, No. 3 (January, 1965), 601.

4. Kaufman, "The New Rochelle Decision: The Facts."

5. Lewis Steel, "Jim Crow in the North," *In These Times*, January 8, 2009; Interview with Lewis Steel, by Author.

6. Plaintiffs, Findings of Fact, *Barksdale v. Springfield School Committee*, November 5, 1964, NAACP Papers, Group V, Box 56, Part 23: Legal Department Case Files, 1956–1965. Series B: The Northeast, Reel 2.

7. Plaintiffs, Findings of Fact, *Barksdale v. Springfield School Committee*.

8. Harvard Center for Law and Education, "A Study of the Massachusetts Racial Imbalance Act" (February 1972), Publication No. 6019, 12–13, 32–33.

9. John F. Kennedy, "Address on Civil Rights," June 11, 1963, Miller Center Presidential Speech Archive, http://millercenter.org/president/speeches/detail/3375.

10. Plaintiffs' Exhibit 17, Regular Session of the School Committee (September 19, 1963), Brief for Appellees, *Springfield School Committee v. Abraham Barksdale, Jr.*, April 15, 1965, p. 36a–38a, NAACP Papers, Reel 1; Plaintiffs, Findings of Fact, November 5, 1964, p. 9, *Barksdale v. Springfield School Committee*, NAACP Papers, Reel 2.

11. Interview with Charlie Ryan, by Author, Springfield, Massachusetts, May 10, 2010.

12. Stenographic Record of *Barksdale v. Ryan*, United States District Court, District Court of Massachusetts, Civil Action No. 64–8, October 23, 1964, p. 3–140 to 3–142, NAACP Papers, Reel 2.

13. Complaint, *Barksdale v. Springfield School Committee*, NAACP Papers, Reel 1.

14. Complaint, *Barksdale v. Springfield School Committee*; "School Board Halts Study of Desegregation," *Springfield Union*, January 31, 1964.

15. "NAACP Official Disagrees With Law Department," *SU*, February 1, 1964.

16. Robert Carter, *A Matter of Law: A Memoir of Struggle in the Cause of Equal Rights* (New York: New Press, 2005), 172, 170.

17. *Barksdale v. Ryan*, October 21, 1964, p. 1–3 to 1–6, NAACP Papers, Reel 1; Robert Levey, "U.S. Court Tests School Segregation," *BG*, October 22, 1964.

18. *Barksdale v. Ryan*, October 21, 1964, 1–23 to 1–26, 1–50 to 1–51, NAACP Papers, Reel 1.

19. *Barksdale v. Ryan*, October 21, 1964, 1–139 to 1–141, 1–153, NAACP Papers, Reel 1; "Brightwood Plans Are Barred at School Segregation Trial," *SU*, October 22, 1964.

20. *Barksdale v. Ryan*, October 23, 1964, NAACP Papers, Reel 2; "5 Take Stand in School Suit," *SU*, October 24, 1964.

21. *Barksdale v. Ryan*, October 26, 1964, 4–70, NAACP Papers, Reel 2; "Plaintiffs Rest in School Suit," *SU*, October 27, 1964.

22. *Barksdale v. Ryan*, October 26, 1964, 4–70, 4–73 to 4–74, 4–79, NAACP Papers, Reel 2.

23. Ellen Lake, "Thomas F. Pettigrew: Faculty Profile," *The Harvard Crimson*, April 9, 1964.

24. Lake, "Thomas F. Pettigrew: Faculty Profile"; *Barksdale v. Ryan*, October 22, 1964, 2–75, NAACP Papers, Reel 1.

25. *Barksdale v. Ryan*, October 22, 1964, 2–108, NAACP Papers, Reel 1.

26. "Merriam Is Ruled Out as Expert Witness in Segregation Suit Here," *SU*, October 23, 1964.

27. Thomas Pettigrew, E-mail correspondence with Author, March 18, 2010; *Barksdale v. Ryan*, October 22, 1964, 2–109, NAACP Papers, Reel 1.

28. *Barksdale v. Ryan*, October 22, 1964, 2–110 to 2–111, NAACP Papers, Reel 1.

29. *Barksdale v. Ryan*, October 22, 1964, 2–113 to 2–114, NAACP Papers, Reel 1.

30. Thomas Pettigrew, E-mail correspondence with Author.

31. *Barksdale v. Ryan*, October 27, 1964, 5–18, NAACP Papers, Reel 2.

32. *Barksdale v. Ryan*, October 27, 1964, 5–21 to 5–23, NAACP Papers, Reel 2.

33. *Barksdale v. Ryan*, October 27, 1964, 5–30 to 5–31, NAACP Papers, Reel 2.

34. *Barksdale v. Ryan*, October 27, 1964, 5–33 to 5–34, NAACP Papers, Reel 2.

35. *Barksdale v. Ryan*, October 27, 1964, 5–37 to 5–38, NAACP Papers, Reel 2.

36. *Barksdale v. Ryan*, October 27, 1964, 5–39, 5–47, NAACP Papers, Reel 2.

37. *Barksdale v. Ryan*, October 27, 1964, 5–61, NAACP Papers, Reel 2.

38. *Barksdale v. Ryan*, October 27, 1964, 5–65, 5–67, NAACP Papers, Reel 2.

39. *Barksdale v. Ryan*, October 27, 1964, 5–69 to 5–70, NAACP Papers, Reel 2.

40. "The School System Goes On," *SU*, October 30, 1964.

41. Decision of the United States District Court, January 11, 1965, Springfield, Massachusetts School Case (*Barksdale, Jr. et al. vs. Springfield School Committee et al.*), NAACP Papers, Reel 2.

42. Decision of the United States District Court, January 11, 1965.

43. News From NAACP: "NAACP Wins School Case in Springfield, Mass.," January 12, 1965, NAACP Papers, Reel 2.

44. "April 30 Deadline Set For Plan to End Race Imbalance in Schools," *SU*, January 12, 1965.

45. "April 30 Deadline Set For Plan to End Race Imbalance in Schools."

46. "Bombshell From the Bench," *SU*, January 13, 1965.

47. "School Board Expected to Appeal Ruling," *SU*, January 14, 1965; "Board Will Appeal Segregation Ruling," *SU*, January 15, 1965.

48. "Negro Leaders Assail Move to Appeal Ruling," *SU*, January 15, 1965.

49. "NAACP Plans to Challenge Aid for Schools," *SU*, January 19, 1965.

50. "Impact of the 'Even If' Clause," *SU*, January 19, 1965.

51. "Impact of the 'Even If' Clause."

52. Findings of the Circuit Court, July 12, 1965, NAACP Papers, Reel 2.

53. "Rights Groups Upset Over School Decision," *SU*, July 13, 1965.

54. "Rights Groups Upset Over School Decision."

55. "Rights Groups Upset Over School Decision."

56. "NAACP to Ask High Court to Review School Decision," *SU*, July 15, 1965.

57. Memorandum, Lewis Steel to Roy Wilkins, Re: *Griffin v. Ryan*—Springfield Demonstration Case, NAACP Papers, Reel 2; "CORE to Sponsor Williams Benefit at Octagon Club," *SU*, July 22, 1965.

58. *Griffin v. Ryan*, Plaintiffs' Post-Trial Brief, p. 3, NAACP Papers, Reel 2.

59. *Griffin v. Ryan*, Plaintiffs' Post-Trial Brief, p. 3.

60. Interview with Charlie Ryan, by Author.

61. Interview with Charlie Ryan, by Author.

62. Interview with Charlie Ryan, by Author.

63. *Griffin v. Ryan*, Plaintiffs' Post-Trial Brief; "Negroes in Massachusetts Charge Brutality By the Police," *NYT*, July 22, 1965.

64. "Negroes Hold Sleep-Out in Bay State," *Chicago Tribune*, July 24, 1965.

65. Interview with Charlie Ryan, by Author.

66. "Springfield, Mass., Negroes Staging Protest at City Hall," *NYT*, August 11, 1965.

67. "Springfield, Mass., Jails 23 Protesters; Two Stores Burned," *NYT*, August 14, 1965; Paul Montgomery, "35 Arrests End Truce in Springfield," *NYT*, August 15, 1965; "U.S. Studies Tensions in Springfield, Mass.," *Los Angeles Times*, August 16, 1965; *Griffin v. Ryan*, Plaintiffs' Post-Trial Brief.

68. Montgomery, "35 Arrests End Truce in Springfield"; *Griffin v. Ryan*, Plaintiffs' Post-Trial Brief.

69. Interview with Lewis Steel, by Author.

70. "Warning on Springfield," *NYT*, August 18, 1965.

71. "CORE Sets Selma-Style March in Springfield," *Los Angeles Times*, August 19, 1965; "Negroes Slate 'Selma' March at Springfield," *Washington Post*, August 19, 1965; *Griffin v. Ryan*, Plaintiffs' Post-Trial Brief; "Rights Leaders Cancel Plans," *Los Angeles Times*, August 20, 1965; "Fire 13 Whites From Negro School Staff," *Chicago Tribune*, August 20, 1965. Adding fuel to the fire, the Springfield police arrested Oscar Bright on a trumped-up narcotics charge earlier in the week.

72. "Priest Urges City Emphasis in Right Fight," *Chicago Tribune*, August 21, 1965; *Griffin v. Ryan*, Plaintiffs' Post-Trial Brief.

73. "Bay State City Prepares For 'Selma' March," *Chicago Tribune*, August 22, 1965; Interview with Charlie Ryan, by Author.

74. John Fenton, "1,000 Troops Keep Springfield Calm," *NYT*, August 23, 1965.

75. "12 Are Convicted at Springfield," *Washington Post*, August 27, 1965.

76. *Griffin v. Ryan*, Plaintiffs' Post-Trial Brief.

77. Interview with Lewis Steel, by Author.

78. Formisano, *Boston Against Busing*, 46.

79. Steel, "Jim Crow in the North." In *Milliken v. Bradley* (1974), the Supreme Court did take up a case on northern school integration. It ruled against Verda Bradley, a black mother in Detroit.

CHAPTER 4: THE COLOR-BLIND COMMONWEALTH?

1. Interview with Edward Brooke, by Renee Pouissant, February 2001, Oral History Archive, National Visionary Leadership Project, http://www.visionaryproject.org/brookeedward/; Interview with Edward Brooke, by Author, by Telephone, December 10, 2009.

2. Interview with Richard Norton Smith, Public Affairs Radio, C-Span, 2007.

3. Interview with Edward Brooke, by Renee Pouissant; Edward Brooke, *Bridging the Divide: My Life* (New Brunswick, NJ: Rutgers University Press, 2007), 4, 22–23.

4. Brooke, *Bridging the Divide*, 54–56.

5. Martin Nolan, "The Last Hurrahs Are Fading," *BG Magazine*, November 6, 1966, 7.

6. John Henry Cutler, *Ed Brooke: Biography of a Senator* (New York: Bobbs-Merrill, Inc., 1972), 55.

7. Brooke, *Bridging the Divide*, 67, "A Negro Runs For State Office," *Look*, November 8, 1960, 112.

8. Brooke, *Bridging the Divide*, 69.

9. Brooke, *Bridging the Divide*, 70.

10. Interview with Edward Brooke, by Author.

11. Brooke, *Bridging the Divide*, 85.

12. Brooke, *Bridging the Divide*, 93.

13. Interview with Edward Brooke, by Author.

14. Brooke, *Bridging the Divide*, 94–95; John Fenton, "Primary Tuesday in Massachusetts," *NYT*, September 16, 1962.

15. Alan Lupo, *Liberty's Chosen Home: The Politics of Violence in Boston* (Boston: Little, Brown, 1977), 135–150.

16. Interview with Edward Brooke, by Author; Edward Sheehan, "Brooke of Massachusetts: A Negro Governor on Beacon Hill?," *Harper's*, June 1964, 46; Peter Cummings, "Boston Groups Plan School Boycott Despite Attorney General's Warning," *The Harvard Crimson*, February 12, 1964; Cutler, *Ed Brooke*, 120.

17. Interview with Edward Brooke, by Author.

18. Interview with Edward Brooke, by Renee Pouissant. Brooke would articulate his views in his 1966 book: Edward Brooke, *The Challenge of Change: Crisis in Our Two-Party System* (Boston: Little, Brown, 1966). Historian Leah Wright argues that Brooke did not embrace Democratic liberalism. She labels his ideology a "progressive conservatism." Leah Wright, "'The Challenge of Change': Edward Brooke, the Republican Party, and the Struggle for Redemption," *Souls*, 13:1 (January-March 2011), 98.

19. John Fenton, "Johnson Carries All New England," *NYT*, November 4, 1964; Elinor Hartshorn, "The Quiet Campaigner: Edward W. Brooke in Massachusetts," Ph.D. Diss., University of Massachusetts, Amherst, 1973, 97; "The Figures," *Time*, November 13, 1964; Peter Carter, "Boston's Brooke," *Newark Sunday News*, December 13, 1964.

20. Interview with Edward Brooke, by Renee Pouissant.

21. David Broder, "Negro Announces for Senate Race," *NYT*, December 31, 1965; "Candidate for Senator," *NYT*, December 31, 1965; Hartshorn, "The Quiet Campaigner," 127–128; Statement by Edward W. Brooke, Box 621, Folder: U.S. Senate, 1966—Announcement of Candidacy and Opening of Campaign Headquarters, Edward Brooke Papers, Manuscript Division, Library of Congress.

22. "The Bay State's Color-Blind Candidate," *Life*, April 8, 1966, 57, 64; "Negro in Mass. Senate Race Stresses Issues," *Newark Sunday News*, February 6, 1966.

23. John Becker and Eugene Heaton Jr., "The Election of Senator Edward W. Brooke," *The Public Opinion Quarterly*, Vol. 31, No. 3 (Autumn 1967), 349, 357; John Becker to Edward Brooke (December 28, 1964), Box 624, Folder—Campaign Materials: U.S. Senate, 1966–Opinion Polls, EB Papers.

24. Ralph, *Northern Protest*, 30–31.

25. James Doyle, "Brooke Alters Campaign Strategy: Drops Slogan, Wants Debate," *BG*, October 9, 1966.

26. Al Gammal to Edward W. Brooke (May 9, 1966), Box 621, Folder: U.S. Senate, 1966—Campaign Literature, EB Papers.

27. "Carmichael Urges Negro Unity," *BSB*, August 27, 1966.

28. Evan Dobelle, Field Report, Box 622, Folder: Campaign Materials: U.S. Senate, 1966, EB Papers; Becker and Heaton, "The Election of Senator Edward W. Brooke," 357.

29. Transcript, *Issues and Answers*, September 4, 1966, Box 562, Folder: Radio and TV Transcripts (1966–1967), EB Papers.

30. Springfield, September 1966, Box 621, Folder: U.S. Senate, 1966—Briefing Book #2, Folder #2, EB Papers; Speakers' Bureau, Notes for Speakers, Box 621, Folder: U.S. Senate, 1966—Briefing Book #2, Folder #2, EB Papers.

31. Interview with Edward Brooke, by Author; Hartshorn, "The Quiet Campaigner," 162; "The Massachusetts Public Appraises Edward W. Brooke," Opinion Research Corporation, Box 624, Folder: Campaign Materials: U.S. Senate, 1966—Opinion Polls, EB Papers.

32. Timothy Rose, "Civic War: People, Politics, and the Battle of New Boston, 1945–1967," Ph.D. Diss., University of California, Berkeley, 2006, 432–433; "G.O.P. on Top," *Time*, September 23, 1966.

33. "Backlash in the Bay State," *The Nation*, September 26, 1966; Tom Wicker, "President Buoyed by Voter Support of Vietnam Policy," *NYT*, September 15, 1966.

34. Speech by Edward W. Brooke, Box 621: U.S. Senate, 1966—Announcement of Candidacy and Opening of Campaign Headquarters, EB Papers; Box 567: Speeches & Writings, Folder: Nomination Acceptance Speech, Republican State Convention (June 25, 1966), EB Papers.

35. "Backlash in the Bay State"; Brooke, *Bridging the Divide*, 138.

36. Hartshorn, "The Quiet Campaigner," 162; Becker and Heaton, "The Election of Senator Edward W. Brooke," 355–356.

37. Becker and Heaton, "The Election of Senator Edward W. Brooke," 356.

38. John Skow, "The Black Man Leading a G.O.P. March on Washington," *Saturday Evening Post*, September 10, 1966; "Running Brooke: He May Become a Senate Leader," *National Observer*, September 19, 1966.

39. David Wilson, "Will Blanks Beat Brooke?," *BG*, October 1, 1966; Lisa McGirr, *Suburban Warriors: The Origins of the New American Right* (Princeton, NJ: Princeton University Press, 2001), 204.

40. Interview with Edward Brooke, by Author.

41. Robert Healy, "Brooke Deals With Backlash," *BG*, October 2, 1966; Hartshorn, "The Quiet Campaigner," 178.

42. Healy, "Brooke Deals With Backlash"; Martin Nolan, "Brooke Hurls 5-Part Challenge," *BG*, October 4, 1966.

43. Cornelius Noonan, "If Anything Divides Brooke-Peabody, It's Vietnam," *BG*, October 30, 1966; Richard Daly, "Brooke, Peabody More Alike Than Not," *Boston Herald*, November 6, 1966.

44. "The Massachusetts Public Appraises Edward W. Brooke," EB Papers.

45. "The Massachusetts Public Appraises Edward W. Brooke," EB Papers.

46. Cal Brumley, "Bay State Backlash," *Wall Street Journal*, October 20, 1966; John Fenton, "Backlash Enters Bay State Race," *NYT*, October 23, 1966.

47. Martin Nolan, "The Shadings of 'Backlash,'" *BG*, October 27, 1966.

48. Timothy Leland, "Senate Rivals Clash on War," *BG*, October 20, 1966; Robert Healy, "Adams' Vote Favors Brooke," *BG*, October 24, 1966.

49. "Both Sides Get Lifts," *BG*, November 1, 1966; Hartshorn, "The Quiet Campaigner," 169, 144; "Clergymen, Professors Come Out for Brooke," *BG*, November 2, 1966; "Candidates Fire Final Rounds as Deadline Nears," *Boston Herald*, November 6, 1966.

50. "Brooke vs. Peabody," *BG*, November 1, 1966.

51. "Brooke Towers Above," *Fitchburg Sentinel*, October 26, 1966. Also see "Brooke for the United States Senate," *Malden News*, October 27, 1966; "Brooke for Senator," *Lowell Sun*, October 1966; "Why We're For Brooke," *Berkshire Eagle*, November 5, 1966.

52. "Unique Opportunity," *BSB*, October 29, 1966; "Worthy Successor," *Holyoke Transcript Telegram*, November 2, 1966; Evan Dobelle to Carmen Durso, Re: Field Report (November 4, 1966), Box 623, Folder: Campaign Materials: U.S. Senate, 1966—Field Reports, EB Papers.

53. Transcript, "Newsmakers: 1966" (October 30, 1966), Box 562, Folder: Radio and TV Transcripts (1966–1967), EB Papers; "Brooke Explains Stand on White Backlash Issue," *BSB*, November 5, 1966.

54. "Brooke Explains Stand on White Backlash Issue"; Robert Healy, "Focus on Senate Race," *BG*, November 6, 1966; Thomas Gallagher, "Tuesday's Vote Called State's Most Crucial," *Boston Sunday Herald*, November 6, 1966.

55. "Innocent Victim?," *Boston Sunday Herald*, November 6, 1966.

56. Interview with Edward Brooke, by Author.

57. "News From Brooke," Box 623, Folder: Campaign Materials: U.S. Senate, 1966, EB Papers.

58. Brooke, *Bridging the Divide*, 143; Jeremiah Murphy, "Brooke Responds to Victory Cheers," *BG*, November 9, 1966.

59. Interview with Edward Brooke, by Author.

60. Hartshorn, "The Quiet Campaigner," 196–197, 208, 217, 222; "Vote for Senate," *BG*, November 9, 1966; John Herbers, "Negro 'Frontlash' Held More Sophisticated and Selective than White Backlash," *NYT*, November 10, 1966; Robert Hanron, "Outcome Became Known Early on Basis of City's Patterns," *BG*, November 9, 1966.

61. Brooke, *Bridging the Divide*, 143; Murphy, "Brooke Responds to Victory Cheers"; Interview with Edward Brooke, by Author.

62. The *Globe's* front page announced that Brooke's win had proved "with stunning impact the myth of white backlash in state politics." S. J. Micciche, "Richardson Joins Big GOP Sweep," *BG*, November 9, 1966; Robert Healy, "Senate Race Pressed on a High Level," *BG*, November 9, 1966; "How Big a Backlash?," *NYT*, November 11, 1966.

63. "People Judge You on Your Merit," *BG*, November 9, 1966; "There She Is," *BG*, November 9, 1966. The *Holyoke Transcript-Telegram* suggested: "Massachusetts, so often a national leader, again is in the forefront." "Edward W. Brooke," *Holyoke Transcript-Telegram*, November 10, 1966.

64. Cutler, *Ed Brooke*, 193; "The Brooke Era," *Silver Lake News*, November 10, 1966.

65. "A New Senator," *The Pilot*, November 12, 1966.

66. *Lewiston Evening Journal*, November 10, 1966; "Heart-Warming Event," *Monitor & Patriot*, November 12, 1966; Edward Berman, "Fine Hour for Massachusetts," *Woonsocket Call*, November 12, 1966.

67. Carolyn Nemrow, Letter to the Editor, *Time*, November 18, 1966.

68. Alyce O'Sullivan, Letter to the Editor, *Time*, February 24, 1967.

69. Malcolm Nash, "Brooke's Win Answers Backlash," *AN*, November 12, 1966.

70. Harold Kaese, "Negro Athletes Helped Brooke," *BG*, November 10, 1966.

71. Jackie Robinson, "A Man We Can Be Proud Of," *Pittsburgh Courier*, December 3, 1966.

72. "Heart-Warming Event"; Berman, "Fine Hour for Massachusetts"; Poppy Cannon White, "History and Brooke," *AN*, November 26, 1966.

73. "The American Dream, Yes!," *Jewish Advocate*, November 1966.

74. Adolph Slaughter, "The Mystique . . . Et cetera . . . ," *Pittsburgh Courier*, December 10, 1966.

75. Stephan Thernstrom, *The Other Bostonians: Poverty and Progress in the American Metropolis, 1880–1970* (Cambridge, MA: Harvard University Press, 1973), 179, 11; Thomas Whalen, *Dynasty's End: Bill Russell and the 1968–69 World Champion Boston Celtics* (Boston: Northeastern University Press, 2004), 4; "The Real Black Power," *Time*, November 17, 1967.

76. Whalen, *Dynasty's End*, 54, 66; Bill Russell and Taylor Branch, *Second Wind: The Memoirs of an Opinionated Man* (New York: Ballantine, 1980), 207–208.

77. "White, Non-White Enrollment, 1965–66," *BG*, November 19, 1966; "More Boston Schools Called Imbalanced," *Boston Herald*, November 8, 1966; Jonathan Kozol, *Death at an Early Age: The Destruction of Hearts and Minds of Negro Children in the Boston Public Schools* (Boston: Houghton Mifflin, 1967); Formisano, *Boston Against Busing*, 46.

78. "The Massachusetts Public Appraises Edward W. Brooke," EB Papers.

79. Mark Grimes, "He That Sitteth on a Hot Stove Shall Surely Rise," *BSB*, March 11, 1967.

80. "The Real Story Behind Those Riots in Boston," *AN*, June 10, 1967.

81. "Boston Gets an Antiriot Prescription," *Washington Post*, July 27, 1967; John Fenton, "Ghetto Report Scores Boston Officials," *NYT*, July 30, 1967; "The Voice of the Ghetto," 2, 16, Box 219, Folder: Massachusetts Commission on Civil Rights, EB Papers.

82. Fenton, "Ghetto Report Scores Boston Officials"; "The Voice of the Ghetto," 6–8, EB Papers.

CHAPTER 5: SHIRLEY CHISHOLM'S PLACE

1. John Kifner, "G.O.P. Names James Farmer for Brooklyn Race for Congress," *NYT*, May 20, 1968.

2. Wayne Dawkins, *City Son: Andrew W. Cooper's Impact on Modern-Day Brooklyn* (Jackson, MS: University Press of Mississippi, 2012), 34; Martin Tolchin, "Brooklyn Shifts, So Do Democrats," *NYT*, June 12, 1968.

3. Tolchin, "Brooklyn Shifts, So Do Democrats."

4. Theodore White, "The Big City Faces Its Decisive Moment," *Life*, October 29, 1965, 77; "Hurrah," *The New Yorker*, September 30, 1972, 34.

5. White, "The Big City Faces Its Decisive Moment," 77.

6. White, "The Big City Faces Its Decisive Moment," 78.

7. Terence Smith, "The Status of Reform," *NYT*, July 8, 1966.

8. Shirley Chisholm, *Unbought and Unbossed* (Washington, DC: Take Root Media, 2010), 65, 67; Gerson, "Building the Brooklyn Machine," 304, 317.

9. Chisholm, *Unbought and Unbossed*, 30, 34; Interview with Shirley Chisholm, Sc Audio C-160, Side 2, Schomburg Oral History Collection, Moving Image & Recorded Sound Division, Schomburg Center for Research in Black Culture.

10. Joshua Guild, "To Make That Someday Come: Shirley Chisholm's Radical Politics of Possibility," in Dayo Gore, Jeanne Theoharis, and Komozi Woodard, eds., *Want to Start a Revolution? Radical Women in the Black Freedom Struggle* (New York: NYU Press, 2009), 251.

11. Chisholm, *Unbought and Unbossed*, 45; Guild, "To Make That Someday Come," 252.

12. Chisholm, *Unbought and Unbossed*, 68.

13. Chisholm, *Unbought and Unbossed*, 71–72. The first black woman in the New York State Assembly was Bessie Buchanan, who represented Harlem from 1955 to 1960.

14. Gerson, "Building the Brooklyn Machine," 329–340.

15. Chisholm, *Unbought and Unbossed*, 73–76.

16. Daphne Sheppard, "Shirley Chisholm: The Saga of a Determined, Hard-Hitting Boro Leader," *AN*, November 16, 1968.

17. Interview with Shirley Chisholm, Sc Audio C-160, Side 1, SOHC.

18. "Biggest Impact Seen Here," *NYT*, December 19, 1967.

19. Interview with Marshall Dubin, Sc Audio C-164, Side 1, SOHC.

20. "Angry Legislator: Edna Flannery Kelly," *NYT*, March 6, 1968.

21. "Bedford-Stuyvesant Is Called a Victim of Gerrymandering," *NYT*, June 24, 1966; Interview with Shirley Chisholm, Sc Audio C-161, Side 2, SOHC; Chisholm, *Unbought and Unbossed*, 65; Dawkins, *City Son*, 34, 50–53.

22. "Celler Is Facing 'A Lovely Lady and a Youngster' in Primary," *NYT*, May 19, 1968; Thomas Ronan, "Rep. Kelly Scores Steingut 'Bossism,'" *NYT*, March 6, 1968.

23. "Let's Help Make Diversity Work," *Greenpoint Weekly Star*, December 22, 1967; "There's Hope For District 14," *Greenpoint Weekly Star*, February 23, 1968. The *Williamsburg News* agreed. These were two communities "where all races, all languages live as the symbol of democracy." *Williamsburg News*, May 10, 1968.

24. "New Lines For 14 C.D. Splits Assembly Dist.," *Greenpoint Weekly Star*, March 1, 1968.

25. "New Lines For 14 C.D. Splits Assembly Dist."; "C.D. Lines Explained, Opposed," *Greenpoint Weekly Star*, March 8, 1968.

26. Editorial, "New District Lines Hurt Greenpoint," *Greenpoint Weekly Star*, March 1, 1968.

27. Interview with Judith Berek, Sc Audio C-163, Side 2, SOHC.

28. Interview with Shirley Chisholm, Sc Audio C-161, Side 2, SOHC.

29. "C.D. Lines Explained, Opposed."

30. "C.D. Lines Explained, Opposed"; Chisholm, *Unbought and Unbossed*, 86.

31. Tolchin, "Brooklyn Shifts, So Do Democrats"; Chisholm, *Unbought and Unbossed*, 19; John Kifner, "Farmer and Woman in Lively Bedford-Stuyvesant Race," *NYT*, October 26, 1968.

32. Murray Schumach, "The Melting Pot Failed in Bedford," *NYT*, July 31, 1967; Tolchin, "Brooklyn Shifts, So Do Democrats."

33. Interview with Shirley Chisholm, Sc Audio C-161, Side 2, SOHC; Sheppard, "Shirley Chisholm: The Saga of a Determined, Hard-Hitting Boro Leader"; "CNC Blasts-Off Chisholm Campaign," *AN*, January 27, 1968; Guild, "To Make That Someday Come," 253–254.

34. "CNC Blasts-Off Chisholm Campaign."

35. Interview with Shirley Chisholm, Sc Audio C-161, Side 2, SOHC.

36. "Thompson Boards Congress Train," *AN*, March 2, 1968; Earl Caldwell, "Three Negroes Weigh House Race in New Brooklyn 12th District," *NYT*, February 26, 1968; "Bertram Baker Backs Mrs. Robinson in Race," *AN*, March 30, 1968; "Robinson Stock Up; Rev. Taylor Falls In," *AN*, April 20, 1968; "Surprise Names Crop Up For Boro Primary Race," *AN*, April 6, 1968.

37. Interview with Shirley Chisholm, Sc Audio C-160–161, SOHC.

38. Tolchin, "Brooklyn Shifts, So Do Democrats"; Caldwell, "Three Negroes Weigh House Race in New Brooklyn 12th District"; Interview with Shirley Chisholm, Sc Audio C-161, Side 2, SOHC.

39. Tolchin, "Brooklyn Shifts, So Do Democrats"; Interview with Shirley Chisholm, Sc Audio C-160, Side 1, and Sc Audio C-161, Side 2, SOHC.

40. Interview with Shirley Chisholm, Sc Audio C-161, Side 2, SOHC; Susan Brownmiller, "This Is Fighting Shirley Chisholm," *NYT Magazine*, April 13, 1969.

41. Gerson, "Building the Brooklyn Machine," 299; Brownmiller, "This Is Fighting Shirley Chisholm"; Interview with Shirley Chisholm, Sc Audio C-160, Side 1–2, SOHC.

42. Brownmiller, "This Is Fighting Shirley Chisholm"; Interview with Shirley Chisholm, Sc Audio C-161, Side 2, SOHC.

43. Interview with Shirley Chisholm, Sc Audio C-160, Side 1, SOHC; Sheppard, "Shirley Chisholm: The Saga of a Determined, Hard-Hitting Boro Leader"; Interview with Shirley Chisholm, Sc Audio C-161, Side 2, SOHC.

44. Interview with Shirley Chisholm, Sc Audio C-161, Side 2, SOHC.

45. Interview with Judith Berek, Sc Audio C-163, Side 2, SOHC.

46. Interview with Shirley Chisholm, Sc Audio C-161, Side 2, SOHC; "Brooklyn Puerto Ricans Meet to Plan Strategy on Complaints," *NYT*, March 18, 1968.

47. Daphne Sheppard, "Bed-Stuy Primary Round-Up Shows Sweep by New Breed," *AN*, June 29, 1968; Martin Tolchin, "Negro Support of O'Dwyer Weighed," *NYT*, June 22, 1968; Interview with Shirley Chisholm, Sc Audio C-161, Side 2, SOHC; Mary Manoni, *Bedford-Stuyvesant: The Anatomy of a Central City Community* (New York: Quadrangle, 1973), 20.

48. Daphne Sheppard, "Ex-Teacher Aims at Congress Seat," *AN*, June 22, 1968; Sheppard, "Bed-Stuy Primary Round-Up Shows Sweep by New Breed."

49. "Campaign Opened by James Farmer," *NYT*, July 26, 1968; Kifner, "G.O.P. Names James Farmer for Brooklyn Race for Congress."

50. Kifner, "Farmer and Woman in Lively Bedford-Stuyvesant Race"; Interview with Shirley Chisholm, Sc Audio C-161, Side 2, SOHC.

51. Interview with Shirley Chisholm, Sc Audio C-161, Side 2, SOHC.

52. Kifner, "Farmer and Woman in Lively Bedford-Stuyvesant Race."

53. Martin Tolchin, "Javits Is Jeered; Farmer Aids Him," *NYT*, September 26, 1968; Interview with Marshall Dubin, Sc Audio C-164, Side 1, SOHC.

54. Shirley Chisholm Street Rally, October 29, 1968, Sc Audio C-170, Side 1, SOHC.

55. Kifner, "Farmer and Woman in Lively Bedford-Stuyvesant Race"; Brownmiller, "This Is Fighting Shirley Chisholm"; Interview with Shirley Chisholm, Sc Audio C-161, Side 2, SOHC.

56. Interview with Shirley Chisholm, Sc Audio C-161, Side 2, SOHC.

57. Interview with Marshall Dubin, Sc Audio C-164, Side 1, SOHC.

58. Shirley Chisholm Street Rally, October 29, 1968, SOHC; Manny Fernandez, "Where Brooklyn Once Triumphed, a Tragic Scene," *NYT*, January 6, 2008.

59. Jerald Podair, *The Strike That Changed New York: Blacks, Whites, and the Ocean Hill-Brownsville Crisis* (New Haven: Yale University Press, 2002).

60. Thomas Sugrue, "Shanker Blows Up the World," *The Nation*, November 12, 2007.

61. Chisholm-Farmer Debate, October 1968, Sc Audio C-166, SOHC.

62. James Farmer, *Lay Bare the Heart: An Autobiography of the Civil Rights Movement* (New York: Arbor House, 1985), 311.

63. George Todd, "Farmer Graciously Bows in Defeat to First Lady," *AN*, November 9, 1968. Chisholm tallied 34,885 votes compared to 13,777 for Farmer. "Statistics of the Presidential and Congressional Election of November 5, 1968," U.S. Government Printing Office (Washington, DC, 1969), 29.

64. Todd, "Farmer Graciously Bows in Defeat to First Lady"; Edith Evans Asbury, "Freshman in Congress Won't Be Quiet," *NYT*, November 6, 1968; Daphne Sheppard, "Chisholm Overwhelms Farmer in House Race," *AN*, November 9, 1968.

65. Asbury, "Freshman in Congress Won't Be Quiet"; Interview with Judith Berek, Sc Audio C-163, Side 2, SOHC.

66. Roy Wilkins, "The Black Vote Was For Inclusion," *AN*, November 23, 1968; Todd, "Farmer Graciously Bows in Defeat to First Lady."

67. George Metcalf, *Up From Within: Today's New Black Leaders* (New York: McGraw-Hill, 1971), 134; Shirley Chisholm, "Coalitions—The Politics of the Future," in Nathan Wright Jr., ed., *What Black Politicians Are Saying* (New York: Hawthorn, 1972), 90.

68. Chisholm, "Coalitions—The Politics of the Future," 93.

69. Stephan Lesher, "The Short, Unhappy Life of Black Presidential Politics," *NYT Magazine*, June 25, 1972; Shirley Chisholm, "Statement of Candidacy for the Office of President of the United States" (January 25, 1972), Folder: Chisholm, Shirley: Candidacy for President, 1972, EB Papers; Guild, "To Make That Someday Come," 265.

70. Dawkins, *City Son*, 99–101; "The Shirley Chisholm Issue," *AN*, September 9, 1978.

71. Andrew Cooper and Wayne Barrett, "Chisholm's Compromise: Politics and the Art of Self-Interest," *Village Voice*, October 30, 1978.

72. Joe Anuta, "'Chisholm' Trail!: Fort Greene Gets Building Named After Legendary Congresswoman," *The Brooklyn Paper*, October 4, 2010.

CHAPTER 6: "THE NORTH IS GUILTY"

1. *CR* (February 9, 1970), 2892.

2. The Reminiscences of Abraham Ribicoff, Interview by Ronald Grele, September 26, 1988, p. 3, Columbia Center for Oral History Collection; Ribicoff, *America Can Make It!*, 51.

3. The Reminiscences of Abraham Ribicoff, September 26, 1988, p. 7, CCOHC.

4. "Ribicoff of Connecticut Dies; Governor and Senator was 87," *NYT*, February 23, 1998; The Reminiscences of Abraham Ribicoff, Interview by Ronald Grele, January 24, 1989, p. 69–70, CCOHC; Martin Weil, "Abraham Ribicoff, 87, Dies," *Washington Post*, February 23, 1998; The Reminiscences of Abraham Ribicoff, Interview by Ronald Grele, June 12, 1989, p. 199, CCOHC; Neal Peirce, *The New England States: People, Politics, and Power in the Six New England States* (New York: Norton, 1976), 196.

5. The Reminiscences of Abraham Ribicoff, Interview by Ronald Grele, May 15, 1989, p. 152, CCOHC.

6. "Ribicoff of Connecticut Dies; Governor and Senator was 87"; Weil, "Abraham Ribicoff, 87, Dies."

7. "Ribicoff of Connecticut Dies; Governor and Senator was 87."

8. *CR* (February 9, 1970), 2890; "The Stennis Proposal Passes the Senate," *HC*, February 20, 1970.

9. Interview with John Koskinen, by C. Christopher Pavek, November 14, 1980, Box 676, Folder: Oral History Transcripts, Abraham Ribicoff Papers, Manuscript Division, Library of Congress.

10. Joseph Crespino, *In Search of Another Country: Mississippi and the Conservative Counterrevolution* (Princeton, NJ: Princeton University Press, 2007), 191,

11. *CR* (February 9, 1970), 2892; Ribicoff, *America Can Make It!*, 23–24.

12. Peter Dreier, John Mollenkopf, and Todd Swanson, *Place Matters: Metropolitics for the 21st-Century* (Lawrence, KS: University Press of Kansas, 2001), 216.

13. *CR* (February 9, 1970), 2892–2893.

14. *CR* (February 9, 1970), 2902. Fulbright represented Arkansas, Baker represented Tennessee, and Russell represented Georgia.

15. *CR* (February 9, 1970), 2901; The Reminiscences of Abraham Ribicoff, Interview by Ronald Grele, May 24, 1989, p. 187, CCOHC.

16. *CR* (February 9, 1970), 2903–2905.

17. *CR* (February 9, 1970), 2904.

18. "Monumental Hypocrisy," *Richmond Times-Dispatch*, February 11, 1970; J. Luther Glass to Abraham Ribicoff (February 13, 1970), Box 575, Folder: Education-Segregation, New Stories Re AR, 1970, AR Papers. Interestingly, Virginia was one southern state that had an aspirational dimension to its history. In this instance, Virginians fit Ribicoff into their story.

19. "Tsk! Tsk! Tsk!," *Denver Post*, Undated, Box 575, Folder: Education-Segregation, New Stories Re AR, 1970, AR Papers.

20. "Is That Me?," *Washington, DC, Daily News*, Reprinted in *Modesto Bee*, February 22, 1970, Box 575, Folder: Education-Segregation, New Stories Re AR, 1970, AR Papers.

21. Richard Rovere, "Letter From Washington," *The New Yorker*, February 21, 1970, 109.

22. "Ribicoff Bares Hypocrisy in North," *Dallas Morning News*, Sent by Martin Gross, Box 575, Folder: Education-Segregation Editorials, 1970, AR Papers.

23. "Ribicoff's Great Discovery," *The Arkansas Gazette*, reprinted in *HC*, March 4, 1970.

24. "Mirror, Mirror on the Wall," *BG*, February 15, 1970; John Averill, "Ribicoff's Motives in Hypocrisy Charge Doubted by Liberals," *BG*, February 15, 1970; "Equality of Injustice," *NYT*, February 22, 1970.

25. James Free, "Mail Reaction Favors Sen. Ribicoff's Stand," Undated, Box 575, Folder: Education-Segregation Editorials, 1970, AR Papers.

26. "Discrimination in the Valley," *Ansonia Sentinel*, March 24, 1970, Box 575, Folder: Education-Segregation Editorials, 1970, AR Papers.

27. "The Beam, the Mote, and Senator Ribicoff," *HC*, February 11, 1970; "The Stennis Proposal Passes the Senate"; "Integration and Politics," *New Haven Journal-Courier*, February 16, 1970; "The Desegregation Dilemma," *Middletown Press*, February 21, 1970.

28. D.J. Doudera, "The Population Mix and Private Schools," Letter to the Editor, *HC*, February 14, 1970.

29. "An Important Distinction," *Meriden Record*, February 11, 1970, Box 575, Folder: Education-Segregation Editorials, 1970, AR Papers.

30. "That Ribicoff Speech," *Hartford Times*, February 12, 1970, Box 575, Folder: Education-Segregation Editorials, 1970, AR Papers.

31. *CR* (February 17, 1970), 3570–3572.

32. *CR* (February 17, 1970), 3579, 3581.

33. *CR* (February 17, 1970), 3582, 3594; Interview with John Koskinen, by C. Christopher Pavek, AR Papers.

34. H. L. Schwartz, "Senate Passes Stennis Amendment Forcing North-South Integration," *BG*, February 19, 1970; Warren Weaver Jr., "Senate, 56–36, Votes Curbs on De Facto Segregation," *NYT*, February 19, 1970.

35. "Congress Votes Down Bias Busing," *HC*, February 20, 1970; "The Stennis Proposal Passes the Senate."

36. David Broder, "Desegregation . . . Is It Dead and Buried?," *BG*, February 25, 1970.

37. Crespino, *In Search of Another Country*, 196; Ribicoff, *America Can Make It!*, 33.

38. Abraham Ribicoff, "Integration in Our Society," University of Pennsylvania, March 2, 1970, Box 575, Folder #2: Education-Segregation, New Stories Re AR, 1970,

AR Papers; *Philadelphia Evening Bulletin*, March 3, 1970, Box 575, Folder #2: Education-Segregation, New Stories Re AR, 1970, AR Papers.

39. Carl Rowan, "Ribicoff Was Duped on Desegregation," February 20, 1970, Box 575, Folder: Education-Segregation Editorials, 1970, AR Papers.

40. Letter from John Morsell to Abraham Ribicoff (April 21, 1970), Box 575, Folder: Education-Segregation Editorials, 1970, AR Papers.

41. Tom Wicker, "The Death of Integration," *NYT*, February 19, 1970.

42. Pat Watters, "Southern Integrationists Feel Betrayed by the North," *NYT Magazine*, May 3, 1970.

43. "Conferees Soften Integration Curbs," *Washington Post*, March 20, 1970; "Stennis' Equal Desegregation Policy Weakened by Conferees," *Los Angeles Times*, March 20, 1970; "Water Down Dixie Curbs in Education Bill," *Chicago Tribune*, March 20, 1970; William Mead, "Senate Tames Stennis Measure, Oks School Aid," *BG*, April 2, 1970; Joseph Crespino, "The Best Defense Is a Good Offense: The Stennis Amendment and the Fracturing of Liberal School Desegregation Policy, 1964–1972," *Journal of Policy History*, Vol. 18, Issue 3 (July 2006), 318.

44. Abraham Ribicoff, "Segregation Is Segregation," San Francisco, CA, May 13, 1970, Box 575, Folder #2: Education-Segregation, New Stories Re AR, 1970, AR Papers.

45. *CR* (April 20, 1971), 10960; "Two Ribicoff Bills Hit North's Racism," *HC*, March 17, 1971; Robert Waters, "Ribicoff Launches Bias Fight," *HC*, April 20, 1971.

46. *CR* (April 21, 1971), 11326; Interview with John Koskinen, by C. Christopher Pavek, AR Papers.

47. David Broder, "Ribicoff's Plan Still Alive," *BG*, April 28, 1971; Tom Wicker, "Mr. Ribicoff Comes Through," *NYT*, March 21, 1971; "Two Ribicoff Bills Hit North's Racism," *HC*, March 17, 1971.

48. "Ribicoff's Defection," *Richmond News-Leader*, December 3, 1970, Box 575, Folder: Education-Segregation Editorials, 1970, AR Papers; J. L. Glass to Abraham Ribicoff (December 3, 1970), Box 575, Folder: Education-Segregation Editorials, 1970, AR Papers; Sun-n-Sand Motor Motel, Unsigned Letter to Abraham Ribicoff (December 1970), Box 575, Folder: Education-Segregation Editorials, 1970, AR Papers.

49. "Only an Inch," *Providence Journal*, December 3, 1970; "Big Erasure," *West Hartford News*, December 10, 1970.

50. David Rosenbaum, "Javits Accused by Ribicoff of 'Hypocrisy' on Schools," *NYT*, April 21, 1971.

51. *CR* (April 21, 1971), 11329, 11331; Spencer Rich, "US Senate Kills Inner City-Suburb School Integration," *BG*, April 22, 1971; *CR* (April 20, 1971), 10949.

52. Thomas Kelley, "Ribicoff Bill," Letter to the Editor, *HC*, May 3, 1971; "Building Committee Head Hits Ribicoff on Busing Proposal," *HC*, April 25, 1971.

53. Mrs. Corrado Puglisi, "Opposes Bussing," Letters to the Editor, *HC*, March 2, 1970.

CHAPTER 7: "THIS BEDEVILING BUSING BUSINESS"

1. Robert Kenney, "The Shift by Brooke and Storm It Brought," *BG*, March 25, 1967; Mary McGrory, "Eloquent Brooke Slams Carswell," *BG*, March 20, 1970; "New Face in the Senate," CBS, November 29, 1966, Box 562, Folder: U.S. Senate, 1966, TV and Radio Appearances—Transcripts, EB Papers.

2. Martin Nolan, "Ed Brooke Joins 'The Club,'" *BG*, January 8, 1967.

3. "Brooke, Ted Deplore Violence," *BG*, June 5, 1967; Robert Anglin, "Brooke Warns NAACP," *BG*, July 12, 1967.

4. *Report of the National Advisory Commission on Civil Disorders* (New York: Bantam Books, 1968), 1–2.

5. Richard Stewart, "Brooke Works for Rights Bill," *BG*, February 26, 1968; Brooke, *Bridging the Divide*, 175, 177; Richard Stewart, "Brooke's Amendment Opens Public Housing to Very Poor," *BG*, September 28, 1969. Historian Thomas Sugrue described the Fair Housing Act as "largely a symbolic gesture." Sugrue, *Sweet Land of Liberty*, 423.

6. Rowland Evans and Robert Novak, "Nixon, Brooke Team Up for GOP Ghetto Rapport," *BG*, September 9, 1968; James Doyle, "Brooke Told 'No' By Agnew," *BG*, September 11, 1968; James Doyle, "Brooke Back With Nixon to Talk About Integration," *BG*, September 14, 1968; Richard Stewart, "Brooke Warns on Tolerance," *BG*, September 27, 1968; "Robinson Charges Secret Nixon Plan," *BG*, October 7, 1968; "What President," *Time*, November 1, 1968.

7. "Mass. Poll: Brooke Favored Over Kennedy," *BG*, September 20, 1969.

8. James Doyle, "The Zig-Zag Year of Senator Brooke," *BG Magazine*, February 4, 1968.

9. *CR* (November 17, 1969), 34448; Brooke, *Bridging the Divide*, 194.

10. "Text of Sen. Brooke's Letter to Nixon," *BG*, October 10, 1969. Two legal scholars concluded that Haynsworth committed no ethical violations. Stephen Wasby and Joel Grossman, "Clement F. Haynsworth, Jr.: New Perspective on his Nomination to the Supreme Court," *Duke Law Journal* (February 1990), 80.

11. Alfonso Narvaez, "Clement Haynsworth Dies at 77; Lost Struggle for High Court Seat," *NYT*, November 23, 1989; *CR* (November 17, 1969), 34448.

12. Rick Perlstein, *Nixonland: The Rise of a President and the Fracturing of America* (New York: Scribner, 2008), 465; Brooke, *Bridging the Divide*, 195.

13. *CR* (April 8, 1970), 10763.

14. S. J. Micciche, "A Portrait of Racism," *BG*, February 8, 1970; *CR* (March 19, 1970), 8060; "Boosters' Club," Box 419, Folder: Carswell #2, EB Papers; Clarence Mitchell to Edward Brooke (January 27, 1970), Box 419, Folder: Carswell #1, EB Papers.

15. Richard Harris, *Decision* (New York: E.P. Dutton, 1971), 14–15, 74.

16. *CR* (February 25, 1970), 4874; Harris, *Decision*, 17–18.

17. Brooke, *Bridging the Divide*, 197; Memo, From: Rich, To: Marilyn (March 18, 1970), Box 419, Folder: Carswell #2, EB Papers.

18. *CR* (March 19, 1970), 8061–8062.

19. *CR* (March 19, 1970), 8061–8067.

20. "Exchange of Letters with Senator William B. Saxbe," April 1, 1970, *The American Presidency Project*, University of California, Santa Barbara, www.presidency.ucsb.edu/ws/index.php?pid=2931#axzz1PDAQA8NT.

21. "New England Can Save the Court," *BG*, April 1, 1970.

22. "Four Crucial Nays: Why They Did It," *Time*, April 20, 1970; Brooke, *Bridging the Divide*, 198; Fred Graham, "A Major Setback," *NYT*, April 9, 1970; Harris, *Decision*, 183.

23. Graham, "A Major Setback"; Brooke, *Bridging the Divide*, 198; Harris, *Decision*, 199.

24. *CR* (April 8, 1970), 10769; Graham, "A Major Setback"; "How the Senators Voted," *NYT*, April 9, 1970; Brooke, *Bridging the Divide*, 198; Harris, *Decision*, 201.

25. *CR* (April 8, 1970), 10769; Graham, "A Major Setback"; "How the Senators Voted"; Brooke, *Bridging the Divide*, 198; Harris, *Decision*, 201–202.

26. "The Carswell Decision," *NYT*, April 9, 1970; "The Rejection of Carswell," *BG*, April 9, 1970; "Senator Brooke's Battles," *BSB*, April 9, 1970.

27. Shirley Chisholm to Edward Brooke (April 17, 1970), Box 178, Folder: General Correspondence: Shirley Chisholm, EB Papers.

28. Interview with Ruth Batson, by Jackie Shearer, November 9, 1988, *Eyes on the Prize II Interviews*, Henry Hampton Collection, Film and Media Archive, Washington University Libraries, http://digital.wustl.edu/e/eii/eiiweb/bat5427.0911.011ruthbatson .html.

29. S.J. Micciche, "Boston School Board, in Capital, Disputes HEW Imbalance Claim," *BG*, February 4, 1972.

30. Francis Sargent, *The Sargent Years: Selected Public Papers of Francis W. Sargent, Governor 1969–1975* (Boston: S.N., 1976), 108, 110, 152; *BSB*, July 13, 1972.

31. Sargent, *The Sargent Years*, 204–205.

32. Michael Ross and William Berg, *"I Respectfully Disagree with the Judge's Order": The Boston School Desegregation Controversy* (Washington, DC: University Press of America, 1981), 123, 127.

33. Sargent, *The Sargent Years*, 260–261.

34. *BSB*, June 13, 1974; Gary Orfield, *Must We Bus?: Segregated Schools and National Policy* (Washington, DC: Brookings Institution, 1978), 118.

35. Interview with Ruth Batson, by Jackie Shearer; Interview with Tom Atkins, by Jackie Shearer, October 11, 1988, *Eyes on the Prize II Interviews*; Formisano, *Boston Against Busing*, 54.

36. Interview with Edward Brooke, by Author.

37. Interview with Edward Brooke, by Author.

38. Orfield, *Must We Bus?*, 267.

39. *CR* (May 15, 1974), 14853–14854; Stephen Wermiel, "Brooke Calls Defeat of Antibusing Plan a 'Victory' in Fight for Desegregation," *BG*, May 16, 1974; Stephen Wermiel, "Mass. Delegation Mixed on Busing," *BG*, May 20, 1974; Orfield, *Must We Bus?*, 262; Edward Brooke, "Dear Friend" letter (June 11, 1974), Box 418, Folder: Subject File—Busing, 1974–1975, EB Papers.

40. *CR* (May 15, 1974), 14878–14880; Wermiel, "Brooke Calls Defeat of Antibusing Plan a 'Victory' in Fight for Desegregation"; "A Scary Squeaker!," *BSB*, May 23, 1974; Wermiel, "Mass. Delegation Mixed on Busing."

41. *CR* (May 15, 1974), 14925.

42. "Sargent's School Plan 'Dead Wrong': Brooke," *BG*, June 2, 1974.

43. Richard Connolly, "Kennedy Jeered by Hub Busing Foes," *BG*, September 9, 1974; Ken Botwright, "A Rally for Parents and Pupils—Not Kennedy," *BG*, September 10, 1974.

44. Connolly, "Kennedy Jeered by Hub Busing Foes"; Mary Thornton, "No One Expected Kennedy at Rally—Including Himself," *BG*, September 10, 1974; Bob Sales, "Sen. Kennedy Jeered from Stage at Rally," *BG*, September 10, 1974.

45. Sales, "Sen. Kennedy Jeered from Stage at Rally"; Thornton, "No One Expected Kennedy at Rally—Including Himself."

46. Lukas, *Common Ground*, 241.

47. Jeanne Theoharis, "'We Saved the City': Black Struggles for Educational Equality in Boston, 1960–1976," *Radical History Review*, Issue 81 (Fall 2001), 78, 82–83.

48. Interview with Tom Atkins, by Jackie Shearer; Eric Moskowitz and Mark Feeney, "Civil Rights Trailblazer Atkins Dies at 69," *BG*, June 29, 2008.

49. Interview with Tom Atkins, by Jackie Shearer; Formisano, *Boston Against Busing*, 112, 63.

50. Lupo, *Liberty's Chosen Home*, 210, 11; Elizabeth Neal, "Southern View," Letter to the Editor, *BG*, September 19, 1974; Barbara Hodges, "Where Were You?," Letter to the Editor, *BG*, October 2, 1974. A resident of Hufsmith, Texas, wrote: "What's the matter with you damn Yankees. We've been enjoying forced busing down here for several years, thanks to your Senator's efforts." Matthew Miertschin, "Thanks to You . . . ," Letter to the Editor, *BG*, September 30, 1974; Jimmy Howle, "Sure Do Admire . . . ," Letter to the Editor, *BG*, September 30, 1974.

51. Jim Evans, "Little Rock's Question," Letter to the Editor, *BG*, October 1, 1974.

52. Peter DiBartolo, "Boston Nightmare," Letter to the Editor, *BG*, September 30, 1974; Mark Brightman, "Damaged Pride," Letter to the Editor, *BG*, September 30, 1974.

53. "Busing Works, N.C. Students Tell Boston," *BG*, October 15, 1974; "Letters to Boston: 'Together, We Get a Surprisingly Lot Done,'" *BG*, October 19, 1974; "4 Boston Students Visiting South 'For Lesson in Racial Relations,'" *BG*, October 21, 1974.

54. Robert Rosenthal and James Ayres, "2000 Busing Foes Rally, Then Harass Democrats," *BG*, October 15, 1974; "Violence Opens 5th Week of School Busing," *BG*, October 16, 1974.

55. Carol Murphy to Gregory Anrig and Edward Brooke (September 25, 1974), Box 216, Folder: Busing, 1974, EB Papers; Carolyn Toronto to Arthur Garrity, Edward Brooke, and Ted Kennedy, Undated, Box 216, Folder: Busing, 1974, EB Papers.

56. Edward Brooke, "Begin busing letter," Box 216, Folder: Busing, 1974, EB Papers.

57. Brooke, "Begin busing letter."

58. Brooke, "Begin busing letter."

59. Stephen Wermiel, "Laws Which Limit Busing Have No Effect on City," *BG*, October 13, 1974.

60. John W. Lewis Jr., "Brooke Blocks Move to Kill Penalties For Disobeying School Mixing Orders," *Pittsburgh Courier*, November 30, 1974; William Robbins, "Senate Cuts Off Filibuster," *NYT*, December 15, 1974.

61. "Block Anti-Busing Move," *CD*, December 19, 1974; "NAACP and Brooke Lead in Holt Amendment Defeat," *AN*, January 11, 1975.

62. Edward Brooke to the Editor of the *Boston Globe* (December 23, 1974), Box 216, Folder: Busing, 1974, EB Papers; Edward Brooke, "Boston Crossroads," *BG*, December 26, 1974; "Brooke Appeals for Peaceful Integration in Hub Schools," *Boston Herald-American*, December 25, 1974.

63. Edward Brooke to the Editor of the *Boston Globe*.

64. Edward Brooke to the Editor of the *Boston Globe*.

65. Edward Brooke to the Editor of the *Boston Globe*.

66. Orfield, *Must We Bus?*, 273; Richard Madden, "Senate Liberals Fail to Shut Off Debate on a Measure That Would Curb Busing," *NYT*, September 24, 1975; "Should School

Busing Be Stopped?," *U.S. News & World Report*, October 20, 1975, 33; Brett Gadsden, *Between North and South: Delaware, Desegregation, and the Myth of American Sectionalism* (Philadelphia: University of Pennsylvania Press, 2013), 1–3, 228.

67. Nick Thimmesch, "Busing: The Hypocrisy in Washington," *Saturday Evening Post*, April 1976, 40.

68. "Antibusing Measure Approved in Senate," *NYT*, September 18, 1975; Martin Nolan, "The Cure and the Ailment," *BG*, September 23, 1975; Madden, "Senate Liberals Fail to Shut Off Debate on a Measure That Would Curb Busing."

69. David Nyhan, "Antibusing Move Decried by Brooke," *BG*, September 19, 1975.

70. John Mathews, "Liberal Flight: Fooling with Busing," *New Republic*, October 11, 1975.

71. Stephen Wermiel, "Liberal Shifts Altering Senate Stand on Busing," *BG*, September 28, 1975.

72. Ralph Neas to Edward Brooke (October 1, 1975), "Interviews on Busing and Last Week's Debate on the Labor-HEW Appropriations Bill," Box 219, Folder: Busing, 1975, EB Papers.

73. Walter Robinson and Stephen Wermiel, "Atkins Says Amendment Won't Affect Boston," *BG*, March 6, 1975.

74. "Should School Busing Be Stopped?"

75. "Should School Busing Be Stopped?"

76. "Should School Busing Be Stopped?"

77. George Croft, "Won't Aid Antibus Amendment, Brooke Tells ROAR Delegation," *BG*, December 24, 1975.

78. Carl Rowan, "Brooke Challenges Revival of 'Separate But Equal' Ploy," *Washington Star*, December 7, 1975.

79. Mrs. John E. Naoum to Edward Brooke (July 11, 1975), Box 219, Folder: Busing, 1975, EB Papers; Edward Brooke to Mrs. John E. Naoum (July 17, 1975), Box 219, Folder: Busing, 1975, EB Papers; Edward Brooke to Irena Greatorex (July 12, 1976), Box 219, Folder: Busing, 1975, EB Papers.

80. "Doctor, Convicted in Abortion, Charges Prejudice Barred Fair Trial in Boston," *NYT*, February 17, 1975. Also see Sara Dubow, *Ourselves Unborn: A History of the Fetus in Modern America* (New York: Oxford University Press, 2010).

81. Joseph Corkery to Edward Brooke (July 30, 1976), Box 223, Folder: Abortion, 1976, EB Papers.

82. Lukas, *Common Ground*, 324–326.

83. Sally Jacobs, "The Unfinished Chapter," *BG Magazine*, March 5, 2000.

84. "Brooke's Role in the Senate," *BG*, August 26, 1978.

85. Memo, August 16, 1978, RE: Roxbury Walk-through for the Cross-Over Effort, Box 633, Folder: Campaign Materials—U.S. Senate, 1978, Memos To and From Staff, EB Papers; "We Need Your Vote," *BSB*, September 14, 1978.

86. Michael Fields, "Sen. Brooke Squeaks by Nelson," *BSB*, September 21, 1978; Norman Lockman, "Brooke Building His Campaign on 12 Years' Experience," *BG*, September 25, 1978.

87. Jack Germond and Jules Witcover, "Race Key to Senate Challenge," *BG*, September 2, 1978.

88. Norman Lockman, "Frank, Reagan Back Brooke; CPPAX Endorses Tsongas," *BG*, October 13, 1978; Robert Healy, "The Biggest Challenge Yet For Tsongas," *BG*, October 13, 1978.

89. Memo, To: Sen. Brooke, From: Rick, RE: The Fall Campaign (September 21, 1978), Box 633, Folder: Campaign Materials—U.S. Senate, 1978, Memos To and From Staff, EB Papers.

90. Brooke, *Bridging the Divide*, 255; "Brooke's Brighter Day," *Washington Post*, October 29, 1978.

91. Norman Lockman, "Brooke, Tsongas in Kid-Gloves Match," *BG*, October 27, 1978.

92. Memo, From: Rick, To: Senator Brooke, RE: Debates—Last Week and Tomorrow Night (October 30, 1978), Box 633, Folder: Campaign Materials—U.S. Senate, 1978, EB Papers; Memo, From: Rick, To: Senator Brooke, Draft of Proposed Opening Statement (October 30, 1978), Box 633, Folder: Campaign Materials—U.S. Senate, 1978, EB Papers.

93. Mary McGrory, "Brooke-Tsongas: Superstar Realist vs. Dogged Idealist," *BG*, November 1, 1978.

94. "Brooke and Tsongas Speak for Themselves," *BG*, November 2, 1978.

95. Barney Frank, Joe Rauh, and Elizabeth Dunn, "Injustice to Brooke," Letter to the Editor, *BG*, November 6, 1978.

96. Norman Lockman, "Brooke Concedes, Praises Tsongas," *BG*, November 8, 1978; "How to Lose, How to Win," *BG*, November 9, 1978.

97. Norman Lockman, "The Demise of Brooke: Six Months of Troubles," *BG*, November 9, 1978; *BSB*, November 9, 1978.

98. Bryant Rollins, "Kennedy Behind Brooke Defeat," *AN*, November 11, 1978; Robert Robinson, "Brooke's Race a Factor?," Letter to the Editor, *BG*, November 15, 1978.

99. Brooke, *Bridging the Divide*, 259.

CHAPTER 8: A TALE OF TWO HARTFORDS

1. Samuel Freedman, "In Hartford, It's the Best and the Worst of Times," *NYT*, April 14, 1983; Matt Bai, "The Great Connecticut Country-Club Crackup," *NYT Magazine*, September 26, 2010, 44.

2. Frank Andrews Stone, *African American Connecticut: African Origins, New England Roots* (Storrs, CT: University of Connecticut, 1991), 248; Jose Cruz, *Identity and Power: Puerto Rican Politics and the Challenge of Ethnicity* (Philadelphia: Temple University Press, 1998), 22.

3. Clayborne Carson, ed., *The Papers of Martin Luther King, Jr., Volume I: Called to Serve, January 1929–June 1951* (Berkeley: University of California Press, 1992), 112, 115, 117; Stephen Oates, *Let the Trumpet Sound: A Life of Martin Luther King, Jr.* (New York: Harper & Row, 1982), 17.

4. Coretta Scott King, *My Life With Martin Luther King, Jr.* (New York: Holt, 1969), 85. King would return to work the tobacco farms in the summer of 1947.

5. Cruz, *Identity and Power*, 26–27.

6. Howard Sherman, "Avenue Is 'Awakening,'" *HC*, July 5, 1981; Stone, *African American Connecticut*, 260. On urban renewal in New Haven, see Fred Powledge, *Model City: A Test of American Liberalism—One Town's Efforts to Rebuild Itself* (New York: Simon

& Schuster, 1970), and Rae, *City*; on Boston, see Tim Rose, *Civic Wars*; on New York, see Joel Schwartz, *The New York Approach: Robert Moses, Urban Liberals, and Redevelopment of the Inner City* (Columbus: Ohio State University Press, 1993), and Robert Caro, *The Power Broker: Robert Moses and the Fall of New York* (New York: Alfred A. Knopf, 1974).

7. Herbert Janick, *A Diverse People: Connecticut, 1914 to the Present* (Chester, CT: The Pequot Press, 1975), 95; Pierre Clavel, *The Progressive City: Planning and Participation, 1969–1984* (New Brunswick, NJ: Rutgers University Press, 1986), 24; Jose Cruz, "A Decade of Change: Puerto Rican Politics in Hartford, Connecticut, 1969–1979," *Journal of American Ethnic History* (Spring 1997), 49–50; Cruz, *Identity and Power*, 56–60; Jose Cruz, "Maria Sanchez: Godmother of the Puerto Rican Community," *Hog River Journal*, Summer 2003.

8. John Rosenberg, "Hartford's Economy Is Buffered by Aetna," *NYT*, August 24, 1980; John Rosenberg, "Employment for Black and Hispanic Residents at Low Ebb," *NYT*, March 22, 1981; Susan Eaton, *The Children in Room E4: American Education on Trial* (Chapel Hill, NC: Algonquin, 2007), 6.

9. Cruz, *Identity and Power*, 20–21, 102; Kirk Johnson, "Corporate Elite a Fading Force Over Hartford," *NYT*, September 7, 1992; Interview with Thirman Milner, by Author, Hartford, Connecticut, January 17, 2012.

10. Pierre Clavel, *Activists in City Hall: The Progressive Response to the Reagan Era in Boston and Chicago* (Ithaca: Cornell University Press, 2010), 19–20; Clavel, *The Progressive City*, 19–56.

11. Alan Dicara, "Wanted: Access to Suburban Jobs," *NYT*, June 29, 1980; Matthew Wald, "Hartford, Facing Many Problems, Awaits Carter," *NYT*, September 11, 1979; Cruz, *Identity and Power*, 26; Clavel, *The Progressive City*, 20; Ellsworth Strong Grant and Marion Hepburn Grant, *The City of Hartford, 1784–1984* (Hartford, CT: Connecticut Historical Society, 1986), 179; Ed Laiscell, "Milner Calls for Employment Policy," *The Hartford Inquirer*, June 2, 1982; Ronald Smothers, "Manchester Sets Hiring Goal," *NYT*, August 16, 1981.

12. Thirman Milner, *Up From Slavery: A History From Slavery to City Hall in New England* (Enumclaw, WA: Pleasant Word, 2009), 85; Interview with Thirman Milner, by Author.

13. Milner, *Up From Slavery*, 27.

14. Milner, *Up From Slavery*, 48.

15. Interview with Thirman Milner, by Author; Jon Sandberg, "Milner Has His Chance to Focus on Issues Besides Race," *HC*, August 2, 1981.

16. Interview with Thirman Milner, by Author; Milner, *Up From Slavery*, 68–69; Bill Grava, "Jubilation Marks Milner Win," *HC*, September 13, 1978.

17. Interview with Thirman Milner, by Author.

18. Milner, *Up From Slavery*, 76.

19. David Barrett and Marc Gunther, "City Democrats Set Sights on Council Posts," *HC*, March 16, 1981; "Milner's Possible Run For Mayor," Letter to the Editor, *HC*, March 18, 1981.

20. Marc Gunther, "Milner Preparing to Run For Mayor," *HC*, April 30, 1981; Jon Sandberg, "Milner Announces Mayoral Bid," *HC*, June 14, 1981.

21. Sandberg, "Milner Has His Chance to Focus on Issues Besides Race"; Interview with Thirman Milner, by Author.

22. Sandberg, "Milner Has His Chance to Focus on Issues Besides Race."

23. "Democratic Mayoral Choice," *HC*, August 26, 1981; "Why Milner?," *HC*, August 26, 1981.

24. Interview with Thirman Milner, by Author.

25. Marc Gunther, "Athanson Target of Opponents' Attacks During Radio Debate," *HC*, September 3, 1981; Marc Gunther, "Athanson's Power Main Issue," *HC*, September 5, 1981.

26. Terese Karmel, "City Mayoral Candidates Predict Victory; Discount Poll," *HC*, September 7, 1981.

27. "Milner Volunteers Shaped Election," *HC*, September 9, 1981; Jon Sandberg and Howard Sherman, "Dissident Black Democrats Buoyed by Milner's Showing," *HC*, September 11, 1981.

28. Kay Cahill, "Cliffhanger Vote Drains Candidates," *HC*, September 9, 1981.

29. Cahill, "Cliffhanger Vote Drains Candidates"; Bruce Kauffman, "The Mayor and the Media," *Hartford Advocate*, April 21, 1982.

30. Marc Gunther, "Athanson Defeats Milner by 94 Votes," *HC*, September 9, 1981; Marc Gunther, "City Votes Split on Racial Lines," *HC*, September 10, 1981.

31. Gunther, "City Votes Split on Racial Lines."

32. Interview with Thirman Milner, by Author.

33. Interview with Thirman Milner, by Author; Milner, *Up From Slavery*, 81. Robert Ludgin claimed no first-hand knowledge of such trickery, but he did not doubt that the Democratic Party leaders had their hands in those absentee ballots. "The machine knew where the votes were." Interview with Robert Ludgin, by Author, by Telephone, June 6, 2012.

34. Kay Cahill, "New Vote Finding Gives Milner Hope," *HC*, September 19, 1981.

35. Kay Cahill and Karlynn Carrington, "Milner Files Suit Challenging Primary," *HC*, September 12, 1981; Milner, *Up From Slavery*, 82.

36. Kay Cahill, "Milner Alleges Vote Conspiracy," *HC*, September 16, 1981; Jeanette DeBrady, "Recap on the Milner Hearings," *Northend Agents*, September 21, 1981.

37. Kay Cahill, "Democrats to Rerun Mayoral Primary," *HC*, September 23, 1981; Jeanette DeBrady, "Milner's Victory Continues," *Northend Agents*, September 28, 1981; Interview with Thirman Milner, by Author.

38. Kay Cahill, "Voting Machine Erasure Criticized by Prosecutor," *HC*, September 24, 1981.

39. Howard Sherman, "Athanson Drive Hit by Fatigue," *HC*, October 5, 1981; "Candidates Volley Charges," *HC*, October 6, 1981.

40. Thomas Sugrue, *Not Even Past: Barack Obama and the Burden of Race* (Princeton, NJ: Princeton University Press, 2010), 16, 25–26, 29–30.

41. Kay Cahill, "Black Ministers Exhort Congregations to Back 'Brother Milner' in Primary," *HC*, October 6, 1981.

42. Suzanne Bilello, "Jackson Makes Milner Pitch at Rally," *HC*, October 6, 1981.

43. Howard Sherman, "Race Issue Dominates Debate of Mayoral Candidates," *HC*, October 6, 1981; Jon Sandberg, "Mayoral Candidates Plow Old Ground in Debate," *HC*, October 7, 1981; Jon Sandberg and Howard Sherman, "Voting Along Racial Lines in Hartford: A Matter of Pride or Bigotry?," *HC*, October 11, 1981; Kay Cahill, "Labor Council Gives Support to Milner in 1st Primary Move," *HC*, October 8, 1981.

44. Cruz, *Identity and Power*, 130–132, 96; Jon Sandberg, "Hispanic Congressman Boosts Milner Campaign," October 10, 1981; Crescent Justin, "Now That the Hartford Democratic Primary Is Over, What Next?," *Northend Agents*, October 19, 1981. The Puerto Rican population was largest in the corridor from Boston to Brooklyn. Their presence shattered any notions of a black-white paradigm. Yet they were often pushed to one side of this binary or the other. For instance, Massachusetts's 1965 Racial Imbalance Act forced public schools to categorize each student as either white or nonwhite. The Boston School Committee tried to exploit this. In majority-black schools, the committee counted Puerto Rican (as well as Chinese) students as "white," so as to lessen the apparent racial imbalance. Massachusetts State Advisory Committee to the United States Commission on Civil Rights, Issues of Concern to Puerto Ricans in Boston and Springfield (Washington, DC: U.S. Commission on Civil Rights, 1972), 50. By 2010, Puerto Ricans would comprise 35 percent of Hartford's population—the highest percentage of any city in the nation. Brad Kane, "Booming Hispanic Market Creates Business Opportunities," *Hartford Business Journal Online*, April 15, 2012.

45. "The Primary, Again!" *HC*, October 9, 1981.

46. Milner, *Up From Slavery*, 84; Interview with Thirman Milner, by Author.

47. Jon Sandberg, "Milner Captures City Primary Rerun," *HC*, October 14, 1981; Kay Cahill, "Milner Savors Win as Citywide Victory," *HC*, October 14, 1981; Matthew Wald, "Milner Discounts Race as Hartford Victory Factor," *NYT*, October 15, 1981.

48. Kay Cahill, "Primary Stays Alive; City Orders Recount," *HC*, October 15, 1981; Howard Sherman, "Milner Is the Winner; But Democrats Unsure of Primary's Effects," *HC*, October 18, 1981; Wald, "Milner Discounts Race as Hartford Victory Factor."

49. Wald, "Milner Discounts Race as Hartford Victory Factor"; Vivian Martin, "3 Mayoral Candidates Spar in Spirited Debate," *HC*, October 28, 1981; "Hartford's Mayoral Candidates Address the Issues," *HC*, November 1, 1981.

50. Ludgin won 27 percent and McGarry won 16 percent. Jon Sandberg, "Landslide Win Caps Milner Drive," *HC*, November 4, 1981; Kay Cahill, "Milner Yet to Turn Popularity Into Clout," *HC*, March 16, 1982.

51. Sandberg, "Landslide Win Caps Milner Drive."

52. Bob Englehart, "Gimme Five!," *HC*, November 4, 1981; Grant and Grant, *The City of Hartford*, 9.

53. "Transcript of Historic Inauguration Address of Thirman Milner," *Northend Agents*, December 7, 1981.

54. "Transcript of Historic Inauguration Address of Thirman Milner."

55. Kevin Thomas, "Milner Urges 3-Way Partnership in City," *HC*, November 12, 1981; "Thirman Milner Mayor," *Northend Agents*, November 9, 1981.

56. Cahill, "Milner Yet to Turn Popularity Into Clout"; Suzanne Bilello, "Milner Challenges Developer on Minority Hiring," *HC*, May 27, 1982.

57. Michael Vitez, "Minority Contractors Out in Cold," *HC*, December 14, 1981; Cahill, "Milner Yet to Turn Popularity Into Clout"; Michael Vitez, "Mayor Pressures Council to Name Minority Company," *HC*, April 3, 1982; Bilello, "Milner Challenges Developer on Minority Hiring"; Gwen Bryant, "Manager's Report on Hartford Plan: Still Not Enough Compliance," *Northend Agents*, May 17, 1982; Jon Turner, "Contractors Voice Concerns," *Hartford Inquirer*, August 4, 1982; Kalu Wilcox, "Federal Grant to City of Hartford Will Aid Minority Businesses," *Northend Agents*, May 20, 1985.

58. Interview with Robert Ludgin, by Author.

59. Robert Hamilton, "NAACP Hosts Mayor Milner in Push for New Members," *Willimantic Chronicle*, Reprinted in *Northend Agents*, June 14, 1982; Jon Sandberg, "Milner Urges U.S. Plan to Share Surplus Food," *HC*, February 9, 1983; Jon Sandberg, "Milner Backed on Food Plan," *HC*, March 5, 1983; Arnold Hirsch, "Harold and Dutch: A Comparative Look at the First Black Mayors of Chicago and New Orleans," in Raymond Mohl, ed., *The Making of Urban America* (Wilmington, DE: Scholarly Resources, 1988).

60. Bob Englehart, "Yes, I Will Run Again," *HC*, February 23, 1983.

61. "What Was the Cartoonist Saying?," *HC*, February 26, 1983; "Editorial Cartoon Castigated, Defended," *HC*, March 1, 1983; Gwen Bryant, "Courant's Cartoon Misses Mark," *HC*, February 28, 1983; "Letter to Ministerial Alliance," *HC*, March 23, 1983.

62. Marilyn Marshall, "Hartford: Blacks Gain Political Clout in Connecticut's Historic Capital," *Ebony*, December 1982, 31–34.

63. "Comments on Political Cartoon," *HC*, March 4, 1983.

64. "Comments on Political Cartoon."

65. Rick Taylor, "Courant Cartoon Called Racist," *HC*, February 28, 1983; Richard Madden, "3 Blacks' Campaigns Point Up Political Change in Connecticut," *NYT*, October 27, 1983.

66. "The Mayor's 'Fishbowl,'" *HC*, October 7, 1983; "The Next Mayor of Hartford," *HC*, October 30, 1983.

67. Jon Sandberg, "Council Passes Development Plan; Milner Threatens Veto," *HC*, December 3, 1983.

68. Jon Sandberg, "Milner Vetoes Key Elements of Downtown Plan," *HC*, December 7, 1983.

69. "Two Avoidable Vetoes," *HC*, December 7, 1983; Bob Englehart, "Milner's Downtown Plan," *HC*, December 8, 1983.

70. Jon Sandberg, "Milner Gains Local Support on Downtown Zoning Vetoes," *HC*, December 10, 1983; "Move Ahead With Zoning," *HC*, February 14, 1984.

71. Jon Sandberg, "Council Backs Downtown Plan," *HC*, February 15, 1984; "Milner Undecided on Zoning Plan," *HC*, February 16, 1985; Joseph Rodriguez, "Mayor Faults Zoning Plan, but Forgoes Veto," *HC*, February 22, 1984.

72. Vivian Martin, "Black Mayors' Group to Meet in Hartford," *HC*, March 28, 1985; Thirman Milner, "Host City Symbolizes the Dream," *HC*, April 17, 1985.

73. Milner, "Host City Symbolizes the Dream"; Richard Benedetto, "Host to Black Mayors Promotes New England," *USA Today*, April 18, 1985; Vivian Martin, "O'Neill Greets Black Mayors, Decries Cutbacks," *HC*, April 19, 1985.

74. Gloria Johnson, Letter to the Editor, *Northend Agents*, April 22, 1985; Tao Woolfe, "City Residents Call Conference Proof of Blacks' New Power," *HC*, April 20, 1985.

75. Lynne Garrett, "Child Learns Dreams Live in City, Too," *HC*, May 10, 1985.

76. Kirk Johnson, "Hartford, Its Boom Over, Sees Downtown Decaying," *NYT*, August 22, 1990; Louise Simmons, *Organizing in Hard Times: Labor and Neighborhoods in Hartford* (Philadelphia: Temple University Press, 1994), 35; Richard Madden, "Two Hartfords Are at Issue in Mayor Race," *NYT*, October 29, 1987.

77. Simmons, *Organizing in Hard Times*, 1–2; Cruz, *Identity and Power*, 154; Segregation in schools led to a landmark lawsuit, *Sheff v. O'Neill*. See Eaton, *The Children in Room E4*; "Hartford at a Glance," *NYT*, February 7, 1988.

78. Freedman, "In Hartford, It's the Best and the Worst of Times."

79. Freedman, "In Hartford, It's the Best and the Worst of Times."

80. Interview with Deval Patrick, by Author, by Telephone, June 4, 2013; James Green, "The Making of Mel King's Rainbow Coalition: Political Changes in Boston, 1963–1983," in James Jennings and Mel King, eds., *From Access to Power* (Cambridge, MA: Schenkman, 1986), 126.

81. Fox Butterfield and Constance Hays, "A Boston Tragedy," *NYT*, January 15, 1990.

CHAPTER 9: THE GHOST OF WILLIE TURKS

1. Joseph Fried, "Jurors Find Slaying of Black in Brooklyn Was Manslaughter," *NYT*, March 9, 1983; Joseph Fried, "Second Brooklyn Youth on Trial in Killing of Black," *NYT*, July 10, 1983; Joseph Fried, "Court Is Told Defendant Struck Victim," March 3, 1983; Leonard Buder, "2 More Suspects Seized by Police in Mob Assault," *NYT*, June 29, 1982.

2. Jim Sleeper, "The Limits of Indignation," *The American Prospect*, December 4, 2000; Sydney Schanberg, "The Walls Still Stand," *NYT*, July 3, 1982.

3. Ken Burns, Sarah Burns, and David McMahon, *The Central Park Five* (Florentine Films, 2012).

4. Nicolaus Mills, "Howard Beach—Anatomy of a Lynching," *Dissent*, Fall 1987, Reprinted in Jim Sleeper, ed., *In Search of New York* (New Brunswick, NJ: Transaction, 1989), 74; John DeSantis, *For the Color of His Skin: The Murder of Yusuf Hawkins and the Trial of Bensonhurst* (New York: Pharos Books, 1991), 34; Irving Howe, "Social Retreat and the *Tumler*," in Sleeper, ed., *In Search of New York*, 1.

5. Robert McFadden, "A 3-Term Mayor as Brash, Shrewd and Colorful as the City He Led," *NYT*, February 2, 2013.

6. McNickle, *To Be Mayor of New York*, 305; Sam Roberts, "A Racial Attack That, Years Later, Is Still Being Felt," *NYT*, December 18, 2011.

7. Charles Hynes and Bob Drury, *Incident at Howard Beach: The Case for Murder* (New York: Putnam, 1990), 11–21; Joseph Fried, "Attacker Describes Death at Howard Beach," *NYT*, October 23, 1987.

8. Hynes and Drury, *Incident at Howard Beach*, 22–24, 168–174; Fried, "Attacker Describes Death at Howard Beach."

9. James Baldwin, "A Report from Occupied Territory," *The Nation*, July 11, 1966.

10. Jeffrey Trachtman, "Howard Beach Turns a Beam on Racial Tensions," Letter to the Editor, *NYT*, January 11, 1987.

11. Roger Wilkins, "Howard Beach Started 200 Years Ago," *NYT*, January 5, 1987.

12. Bruce Schulman, *The Seventies: The Great Shift in American Culture, Society, and Politics* (New York: Free Press, 2001), 213–214.

13. Michael Oreskes, "Why Howard Beach?; Notoriety of the Queens Attack Builds on Anger Left From Earlier Assaults," *NYT*, January 15, 1987.

14. Hynes and Drury, *Incident at Howard Beach*, 35; "Howard Beach: Judged and Prejudged," *NYT*, December 23, 1987.

15. Howard French, "Hatred and Social Isolation May Spur Acts of Racial Violence, Experts Say," *NYT*, September 4, 1989.

16. White, *Here Is New York*, 26.

17. White, *Here Is New York*, 43.

18. Sarah Burns, *The Central Park Five: A Chronicle of a City Wilding* (New York: Alfred A. Knopf, 2011).

19. Michael Stone, "What Really Happened in Central Park," *New York*, August 14, 1989, 30; Sam Roberts, "Park Rampage and Mayor Race: Fear and Politics," *NYT*, May 1, 1989; Lisa Foderado, "Angered by Attack, Trump Urges Return of the Death Penalty," *NYT*, May 1, 1989; Joan Didion, "New York: Sentimental Journeys," *New York Review of Books*, January 17, 1991; "Lunging for Death," *NYT*, May 4, 1989; "The Jogger and the Wolf Pack," *NYT*, April 26, 1989; Burns, Burns, and McMahon, *The Central Park Five*.

20. Burns, *The Central Park Five*, 118.

21. Spike Lee with Lisa Jones, *Do the Right Thing* (New York: Fireside, 1989), 24, 34; Michael Kaufman, "In a New Film, Spike Lee Tries to Do the Right Thing," *NYT*, June 25, 1989; Michael Marriott, "Raw Reactions to Film on Racial Tension," *NYT*, July 3, 1989; *Do the Right Thing* (Forty Acres and a Mule Productions, 1989).

22. Michael Stone, "What Really Happened in Bensonhurst," *New York*, November 6, 1989, 47; Celestine Bohlen, "In Bensonhurst, Grief Mixed With Shame and Blunt Bias," *NYT*, August 28, 1989.

23. Stone, "What Really Happened in Bensonhurst," 54.

24. Stone, "What Really Happened in Bensonhurst," 54; Ralph Blumenthal, "Black Youth Is Killed by Whites; Brooklyn Attack Is Called Racial," *NYT*, August 25, 1989.

25. *Frontline: Seven Days in Bensonhurst* (PBS, May 1990).

26. Blumenthal, "Black Youth Is Killed by Whites."

27. *Frontline: Seven Days in Bensonhurst*; Nick Ravo, "Marchers and Brooklyn Youths Trade Racial Jeers," *NYT*, August 27, 1989.

28. DeSantis, *For the Color of His Skin*, 117; Kirk Johnson, "A New Generation of Racism Is Seen," *NYT*, August 27, 1989; Nick Ravo, "Marchers and Brooklyn Youths Trade Racial Jeers," *NYT*, August 27, 1989.

29. Robert Carter, "Thirty-Five Years Later: New Perspectives on *Brown*," in Herbert Hill and James E. Jones Jr., eds., *Race in America: The Struggle for Equality* (Madison, WI: University of Wisconsin Press, 1993), 84, 83.

30. *Frontline: Seven Days in Bensonhurst*; "What the Mayor Didn't Say," *NYT*, August 30, 1989; Neil Lewis, "Bishop Questions Protest Marches in Racial Slaying," *NYT*, August 30, 1989.

31. Felicia Lee, "At Youth's Wake, Grief, Anger and Talk of Racism," *NYT*, August 30, 1989; *Frontline: Seven Days in Bensonhurst*.

32. *Frontline: Seven Days in Bensonhurst*; Elizabeth Kolbert, "Youth's Funeral Focuses on Racial Divisions," *NYT*, August 31, 1989.

33. Michael Oreskes, "Blacks in New York: The Anguish of Political Failure," *NYT*, March 31, 1987.

34. Joe Klein, "Can Dinkins Do It?," *New York*, July 31, 1989, 33.

35. Sam Roberts, "Dinkins Is Customizing His Stock Message," *NYT*, August 23, 1989; McNickle, *To Be Mayor of New York*, 295; Earl Caldwell, "Dinkins—The Man and the Moment," *New York Daily News*, February 15, 1989.

36. Marttila & Kiley, Inc., "The David Dinkins Book of Numbers" (March 1989), Box 15, Folder 5, DD Papers, Columbia University Rare Book & Manuscript Library; Dennis Duggan, "Quiet Man Sizes Up the Mayor," *New York Newsday*, January 19, 1989.

37. Asher Arian, Arthur Goldberg, John Mollenkopf, and Edward Rogowsky, *Changing New York City Politics* (New York: Routledge, 1990), 6, 77. Asian Americans comprised roughly 7 percent of the city's overall population.

38. "Robert Abrams Endorsing Borough President David Dinkins," May 2, 1989, Box 15, Folder 7, DD Papers; David Dinkins, "Dear Friend," May 11, 1989, Box 14, Folder 8, DD Papers; Leonard Wacholder to David Dinkins (May 16, 1989), Box 24, Folder 3, DD Papers.

39. Barbara Ross, "Latino Poll: Dave Tops Rudy," *New York Daily News*, April 20, 1989; Tom Wicker, "Dinkins Out Front," *NYT*, June 23, 1989.

40. Roberts, "Dinkins Is Customizing His Stock Message."

41. Joe Klein, "Gandhi v. Gumby," *New York*, November 6, 1989; Letter from Richard Nygaard to David Dinkins, Undated, Box 16, Folder 2, DD Papers.

42. "Statement of Senator Edward M. Kennedy Endorsing David Dinkins for Mayor of New York City," September 5, 1989, Box 14, Folder 6, DD Papers.

43. David N. Dinkins, Press Conference with Jewish Supporters, September 6, 1989, Box 24, Folder 3, DD Papers; Rabbi Gilbert Klaperman, September 6, 1989, Box 24, Folder 4, DD Papers.

44. Celestine Bohlen, "Dinkins and Friends Exult in Victory," *NYT*, September 13, 1989.

45. Arian et al., *Changing New York City Politics*, 77, 84, 82; Frank Lynn, "Mayor Offers Help," *NYT*, September 13, 1989; "David Dinkins, With a Roar," *NYT*, September 13, 1989.

46. "Excerpt of the Victory Speeches of Dinkins and Giuliani," *NYT*, September 14, 1989.

47. Sam Roberts, "A Sense of Quiet Strength," *NYT*, September 13, 1989; Letter from Katsuya Abe to David Dinkins (September 27, 1989), Box 16, Folder 12, DD Papers.

48. McNickle, *To Be Mayor of New York*, 306.

49. Adam Clymer, "New York Mayoral Poll: Ethnic Groups' Variables," *NYT*, June 23, 1989.

50. Letter from Hugh Rubin to David Dinkins (September 13, 1989), Box 24, Folder 1, DD Papers.

51. Klein, "Gandhi v. Gumby"; Todd Purdum, "Giuliani Has Taunt for Dinkins: He's a Jesse Jackson Democrat," *NYT*, September 26, 1989; "David Dinkins for Mayor," *Jewish Daily Forward*, October 6, 1989.

52. Address by David N. Dinkins, Jewish Leadership Breakfast, October 12, 1989, Box 23, Folder 10, DD Papers; McNickle, *To Be Mayor of New York*, 308.

53. McNickle, *To Be Mayor of New York*, 309–312; "The Finish Line," *NYT*, November 4, 1989; Sam Roberts, "Giuliani Discounts Color as an Issue," *NYT*, November 1, 1989; Sam Roberts, "Giuliani Still Jabbing in Last Days of Race," *NYT*, November 4, 1989.

54. Statement by David N. Dinkins, On the Endorsements of Crown Heights Jewish Community Leaders & United States Senator Joseph Lieberman, October 30, 1989, Box 23, Folder 10, DD Papers.

55. Kevin Sack, "Dinkins's Vote-Getter in Brooklyn Has Big Army," *NYT*, November 6, 1989.

56. Sam Roberts, "Almost Lost at the Wire," *NYT*, November 9, 1989; Sam Roberts, "First Black Mayor," *NYT*, November 8, 1989; Joe Klein, "The New Mayor and the Crisis

of New York," *New York*, November 20, 1989, 38; "Final Tally: Still Dave," *New York Daily News*, December 14, 1989; McNickle, *To Be Mayor of New York*, 313; Arian et.al., *Changing New York City Politics*, 95.

57. McNickle, *To Be Mayor of New* York, 313; Arian et al., *Changing New York City Politics*, 95; Klein, "The New Mayor and the Crisis of New York," 38, 40.

58. "From Protest to Politics," *NYT*, November 9, 1989; Interview with David Dinkins, *National Visionary Leadership Project*, www.visionaryproject.org/dinkinsdavid/.

59. "Excerpt From Speech by Dinkins: A New Link," *NYT*, November 8, 1989; McNickle, *To Be Mayor of New* York, 313.

60. John Kifner, "The Mayor-Elect Inspires Pride, but It's Hardly Universal," *NYT*, November 9, 1989.

61. Letter from Robert Gentile to David Dinkins (November 9, 1989), Box 16, Folder 10, DD Papers.

62. Letter from David Wells to David Dinkins (November 8, 1989), Box 16, Folder 10, DD Papers.

63. R. W. Apple Jr., "Black Success With Measured Approach," *NYT*, November 8, 1989; Jonathan Yardley, "Virginia's Election: No Small Victory," *Washington Post*, November 20, 1989.

64. Mylon Winn, "The Election of Norman Rice as Mayor of Seattle," *PS: Political Science and Politics*, Vol. 23, No. 2 (June 1990), 158.

65. Christopher Daly, "Old-Line Ethnic 'Machine' Humbled in New Haven," *Washington Post*, September 14, 1989; Nick Ravo, "Ex-Athlete Revisits City Hall, but as Mayor," *NYT*, November 10, 1989; Mary Summers and Philip Klinkner, "The Daniels Election in New Haven and the Failure of the Deracialization Hypothesis," *Urban Affairs Quarterly*, Vol. 27, No. 2 (December 1991), 205, 213; Robert Dahl, *Who Governs?: Democracy and Power in an American City* (New Haven, CT: Yale University Press, 1961), 293; Douglas Rae, *City: Urbanism and Its End* (New Haven, CT: Yale University Press, 2003), 414; "The Parade of Cities," *Ebony*, February 1990, 31.

66. "Two Tyrannies," *NYT*, November 12, 1989. Hartford mayor Carrie Saxon Perry said, "The election of black politicians in states and cities that are majority white is of the same historical significance as the tearing down of the Berlin Wall. . . . It is a sign that we are moving towards a color-blind society." "What did 'Rainbow Tuesday' Mean?," *Ebony*, February 1990, 32.

67. Joe Klein, "Race: The Mess—A City on the Verge of a Nervous Breakdown," *New York*, May 28, 1990, 33; Andrew Maykuth, "N.Y. Mayor Seeks Calm as Racial Tensions Rise," *Philadelphia Inquirer*, May 12, 1990; William Glaberson, "The Bensonhurst Case," *NYT*, May 18, 1990; "The Charges Against Keith Mondello," *NYT*, May 19, 1990.

68. "'This City Is Sick of Violence': Dinkins's Address," *NYT*, May 12, 1990; Klein, "Race: The Mess," 32.

69. Klein, "Race: The Mess," 36.

70. Chris McNickle, *The Power of the Mayor: David Dinkins, 1990–1993* (New Brunswick, NJ: Transaction, 2013), 355; "Lee Brown's Legacy," *NYT*, August 4, 1992; Joseph Berger, "So, How'd He Do?," *NYT*, February 3, 2013.

71. Interview with David Dinkins, *National Visionary Leadership Project*.

72. Edward Shapiro, *Crown Heights: Blacks, Jews, and the 1991 Brooklyn Riot* (Waltham, MA: Brandeis University Press, 2006), 1–5.

73. James Barron, "Fear, Loss and Rage Tear Area," *NYT*, August 22, 1991; "Crown Heights—A Chronology," Box 40, Folder 7, DD Papers.

74. Shapiro, *Crown Heights*, 5–11.

75. Todd Purdum, "A Frustrated Dinkins Appeals for Peace," *NYT*, August 23, 1991; "He's the Mayor, Not a Magician," *NYT*, August 23, 1991.

76. James McKinley, "Dinkins, in TV Speech, Defends Handling of Crown Heights Tension," *NYT*, November 26, 1992.

77. McKinley, "Dinkins, in TV Speech, Defends Handling of Crown Heights Tension"; "Excerpts from Mayor Dinkins's Speech on Crown Hts. and Race," *NYT*, November 26, 1992.

78. "Excerpts from Mayor Dinkins's Speech on Crown Hts. and Race"; "A Stirring Holiday Sermon," *NYT*, November 26, 1992.

79. David Dinkins to Margie Ellenbogen, "Standard Crown Heights Response," Box 40, Folder 7, DD Papers; Robert McFadden, "Dinkins Plans Major Appeal for Harmony," *NYT*, November 25, 1992.

80. "Excerpts from Mayor Dinkins's Speech on Crown Hts. and Race."

81. Todd Purdum, "Crown Hts. Drives Contest for Mayor," *NYT*, December 7, 1992; Michael Powell, "In a Volatile City, a Stern Line on Race and Politics," *NYT*, July 22, 2007.

82. Todd Purdum, "Rudolph Giuliani and the Color of Politics in New York City," *NYT Magazine*, July 25, 1993; Sam Roberts, "The Murky Mix of Race, Competence and Politics," *NYT*, October 4, 1993.

83. Andrew Kirtzman, *Rudy Giuliani: Emperor of the* City (New York: William Morrow, 2000), 39–40; Jonathan Mahler, "The Making of Andrew Cuomo," *NYT Magazine*, August 11, 2010.

84. Elizabeth Kolbert, "Two Candidates Present Two New Yorks," *NYT*, October 7, 1993; Todd Purdum, "Giuliani on Race," *NYT*, October 7, 1993.

85. Kirtzman, *Rudy Giuliani*, 58; Bob Herbert, "Dangerous Turf," *NYT*, October 3, 1993.

86. In addition, more Latino voters began to support Giuliani. Scholar Richard Wade described Latinos as "the swing vote" in 1993. Dinkins would win 60 percent of their votes in 1993, compared with 70 percent in 1989. McNickle, *The Power of the Mayor*, 310, 331.

87. Felicia Lee, "Viewing a Verdict as Based on Race," *NYT*, November 3, 1993; Felicia Lee, "For Blacks, Loss by Dinkins Undermines Hopes of Change," *NYT*, November 4, 1993; Nicholas Lemann, "Race, Reform and Urban Voters," *NYT*, November 4, 1993.

88. "Never Delivered Victory Speech, '93: Remarks by David N. Dinkins, Election Night '93," November 2, 1993, Box 45, Folder 9, DD Papers.

CHAPTER 10: THE NORTH RISES AGAIN

1. Deval Patrick, *A Reason to Believe: Lessons from an Improbable Life* (New York: Broadway Books, 2011), 32; "Barack Obama's Speech on Race," *NYT*, March 18, 2008; "Obama's Victory Speech" *NYT*, November 5, 2008.

2. Michael Paulson, "Patrick Takes Historic Oath of Office," *BG*, January 4, 2007.

3. "On Values, Mobility, a Hardscrabble Past," *BG*, March 29, 2006; Patrick, *A Reason to Believe*, 6; Taylor Branch, *At Canaan's Edge: America in the King Years*, 1965–68 (New York: Simon & Schuster, 2006), 511.

4. Patrick, *A Reason to Believe*, 57, 39, 35; "On Values, Mobility, a Hardscrabble Past"; Gwen Ifill, *The Breakthrough: Politics and Race in the Age of Obama* (New York: Doubleday, 2009), 183; Charles Pierce, "The Optimist," *BG Magazine*, December 31, 2006.

5. Patrick, *A Reason to Believe*, 149.

6. Scott Helman, "Activism, Soaring Language, Disputes Mark Patrick's Career," *BG*, September 6, 2006; Stephen Labaton, "Denny's Restaurants to Pay $54 Million in Race Bias Suits," *NYT*, May 25, 1994; Jeffrey Rosen, "Is Affirmative Action Doomed?," *The New Republic*, October 17, 1994.

7. Wil Haygood, "A Long Way From Home," *Washington Post*, October 25, 2006; Ifill, *The Breakthrough*, 186.

8. Scott Helman, "Patrick Faces Challenge in Black Community," *BG*, January 15, 2006; Jeff Jacoby, "End to One Troubling Chapter, But a Reopening of Another One," *BG*, November 7, 2006.

9. Patrick, *A Reason to Believe*, 207.

10. Frank Phillips and Scott Greenberger, "Patrick Wins Big Among Delegates," *BG*, February 5, 2006; Elizabeth Mehren, "Blue for Beacon Hill?," *Los Angeles Times*, October 31, 2006.

11. Adrian Walker, "Campaign's Invisible Foe," *BG*, June 1, 2006.

12. Deval Patrick, Convention Speech, June 3, 2006, Worcester, MA, Project Vote Smart, votesmart.org/public-statement/203608/convention-speech#.UZrNo-A5WfQ; Haygood, "A Long Way From Home."

13. Derrick Z. Jackson, "Sweeping Race Out the Door," *BG*, September 16, 2006.

14. Frank Phillips, "Patrick Roars to Nomination," *BG*, September 20, 2006.

15. Glen Johnson, "Patrick Assures Independence as Democrats Come to His Aid," *BG*, October 10, 2006; Steve LeBlanc, "New Healey Ad Links Patrick Record to Women's Fears of Rape," *BG*, October 18, 2006; Ben Arnoldy, "Attack Ads Sometimes Backfire," *Christian Science Monitor*, October 31, 2006.

16. DeWayne Wickham, "In Boston, the Smell of a Dirty Trick," *USA Today*, October 17, 2006; Patrick, *A Reason to Believe*, 178–180.

17. Statement from Deval Patrick, *BG*, October 13, 2006.

18. Deval Patrick, "Rally for Change," Boston, MA, October 15, 2006; Adrian Walker, "A Big Week for Patrick," *BG*, October 16, 2006.

19. Alex Chadwick, "Day to Day," *NPR*, October 13, 2006; Wickham, "In Boston, the Smell of a Dirty Trick." With his mention of Willie Horton, Dukakis was referring to the 1988 presidential campaign. Vice President George Bush (the Republican nominee) aired a television advertisement alleging that Dukakis (the Democratic nominee) was soft on crime. The ad featured an image of Willie Horton, an African American who had been convicted of rape and then furloughed. See *The Living Room Candidate*, www.livingroomcandidate.org/commercials/1988/willie-horton.

20. Arnoldy, "Attack Ads Sometimes Backfire"; Kimberly Atkins, "Deval Turns Up Heat on Healey," *Milford Daily News*, October 19, 2006.

21. Arnoldy, "Attack Ads Sometimes Backfire."

22. Mehren, "Blue for Beacon Hill?"; Pierce, "The Optimist"; Susan Page, "Election Tests How Much Race Matters," *USA Today*, November 1, 2006; Interview with Deval Patrick, by Author.

23. Charles Pierce wrote, "Race was intrinsic to the geology of the Patrick campaign, strengthening it at its depths rather than weakening it on the surface." Pierce, "The Optimist."

24. "Transcript of Wednesday's Gubernatorial Debate," *BG*, November 2, 2006; Interview with Deval Patrick, by Author.

25. Angela K. Lewis, "Between Generations: Deval Patrick's Election as Massachusetts' First Black Governor," in Andra Gillespie, ed., *Whose Black Politics?: Cases in Post-Racial Black Leadership* (New York: Routledge, 2010), 189.

26. "Transcript of Deval Patrick's Acceptance Speech," *BG*, November 8, 2006.

27. Jacoby, "End to One Troubling Chapter, But a Reopening of Another One"; "Vision for a Diverse Boston," *BG*, May 11, 2007. Perhaps the wounds of the busing crisis festered among white liberals more than they did among African Americans. By 2004, 80 percent of Boston's blacks had not resided in the city when busing took place. Louis Masur, *The Soiling of Old Glory: The Story of a Photograph that Shocked America* (New York: Bloomsbury, 2008), 197.

28. Lisa Wangsness, "Patrick Urges Iowa to Put Hope in Obama," *BG*, December 30, 2007.

29. David Remnick, *The Bridge: The Life and Rise of Barack Obama* (New York: Alfred A. Knopf, 2010), 493–494.

30. Mark Danner, "Obama & Sweet Potato Pie," *New York Review of Books*, November 20, 2008.

31. "Barack Obama's Speech on Race."

32. "Barack Obama's Speech on Race."

33. Interview with Deval Patrick, by Author.

34. "Obama's Victory Speech."

35. See Remnick, *The Bridge*; Sugrue, *Not Even Past*; David Remnick, "The Joshua Generation," *The New Yorker*, November 17, 2008; Peniel Joseph, *Dark Days, Bright Nights: From Black Power to Barack Obama* (New York: BasicCivitas Books, 2010); James Kloppenberg, *Reading Obama: Dreams, Hope, and the American Political Tradition* (Princeton, NJ: Princeton University Press, 2011); David Maraniss, *Barack Obama: The Story* (New York: Simon & Schuster, 2012); Ifill, *The Breakthrough*.

36. Chuck Todd and Sheldon Gawiser, *How Barack Obama Won: A State-by-State Guide to the Historic 2008 Presidential Election* (New York: Vintage, 2009), 58, 247–248. Aside from New England and New York, there were nine other states where Obama won a majority of white votes.

37. Stephanie Barry, "Judge: Michael Jacques, Others 'Shiftless and Pathetic' in Racially Motivated Springfield Church Arson," *Springfield Republican*, December 23, 2011.

38. George Graham, "Post-election Church Arson at Predominantly Black Parish Probed as Possible Hate Crime," Springfield Republican, November 5, 2008; "Faith, Justice Prevail for Macedonia Church of God in Christ in Springfield," *Springfield Republican*, April 27, 2011; "Macedonia Church of God in Christ, Springfield Celebrate a New Day," *Springfield Republican*, September 28, 2011.

39. Stephanie Barry, "Prosecutor Paints Portrait of Benjamin Haskell," *Springfield Republican*, June 17, 2010; Dan Barry, "Up from the Ashes, a Symbol that Hate Does Not Win," *NYT*, September 26, 2011.

40. Fredrick Harris, "The Price of a Black President," *NYT*, October 28, 2012; Fredrick Harris, *The Price of the Ticket: Barack Obama and the Rise and Decline of Black Politics* (New York: Oxford University Press, 2012).

41. Randall Kennedy, *The Persistence of the Color Line: Racial Politics and the Obama Presidency* (New York: Pantheon, 2011), 277; William Julius Wilson, "Obama Heads the Right Way on Poverty, Jobs," *The Root*, January 9, 2013; Lawrence Bobo, "Does Obama Owe a Debt to Black America?," *The Root*, February 20, 2013.

42. Matt Viser, "Rev. Rivers Raps Governor's Record on Black Issues," *BG*, June 10, 2009; Brian Wright O'Connor, "Deval, DiMasi Debated at Mass. Dem Meeting," *BSB*, June 11, 2009; Bruce Mohl, "Article Examines Patrick's Representation of Blacks," *Commonwealth*, May 2, 2012.

43. Patrick, *A Reason to Believe*, 222–223; Ifill, *The Breakthrough*, 204.

44. Jodi Kantor, "For President, a Complex Calculus of Race and Politics," *NYT*, October 21, 2012.

45. Jackie Calmes, "When a Boy Found a Familiar Feel in a Pat of the Head of State," *NYT*, May 23, 2012.

46. Interview with Deval Patrick, by Author.

47. *NewsHour with Jim Lehrer*, PBS, January 19, 2009.

48. Ta-Nehisi Coates, "Fear of a Black President," *The Atlantic*, September 2012.

49. "Governor Patrick's First Year," *BG*, January 4, 2008; Ifill, *The Breakthrough*, 196.

50. Joan Vennochi, "A Massachusetts Miracle," *BG*, November 3, 2010; Tim Murray and Deval Patrick, televised victory speech, Boston, MA, November 2, 2010.

51. Interview with Deval Patrick, by Author.

52. Murray and Patrick, Boston, MA, November 2, 2010.

53. Brian Mooney, "An Incumbent Defies Odds to the End," *BG*, November 3, 2010.

54. Kantor, "For President, a Complex Calculus of Race and Politics."

55. "Deval Patrick Speech Text," *Huffington Post*, September 4, 2012.

56. Sarah Wheaton, "For First Time on Record, Black Voting Rate Outpaced Rate For Whites in 2012," *NYT*, May 9, 2013.

57. Callum Borchers, "Since '60, No Road to Oval Office From Mass.," *BG*, November 8, 2012; Charles Blow, "Election Data Dive," *NYT*, November 10, 2012.

58. President Exit Polls, *NYT*, elections.*ny*times.com/2012/results/president/exit -polls; Blow, "Election Data Dive"; Nate Cohn, "Why a Democratic Majority Has Yet to Materialize," *NYT*, April 24, 2014.

59. "Transcript of President Obama's Election Night Speech," *NYT*, November 7, 2012.

60. Joseph Stiglitz, "Equal Opportunity, Our National Myth," *NYT*, February 17, 2013; Sabrina Tavernise, "Soaring Poverty Casts Spotlight on 'Lost Decade,'" *NYT*, September 13, 2011.

61. Interview with Deval Patrick, by Author.

Bibliography

ARCHIVAL COLLECTIONS

Brooklyn Collection, Brooklyn Public Library
Columbia University Rare Book & Manuscript Library
  David Dinkins Papers
Columbia University Center for Oral History Collection
  The Reminiscences of Abraham Ribicoff
Hartford History Center, Hartford Public Library
Howard Gotlieb Archival Research Center, Boston University
  Edward W. Brooke Collection
Library of Congress
  Manuscripts Division:
  Edward Brooke Papers
  Abraham Ribicoff Papers
  Jackie Robinson Papers
Schomburg Center for Research in Black Culture
  Schomburg Oral History Collection
Papers of the National Association for the Advancement of Colored People (Microfilm)

INTERVIEWS BY AUTHOR

Edward Brooke
Robert Ludgin
Thirman Milner
Deval Patrick

Charlie Ryan
Lewis Steel

SELECTED NEWSPAPERS
Amsterdam News
Bay State Banner
Boston Globe
Brooklyn Eagle
Chicago Defender
Greenpoint Weekly Star
Hartford Courant
New York Times
Northend Agents
Springfield Union
Williamsburg News

BOOKS
Abrams, Charles. *Forbidden Neighbors: A Study of Prejudice in Housing*. New York: Harper, 1955.

Alland, Alexander and James Waterman Wise. *The Springfield Plan*. New York: The Viking Press, 1945.

Baldwin, James. *Collected Essays*. New York: Library of America, 1998.

Baldwin, James. *Nobody Knows My Name: More Notes of a Native Son*. New York: Dial Press, 1961.

Baldwin, James. *Notes of a Native Son*. New York: Bantam Books, 1955.

Bass, Paul and Douglas W. Rae. *Murder in the Model City: The Black Panthers, Yale, and The Redemption of a Killer*. New York: Basic Books, 2006.

Bilbo, Theodore. *Take Your Choice: Separation or Mongrelization*. Poplarville, MS: Dream House Publishing Company, 1947.

Biondi, Martha. *To Stand and Fight: The Struggle for Civil Rights in Postwar New York City*. Cambridge, MA: Harvard University Press, 2003.

Branch, Taylor. *At Canaan's Edge: America in the King Years, 1965–68*. New York: Simon & Schuster, 2006.

Breitman, George, ed. *Malcolm X Speaks*. New York: Grove Press, 1965.

Brooke, Edward. *Bridging the Divide: My Life*. New Brunswick, NJ: Rutgers University Press, 2007.

Brooke, Edward. *The Challenge of Change: Crisis in Our Two-Party System*. Boston: Little, Brown, 1966.

Brown, Richard and Jack Tager. *Massachusetts: A Concise History*. Amherst, MA: University of Massachusetts Press, 2000.

Brownmiller, Susan. *Shirley Chisholm: A Biography*. Garden City, NY: Doubleday, 1970.

Bryant, Howard. *Shut Out: A Story of Race and Baseball in Boston*. Boston: Beacon Press, 2002.

Burkholder, Zoe. *Color in the Classroom: How American Schools Taught Race, 1900-1954*. New York: Oxford University Press, 2011.

Burns, Constance K. and Ronald P. Formisano, eds. *Boston 1700–1980: The Evolution of Urban Politics*. Westport, CT: Greenwood Press, 1984.

Bysiewicz, Susan. *Ella: A Biography of Governor Ella Grasso*. Old Saybrook, CT: Peregrine, 1984.

Campanella, Roy. *It's Good to Be Alive*. Boston: Little, Brown, 1959.

Caro, Robert. *The Power Broker: Robert Moses and the Fall of New York*. New York: Alfred A. Knopf, 1974.

Carter, Robert. *A Matter of Law: A Memoir of Struggle in the Cause of Equal Rights*. New York: New Press, 2005.

Celler, Emanuel. *You Never Leave Brooklyn*. New York: John Day Company, 1953.

Chafe, William. *Civilities and Civil Rights: Greensboro, North Carolina, and the Black Struggle for Freedom*. New York: Oxford University Press, 1980.

Chatto, Clarence I. and Alice L. Halligan. *The Story of the Springfield Plan*. New York: Barnes & Noble, 1945.

Chisholm, Shirley. *The Good Fight*. New York: Harper & Row, 1973.

Chisholm, Shirley. *Unbought and Unbossed, Expanded 40th Anniversary Edition*. Washington, DC: Take Root Media, 2010.

Clark, Kenneth. *Prejudice and Your Child*. Boston: Beacon Press, 1963.

Clavel, Pierre. *Activists in City Hall: The Progressive Response to the Reagan Era in Boston and Chicago*. Ithaca, NY: Cornell University Press, 2010.

Clavel, Pierre. *The Progressive City: Planning and Participation, 1969–1984*. New Brunswick, NJ: Rutgers University Press, 1986.

Cobb, James. *Away Down South: A History of Southern Identity*. New York: Oxford University Press, 2005.

Cobb, William Jelani. *The Substance of Hope: Barack Obama and the Paradox of Progress*. New York: Walker & Company, 2010.

Cohen, Lizabeth. *A Consumers' Republic: The Politics of Mass Consumption in Postwar America*. New York: Alfred A. Knopf, 2003.

Coles, Robert. *The South Goes North*. Boston: Little, Brown, 1971.

Connolly, Harold X. *A Ghetto Grows in Brooklyn*. New York: New York University Press, 1977.

Countryman, Matthew. *Up South: Civil Rights and Black Power in Philadelphia*. Philadelphia: University of Pennsylvania Press, 2006.

Crespino, Joseph. *In Search of Another Country: Mississippi and the Conservative Counterrevolution*. Princeton, NJ: Princeton University Press, 2007.

Cripps, Thomas. *Making Movies Black: The Hollywood Message Movie from World War II to the Civil Rights Era*. New York: Oxford University Press, 1993.

Cruz, José. *Identity and Power: Puerto Rican Politics and the Challenge of Ethnicity*. Philadelphia: Temple University Press, 1998.

Current, Richard. *Northernizing the South*. Athens, GA: University of Georgia Press, 1983.

Cutler, John Henry. *Ed Brooke: Biography of a Senator*. New York: Bobbs-Merrill, 1972.

Dahl, Robert. *Who Governs?: Democracy and Power in an American City*. New Haven, CT: Yale University Press, 1961.

Daniels, Jonathan. *A Southerner Discovers New England*. New York: Macmillan, 1940.

Dawkins, Wayne. *City Son: Andrew W. Cooper's Impact on Modern-Day Brooklyn*. Jackson, MS: University Press of Mississippi, 2012.

DeBerry, William, ed. *Sociological Survey of the Negro Population of Springfield, Massachusetts*. Springfield, MA: The Dunbar Community League, 1940.

Demerath III, N. J. and Rhys Williams. *A Bridging of Faiths: Religion and Politics in a New England City*. Princeton, NJ: Princeton University Press, 1992.

Dinkins, David with Peter Knobler. *A Mayor's Life: Governing New York's Gorgeous Mosaic*. New York: PublicAffairs, 2013.

Doherty, Thomas. *Projections of War: Hollywood, American Culture and World War II*. New York: Columbia University Press, 1999.

Dorinson, Joseph and Joram Warmund, eds. *Jackie Robinson: Race, Sports, and the American Dream*. Armonk, NY: M.E. Sharpe, 1998.

Douglas, Davison. *Jim Crow Moves North: The Battle Over Northern School Desegregation, 1865–1954*. New York: Cambridge University Press, 2005.

Dreier, Peter, John Mollenkopf, and Todd Swanson. *Place Matters: Metropolitics for the 21st-Century*. Lawrence, KS: University Press of Kansas, 2001.

Duckett, Alfred. *Changing of the Guard: The New Breed of Black Politicians*. New York: Coward, McCann & Geoghegan, 1972.

Duffy, Susan, ed. *Shirley Chisholm: A Bibliography of Writings By Her and About Her*. Metuchen, NJ: Scarecrow Press, 1988.

Dukakis, Michael and Rosabeth Moss Kanter. *Creating the Future: The Massachusetts Comeback and Its Promise for America*. New York: Summit Books, 1988.

Edel, Matthew, Elliott Sclar and Daniel Luria. *Shaky Palaces: Homeownership and Social Mobility in Boston's Suburbanization*. New York: Columbia University Press, 1984.

Egerton, John. *The Americanization of Dixie: The Southernization of America*. New York: Harper's Magazine Press, 1974.

Eig, Jonathan. *Opening Day: The Story of Jackie Robinson's First Season*. New York: Simon & Schuster, 2007.

Einhorn, Robin. *American Taxation, American Slavery*. Chicago: University of Chicago Press, 2008.

Eliot, Marc. *Song of Brooklyn: An Oral History of America's Favorite Borough*. New York: Broadway Books, 2008.

Englehart, Bob. *A Distinguished Panel of Experts: A Collection of Cartoons by Bob Englehart*. Hartford, CT: Hartford Courant Books, 1985.

Erskine, Carl. *What I Learned From Jackie Robinson: A Teammate's Reflections On and Off the Field*. New York: McGraw-Hill, 2005.

Falkner, David. *Great Time Coming: The Life of Jackie Robinson, from Baseball to Birmingham*. New York: Simon & Schuster, 1995.

Farmer, James. *Lay Bare the Heart: An Autobiography of the Civil Rights Movement*. New York: Arbor House, 1985.

Farrell, John. *Tip O'Neill and the Democratic Century*. Boston: Little, Brown, 2001.

Formisano, Ronald. *Boston Against Busing: Race, Class, and Ethnicity in the 1960s and 1970s*. Chapel Hill, NC: University of North Carolina Press, 1991.

Franklin, John Hope. *Mirror to America: The Autobiography of John Hope Franklin*. New York: Macmillan, 2006.

Freeman, Joshua. *Working Class New York*. New York: The New Press, 2000.

Frommer, Myrna and Harvey Frommer. *It Happened in Brooklyn: An Oral History of Growing Up in the Borough in the 1940s, 1950s, and 1960s.* New York: Harcourt Brace, 1993.

Gadsden, Brett. *Between North and South: Delaware, Desegregation, and the Myth of American Sectionalism.* Philadelphia: University of Pennsylvania Press, 2013.

Gaines, Richard and Michael Segal. *Dukakis and the Reform Impulse.* Boston: Quinlan Press, 1987.

Gamm, Gerald. *Urban Exodus: Why the Jews Left Boston and the Catholics Stayed.* Cambridge, MA: Harvard University Press, 1999.

Gans, Herbert J. *The Urban Villagers: Group and Class in the Life of Italian-Americans.* New York: Free Press of Glencoe, 1962.

Gillespie, Andra, ed. *Whose Black Politics?: Cases in Post-Racial Black Leadership.* New York: Routledge, 2010.

Glasser, Ruth. *Aqui Me Quedo: Puerto Ricans in Connecticut.* Hartford, CT: Connecticut Humanities Council, 1997.

Glazer, Nathan and Daniel P. Moynihan. *Beyond the Melting Pot: The Negroes, Puerto Ricans, Jews, Italians, and Irish of New York City.* Cambridge, MA: MIT Press, 1963.

Golenbock, Peter. *Bums—An Oral History of the Brooklyn Dodgers.* New York: Putnam, 1984.

Golenbock, Peter. *In the Country of Brooklyn: Inspiration to the World.* New York: William Morrow, 2008.

Goodwin, Doris Kearns. *Wait Till Next Year: A Memoir.* New York: Simon & Schuster, 1997.

Gore, Dayo, Jeanne Theoharis, and Komozi Woodard, eds. *Want to Start a Revolution? Radical Women in the Black Freedom Struggle.* New York: New York University Press, 2009.

Gottmann, Jean. *Megalopolis; The Urbanized Northeastern Seaboard of the United States.* New York: Twentieth Century Fund, 1961.

Grant, Ellsworth Strong and Marion Hepburn Grant. *The City of Hartford, 1784–1984.* Hartford, CT: Connecticut Historical Society, 1986.

Greenberg, Cheryl L. *Troubling the Waters: Black-Jewish Relations in the American Century.* Princeton, NJ: Princeton University Press, 2006.

Halsey, Margaret. *Colorblind: A White Woman Looks at the Negro.* New York: Simon & Schuster, 1946.

Harris, Fredrick. *The Price of the Ticket: Barack Obama and the Rise and Decline of Black Politics.* New York: Oxford University Press, 2012.

Harris, Richard. *Decision.* New York: E.P. Dutton, 1971.

Haygood, Wil. *King of the Cats: The Life and Times of Adam Clayton Powell, Jr.* Boston: Houghton Mifflin, 1993.

Hentoff, Nat. *Boston Boy.* New York: Alfred A. Knopf, 1986.

Higgins, George. *Style Versus Substance: Boston, Kevin White, and the Politics of Illusion.* New York: Macmillan, 1984.

Hirsch, Arnold. *Making the Second Ghetto: Race and Housing in Chicago, 1940–1960.* New York: Cambridge University Press, 1983.

Hill, Herbert and James E. Jones Jr., eds. *Race in America: The Struggle for Equality.* Madison, WI: University of Wisconsin Press, 1993.

Hollinger, David. *Postethnic America: Beyond Multiculturalism.* New York: Basic Books, 1995.

Ifill, Gwen. *The Breakthrough: Politics and Race in the Age of Obama*. New York: Doubleday, 2009.

Jackson, Kenneth. *Crabgrass Frontier: The Suburbanization of the United States*. New York: Oxford University Press, 1985.

Jackson, Kenneth. *The Neighborhoods of Brooklyn*. New Haven, CT: Yale University Press, 2004.

Janick, Herbert. *A Diverse People: Connecticut, 1914 to the Present*. Chester, CT: Pequot Press, 1975.

Jeffries, John. *Testing the Roosevelt Coalition: Connecticut Society and Politics in the Era of World War II*. Knoxville, TN: University of Tennessee Press, 1979.

Jennings, James and Mel King, eds. *From Access to Power: Black Politics in Boston*. Cambridge, MA: Schenkman Books, 1986.

Jones, Patrick. *The Selma of the North: Civil Rights Insurgency in Milwaukee*. Cambridge, MA: Harvard University Press, 2009.

Joseph, Peniel E. *Dark Days, Bright Nights: From Black Power to Barack Obama*. New York: BasicCivitas Books, 2010.

Kahn, Roger. *The Boys of Summer*. New York: Harper & Row, 1971.

Kelley, Robin. *Race Rebels: Culture, Politics, and the Black Working Class*. New York: Free Press, 1994.

Kennedy, Randall. *The Persistence of the Color Line: Racial Politics and the Obama Presidency*. New York: Pantheon, 2011.

King, Mel. *Chain of Change: Struggles for Black Community Development*. Boston: South End Press, 1981.

Kirtzman, Andrew. *Rudy Giuliani: Emperor of the City*. New York: William Morrow, 2000.

Kluger, Richard. *Simple Justice: The History of* Brown v. Board of Education *and Black America's Struggle for Equality*. New York: Alfred A. Knopf, 1977.

Kountze, Mabe. *Fifty Sports Years Along Memory Lane: A Newspaperman's Research, Views, Comment & Career Story of United States, Hometown, National & International Afro-American Sports History*. Medford, MA: Mystic Valley Press, 1979.

Kozol, Jonathan. *Death at an Early Age: The Destruction of Hearts and Minds of Negro Children in the Boston Public Schools*. Boston: Houghton Mifflin, 1967.

Kranzler, George. *Williamsburg: A Jewish Community in Transition: A Study of the Factors and Patterns of Change in the Organization and Structure of a Community in Transition*. New York: P. Feldheim, 1961.

Krase, Jerome and Charles LaCerra. *Ethnicity and Machine Politics*. Lanham, MD: University Press of America, 1991.

Landesman, Alter. *Brownsville: The Birth, Development and Passing of a Jewish Community in New York*. New York: Bloch, 1969.

Lassiter, Matthew and Joseph Crespino, eds. *The Myth of Southern Exceptionalism*. New York: Oxford University Press, 2010.

Lee, Alfred. *Race Riot*. New York: Octagon Books, 1943.

Lee, Frank. *Negro and White in Connecticut Town*. New York: Bookman, 1961.

Levy, Frank. *Northern Schools and Civil Rights: The Racial Imbalance Act of Massachusetts*. Chicago: Markham, 1971.

Lieberman, Joseph. *The Power Broker; A Biography of John M. Bailey, Modern Political Boss*. Boston: Houghton Mifflin, 1966.

Litwack, Leon. *North of Slavery: The Negro in the Free States*. Chicago: University of Chicago Press, 1961.

Loewen, James W. *Sundown Towns: A Hidden Dimension of American Racism*. New York: New Press, 2005.

Long, Michael, ed. *First Class Citizenship: The Civil Rights Letters of Jackie Robinson*. New York: Times Books, 2007.

Lukas, J. Anthony. *Common Ground: A Turbulent Decade in the Lives of Three American Families*. New York: Alfred A. Knopf, 1985.

Lupo, Alan. *Liberty's Chosen Home: The Politics of Violence in Boston*. Boston: Little, Brown, 1977.

Mahler, Jonathan. *Ladies and Gentlemen, the Bronx Is Burning: 1977, Baseball, Politics, and the Battle for the Soul of a City*. New York: Farrar, Straus, and Giroux, 2005.

Manoni, Mary. *Bedford-Stuyvesant: The Anatomy of a Central City Community*. New York: Quadrangle, 1973.

Marable, Manning. *Malcolm X: A Life of Reinvention*. New York: Viking, 2011.

March, Charles. *Daniel Webster and His Contemporaries*. New York: C. Scribner, 1852.

Massachusetts State Advisory Committee to the United States Commission on Civil Rights. *Issues of Concern to Puerto Ricans in Boston and Springfield*. Washington, DC: U.S. Commission on Civil Rights, 1972.

Masur, Louis. *The Soiling of Old Glory: The Story of a Photograph that Shocked America*. New York: Bloomsbury Press, 2008.

McGreevey, John. *Parish Boundaries: The Catholic Encounter with Race in the Twentieth-Century Urban North*. Chicago: University of Chicago Press, 1996.

McNickle, Chris. *To Be Mayor of New York: Ethnic Politics in the City*. New York: Columbia University Press, 1993.

McNickle, Chris. *The Power of the Mayor: David Dinkins, 1990–1993*. New Brunswick, NJ: Transaction Publishers, 2013.

Melish, Joanne Pope. *Disowning Slavery: Gradual Emancipation and "Race" in New England, 1780–1860*. Ithaca, NY: Cornell University Press, 1998.

Metcalf, George R. *Black Profiles*. New York: McGraw-Hill, 1968.

Metcalf, George R. *Up From Within: Today's New Black Leaders*. New York: McGraw-Hill, 1971.

Miller, Rita Seiden, ed. *Brooklyn USA: The Fourth Largest City in America*. New York: Brooklyn College Press, 1979.

Milner, Thirman. *Up From Slavery: A History From Slavery to City Hall in New England*. Enumclaw, WA: Pleasant Word, 2009.

Mollenkopf, John. *A Phoenix in the Ashes: The Rise and Fall of the Koch Coalition in New York City Politics*. Princeton, NJ: Princeton University Press, 1992.

Morris, Willie. *North Toward Home*. Boston: Houghton Mifflin, 1967.

Mumford, Kevin. *Newark: A History of Race, Rights, and Riots in America*. New York: New York University Press, 2007.

Myrdal, Gunnar. *An American Dilemma: The Negro Problem and Modern Democracy*. New York: Harper, 1944.

Naison, Mark. *White Boy: A Memoir*. Philadelphia: Temple University Press, 2002.

Newcomb, Theodore and Eugene Hartley, eds. *Readings in Social Psychology*. New York: Holt, 1947.

Newfield, Jack. *Somebody's Gotta Tell It: The Upbeat Memoir of a Working-Class Journalist*. New York: St. Martin's Press, 2002.

Normen, Elizabeth, ed. *African American Connecticut Explored*. Middletown, CT: Wesleyan University Press, 2013.

Obama, Barack. *The Audacity of Hope: Thoughts on Reclaiming the American Dream*. New York: Crown, 2006.

Obama, Barack. *Dreams From My Father: A Story of Race and Inheritance*. New York: Times Books, 1995.

Oliphant, Thomas. *Praying for Gil Hodges: A Memoir of the 1955 World Series and One Family's Love of the Brooklyn Dodgers*. New York: Thomas Dunne Books/St. Martin's Press, 2005.

Orfield, Gary. *Must We Bus?: Segregated Schools and National Policy*. Washington, DC: Brookings Institution, 1978.

Patrick, Deval. *A Reason to Believe: Lessons from an Improbable Life*. New York: Broadway Books, 2011.

Patrick, Deval. *Faith in the Dream: A Call to the Nation to Reclaim American Values*. New York: Hyperion E-Book, 2012.

Peirce, Neal. *The New England States: People, Politics, and Power in the Six New England States*. New York: Norton, 1976.

Perlstein, Rick. *Nixonland: The Rise of a President and the Fracturing of America*. New York: Scribner, 2008.

Phillips, Kevin. *The Emerging Republican Majority*. Garden City, NY: Anchor Books, 1970.

Pitt, James. *Adventures in Brotherhood*. New York: Farrar, Straus and Company, 1955.

Podair, Jerald. *The Strike That Changed New York: Blacks, Whites, and the Ocean Hill-Brownsville Crisis*. New Haven, CT: Yale University Press, 2002.

Powledge, Fred. *Model City: A Test of American Liberalism: One Town's Efforts to Rebuild Itself*. New York: Simon & Schuster, 1970.

Prince, Carl. *Brooklyn's Dodgers: The Bums, the Borough, and the Best of Baseball, 1947–1957*. New York: Oxford University Press, 1996.

Pritchett, Wendell. *Brownsville, Brooklyn: Blacks, Jews, and the Changing Face of the Ghetto*. Chicago: University of Chicago Press, 2002.

Purnell, Brian. *Fighting Jim Crow in the County of Kings: The Congress of Racial Equality in Brooklyn*. Lexington, KY: University of Kentucky Press, 2013.

Rae, Douglas. *City: Urbanism and Its End*. New Haven, CT: Yale University Press, 2003.

Ralph, James. *Northern Protest: Martin Luther King, Jr., Chicago, and the Civil Rights Movement*. Cambridge, MA: Harvard University Press, 1993.

Rampersad, Arnold. *Jackie Robinson: A Biography*. New York: Alfred A. Knopf, 1997.

Ravitch, Diane. *The Great School Wars, New York City, 1805–1973: A History of the Public Schools as Battlefield of Social Change*. New York: Basic Books, 1974.

Reiter, Howard and Jeffrey Stonecash. *Counter Realignment: Political Change in the Northeastern United States*. New York: Cambridge University Press, 2011.

Remini, Robert. *Daniel Webster: The Man and His Time*. New York: W.W. Norton & Co., 1997.

Remnick, David. *The Bridge: The Life and Rise of Barack Obama*. New York: Alfred A. Knopf, 2010.

Ribicoff, Abraham. *America Can Make It!* New York: Atheneum, 1972.

Ribicoff, Abraham. *Politics: The American Way*. Boston: Allyn and Bacon, 1967.

Rieder, Jonathan. *Canarsie: The Jews and Italians of Brooklyn Against Liberalism*. Cambridge, MA: Harvard University Press, 1985.

Robbins, Michael, ed. *Brooklyn: A State of Mind*. New York: Workman, 2001.

Roberts, Gene and Hank Klibanoff. *The Race Beat: The Press, the Civil Rights Struggle, and the Awakening of a Nation*. New York: Alfred A. Knopf, 2006.

Robinson, Jackie. *Baseball Has Done It*. Philadelphia: Lippincott, 1964.

Robinson, Jackie. *I Never Had It Made*. New York: Putnam, 1972.

Robinson, Jackie. *Jackie Robinson, My Own Story*. New York: Greenberg, 1948.

Robinson, Rachel with Lee Daniels. *Jackie Robinson: An Intimate Portrait*. New York: Harry N. Abrams, 1996.

Ross, J. Michael and William M. Berg. *"I Respectfully Disagree with the Judge's Order": The Boston School Desegregation Controversy*. Washington, DC: University Press of America, 1981.

Rowan, Carl with Jackie Robinson. *Wait Till Next Year*. New York: Random House, 1960.

Russell, Bill with Taylor Branch. *Second Wind: The Memoirs of an Opinionated Man*. New York: Ballantine, 1980.

Sale, Kirkpatrick. *Power Shift: The Rise of the Southern Rim and Its Challenge to the Eastern Establishment*. New York: Random House, 1975.

Sargent, Francis. *The Sargent Years: Selected Public Papers of Francis W. Sargent, Governor 1969–1975*. Boston: S.N., 1976.

Scarrow, Howard. *Parties, Elections and Representation in the State of New York*. New York: New York University Press, 1983.

Schroeder, Oliver and David Smith, eds. *De Facto Segregation and Civil Rights*. Buffalo, NY: W.S. Hein, 1965.

Schulman, Bruce J. *The Seventies: The Great Shift in American Culture, Society, and Politics*. New York: Free Press, 2001.

Schultz, Kevin. *Tri-Faith America: How Catholics and Jews Held Postwar America to Its Protestant Promise*. New York: Oxford University Press, 2011.

Schwartz, Joel. *The New York Approach: Robert Moses, Urban Liberals, and Redevelopment of the Inner City*. Columbus, OH: Ohio State University Press, 1993.

Scott, Daryl Michael. *Contempt and Pity: Social Policy and the Image of the Damaged Black Psyche, 1880–1996*. Chapel Hill, NC: University of North Carolina Press, 1997.

Selig, Diana. *Americans All: The Cultural Gifts Movement*. Cambridge, MA: Harvard University Press, 2008.

Shapiro, Edward. *Crown Heights: Blacks, Jews, and the 1991 Brooklyn Riot*. Waltham, MA: Brandeis University Press, 2006.

Shapiro, Michael. *The Last Good Season: Brooklyn, the Dodgers, and Their Final Pennant Race Together*. New York: Doubleday, 2003.

Siegel, Fred. *The Prince of the City: Giuliani, New York and the Genius of American Life*. San Francisco: Encounter Books, 2005.

Simmons, Louise. *Organizing in Hard Times: Labor and Neighborhoods in Hartford*. Philadelphia: Temple University Press, 1994.

Sleeper, Jim. *The Closest of Strangers: Liberalism and the Politics of Race in New York*. New York: W.W. Norton, 1990.

Smith, Anna Deavere. *Fires in the Mirror: Crown Heights, Brooklyn and Other Identities.* New York: Anchor Books, 1993.

Springfield Council of Social Agencies. *The Social Needs of Negroes in Springfield, Massachusetts.* Springfield, MA: Springfield Council of Social Services, 1942.

Stave, Sondra Astor. *Achieving Racial Balance: Case Studies of Contemporary School Desegregation.* Westport, CT: Greenwood Press, 1995.

Stegner, Wallace. *One Nation.* Boston: Houghton Mifflin Company, 1945.

Stetler, Henry. *Attitudes Toward Racial Integration in Connecticut.* Hartford, CT: Hartford Commission on Civil Rights, 1961.

Stone, Frank Andrews. *African American Connecticut: African Origins, New England Roots.* Storrs, CT: University of Connecticut, 1991.

Sugrue, Thomas. *Not Even Past: Barack Obama and the Burden of Race.* Princeton, NJ: Princeton University Press, 2010.

Sugrue, Thomas. *The Origins of the Urban Crisis: Race and Inequality in Postwar Detroit.* Princeton, NJ: Princeton University Press, 1996.

Sugrue, Thomas. *Sweet Land of Liberty: The Forgotten Struggle for Civil Rights in the North.* New York: Random House, 2008.

Sugrue, Thomas J. and Kevin M. Kruse, eds. *The New Suburban History.* Chicago: University of Chicago Press, 2006.

Sullivan, Neil. *The Dodgers Move West.* New York: Oxford University Press, 1987.

Taba, Hilda, Elizabeth Hall Brady, and John T. Robinson. *Intergroup Education in Public Schools.* Washington, DC: American Council on Education, 1952.

Taylor, Clarence, ed. *Civil Rights in New York City: From World War II to the Giuliani Era.* New York: Fordham University Press, 2011.

Taylor, William. *Cavalier and Yankee: The Old South and American National Character.* Cambridge, MA: Harvard University Press, 1979.

Thabit, Walter. *How East New York Became a Ghetto.* New York: New York University Press, 2003.

Theoharis, Jeanne and Komozi Woodard, eds. *Freedom North: Black Freedom Struggles Outside the South, 1940–1980.* New York: Palgrave Macmillan, 2003.

Thernstrom, Stephan. *The Other Bostonians: Poverty and Progress in the American Metropolis, 1880–1970.* Cambridge, MA: Harvard University Press, 1973.

Thomas, J. Phillip. *Double Trouble: Black Mayors, Black Communities, and the Call for a Deep Democracy.* New York: Oxford University Press, 2005.

Todd, Chuck and Sheldon Gawiser. *How Barack Obama Won: A State-by-State Guide to the Historic 2008 Presidential Election.* New York: Vintage, 2009.

Tygiel, Jules. *Baseball's Great Experiment: Jackie Robinson and His Legacy.* New York: Oxford University Press, 1983.

Washington, James, ed. *A Testament of Hope: The Essential Speeches and Writings of Martin Luther King, Jr.* New York: Harper Collins, 1986.

Whittemore, Katharine and Gerald Marzorati, eds. *Voices in Black & White: Writings on Race in America from Harper's Magazine.* New York: Franklin Square Press, 1993.

Wakefield, Dan. *Revolt in the South.* New York: Grove, 1960.

Warner, Robert. *New Haven Negroes: A Social History.* New Haven, CT: Yale University Press, 1940.

Weinberg, Martha Wagner. *Managing the State.* Cambridge, MA: MIT Press, 1977.

Weld, Ralph Foster. *Brooklyn Is America*. New York: Columbia University Press, 1950.

Whalen, Thomas J. *Dynasty's End: Bill Russell and the 1968–69 World Champion Boston Celtics*. Boston: Northeastern University Press, 2004.

Wiese, Andrew. *Places of Their Own: African American Suburbanization in the Twentieth Century*. Chicago: University of Chicago Press, 2004.

Wilder, Craig. *A Covenant With Color: Race and Social Power in Brooklyn*. New York: Columbia University Press, 2000.

Wilkerson, Isabel. *The Warmth of Other Suns: The Epic Story of America's Great Migration*. New York: Random House, 2010.

Williams, Yohuru. *Black Politics/White Power: Civil Rights, Black Power, and the Black Panthers in New Haven*. St. James, NY: Brandywine Press, 2000.

Wilsey, Sean, ed. *State by State: A Panoramic Portrait of America*. New York: Ecco, 2008.

Winslow, Barbara. *Shirley Chisholm: Catalyst for Change, 1926–2005*. Boulder, CO: Westview Press, 2014.

Wolfinger, James. *Philadelphia Divided: Race and Politics in the City of Brotherly Love*. Chapel Hill, NC: University of North Carolina Press, 2007.

Woodward, C. Vann. *The Burden of Southern History*. Baton Rouge, LA: Louisiana State University Press, 1960.

Wright, Nathan Jr. *What Black Politicians Are Saying*. New York: Hawthorn, 1972.

Zeiler, Thomas. *Jackie Robinson and Race in America*. Boston: Bedford/St. Martin's, 2014.

Zinn, Howard. *The Southern Mystique*. New York: Alfred A. Knopf, 1964.

Index

A. M. E. Zion Church, 245
Abe, Katsuya, 276
Abortion, 222, 223
Abrams, Robert, 274
Adams, Mildred, 82
Adams, Thomas Boylston, 122
Aetna, 236
Aldrich, Bailey, 91, 92
Alexander v. Holmes County, 185, 197
Alice B. Beal elementary school, 74
Alland, Alexander, 21–22
Allen, James, 79, 82–85, 215
Amelia, James, 147
America First Party, 6
Amoros, Sandy, 57, 68
Anderson, David, 66
Apple, R. W., 281
Arkansas Gazette, 179–180
Arnold, Rudolph, 242
Ashmore, Harry, xviii–xix
Athanson, George, 237, 239, 244
Atkins, Tom, 206, 211, 220

Bailey, John M., 244
Baker, Bertram, 50, 61–62
  on housing, 62
  Robinson, Dollie, endorsed by, 151

state assembly campaign, 52–53
  support for, 51
Baker, Charlie, 311
Baker, Howard, 176
Baldwin, James, x, xv, xxii
Banner, Troy, 267–268
Barksdale, Abraham, Jr., 79
Barksdale v. Ryan, 79–89
  appealing, 89–90
  Springfield Union on, 90–91
Baseball integration
  Burley on, 39–40, 43–44
  Kountze on, 30
  Smith, Wendell, on, 29–30
  Yawkey opposing, 30
Baseball Writers Association, 40–41
Batson, Ruth, 204
Bay State Banner, 123–124
Beame, Abe, 166
Beauford, Fred, 164
Bedford-Stuyvesant
  Chisholm on, 146
  Newfield on, 48
  political fragmentation of, 138
  population of, 48
Bedford-Stuyvesant Political League, 141
"The Beginnings of Mankind," 9

Belson, Jon, 56
Berek, Judith, 148, 155, 164
Berger, Joel, 31
Berger, Meyer, 3
Berlin Wall, 281
Berman, Edward, 128–129
Bernard, Edward, 9–10
Berra, Yogi, 68
A Better Chance, 293
Biden, Joseph, 217–218, 220–221
Biden II, 219
Bieluch, William, 243
Bilbo, Theodore, 23
Billington, Clyde, 239
Binder, Frederick, xvi
Black, Joe, 56
Black Power
    Beauford on, 164
    Brooke on, 115, 116, 194
    Farmer and, 159
Blackmun, Harry, 203
Bonadies, Nicholas, 244
Bostic, Joe, 41
Boston
    Brooke's letter to, 216–217
    busing riots, 210
    busing start date, 209
    Curry on, xi
    DiBartolo on, 212
    Evans, J., on, 212
    Hodges on, 212
    Howle on, 212
    Lupo on, 211
    Neal on, 212
    Russell, B., on, 132–133
    segregated schools in, 133
Boston Braves, 29
Boston City Council, 16
Boston Finance Commission, 107
Boston Globe, 127
Boston Red Sox, 29
Boston School Committee, 16
Bova, Gino, 260
Bowker, Rosa, 9–10
Braun, Carol Moseley, 131
Breslin, Jimmy, 47

Bright, Oscar, 88, 90, 93, 97
Brightman, Mark, 212–213
Brooke, Ed, ix, 79, 97
    on abortion, 223
    approval ratings, 196
    background of, 104–105
    on backlash, 120–121
    Bay State Banner on, 123–124
    on Black Power, 115, 116, 194
    Boston Globe on, 127
    Boston letter from, 216–217
    on busing, 207–209, 214–217,
        221–222
    campaign of, 106–109, 118–126
    campaign slogan of, 113–114, 121
    on Carswell, 199–201
    Committee of Religious Concern
        About Vietnam endorsing, 123
    The Crisis on, 127
    on defeat, 228, 229
    divorce of, 223–224, 226
    Doyle on, 113
    Dunn on, 228
    Eaton on, 110
    election of, 126
    Fitchburg Sentinel on, 123
    Frank on, 227–228
    Guscott on, 129
    Healy on, 120–121
    Holland on, 228
    Holyoke Transcript-Telegram on, 124
    international coverage of, 122
    Jackson, J., on, 228
    Jewish Advocate on, 130–131
    Kaese on, 130
    King, C. S., on, 228
    Lockman on, 228
    on Massachusetts, 115
    Massachusetts Political Action for
        Peace endorsing, 122–123
    McGrory on, 193, 200–201, 227
    Mitchell on, 196
    Nemrow on, 129
    O'Sullivan on, 129
    other states reacting to, 128–129
    Pilot on, 128

Pittsburgh Courier on, 131–132
Rauh on, 228
Republican nomination of, 117–118
Robinson, Jackie, on, 130
Rowan on, 221
school boycott outlawed by, 110
school segregation and, 109–110
Senate candidacy declared by, 112
Silver Lake News on, 127–128
Slaughter on, 131–132
on Smith, M. C., 201–202
Spingarn Medal awarded to, 194
Swan on, 129
traveling with Nixon, 195–196
Tsongas debate with, 226–227
on Vietnam War, 122
White, P. C., on, 130
Wilson on, 119
Brooke Amendment, 195
Brooklyn
Dorinson on, 37
Golenbock on, 34
Hametz on, 34
Newfield on, 33, 37
nostalgia for, 32, 68–69
Oliphant on, 34
population of, 46–47
Reddy on, 67
Taylor, G. C., on, 34, 50
trolley operators, 35
Warmund on, 37
Weld, R. F., on, 33, 38–39
Brooklyn Dodgers, 29
Clark, K., and, 44
departure of, 68–69
Robinson, Jackie, on, 57
tryouts, 39–40
in World Series, 45–46, 68
Brooklyn is America (Weld, R. F.), 33
Brooklyn Navy Yard, 47–48
Brown, Dominic, 270
Brown, John, 4
Brown, Martha, 58
Brown, Scott, 310
Brown v. Board of Education, 11, 13, 60,
71–72

Brumley, Cal, 122
Brunton, Daniel, 25
Bucke, Emory Stevens, 28
Bulkley, James, 95
Bunderick, Tom "Duke," 42
Buntin, Frank, 78, 80–81, 88–90
Burley, Dan, 39–40, 43–44
Burns, Ben, 22
Busing
amendments, 208
Atkins on, 211, 220
Biden on, 217–218, 220–221
Boston riots, 210
Boston start date, 209
Brightman on, 212–213
Brooke on, 207–209, 214–217,
221–222
Charlotte, 213
failures of, 207
Javits on, 182–183
Kennedy, T., on, 208, 209–210
McGovern on, 218
U.S. News and World Report on,
220–221
Butler, Jane, 16
Butts, Calvin, 261
Byrd, Robert, 219

Cadrow, Boris, 280
Caldwell, Earl, 272
Caldwell, Gilbert, 135
Campanella, Roy, 54, 55
Canada, Geoffrey, 290
Canning, Thomas, 59
Cannon, Jimmy, 47
Cao, Tuan Ana, 284–285
Carbone, Nicholas, 236–237
Carmichael, Stokely, 114–115, 119
Carney, Vincent, 141
Caron, Michael, 305
Carson, Sonny, 278
Carswell, G. Harrold, 198–199
Brooke on, 199–201
Gravel on, 201
rejection of, 203
Seymour on, 200

Carter, Robert, 81, 269
  on color blindness, 86–87
  on neighborhood school, 86
  on school segregation, 78
Cato, Angela, 285–286
Cato, Gavin, 285–286
Celler, Emanuel, 146, 156, 161
Chandler, Albert "Happy," 40–41
Charlotte, North Carolina, 213
Chatto, Clarence, 7, 8, 22
Chicago Defender, 18
  on *It Happened in Springfield*, 21
Children's prejudice, 6, 11–13
Chisholm, Shirley
  background of, 142–143
  on Bedford-Stuyvesant, 146
  Berek on, 155, 164
  campaign of, 139, 150–151
  campaign slogan of, 152
  Cooper on, 166
  Dubin on, 160–161
  election of, 163
  on financing, 158
  on gender, 160
  goals of, 165
  Guild on, 166
  on Holder, 153
  Jeffries on, 167
  on Kings County Democratic Party,
    151–152
  legacy of, 166–167
  on Ocean Hill-Brownsville, 162–163
  presidential campaign of, 165–166
  Spanish campaign of, 155–156
  speeches by, 157
  on Thompson, 152
  on Vietnam War, 165
Civil disobedience, 110
Civil War, xv
Civilian Complaint Review Board, 127,
  288
Clampit, Ralph, 27
Clark, John, 235
Clark, Kenneth, 11–13, 44
Clarkson, Clifford, 79
Cleveland Indians, 54

Clinton, Bill, 289
CNC. *See* Committee for a Negro
  Congressman from Brooklyn
Coates, Ta-Nehisi, 310
Cobb, Charles, 93, 94
Cobb, James, xviii
COCR. *See* Council of Organizations
  of Civil Rights
Coleman, John, 51
Collins, John, 116–117
Color blindness, 72
  Carter on, 86–87
  malleability of, 73
  Tsongas on, 225
*Colorblind: A White Woman Looks at the
  Negro* (Halsey), xiv–xv
Committee for a Negro Congressman
  from Brooklyn (CNC), 150
Committee for Democratic Voters, 141
Committee of Religious Concern About
  Vietnam, 123
Committee on Education for Democracy,
  6
Community Development Block Grants,
  237
Congressional Black Caucus, 165
"The Contributions of Nationalities to
  Springfield," 8
Cook, Marlow, 202
Cooper, Andrew, 145–146, 166
Cosme, Felix, 149
Coughlin, Rosemarie, 77, 89, 90, 92
Council of Organizations of Civil Rights
  (COCR), 94
Cowan, William "Mo," 310
The Crisis
  on Brooke, 127
  on Springfield Plan, 17
Crowley, James, 242, 247
Crown Heights, 61
Cuomo, Andrew, 289
Cuomo, Mario, 265, 266
Current, Richard, xix
Curry, Michael, xi
Curtis, Constance, 21–22
Curtis Bill, 27

Custis, Lemuel Rodney, 62–63
Cyr, Romeo, 76, 89, 92

Daley, Richard, 174
Daniels, John, 282
Darien, Connecticut, 66
De facto segregation, 72, 79
De jure segregation, 79
De Sapio, Carmine, 261
DeBerry, William, 14
DeBra, Arthur, 21
Democratic Convention 1968, 173–174
DeRosa, Anthony, 147–148
DiBartolo, Peter, 212
Dimauro, Theodore, 74, 76
DiMonaco, Vincent, 77, 80, 92
Dinkins, David
  Abrams endorsed by, 274
  background of, 272
  Caldwell, E., on, 272
  campaign of, 276–279
  City Hall speech, 284
  Clinton on, 289
  on crime, 278
  Democratic nomination of, 276
  election of, 279–281
  finances of, 278
  on Hawkins, 275
  Jackson, J., and, 275, 277, 278
  Kennedy, T., endorsing, 275
  Klaperman on, 275
  Klein on, 284
  Longiaru on, 279
  Thanksgiving Eve speech, 287–288
  Wilder compared with, 282–283
Dixon, Dennis, 260
Do the Right Thing (Lee), 267
Dobbins, James J., 124–125
Dobelle, Evan, 115
Doby, Larry, 54
Dodd, Thomas, 201
Dorinson, Joseph, 37
Doudera, D. J., 181–182
Douglas, Paul, 127
Downtown Development Plan, 254
Doyle, James, 113

Dubin, Marshall, 145
  on Chisholm, 160–161
  on Farmer, 159
Dukakis, Michael, 292
Dunn, Elizabeth, 228
Dwyer, Jim, 260

Eagleton, Thomas, 218
Eaton, Cornell, 110
Ebbets Field
  Berger, J., on, 31
  final game at, 68–69
  Glasser on, 37–38
  Rodney on, 38
Ebbets Field Apartments, 161
Ebony, 17–18
Edelin, Kenneth, 222
Eisenhower, Dwight, 71
Elementary and Secondary Education
    Act, 174
Ellison, Ralph, xxiii–xxiv
Englehart, Bob, 252–253
Equal employment
  DeBerry on, 14
  Springfield Plan and, 10
Esposito, Meade, 166
Evans, Charles, 135
Evans, Jim, 212
Evers, Medgar, 76

Fair Employment Practices Committee
    (FEPC), 27, 28, 39
Fair Housing Act, 176, 195
Fair Housing Administration (FHA), 61
Fama, Joseph, 268, 283
Farmer, James, 156–157
  background of, 157
  Black Power and, 159
  Dubin on, 159
  on Ocean Hill-Brownsville, 162
  speeches by, 157
Farragut Houses, 58
Farrell, Denny, 272
FEPC. *See* Fair Employment Practices
    Committee
Festival of Lights, 9–10

FHA. *See* Fair Housing Administration
Fine, Benjamin, 8
  on Springfield, Massachusetts, 5
  on Springfield Plan, 15, 18
Fitchburg Sentinel, 123
Flagg, Lewis, 141
Flagg, Nancy, 7
Flaherty, Joe, 36
Flake, Floyd, 262
Fongemie, Jacqueline, 256
Ford, John, 43
Forman, Stanley, 223
Fortas, Abe, 197
Frank, Barney, 225, 227–228
Frigand, Sid, 60, 61
Fritchman, Stephen, 27
Fulbright, J. William, 176, 202

Gabrieli, Chris, 295
Gammal, Al, 113–114, 117
Gans, Herbert, 276
Garcia, Robert, 246
Garrity, W. Arthur, 206–207
Germond, Jack, 225
Gilliam, Junior, 57
Giuliani, Rudy
  campaign of, 276–279
  on Civilian Complaint Review Board,
    288
  Hacker on, 288–289
Glass, J. Luther, 177, 189
Glasser, Ira, 37–38
Goetz, Bernhard, 263
Goldin, Harrison, 273
Goldwater, Barry, 111
Golenbock, Peter, 34, 43
Goodson, Gadson, 35
Goodwin, Anne Stockton, 18–19
Gordon, James, 35
Gore, Albert, 202
Goring, Ruth, 143
Gottmann, Jean, xx
Gouge, Tina, 213
Government Facilities Location Act, 188
Gowanus Houses, 58

Granrud, John, 5, 25
Grant, Albert, 250
Gravel, Mike, 201, 202
Greater Hartford Affirmative Action Plan,
  250
Greater Hartford Corporation, 236
Greater Hartford Labor Council, 246
Greatorex, Irena, 222
Greenwich Real Estate Board's bylaws,
  64
Griffin, Juanita, 93, 94
Griffin v. Ryan, 98
Griffith, Michael, 262
  Koch on, 265
  murder of, 263–264
Grimes, Mark, 134
Grimes, Timothy, 262, 263
Gross, Milton, 56–57
Gruber, Robert, 36, 37, 42
Guild, Joshua, 166
Gunnar, Benedict, 65
Guscott, Kenneth, 129

Haag, Ernest van den, 13
Hacker, Andrew, 288–289
Halligan, Alice, 7, 8, 10, 22
Halsey, Margaret, xiv–xv
Hametz, Ivan, 34
Hamill, Pete, 32
Harlan, John Marshall, 72
Harlow, Bryce, 202
Harriman, Averell, 62
Harris, Frederick, 306
Hartford, Connecticut
  Hogg on, 256–257
  insurance industry in, 236
  King, M. L., Jr., on, 235
  Milner on, 236
  population of, 235
  poverty of, 233, 256
  riots, 236
Hartford Courant
  on Milner, 239, 248, 252–253
  Milner endorsed by, 240–241, 246–247,
    253–254

on Ribicoff, 181
  Wright, T., on, 253
Hartford Food System, 237
Hartford Times, 182
Hawkins, Yusuf, 267–268, 274–275
  Dinkins on, 275
  funeral for, 270
  Koch on, 268, 270
Haynsworth, Clement F., Jr., 197–198
Healey, Kerry, 296, 297
Healy, Robert, 120–121
Helms, Jesse, 218
Hennigan, James, 206–207
Herbert, Bob, 269, 289
Here is New York (White, E. B.), 265
Herter, Christian, 106
Hicks, Louise Day, xxiv, 109–110, 204
Hodges, Barbara, 212
Hogg, Flora, 256–257
Holder, Wesley "Mac," 141, 153
Holland, Alvin, 228
Holmes, Oliver Wendell, xvi
Holt, Marjorie, 215
Holt Amendment, 215
Holyoke Transcript-Telegram, 124
Hooker, Thomas, 249
Hopkins, J. G. E., 10
Housing
  Baker, B., on, 62
  Brown, M., on, 58
  Darien, Connecticut, 66
  projects, 58, 59
  Robinson, Rachel, on, 53–54, 63–66
  segregated, 58–59
  Stamford, Connecticut, 64–66
  Thompson on, 58
  White, W., on, 60
Howard Beach, 262–265
  Lee and, 267
  Paterson on, 265
  Wilkins, Roger, on, 264
Howe, Irving, 261
Howle, Jimmy, 212
Hoyt, Thomas, Jr., 252–253
Humphrey, Hubert, 196

It Happened in Springfield, 19–21
  Zack on, 24

Jackie Robinson Day, 45
Jackson, Ada, 52
Jackson, Derrick Z., 296
Jackson, Jesse
  on Brooke, 227
  Dinkins and, 275, 277, 278
  Milner endorsed by, 245
Jackson, Scoop, 218
Jacoby, Jeff, 299
Jansen, William, 71–72
Jasper Houses, 59
Javits, Jacob, 190, 202
  on busing, 182–183
  on Stennis Amendment, 176
Jeffries, Hakeem, 167
Jensen, Noma, 17
Jethroe, Sam, 29
Jewish Advocate, 130–131
Jewish Community Council, 28
Joe's Restaurant, 139–140
Johnson, Lyndon, 111
Johnson, Rebecca, 18
Jones, Madison, 62
Jones, Thomas, 141–144
Journal-Courier, 181

Kaese, Harold, 130
Kahn, Roger, 36–37, 41–42
Kantor, Jodi, 308
Kaufman, Irving R., 73–74
Kelley, Thomas, 191
Kelling, George, 289
Kelly, Edna, 145
Kelly, Francis, 108
Kennedy, John F., xxi, 76, 106–107
Kennedy, Randall, 308
Kennedy, Ted, 108–109, 202, 228
  on busing, 208, 209–210
  Dinkins endorsed by, 275
  image of, 223
Kent Village Urban Renewal Project, 147
Kerner Commission, 195

Kerrigan, Paul, 148–149
King, Coretta Scott, 227–228
King, Martin Luther, Jr., 72
    on American schizophrenia, xvii
    on civil disobedience, 110
    on Hartford, 235
King, Mel, 206, 257–258, 292
Kings County Democratic Party, 139,
    151–152
Kissinger, Henry, 225
Klaperman, Gilbert, 275
Klein, Joe, 277, 284
Koch, Ed, 166
    Butts on, 261
    on Griffith, 265
    on Hawkins murder, 268, 270
    Lee on, 261
    Sydenham Hospital closed by, 260–261
Korean grocery boycott, 283–285
Koskinen, John, 174–175
Kountze, Mabe "Doc," 30

La Guardia, Fiorello, 39
Ladone, Jason, 263
Lally, William, 134
Landsmark, Ted, 223
Law, Ruby, 238
Lawrence, Bill, 115
Lawrence, Geoffrey, 61
Lawrence, Linda, 213
Lee, Spike, 261, 267
Lehman, Herbert, 4, 141
Leigh, Margaret Ross, 49
Lentol, Edward, 147–148
Lester, Jon, 262
"Letter From Birmingham Jail" (King),
    110
Lexington Democratic Club, 140–141
Lifsh, Yosef, 285–286
Lindsay, John, 162
Litwack, Leon, xix
Lockman, Norman, 228
Lodge, John Davis, 172, 173
Longiaru, Dan, 279
Louis X, 114
Lowery, Joseph, 309

Ludgin, Robert, 241, 244, 251
Lupo, Alan, 211
Lynch, John Pierce, 76–77
Lynch, Mary, 79–80
Lyons, John, 97

Macedonia Church of God, 304–306
Magnuson, Warren, 218
Malcolm X, xix
Mann, Arthur, 41, 43
Mansfield, Mike, 218
Marshall, Thurgood, 13
Martin, Joel, 36
Marttila, John, 273
Mary L. Lynch elementary school, 74
Mason-Dixon line, xix
Massachusetts Council of Churches, 28
Massachusetts Political Action for Peace,
    122–123
McCook, Thomas, 76, 80, 81
McCray, Fred, 285
McDuffie, Terris, 29
McGarry, Michael, 247
McGovern, George, 218
McGrory, Mary, 193, 200–201, 227
McSherry, Elizabeth, 106
Megalopolis, xx
Meili, Trisha, 266
Menino, Thomas, 294
Meriden Record, 182
Metcalf, George, 61–62
Metcalf-Baker bill, 61–62
Meyers, Michael, 287
Miller, Clyde, 6
Milner, Thirman, 234
    background of, 237–239
    campaign slogan of, 239, 240
    Democratic nomination of, 247
    Downtown Development Plan vetoed
        by, 254
    election challenged by, 242–244
    election of, 248
    Englehart cartoons, 248, 252–253, 254
    Grant on, 250
    Greater Hartford Labor Council
        endorsing, 246

on Hartford, 236
Hartford Courant endorsing, 240–241, 246–247, 253–254
Hartford Courant on, 239, 248, 252–253
Jackson, J., endorsing, 245
Ludgin on, 251
mayor campaign, 240
on Parks, 249
Perry supported by, 257
on Reagan, 251
symbolism of, 255–256
Mitchell, Clarence, 189, 196, 225
Mondale, Walter, 176–177, 202
Mondello, Keith, 268, 283
Monroe, Jim, 239
Montiero, Clifford, 97
Montreal Royals, 40
Mooney, Brian, 312
Morgan, Tallulah, 206–207
Morgan v. Hennigan, 206–207
Morial, Ernest "Dutch," 251
Morris, Barbara, 80
Morris, William, 35
Morris, Willie, xvi
Morsell, John, 185–186
Morton, Franklin W., Jr., 51–52
Moses, Robert, 68
Mothers for Adequate Welfare, 134–135
Muchnick, Isadore, 29
Murphy, Carol, 213–214
Murphy, Johanna, 241
Myrdal, Gunnar, xxiv–xxv

National Conference of Black Mayors, 255
National Conference of Christians and Jews, 6
Naval Clothing Depot, 47
Neal, Elizabeth, 212
Neas, Ralph, 219
"The Negro in Brooklyn" (Frigand), 60, 61
Nelson, Avi, 224
Nelson, Gaylord, 218
Nelson, Lemrick, 287
Nemrow, Carolyn, 129

New Federalism, 251
New York Plan, 17
New York Yankees, 45–46, 56
Newcombe, Don, 54, 55
Newfield, Jack, 33, 37, 48
Newkirk, Pamela, 270
Nieman, Joseph, 191
Nixon, Richard, 195–196, 197
Nolan, Martin, 105–106

Obama, Barack, 294
acceptance of, 303
accomplishments of, 312–313
Coates on, 310
in Deep South, 304
Harris on, 306
Kantor on, 308
Kennedy, R., on, 308
Lowery on, 309
Patrick on, 312–313
symbolism of, 306–307
victory speech of, 300, 313
on Wright, J., 301–302
Ocean Hill-Brownsville, 162–163
Octagon Lounge, 92–93, 95
Oliphant, Thomas, 34
Oliver, Lillian, 35
O'Malley, Walter, 68
One Man, One Vote, 138
O'Sullivan, Alyce, 129
Owens, Bill, 224

Paige, Myles, 50–51
Parents' Magazine, 16
Parks, Rosa Lee, 249
Participatory democracy, 140
Paterson, Basil, 265
Patrick, Deval, xiii, 258
accomplishments of, 310
on American Dream, 291
background of, 292–294
Boston Common speech, 297
on Healey, 297
inauguration of, 292
in Iowa, 300
Jackson, D. Z., on, 296

Patrick, Deval *(continued)*
  Jacoby on, 299
  Mooney on, 312
  on Obama, 312–313
  Pierce, C., on, 298
  reelection of, 311–312
  Rivers on, 307
  Rosen, J., on, 294
  victory speech, 299
  Walker, A., on, 295
Payne, E. George, 18
Peabody, Endicott "Chub," 116–117
Pearl Harbor, 15
Perry, Carrie Saxon, 241–242, 257
Pettigrew, Thomas Fraser, 82–84
Philadelphia, Carlton, 308–309
Philadelphia, Jacob, 308–309
Phillips, A. Robert, 135
Pierce, Charles, 298
Pierce, Lawrence, 51
Pilot, 128
Pioneer Democratic Club, 149
Pioneer Spirits, 8–9
Pittsburgh Courier, 29–30
  on Brooke, 131–132
Plessy v. Ferguson, 72
Podres, Johnny, 68
Powell, Adam Clayton, 50
Powell, Lewis, 203
Prejudice testing, 9, 11–13
Prouty, Winston, 201, 202
Providence Journal, 190
Puglisi, Corrado, 191–192
Purdum, Todd, 288

Racial Imbalance Act, 99, 204
  approval of, 133
  Sargent on, 205–206
Rainey, Olive, 5
Rauh, Joe, 227–228
Ravitch, Richard, 273
Reagan, Ronald, 120, 126–127, 225, 251
Reddy, Bill, 36, 67
Reform clubs, 140–141
Rehnquist, William, 203
Reid, Herbert, 89

Reilly, Thomas, 295
Reimers, David, xvi
Restore Our Alienated Rights (ROAR),
  221
Reyes, Matias, 266–267
Reynolds v. Sims, 138
Ribicoff, Abraham
  American Dream speech of, 172–173
  Arkansas Gazette on, 179–180
  background of, 172
  cartoons, 177–179
  Connecticut responses to, 180–182
  at Democratic Convention 1968,
    173–174
  on Fair Housing Act, 176
  Hartford Courant on, 181
  Hartford Times on, 182
  Journal-Courier on, 181
  Meriden Record on, 182
  Morsell on, 185–186
  Nieman on, 191
  Providence Journal on, 190
  Rowan on, 185
  Sherrill on, xxv–xxvi
  southern responses to, 177–180
  speaking tour of, 185, 187–188
  on Stennis Amendment, xxv, 175–176
  Watters on, 186–187
  Weicker on, 173
  West Hartford News on, 190
  Wicker on, 186, 189
Rice, Norm, 281–282
Richardson, Elliot, 107
Richardson, Maude, 52
Rickey, Branch, 29
Riley, Robert, 262, 263
Rivers, Eugene, 307
ROAR. *See* Restore Our Alienated Rights
Robinson, Bryant, Jr., 304–306
Robinson, Dollie, 151
Robinson, Dorothy, 76, 77
Robinson, Jackie
  Bostic on, 41
  on Brooke, 130
  on Brooklyn Dodgers, 57
  Bunderick on, 42

contract, 40
Ford on, 43
Golenbock on, 43
Gross on, 56–57
Gruber on, 37, 42
on Humphrey, 196
Kahn on, 36–37, 41–42
Most Valuable Player, 55
Smith, G. G., correspondence with, 44–45
tryout, 29, 39
Wilder on, 42
Robinson, John, 257
Robinson, Rachel, 53–54, 63–66
Robinson, Robert, 228–229
Rodney, Lester, 38
Roe v. Wade, 203, 222
Romeo J. Cyr Arena, 74
Rooney, John, 147
Roosevelt, Eleanor, 141
Rosen, Jeffrey, 294
Rosen, Marvin, 68
Rosen, Walter, 68
Rosenbaum, Yankel, 286, 287
Ross, Herb, 56
Rovere, Richard, 179
Rowan, Carl, 185, 221
Rubin, Hugh, 277
Russell, Bill, 132–133
Russell, Richard, 176
Ryan, Charlie, 74, 76–77, 93–94

Safe Streets, Safe City, 285
Sale, Kirkpatrick, xix–xx
Saltonstall, Leverett, 107, 111–112
Sanders, William, 26
Sandiford, Cedric, 262, 263
Sargent, Frank, 204–206
Satlow, Archie, 53–54
Satlow, Sarah, 53–54
Savino, Joseph, 148
Schneerson, Menachem, 285
School segregation
  in Boston, 133
  Brooke and, 109–110
  Carter on, 78

Coughlin on, 89, 92
Cyr on, 92
DiMonaco on, 92
Hicks on, 109–110
Jansen on, 71–72
New York Times on, 72
in Springfield, Massachusetts, 14, 74–99
Springfield Union on, 89
Sweeney on, 87–88
Search for Education, Elevation, and
  Knowledge (SEEK), 144
Second Great Migration, 46
SEEK. *See* Search for Education,
  Elevation, and Knowledge
Seminoles Booster Club, 199
Seymour, Richard, 200
Shanker, Albert, 162
Sharpton, Al, 268–269
Shays, Daniel, 4
Sherrill, Robert, xxv–xxvi
Siler, Wade, 44
Silver Lake News, 127–128
Simmons, George, 28
Simon, Andrea, 65
Simon, Richard, 65
Slaughter, Adolph, 131–132
Smith, G. Gilbert, 44–45
Smith, Gerald L. K., 6
Smith, Helena Huntington, 19
Smith, Henry, 280
Smith, Margaret Chase, 201–202, 203
Smith, Wendell, 29–30, 39
Smith, Wilber, 238–239, 241, 251–252
Smith & Wesson, 4
Smyth, Paul, 305
"The Soiling of Old Glory" (Forman), 223
Spong, William, 202, 203
Springfield, Massachusetts, 4–5
  Fine on, 5
  National Guard in, 97–98
  population of, 5
  protests, 93–98
  public school system, 5
  school segregation in, 14, 74–99
  sleep-out, 94–95
Springfield Council on Social Agencies, 10

Springfield Plan, 4
  adult education, 10
  Allen on, 83–84, 85
  barriers to, 9–10
  Boston City Council voting down, 16
  Boston School Committee on, 16
  Burns on, 22
  Butler on, 16
  The Crisis on, 17
  demographic change from, 26
  Ebony on, 17–18
  equal employment and, 10
  failure of, 24, 25–26
  Fine on, 15, 18
  Goodwin on, 18–19
  high schools, 9
  Jensen on, 17
  junior high schools, 8–9
  NAACP Youth Council on, 25–26
  New York Times on, 15
  northern cities adopting, 17
  Pettigrew on, 83–84
  Placement Bureau and, 10
  Sanders on, 26
  shortcomings of, 23
  Smith, Helena Huntington, on, 19
  Stegner on, 22–23
  Washington Post on, 18
  Wilmington, Delaware adopting, 17
  Zack on, 24
The Springfield Plan (Wise), 21–23
Springfield School Committee, 5
Springfield Union
  on *Barksdale v. Ryan*, 90–91
  on school segregation, 89
Stamford, Connecticut, 64–66
Stark, Abe, 59–60
State Commission Against Discrimination
  (NY), 61
Steel, Lewis, xxii–xxiii, 74, 96, 98–99
Stegner, Wallace, 22–23
Steinem, Gloria, 225
Steingut, Irwin, 145
Steingut, Stanley, 139–140, 144
  district redrawing by, 146
Stennis, John, 174, 179

Stennis Amendment
  Javits on, 176
  Koskinen on, 174–175
  Mondale on, 176–177
  passing of, 183–184
  Ribicoff on, xxv, 175–176
Stewart, Moses, 268
Stewart, Rowena, 135
Stichman, Herman, 59
The Story of the Springfield Plan (Halligan
  & Chatto), 22
Stuart, Charles, 258
Sugrue, Thomas, xix
Summons, Doraleena, 228
Sutton, Percy, 166, 271–272
Swan, Ben, 93, 97, 129
Sweeney, George, 79, 87–88
Sydenham Hospital, 260–261
Sylvester, Curtis, 262
Symington, Stuart, 218

*Take Your Choice: Separation or
  Mongrelization* (Bilbo), 23
Taylor, Gardner Calvin, 48–49
  on Brooklyn, 50
  on Brooklyn Jews, 34
  Robinson, Dollie, endorsed by, 151
Taylor, John H., 27–28
Taylor v. New Rochelle Board of Education,
  73–74
Tea Party, 310
Theinert, Helen, 80–81
Thomas, Dave "Showboat," 29
Thompson, William C., 58, 151–152
Thomson, Bobby, 55–56
Tobacco, 234–235
Tolchin, Martin, 149–150
Townsend, Willard, 44
Trachtman, Jeffrey, 264
Travia, Anthony, 144
A Tribe Called Quest, 279
Trump, Donald, 266
Tsongas, Paul, 225–228
  Brooke debate with, 226–227
  on color blindness, 225
Turbyhill, Don, 213

Turks, Willie, 259–260
Tweedy, Richard, 66
Tyrus, Derek, 265

UADA. *See* United Action Democratic Association of Kings County
UDC. *See* Unity Democratic Club
UFT. *See* United Federation of Teachers
Union Baptist Church, 245
United Action Democratic Association of Kings County (UADA), 51
United Federation of Teachers (UFT), 162
United States Commission on Civil Rights 1975 report, 210
United States National Armory, 4
Unity Democratic Club (UDC), 141–142
Urban Education Improvement Act, 189–191
U.S. News and World Report, 220–221

VA. *See* Veterans Administration
Vargas, Edwin, 246
Veterans Administration (VA), 61
Vietnam War, 122–123, 165
Volpe, John, 97, 204
Voting Rights Act, 95

Wacholder, Leonard, 274
Wagner, Robert, 144
Walker, Adrian, 295
Walker, Dixie, 43
Wallace, George, 74–75, 131
Wallace, Lurleen, 120, 126
Walsh, John, 52
Ward, Benjamin, 268
Wardlaw, John, 255
Warmund, Joram, 37
Warner, Henry, 19
Washington, Harold, 253
Washington Post, 18
Watters, Pat, 186–187
Watts riots, 95
Weicker, Lowell, 173
Weissman, Henry, 79–80, 92
Weld, Ralph Foster, 33, 38–39

Weld, William, 292
Wells, Curtis, 270
Wells, David, 281
West Hartford News, 190
Weusi, Jitu, 278
White, Alfred, 245
White, E. B., xvi, 3–4, 265
White, Kevin, 106–107
White, Poppy Cannon, 130
White, Walter, 60
Wicker, Tom, 186, 189
Wilbur, Crane, 19
Wilder, Douglas, 131, 281, 292
    Dinkins compared with, 282–283
    on Robinson, Jackie, 42
Wiley, George, 98
Wilkins, Roger, 264
Wilkins, Roy, 164
Williams, A. Roger, 245
Williams, G. Mennen, 127
Williams, Jerry, 108
Williams, Lester, 93
Williams, Marvin, 29
Williams, Oliver D., 51
Williams, Robert, xxiii
Williams, Roger, 77
Wilmington, Delaware, 17
Wilson, David, 119
Winthrop, John, xvi
Wise, James Waterman, 21–22
Witcover, Jules, 225
Wood, Francis Alden, 108
Woodward, C. Vann, xvi
World's Fair, 3–4
Wright, Douglass, 244
Wright, Jeremiah, 301–302
Wright, Thomas, 253

Yarborough, Ralph, 202, 203
Yardley, Jonathan, 281
Yawkey, Tom, 30
Young, Coleman, 245

Zack, Eugene, 24
Zinn, Howard, xix

JASON SOKOL is Arthur K.Whitcomb Associate Professor of History at the University of New Hampshire. He grew up in Springfield, Massachusetts, attended Oberlin College, and earned his PhD in history from the University of California at Berkeley. Sokol has received fellowships from Harvard, the University of Pennsylvania, and Cornell. He is author of *There Goes My Everything: White Southerners in the Age of Civil Rights, 1945–1975*.